The Data Model Resource Book Revised Edition Volume 1

A Library of Universal Data Models for All Enterprises

Len Silverston

Wiley Computer Publishing

John Wiley & Sons, Inc.

NEW YORK · CHICHESTER · WEINHEIM · BRISBANE · SINGAPORE · TORONTO

Publisher: Robert Ipsen
Editor: Robert M. Elliott
Assistant Editor: Emilie Herman
Managing Editor: John Atkins
Associate New Media Editor: Brian Snapp
Text Design & Composition: Publishers' Design and Production Services, Inc.

Designations used by companies to distinguish their products are often claimed as trademarks. In all instances where John Wiley & Sons, Inc., is aware of a claim, the product names appear in initial capital or ALL CAPITAL LETTERS. Readers, however, should contact the appropriate companies for more complete information regarding trademarks and registration.

This book is printed on acid-free paper. ∞

Published by John Wiley & Sons, Inc.

Published simultaneously in Canada.

This publication is designed to provide accurate and authoritative information in regard to the subject matter covered. It is sold with the understanding that the publisher is not engaged in professional services. If professional advice or other expert assistance is required, the services of a competent professional person should be sought.

Library of Congress Cataloging-in-Publication Data:

ISBN: 0-471-38023-7

Printed in the United States of America.

10 9 8 7

Advance Praise for *The Data Model Resource Book, Revised Edition, Volume 1*

"*The Data Model Resource Book, Revised Edition, Volume 1*, is the best book I've seen on data architecture. It does not merely address the top levels of a data architecture (Zachman Framework row one or two); it provides both common and industry-specific logical models as well as data designs that may be customized to meet your requirements. The end result is a rich framework whose models span the higher and lower levels of a data architecture, including high-level models, logical models, warehouse designs, star schemas, and SQL scripts. You can use the data models, designs, and scripts as templates or starting points for your own modeling, an introduction to subject areas you might not be familiar with, a reference to validate your existing models, and a help to building an enterprise data architecture. The book provides techniques to transform models from one level to another, as well as tips and techniques for getting the appropriate levels of abstraction in the models. Instance tables (sample data) help bring the models to life. I have customized and used the models from the first edition on many projects in the last two years—it is an invaluable resource to me."

Van Scott
President, Sonata Consulting, Inc.

"Len Silverston has produced an enormously useful two-volume compendium of generic (but not *too* generic) data models for an extensive set of typical enterprise subject areas, and for various industries that any data modeler will likely encounter at some point in his or her career. The material is clearly written, well organized, and goes below the obvious to some of the more perverse and difficult information requirements in an enterprise. This is an invaluable resource for doing one's homework before diving into any modeling session; if you can't find it here, there is certainly a very similar template that you can use for just about any situation with which you might be faced."

William G. Smith
President, William G. Smith & Associates

"In today's fast-paced e-oriented world, it is no longer acceptable to bury business constraints in hard-to-change data structures. Data architects must comprehend complex requirements and recast them into data architecture with vision for unforeseen futures. Len's models provide an outstanding starting point for novice and advanced data architects for delivering flexible data models. These models position an organization for the business rule age. Their proper implementation and customization allows the organization to externalize and manage business policies and rules so that the business can proactively change itself. In this way, the data architecture, based on Len's models and procedures for customizing them, becomes by design the foundation for business change."

Barbara von Halle
Founder, Knowledge Partners, Inc.
Co-author of Handbook of Relational Database Design

"These books are long overdue and a must for any company implementing universal data models. They contain practical insights and templates for implementing universal data models and can help all enterprises regardless of their level of experience. Most books address the needs for data models but give little in the way of practical advice. These books fill in that void and should be utilized by all enterprises."

Ron Powell
Publisher, DMReview

"Businesses across the world are demanding quality systems that are built faster by IT shops. This book provides a foundation of patterns for data modelers to expand upon and can cut days, if not weeks, off a project schedule. I have found *The Data Model Resource Book, Revised Edition, Volume 1*, valuable as a resource for my modeling efforts at L.L. Bean, Inc. and feel it is an essential component in any modelers toolkit."

Susan T. Oliver
Enterprise Data Architect, L.L. Bean, Inc.

"I was first introduced to *The Data Model Resource Book* three years ago when I was hired by a firm who wanted an enterprise data model. This company did not believe the dictum that 'all companies are basically the same'; they felt they were somehow unique. After a little analysis with Len Silverston's help, we found that we were actually quite a bit the same: we had customers, accounts, employees, benefits, and all the things you'd find in any corporation. All we had to do was adapt the *product* component of Len's book and we were ready to move ahead with a great framework for all of our data. A CD-ROM (that can be purchased separately) provides scripts to build the model in Oracle very quickly. We then began mapping all of our detailed data types to the enterprise model and, voila, we could find a place for all of those various spellings and misspellings of Account Number.

"Volume 2 of this revised edition provided even more exciting features: models of industry-specific data. I began to see interesting patterns that permeated this volume. For example, a reservation is a reservation, whether you're an airline, a restaurant, or a hotel. (We even have something similar in the oil industry—the allocation.)

"Another concept from the book that has changed my thinking and vocabulary is the word 'party.' I recently managed a project in which an employee could also function as a customer and as an on-line computer user. The team was in disagreement regarding a name for this entity; but after checking *The Data Model Resource Book*, we realized that here we had a party playing three roles.

"Whether your job is to jump-start a data warehouse project or borrow ideas for any subject area in your next operational database, I highly recommend *The Data Model Resource Books, Revised Edition, Volumes 1 and 2*, as your bible for design."

Ted Kowalski
Equilon Enterprises LLC
Author of Opening Doors: A Facilitator's Handbook

Contents

Chapter 10   Creating the Data Warehouse Data Model from the
Enterprise Data Model

Foreword

When I first became involved in data modeling in the mid-1970s, I was taught a set of diagramming conventions, the rules of normalization, and a few principles of good design. It did not take me long to discover that my education had covered only the easy part. The real challenge, as any experienced modeler knows, lies in understanding business requirements and choosing an appropriate set of concepts and structures to support them. The traditional advice to "ask which things the enterprise needs to keep information about and how they are related" is a gross over-simplification of the often very difficult process of identifying entities and relationships.

Research in the last few years has supported what practitioners have known for a long time: rather than modeling from first principles, experienced data modelers re-use and adapt models and parts of models from their previous work. In fact, their "experience" may well reside more in their personal library of models—typically remembered rather than documented—than in greater facility with the basic techniques. The use of pre-existing templates also changes the nature of the dialog between the business experts and modelers: modelers will seek to discover which model or models from their repertoire may be appropriate to the situation, then to check the detail of those models. This is a far more proactive role for modelers than that traditionally described, and recognizes that both parties can contribute ideas and content to the final model.

Of course, it takes time and exposure to a wide variety of business requirements for an individual to build up anything approaching a comprehensive library of models. Only specialist data modelers are likely to have this opportunity, and the reality is that much data modeling is performed by non-specialists.

The obvious step forward from this rather haphazard individual approach is for experienced modelers to develop and publish models for the most commonly encountered business requirements, so that solutions can be shared, reviewed and improved. Almost every commercial enterprise needs to keep data about customers, about staff, about sales. And almost every data modeler has spent time wrestling with these common—but by no means simple—situations, painfully aware that he or she is re-inventing the wheel, but without any confidence that any particular modeler has done a better job.

Such additions to data modeling's "body of knowledge" have been a long time coming. Books, papers, and educational material have continued to focus on the foundations of data modeling: modeling paradigms, diagramming conventions, and normalization. These are important topics, to be sure, but the absence of more developed material lends credence to the argument that data modeling does not deserve the status of a fully-fledged discipline.

Perhaps the reason for the gap in the literature is that the individuals best placed to recognize common situations and to develop models for them are data modeling *practitioners*—more particularly consultants who have had the opportunity to see a range of different business requirements. The models that they have developed over the years are a valuable professional resource, more profitably deployed on consulting assignments than as material for general publication. It also takes some courage to present one's own solutions for scrutiny by peers, all of whom will turn naturally to the problems for which they have personally developed the most elegant solutions!

I am therefore delighted that Len Silverston has chosen to publish a second and substantially expanded edition of *The Data Modeling Resource Book*. The first edition was essential reading for anyone charged with developing data models for business information systems, and was particularly notable for including contributions by specialists in particular data modeling domains. The second edition retains this feature, covers new business areas, and updates the original material. Len's willingness to continue to improve the material gives me hope that the core models will acquire a deserved status as standard starting points.

The second edition of *The Data Modeling Resource Book* is an excellent answer to the question "what is the *second* data modeling book I should purchase, once I've learned the basics?"—and every practitioner of data modeling should own at least two books on the subject!

Graeme Simsion
1 January 2001

Acknowledgments

I wrote this book because I deeply feel that universal data models can provide effective solutions to many important data management and integration issues. However, this book would not have been possible without the insights and knowledge gained through my rewarding interactions and relationships with clients over the past 20 years. I am extraordinarily grateful to these clients who allowed me to provide service for them, while expanding my knowledge of business and information management. Their use, implementation of and modifications to universal data model constructs have greatly contributed to the content of this book. From among the many people that have contributed, I want to thank Regina Pieper, Howard Jenkins, Rob Jacoby, Chris Nickerson, Jay Edson, Dean Boyer, Joe Misiaszek, Paul Zulauf, Steve Seay, Ken Haley, Ted Kowalski, Mike Brightwell, Dan Adler, Linda Abt, Joe Lakitsky, Trent Hampton, Kevin Morris, Karen Vitone, Tracy Muesing, Steve Lark, and Chuck Dana. I also want to thank the many client organizations that have added to and supported the universal data model paradigm.

I am very thankful to the people who added to the content of this current edition of the book. A person that made a significant contribution is Bob Conway, who took time to review these models out of a very busy consulting schedule and who scrupulously reviewed the models, making insightful suggestions as only Bob could have done. I greatly appreciate the work that Burt Holmes has done in implementing these universal data models at numerous clients and in providing valuable feedback regarding changes required for practical implementation of these models. I am very grateful to Natalie Arsenault, who provided ongoing ideas about the universal data models based upon her extensive data modeling background and who also drafted the first cut of the Implementing Universal Data Models chapter. I thank David Templeton, who reviewed the Implementing Universal Data Model chapter.

I want to thank several people who were instrumental in the first edition of this book. A great deal of thanks is due to Bill Inmon for suggesting the first edition of this book to Wiley; if not for him, *The Data Model Resource Book* may not have been published. Bill Inmon has added to this book through his visionary perspectives on data warehousing and his method of how to convert logical data models to data warehouse designs. I am grateful to Kent Graziano whose discipline and writing contributions added a tremendous amount to the first edition of this book, and whose Designer 2000 expertise was instrumental in the creation of the first edition CD-ROM. I thank Claudia Imhoff for her help in data warehousing on the first edition as well as her positive foreword in the first edition.

There were mentors that helped guide me and helped me see this work through completion. I am grateful to Richard Flint for his inspiration, guidance and encouragement to follow my visions. I am very thankful to John DeMartini for helping me to view my life more holistically and for inspiring me to continually learn and write about holistic, integrated systems.

I feel honored to have been able to work on this book with Bob Elliott, the finest editor I know, at John Wiley & Sons and I appreciate his excellent vision, management, editing, and support for this book as well as his ongoing encouragement to me. I want to thank Emilie Herman from John Wiley & Sons for taking care of a great number of tasks at Wiley in publishing this book.

I am thankful to my mom, Dede Silverston, a writer herself, who inspired and supported me in my writing; my dad, Nat Silverston, who has been a great father; my brother and great friend, Steve Silverston, who has lifted my spirits and been there for me; and my sister, Betty Silverston, who has such a big heart. Most of all, I am blessed to have had the support, patience, and love of my beautiful wife, Annette, and daughters, Danielle and Michaela, throughout the trial and tribulations of writing this book.

About the Author

Len Silverston is an author, lecturer, consultant, and pioneer in the field of data management. He has devoted the last 20 years to helping organizations build and integrate information systems, using his unique approaches to develop information architectures, design databases, and solve data management issues.

Mr. Silverston has been an invited speaker at numerous national and international conferences and has written many articles on database design and data warehousing in publications such as *Data Management Review* and Data Warehouse Institute's *Journal of Data Warehousing*.

Len Silverston is the founder and owner of Universal Data Models, LLC (www.universaldatamodels.com), a Colorado-based firm providing consulting and training to help enterprises customize and implement "universal data models" and develop holistic, integrated systems. Universal Data Models, LLC, has helped many diverse organizations develop data architectures and designs in a fraction of the typical time through its extensive repository of reusable data models and data warehouse designs. The company offers several seminars that provide tools to deliver higher quality databases and information systems in less time.

Mr. Silverston lives in Castle Rock, Colorado, with his wife Annette and his daughters, Danielle and Michaela. He holds a masters degree in Computer Science from Renssellear Polytechnic Institute with a specialization in database management systems.

He can be reached at lsilverston@univdata.com.

About the Contributors

Kent Graziano (graziano@bewellnet.com) is a Senior Technical Architect for Aris Corporation in Denver, Colorado, and is the current president of the Oracle Development Tools User Group. He has over 18 years of experience, with the last 12 years devoted to Oracle data modeling and data warehousing. Kent was the recipient of the 1999 Chris Wooldridge Award from the International Oracle Users Group for outstanding contributions to the Oracle user community.

W. H. Inmon, the acknowledged "father of data warehousing," is a partner in www.billinmon.com, a Web site for the corporate information factory and modern systems architecture. He has written more than 40 books on databases, database management, and data warehouse technology, including the recently published *Exploration Warehousing* (Wiley). Bill is also a frequent speaker at leading industry conferences and contributes to *DM Review*.

Natalie Arsenault has worked for major Fortune 100 companies in database administration, design, and modeling for most of her 20-year career. Her current work supports an enterprise data framework that is consistently leveraged throughout the company. She is involved with data standards, metadata planning and is a member of the enterprise technical architecture team.

Ms. Arsenault has been a conference speaker at several international conferences on data modeling, and her colleagues seek her expertise.

CHAPTER 1

Introduction

*If you see can see more of the whole,
you are moving closer towards the truth.*

Why Is There a Need for This Book?

On many data modeling consulting engagements, clients have asked the same
question: "Where can we find a book showing a standard way to model this
structure? Surely, we are not the first company to model company and address
information."

Many organizations develop their data models or data warehouse designs
with very few outside reference materials. A large cost is associated with either
hiring experienced consultants or using internal staff to develop this critical
component of the system design. Often there is no objective reference material
that the company can use to validate its data models or data warehouse designs
or to seek alternate options for database structures.

Based on numerous experiences of using template or "universal data models" and customizing them for various enterprises, we have concluded that usually more than 50 percent of the data model (corporate or logical) consists of
common constructs that are applicable to most organizations, another 25 percent of the model is industry specific (these models are covered in *The Data*

Model Resource Book, Volume 2), and, on average, about 25 percent of the enterprise's data model is specific to that organization. This means that most data modeling efforts are recreating data modeling constructs that have already been created many times before in other organizations.

With this in mind, doesn't it make sense to have a source to use to get a head start on your data model so that you are not "reinventing the wheel" each time a company develops a new system? Organizations can save time and money by leveraging the use of common or universal database structures. Even if a company has data models from its previous systems development efforts, it is very helpful to be able to check the designs against an unbiased source in order to evaluate alternative options.

Although a large number of publications describe how to model data, very few compilations of data model examples exist in published form. This book provides both a starting point and a source for validating data models. It can help data modelers minimize design costs and develop more effective and integrated database designs.

Who Can Benefit from Reading This Book?

This book can assist many different systems development professionals: data administrators, data modelers, data analysts, database designers, data warehouse administrators, data warehouse designers, data stewards, corporate data integrators, or anyone who needs to analyze or integrate data structures. Systems professionals can use the database constructs contained in this book to increase their productivity and provide a checkpoint for quality designs.

The Need for Universal Data Models

Data modeling first gained recognition in Dr. Peter Chen's 1976 article, "Entity-Relationship Modeling," which illustrated his newfound approach. Since then data modeling has become the standard approach used to design databases. By properly modeling an organization's data, the database designer can eliminate data redundancies, which are a key source of inaccurate information and ineffective systems.

Currently, data modeling is a well-known and accepted method for designing effective databases. Therefore, there is a great need to provide standard templates to enterprises (the term "enterprise" is used to describe the organizations for whom the models and systems are being developed) so that they can refine and customize their data models instead of starting from scratch.

Although many standards exist for data modeling, there is a great need to take data modeling to the next step: providing accessibility to libraries of common data model examples in a convenient format. Many different organizations and industries should be able to use these libraries of data models. Such *universal data models* can help save tremendous amounts of time and money spent in the systems development process.

A Holistic Approach to Systems Development

One of the greatest challenges to building effective systems is integration. Systems are often built separately to meet particular needs at different times within each enterprise. Enterprises need to build many systems: contact management systems, sales order systems, project management systems, accounting systems, budgeting systems, purchase order systems, and human resources systems, to name a few.

When systems are built separately, separate pools of information are created for each system. Many of these systems will use common information about organizations, people, geographic locations, or products. This means that each separate system will build and use its own source of information. A huge problem with this approach is that it is almost impossible to maintain accurate, up-to-date information because the same type of information is stored redundantly across many systems. In large organizations, it is not uncommon to see information about customers, employees, organizations, products, and locations stored in dozens of separate systems. How is it possible to know which source of information is the most current or most accurate?

Another disadvantage of building separate systems with non-integrated data structures is that the enterprise (the organization for which the models and systems are being designed) does not have the benefit of viewing integrated information. Being able to see a complete profile for a person, organization, product, or inventory item is an enormous benefit. Imagine systems that are built so that each part of an organization knows what the other part is doing, where the customer service, sales, purchasing, and accounting departments of an organization have integrated information about the people, organizations, and products of the enterprise. This integration can make a big different in the service, sales, and performance of an enterprise.

Another way to approach systems development is from a perspective that an enterprise's systems are connected and, in fact, may be viewed as one interconnected system. From this perspective, there are tremendous benefits to building an enterprise-wide framework so that systems can work together more effectively. Part of this framework should include a corporate data model (i.e., an enterprise data model) that can assist the enterprise in maintaining one of its most valued assets: information. Because each system or application may use similar information about people, organizations, products, and geographic locations, a shared information architecture can be invaluable.

The IS (information systems) industry has recognized the need for integrated designs, prompting the many corporate data modeling and corporate data warehouse modeling efforts. Unfortunately, the IS track record for building and implementing corporate data models has been very poor. Enterprises have realized that it takes a tremendous amount of time and resources to build these models.

Enter CASE (Computer-Aided Systems Engineering) tools. These tools claimed tremendous productivity and time savings when used for corporate-wide modeling efforts. While these tools help document the models, unfortunately they do not reduce the time needed to develop good corporate models.

Many enterprises have stopped building corporate data models because of their time constraints. They are looking at the track record of corporate data modeling and CASE efforts and choosing other alternatives.

Enter *data warehousing*. Finally, here is an approach to provide executives with the management information they need, without all the time and expense of corporate data modeling. Enterprises are now extracting the various pieces of information they need directly from their operational systems in order to build decision support systems.

The only problem with this approach is that *the same problem exists!* First of all, the information in the data warehouse may be extracted from several different, inconsistent sources. If there are multiple places where customer information is being held, which system represents the most accurate source of information?

According to data warehousing principles, the transformation routines are responsible for consolidating and *cleansing* the data. If different departments have different needs for various pieces of data, then each department may build its own extracts from the operational systems. One department may transform the information using one algorithm; a different department may use another algorithm. For example, if two departments are extracting sales analysis information, one department may use the order entry system as its source and another department may use the invoicing system as its source. A high-level manager may view information from both data warehouses and see inconsistent results, thus questioning the credibility of *all* the information. This type of scenario actually compounds the initial problem of many data sources by creating even more *slices of data*.

This is not to say that data warehousing is the wrong approach. It is an ingenious approach that can be used extremely effectively not only to create decision support systems but also to build a migration path to an integrated environment. The data warehouse transformation process helps to identify where there are data inconsistencies and data redundancies in the operational environment. It is imperative, though, to use this information to migrate to more integrated data structures.

The answer is still to build integrated data structures in order to provide good, accurate information. The only effective way to do this is to understand how the data within an enterprise and the relationships fit together and to be able to see the data in a holistic integrated manner. It is necessary to understand the nature of the data in order to build effective systems. Instead of saying that corporate data modeling or CASE is the wrong approach because it just takes too long, the IS community needs to find a way to make it work effectively. By building common, reusable data structures, the IS community can produce quicker results and move toward integrated structures in both the transaction processing and data warehouse environments.

What Is the Intent of This Book and These Models?

Most data modeling books focus on the techniques and methodologies behind data modeling. The approach behind this book is dramatically different. This book assumes that the reader knows how to model data. Data modeling has been around long enough that most information systems professionals are familiar with this concept and will be able to understand this book. Therefore, this book makes no efforts to teach data modeling principles, except by example. Data modelers can use this book, and their previous experience, to build on and refine the data model examples contained within the book in order to develop more customized data models. Essentially, it gives the modeler fundamental tools and building blocks that can be reused. Therefore, the modeler can be more productive and save a great deal of time by starting with standard data models instead of building data models from scratch.

Furthermore, the reader can also benefit from the data warehouse models that are applicable to decision support environments. This book not only presents examples of data warehouse designs, but it also explains in detail how to convert the logical data models to an enterprise-wide data warehouse, then to departmental data marts. The logical data models and data warehouse models presented here are applicable across a wide variety of enterprises.

These models are intended to be a *starting point* for developing logical and data warehouse data models for an enterprise. Each enterprise will have its own detailed requirements; the models will need to be modified and customized in order to be implemented for a specific enterprise. Because the data warehouse data models reflect actual database designs (as opposed to logical data models), they are even more dependent on the business needs of the specific enterprise wishing to use these models. In addition, the models in this book can be used to validate an enterprise's existing data models.

The models presented in the first part of this book (Chapters 2 through 9) are logical data models, not physical database designs. Therefore, these models are normalized and may require some denormalization when designing the physical database. Consistent with this point, the logical data models do not include any derived attributes because derived attributes do not add anything to the information requirements of a business. They merely serve to enhance performance of the physical database.

These logical data models represent possible data requirements for enterprises. They do not include many of the business processing rules that may accompany data models. The data models generally provide all the information needed to enforce business rules; however, the reader is advised in many cases that additional business rules may need to be developed to supplement the data models. Examples of the need for business rules are provided throughout this book.

These data models were designed to benefit many different industries and enterprises. They were picked specifically because they represent very common data constructs that appear in most organizations. Within these models, whenever there was a data modeling decision that may have been dependent on a specific enterprise, the most flexible data modeling option was chosen in order to accommodate many different enterprises.

Furthermore, the chapter on Implementing Universal Data Models provides an explanation on how to use the data models to build an enterprise data model, logical data models, and physical database designs. Detailed examples are provided for how to transform the data models into a physical database design that can be implemented for a database management system.

What Is New in the Second Edition of the *Data Model Resource Book*?

The second edition of the *Data Model Resource Book* provides many enhancements and additional models. There are a great number of updates and additions; the following points describe them at a high level.

A great majority of the data models in the original *Data Model Resource Book* have been significantly enhanced with additional entities, attributes, and relationships.

Many of the data models have slightly different and more enhanced data structures. Based on numerous usages and implementations of these models, the models have been updated to reflect even more effective data structures.

A number of new chapters have been added to the second edition. Chapter 14 provides additional star schemas that can be used as templates for data analysis solutions. Chapter 15 provides an explanation of how to use the universal data models to create an enterprise data model, a logical data model, and a physical database design. This chapter provides examples of customizing enterprise and logical data models and several physical database design examples for implementing one of the universal data models. A great number of new universal data models have been added to the already existing comprehensive library from the first edition. Table 1.1 provides a listing of the new models.

Table 1.1 Data Models Added in Second Edition

CHAPTER	NEW DATA MODELS THAT HAVE BEEN ADDED FROM THE FIRST EDITION TO THE SECOND EDITION
2 Parties	2b Person—alternate model 2.4 Party roles 2.5 Specific party relationships 2.6 Common party relationships 2.11 Facility versus contact mechanism 2.12 Party communication event 2.13 Communication event follow up event
3 Products	3.4 Product feature 3.10a Products and parts 3.10b Products and parts—alternate model
4 Orders	4.3 Sales order parties and contact mechanisms 4.4 Purchase order parties and contact mechanisms 4.6 Order adjustments 4.12 Agreement roles
5 Shipments	5.4 Shipment receipt for incoming shipments 5.5 Item issuances for outgoing shipments 5.6 Shipping documents 5.7 Shipment route segments
6 Work Efforts	6.1 Work requirement 6.2 Work requirement roles 6.12 Work effort results
7 Invoices	7.8a Invoice payments 7.8b Invoice payments—alternate model 7.9 Financial accounts, withdrawals and deposits
8 Accounting	8.2 Business transactions versus accounting transactions 8.4 General ledger account associations and subsidiary ledger accounts 8.7 Budget revision 8.8 Budget revision review 8.9 Budget scenario

Continues

Table 1.1 Data Models Added in Second Edition *(Continued)*

CHAPTER	NEW DATA MODELS THAT HAVE BEEN ADDED FROM THE FIRST EDITION TO THE SECOND EDITION
9 Human Resources	9.8 Benefits tracking 9.10 Employee application 9.11 Employee skills and qualifications 9.12 Employee performance 9.13 Employee termination
12 Star Schema Designs for Sales Analysis Star Schema Designs	12.2 Transaction oriented sales data mart
14 Additional Star Schema Designs	14.1 Inventory management star schema 14.2 Purchase order star schema 14.3 Shipment star schema 14.4 Work effort star schema 14.5 Financial analysis star schema
15 Implementing Universal Data Models	15.2. Customized party contact mechanism (using different terms) 15.3 Additions to the party contact mechanism model 15.4 Detailed model for sales force (showing a customized version for a particular application) 15.6 Party roles and relationships physical design option 1 15.7 Party roles and relationships physical design option 2 15.8 Party roles and relationships physical design option 3

Conventions and Standards Used in This Book

The following section describes the naming standards and diagramming conventions used for presenting the models in this book. Details are provided for entities, subtypes, attributes, relationships, foreign keys, physical models, and illustration tables.

Entities

An *entity* is something of significance about which the enterprise wishes to store information. Whenever entities are referenced throughout the book, they are shown in capital letters. For example, ORDER represents an entity that stores information about a commitment between parties to purchase products. When the name of an entity is used in a sentence to illustrate concepts and busi-

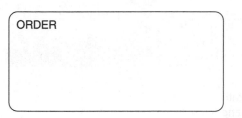

Figure 1.1   An entity.

ness rules, it may be shown in normal text—for example, "Many enterprises have mechanisms such as a sales order form to record sales order information."

The naming conventions for an entity include using a singular noun that is as meaningful as possible to reflect the information it is maintaining. Additionally, the suffix TYPE is added to the entity name if the entity represents a classification of information such as an ORDER TYPE (i.e., sales versus purchase order) rather than a specific instance of a real thing such as an ORDER ("order #23987").

The data models in this book include TYPE entities on the diagrams, even though they usually have only an **id** and a **description.** These entities are included for completeness and to show where allowable values or look-ups are stored.

Entities are included in the data model if it is a requirement of the enterprise to maintain the information included in the entity. For example, if an enterprise doesn't really care about tracking the tasks associated with a shipment, then even though this information exists in the real world, the data model should not incorporate this information because it may not be important enough information for the enterprise to maintain.

Entities are represented by rounded boxes. Figure 1.1 shows an example of the entity ORDER.

Subtypes and Supertypes

A *subtype*, sometimes referred to as a subentity, is a classification of an entity that has characteristics such as attributes or relationships in common with the more general entity. LEGAL ORGANIZATION and INFORMAL ORGANIZATION are, for example, subtypes of ORGANIZATION.

Subtypes are represented in the data modeling diagrams by entities inside other entities. The common attributes and relationships between subtypes are shown in the outside entity, which is known as the *supertype*. The attributes and relationships of the supertype are therefore inherited by the subtype. Figure 1.2 shows the supertype ORGANIZATION and its sub-types LEGAL ORGANIZATION and INFORMAL ORGANIZATION. Notice that the **name** applies to the

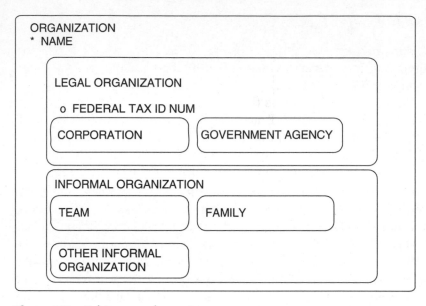

Figure 1.2 Subtypes and supertypes.

supertype ORGANIZATION and the **federal tax ID** applies only to the LEGAL ORGANIZATION subtype. It is therefore shown at the subtype level of LEGAL ORGANIZATION because it applies only to that subtype. Both LEGAL ORGANIZATION and INFORMAL ORGANIZATION would have a **name** because they will inherit the values of the supertype.

Supertypes may have many levels. Figure 1.2 shows that a CORPORATION and GOVERNMENT AGENCY are subtypes of LEGAL ORGANIZATION, which is also a subtype of ORGANIZATION. Thus boxes may be in boxes down to any level to illustrate which subtypes inherit the attributes and relationships of the parent supertype (its outer box).

The subtypes within an entity should represent a complete set of classifications (meaning that the sum of the subtypes covers the supertype in its entirety) and at the same time be mutually exclusive of each other (an exception of handling separate sets of non-mutually exclusive subtypes will be covered in the next section). Many times the data model includes an OTHER...subtype to provide for other possible classifications of the entity that may be defined by the enterprise using the model. For example, each INFORMAL ORGANIZATION may be a TEAM, FAMILY, or OTHER INFORMAL ORGANIZATION.

While the subtypes represent a complete set of possible classifications, there may be more detailed subtypes that are not included in the data model; instead, they may be included in a TYPE entity. In this case, subtypes are shown in two places on a model: as a subtype and in a TYPE entity that shows the domain of allowed types for the entity.

Non-Mutually Exclusive Sets of Subtypes

Sometimes, subtypes are not mutually exclusive; in other words, supertypes may be subtyped different ways and more than one set of subtypes may apply to the same supertype.

Consider Figure 1.3, which shows that a REQUIREMENT may be subtyped different ways. A REQUIREMENT may be from a customer (CUSTOMER REQUIREMENT) or may represent an internal requirement of the enterprise (INTERNAL REQUIREMENT). At the same time, the REQUIREMENT may be a requirement that states the need for a specific product (PRODUCT REQUIRE-MENT) or a requirement that states the need for work to be done (WORK REQUIREMENT).

Therefore, more than one subtype could occur for a REQUIREMENT; for instance, it could be a CUSTOMER REQUIREMENT and PRODUCT REQUIRE-MENT. Figure 1.3 illustrates a convention to show mutually exclusive sets of subtypes by having a box around each set of possible subtypes with no name for the box. The boxes merely serve to establish when there is more than one set of subtypes for a supertype.

Attributes

An *attribute* holds a particular piece of information about an entity, such as the **order date** on an order. Attributes are identified in the text of the book by boldface, lowercase letters such as the previous **order date** example.

Attributes may be part of the unique identifier of an entity (also referred to as a primary key), mandatory, or optional. The primary key attribute(s) is identi-

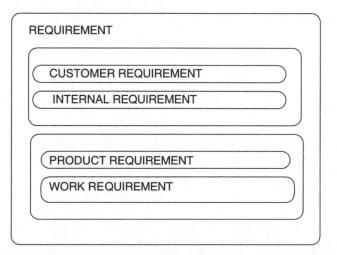

Figure 1.3 Non-mutually exclusive subtypes and supertypes.

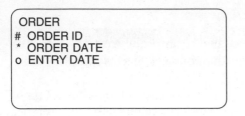

Figure 1.4   Attributes.

fied by a "#" sign preceding the attribute name on the diagram. Mandatory attributes are signified by a "*" before the attribute name. Optional attributes have an "o" before the attribute. Figure 1.4 shows that the ORDER entity has **order ID** as a primary key attribute, **order date** as a mandatory attribute, and **entry date** as an optional attribute.

Certain strings included in an attribute's name have meanings based on the conventions shown in Table 1.2.

Relationships

Relationships define how two entities are associated with each other. When relationships are used in the text, they are usually shown in lowercase as a normal part of the text. In some situations, where they are specifically highlighted, they are identified by boldface lowercase letters. For example, **manufactured by** could be the way a relationship may appear in the text of this book.

Relationship Optionality

Relationships may be either optional or mandatory. A dotted relationship line next to an entity means that the relationship from that entity is optional, and a continuous line means that the relationship is mandatory (the relationship has to exist for all occurrences of each entity). Figure 1.5 shows a relationship that "each SHIPMENT *must be* **shipped from** one and only one POSTAL ADDRESS." This means that the postal address for each shipment must be specified in order to create a shipment instance. The same relationship has an optional aspect when read in the other direction: "Each POSTAL ADDRESS *may be* **the source of** one or more SHIPMENTs." Hence, there could be a postal address which has not been used for a shipment yet.

Relationship Cardinality

Relationships may be one-to-one, one-to-many, or many-to-many. This is generally known as the cardinality of the relationship. The presence of a *crowsfoot* (a three-pronged line that looks like a crow's foot) defines whether an entity points

Table 1.2   Conventions Used in Attribute Naming

STRING WITHIN ATTRIBUTE NAME	MEANING
ID	System-generated sequential unique numeric identifier (i.e., 1, 2, 3, 4,...)
Seq id	System-generated sequence within a parent ID (e.g., order line sequence number)
Code	Unique mnemonic—used to identify user-defined unique identifiers that may have some meaning embedded in the key (i.e., an example of a geo code to store Colorado may be "CO")
Name	A proper pronoun such as a person, geographical area, organization
Description	The descriptive value for a unique code or identifier
Ind (indicator)	A binary choice for values (i.e., yes/no or male/female)
from date	Attribute that specifies the beginning date of a date range and is inclusive of the date specified
thru date	Attribute that specifies the end date of a date range and is inclusive of the date specified (**to date** is not used because **thru date** more clearly represents an inclusive end of date range)

to more than one occurrence of another entity. Figure 1.6 shows that "each ORDER must be **composed of** *one or more* ORDER ITEMs" because the crowsfoot is at the ORDER ITEM side. The other relationship side states that "each ORDER ITEM must be **part of** *one and only one* ORDER." A one-to-one relationship doesn't have any crowsfeet on the relationship, and a many-to-many relationship has crowsfeet at both ends of the relationship. Sometimes, one-to-many relationships are referred to as parent-child relationships.

Sometimes the term "over time" needs to be added to the relationship sentence to verify whether the relationship is one-to-many. For instance, an ORDER may appear to have only one ORDER STATUS; however, if status history is required, then each ORDER may be in the status of by one or more ORDER STATUSes, *over time*.

The data models in the book have very few one-to-one relationships because most of the time one-to-one relationships can be grouped together into a single entity when normalized. The data model diagrams do not show many-to-many relationships because many-to-many-relationships are almost always broken out into *intersection* entities.

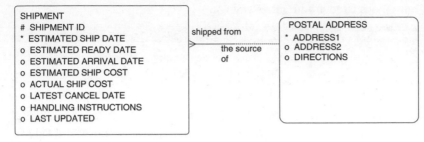

Figure 1.5 Mandatory versus optional relationships.

Foreign Key Relationships

A *foreign key* is defined as the presence of another entity's (or table's) primary key in an entity (or table). For example, in Figure 1.6 the **order ID** from the ORDER entity is part of the ORDER ITEM entity; therefore, it is a foreign key. Any one-to-many relationship indicates that the primary key of the entity on the *one* side of the relationship is brought into the entity on the *many* side of the relationship. Some data modelers show this foreign key as an attribute of the entity (this is sometimes known as key migration). *The data models in this book do not show the foreign keys of entities as attributes because this is redundant.*

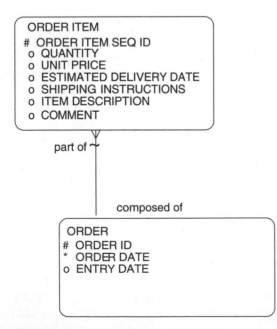

Figure 1.6 One-to-many relationship.

Instead, the relationship itself identifies the foreign key. In Figure 1.6, the **order ID** is not shown as an attribute in the ORDER ITEM entity because the one-to-many nature of the relationship reveals that it is a foreign key.

Foreign Key Inheritance

A diagramming convention in this book is to use a tilde ("~") relationship line to indicate that the inherited foreign key is part of the primary key of the child entity. The tilde ("~") line across the relationship in Figure 1.6 indicates that the **order ID** *is part of the ORDER ITEM entity primary key.* This convention allows a shorthand notation, providing for the primary key to be identified as a combination of the primary key attributes (identified with a "#") as well as the primary keys of the entity to which the relationship with a tilde is pointing.

Therefore the primary key to the ORDER ITEM is the **order item seq ID** plus the primary key of the order, **order id**.

This convention allows a shorthand notation to document the primary keys of each entity without taking up a great deal of space by repeated foreign keys that form part of another entity's primary key. This notation also shows the semantics of the primary key by clearly specifying the relationships that make up the primary key as well as any attributes with a "#" symbol next to them.

Intersection or Association Entities to Handle Many-to-Many Relationships

Intersection entities are also known as associative entities or cross-reference entities. They are used to resolve many-to-many relationships by cross-referencing one entity to another. Often they include additional attributes that may further delineate the relationship. Figure 1.7 shows a many-to-many relationship between a PARTY and a CONTACT MECHANISM that is resolved in this way. The diagram indicates that a PARTY may be **contacted via** *more than one* CONTACT MECHANISM such as a POSTAL ADDRESS, TELECOMMUNICATIONS NUMBER, or ELECTRONIC ADDRESS because a party may have many ways to be contacted. Conversely, a CONTACT MECHANISM may be **used by** *more than one* PARTY. For instance, many people may have the same work address or work phone number. This many-to-many relationship is resolved by the intersection entity PARTY CONTACT MECHANISM.

Each associative entity inherits the key to each of the entities it intersects. Therefore the tilde ("~") is always used in the reference relationships of an associative entity to show that the associative entity inherits the key of each of the referenced entities (see "foreign key inheritance" mentioned in the last section). For example, the **party id** and the **contact mechanism id** are parts of the primary key to PARTY CONTACT MECHANISM, along with the **from date**.

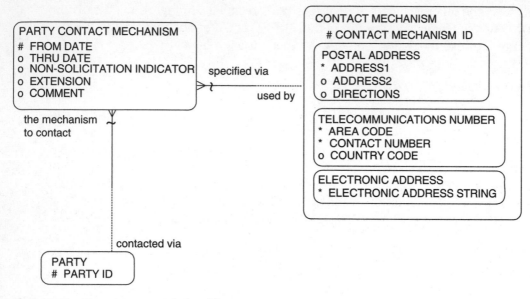

Figure 1.7 Many-to-many relationships.

Notice that in all the examples given, each relationship has two relationship names associated with it that describe the relationship in both directions. The relationship names should be combined so that they read as a complete sentence, as shown in the following format: "Each ENTITY {must be/may be} relationship name {one and only one/one or more} ENTITY, over time," where the appropriate choices are filled in.

In the models presented, the crowsfeet on the relationships generally point up and to the left in order to provide a consistent mechanism for reading the diagrams. This tends to organize the data models in a more understandable format.

Exclusive Arcs

Exclusive arcs are used to identify relationships where an entity is related to two or more other entities, but only one relationship can exist for a specific entity occurrence. The exclusive arc is represented by a curved line going through two or more relationship lines. Figure 1.8 shows an example of an exclusive arc. The relationships are read as "Each INVENTORY ITEM must be *either* located at one and only FACILITY or must be located within one and only one CONTAINER, *but not both.*" This communicates that inventory items are stored at one of two types of levels: They are either located at facilities such as a warehouse or stored within containers such as a bin that is located within a facility.

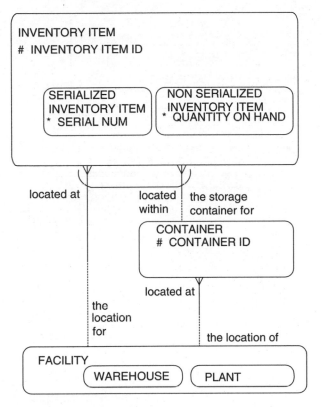

Figure 1.8 Exclusive arcs.

Recursive Relationships

Recursive relationships are relationships that show how one entity is related to itself. For example, a recursive relationship could be modeled either via a relationship pointing from an entity to itself or via a many-to-many-relationship. This depends on if it is a many-to-many recursion or a one-to-many recursion. It is possible for an entity to have many recursive relationships.

Figure 1.9 shows an example of a one-to-many recursion around the WORK EFFORT entity to show that work efforts may be redone. It also shows a many-to-many recursion that is resolved by the intersection entity WORK EFFORT ASSOCIATION to show that work efforts may be either dependent on other work efforts (WORK EFFORT DEPENDENCY subtype) or broken down into several lower-level work efforts (WORK EFFORT BREAKDOWN subtype).

Physical Models

The data warehouse models and diagrams (Chapters 10 through 14) as well as some of the models in Chapter 15, represent physical database designs. The

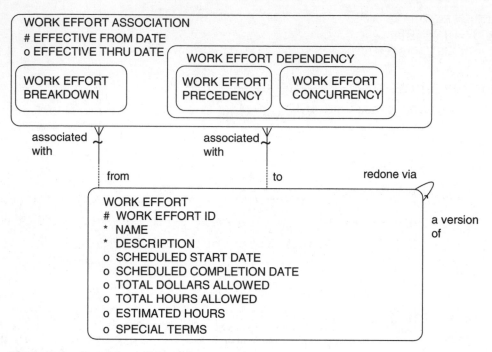

Figure 1.9   Recursive relationships.

same notations can be used as previously stated with the exception that because these models represent physical database designs, each box represents a table, and the field names are columns.

Conventions Used for Illustration Tables

Many parts of the data models are illustrated via tables that contain possible values for attributes. Each illustration table is normally defined to show a specific entity and the relevant information from related entities. For instance, there may be a table illustrating the ORDER ITEM entity, as shown in Table 1.3.

In order to illustrate the details of an ORDER ITEM, Table 1.3 brings in some attribute information from the ORDER entity. Whenever data from each illus-

Table 1.3   Order Item

ORDER ID	ORDER DATE	ORDER ITEM SEQ ID	COMMENT
12930	April 30, 1995	1	Need this item urgently
		2	There's no time pressure at all on this item

tration table is referenced in the text of this book, it is surrounded by double quotes. For instance, the text may refer to specific order "12930," order item seq id "1", which has a comment of "Need this item urgently."

Conventions Used to Reference Figures

Because there are two volumes for the *Data Model Resource Book*, figures are referenced by the following notation:

Vx:Figure x.x

Where   Vx signifies a reference to either Volume 1 or Volume 2

and   Figure x.x references a specific figure in that volume.

For example, V1:2.1 references Figure 2.1 in Volume 1, the Organization data model. V2:2.2 references Figure 2.2 (Parts and products) in the second volume. If there is no Vx in front of the reference, then the reader may assume that the figure is in the current volume.

The Companion Electronic Product

This book and its appendices provide very detailed descriptions of the models discussed. The diagrams lay out all the relationships, the mandatory attributes and columns, the primary keys, and they even include some optional attributes. The appendices include the physical details for the attributes and columns, such as the datatype and size. With this information, it would be possible for a data modeler or database designer to recreate these models in the tool of his or her choice or write the SQL code to build them in a database.

This, however, would take a substantial amount of time and opens the possibility of data entry errors. To assist those interested in quickly implementing the models described in these pages, the models are provided in electronic form. The Demo CD-ROM that accompanies this book offers a free demonstration of the electronic models. The full set of models for Volume 1 is sold separately. See "How to Use the Electronic Product" at the end of this book for details on purchasing, accessing, and using the CD-ROM.

The demo files on this CD-ROM contain a sample of SQL scripts derived directly from the models in the book. In the full version, all the entities, attributes, tables, and columns discussed are implemented with this code. Scripts are provided for several database platforms. There are also generic standard SQL scripts that could be used with other ODBC databases.

Because the CD-ROM includes standard SQL scripts, they should work with not only the current versions of these database management systems but also with future versions. This includes object-relational databases assuming that they support relational designs. The constructs in the book are, of course, also generally applicable to any relational or object-relational database.

Use of the scripts on the CD-ROM will allow an enterprise to more rapidly deploy the models presented in this book. In addition to the time savings, there is obviously a cost savings as well (nobody has to type in all the definitions or write SQL scripts). Once the scripts have been run, the models could be reverse-engineered into the enterprise's favorite CASE tool (most popular CASE tools provide a reverse-engineering feature). Once the models have been brought into a repository, they are easily accessible and may be customized for a specific enterprise's needs. Additionally, they can be used to jump-start the development of corporate data models, new applications, data warehouse designs, or decision support systems.

The CD-ROM also contains the data model diagrams in elecronic formats and a series of reports that list and cross-reference the subject data areas, entities, attributes, tables, and columns of the data models.

The remainder of this book will provide many examples of universal data models and data warehouse designs that can assist in increasing the productivity of system development efforts. Detailed examples of how to implement these models will be provided in chapter 15, "Implementing Universal Data Models."

CHAPTER

2

People and Organizations

The most frequent business information need is to ask questions about people and organizations and to be able to rely on accurate answers to these questions. For instance:

- What are the attributes or characteristics of the people and organizations that are involved in the course of conducting business?

- What relationships exist between various people, between various organizations, and between people and organizations?

- What are the addresses, phone numbers, and other contact mechanisms of people and organizations, and how can they be contacted?

- What types of communication or contacts have occurred between various parties, and what is necessary to effectively follow up on these communications?

Almost all business applications track information about people and organizations, recording information about customers, suppliers, subsidiaries, departments, employees, and contractors redundantly in many different systems. For this reason, it is very difficult to keep key information such as client contact data consistent and accurate. Examples of applications that store information about people and organizations include sales, marketing, purchasing, order entry, invoicing, project management, and accounting.

The data model within this chapter can be used for most organizations and applications. Subsequent chapters use this data model as a basis on which to add more detail. This chapter includes data models on the following:

- Organization
- Person (alternate model also provided)
- Party (organizations or people)
- Party roles (i.e., customers, suppliers, internal organizations)
- Specific party relationships (i.e., customer relationship, supplier relationship, employment)
- Common party relationships
- Party relationship information
- Postal address information (postal addresses and geographic boundaries)
- Party contact mechanism—telecommunications numbers and electronic addresses
- Party contact mechanism (expanded)
- Facility versus contact mechanism
- Party communication event (i.e., phone calls, support calls, meetings)
- Communication event follow-up

Organization

Most data models maintain organizational information in various entities that are portrayed as completely separate entities. For instance, there may be a customer entity, a vendor entity, and a department entity. Each application within an enterprise has its own needs; therefore, the data modeler will often base the model on the needs of a particular application. For example, when building an order entry application, the customer information is crucial; therefore, the data modeler shows a separate entity for customer. Likewise, the supplier information is critical when building a purchasing application; hence, there is normally a supplier entity. For a human resources system, the data modeler might show an entity called a department within which the employees work.

The problem is that an organization may play many roles, depending on the particular circumstance. For instance, in larger companies, internal organizations sell to each other. The property management division may be a supplier to the product sales division. The property management division may also be a customer of the product sales division. In this case, there would normally be both a customer and supplier record, with redundant data, for each of these divisions. Not only could there be a customer and a supplier record, but there could also be many additional records for the organization depending on how many roles the organization plays within the enterprise.

When an organization's information changes—such as a change in address—the information might be updated in only one of the many systems where organization information is stored. This, of course, results in inconsistent information within the enterprise. It may also result in major frustration on the part of managers, customers, suppliers, and anyone who might want to generate a correct mailing list!

The solution to this redundancy problem is to model an entity called ORGANIZATION that stores information about a group of people with a common purpose such as a corporation, department, division, government agency, or nonprofit organization. Basic organizational information, such as its **name** and **federal tax ID num** (for legal entities), is stored once within this entity, reducing redundancy of information and eliminating possible update discrepancies.

Figure 2.1 shows the data model for organization information. An organization is defined as a group of individuals that, together, have an informal or for-

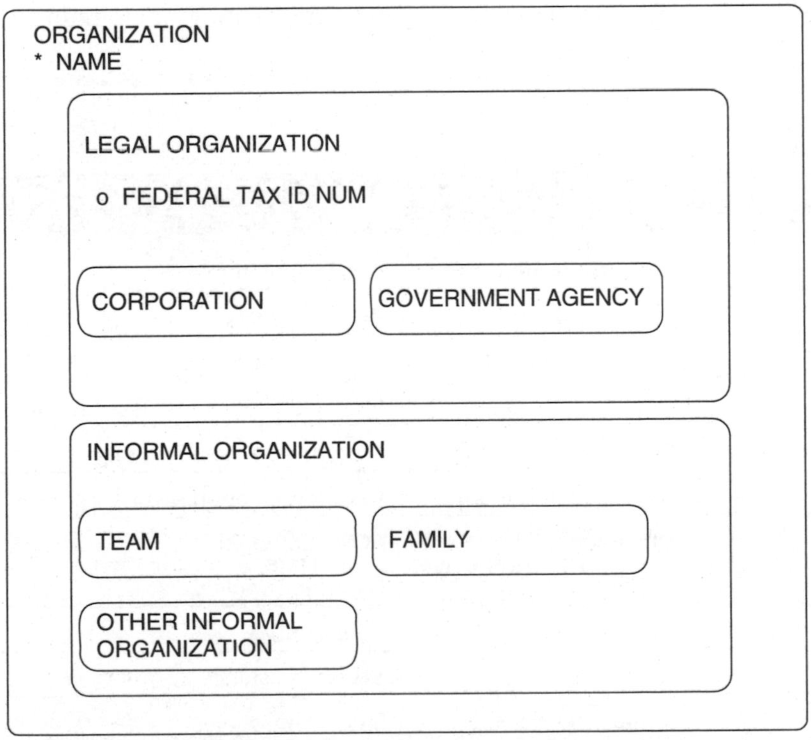

Figure 2.1   Organization.

mal association. An ORGANIZATION may be a LEGAL ORGANIZATION, such as a CORPORATION or GOVERNMENT AGENCY, or an INFORMAL ORGANIZATION, such as a FAMILY, TEAM, or OTHER INFORMAL ORGANIZATION. Both legal and informal organizations may share many relationships because they may both be assigned to various roles and responsibilities and may be managed by people. While they share many things in common, they also have differences. For instance, a legal organization is the only type of organization that may be a party to a contract.

This model reduces redundancy because the organization information is stored only once, as opposed to storing this information redundantly in a customer entity, a supplier entity, a department entity, or any other entity storing organization information.

Table 2.1 gives examples of data in the ORGANIZATION entity. ABC Corporation and ABC Subsidiary are examples of legal organizations that happen to be internal organizations of the enterprise being modeled. "Accounting Division," "Information Systems Department," and "Customer Service Division" are informal organizations and internal to the enterprise. "Fantastic Supplies," "Hughs Cargo," and "Sellers Assistance Corporation" are legal corporations that represent companies with whom the enterprise engages in business. The "Smith family" is an organization because it represents a group of individuals that are associated by family, and it may be useful for recording demographic informa-

Table 2.1   Organizations

ORGANIZATION ID	ORGANIZATION SUBTYPE	NAME
100	Legal organization	ABC Corporation
200	Legal organization	ABC Subsidiary
300	Informal organization	Accounting Division
400	Informal organization	Information Systems Department
500	Informal organization	Customer Service Division
600	Informal organization	Customer Support Team
700	Legal organization	ACME Corporation
800	Legal organization	Fantastic Supplies
900	Legal organization	Hughs Cargo
1000	Legal organization	Sellers Assistance Corporation
1100	Informal organization	Smith Family
1200	Legal organization	Government Quality Commission

tion. The "Government Quality Commission" is a government agency that is involved in monitoring the operations of the enterprise.

For the remainder of this book, the term "enterprise" will be used to refer to all the internal organizations for whom the data model is being developed. For instance, each enterprise will have its own specific needs and business rules that will determine how the enterprise will customize these models for its own use.

Person

Just as most data models show separate entities for various types of organizations, they also show separate entities for various types of people such as employees, contractors, supplier contacts, and customer contacts. The problem with keeping this information in separate entities is that people may also have different jobs and roles that change over time. Most systems will record redundant information about a person because they store a record each time the person's role changes.

For example, John Smith was a good customer of ABC Corporation. John then decided to perform contract labor for ABC Corporation. The people at ABC Corporation liked his work so much that they then hired him as an employee. For most systems, there would be a separate record for John Smith as a customer contact, then as a contractor, then as an employee. Much of John Smith's information has remained the same, such as his name, gender, birth date, skills, and other demographics. Because John Smith's information is stored in several locations, many systems would have trouble keeping his information accurate and consistent.

Another problem is that the same person may have many different roles *at the same time*. For instance, ABC Corporation is a large company with many divisions. Shirley Jones is an employee and manager of the transportation division. She is also considered a customer of the supplies division. At the same time, she is the supplier for the publishing division, which needs her services to transport catalogues. Therefore, Shirley is an employee of one division, a customer contact of another division, and a supplier contact of yet another division. Rather than have three separate records for Shirley with redundant information, there should be only one record.

To address this issue, Figure 2.2a shows a PERSON entity that stores a particular person's information, independent of his or her jobs or roles. Attributes of the PERSON entity may include current last name, current first name, current middle initial, gender, birth date, height, weight, and many other attributes that are listed in Figure 2.2a and describe the person.

Table 2.2 shows some example data for the PERSON entity. The table shows key information about John Smith, Judy Smith, Nancy Barry, Marc Martinez,

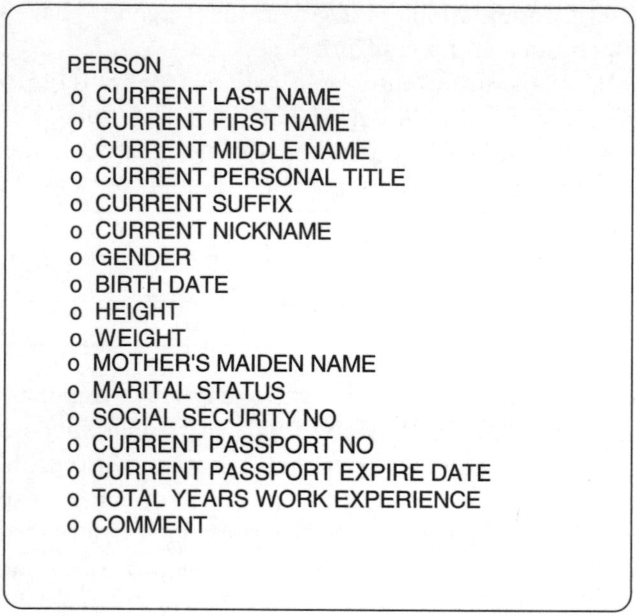

```
PERSON
  o CURRENT LAST NAME
  o CURRENT FIRST NAME
  o CURRENT MIDDLE NAME
  o CURRENT PERSONAL TITLE
  o CURRENT SUFFIX
  o CURRENT NICKNAME
  o GENDER
  o BIRTH DATE
  o HEIGHT
  o WEIGHT
  o MOTHER'S MAIDEN NAME
  o MARITAL STATUS
  o SOCIAL SECURITY NO
  o CURRENT PASSPORT NO
  o CURRENT PASSPORT EXPIRE DATE
  o TOTAL YEARS WORK EXPERIENCE
  o COMMENT
```

Figure 2.2a   Person.

William Jones, Shirley Jones, Barry Cunningham, and Harry Johnson. This model helps reduce redundancy because the person's base information is maintained only once, even though the person may play many different roles. The "Party Roles" section later in this chapter will describe how to model the various roles each person and organization can play and the "Party Relationship" section will show how to model the interrelationships between party roles.

Some of these attributes in the PERSON entity may be repeating attributes and may need to be separated into their own entity, depending on whether the enterprise has the will and means to store many instances of that attribute.

Person—Alternate Model

Figure 2.2b shows an alternate model for PERSON with the repeated attributes separated into their own entities. For instance, the MARITAL STATUS entity allows the maintenance of the history of marital changes, and the MARITAL STATUS TYPE entity could store instances such as "single," "married," "divorced," and "widowed."

To reiterate the diagramming convention from Chapter 1, a tilde ("~") across the relationship line indicates that the inherited foreign key is part of the primary key of the child entity. For instance, the tildes ("~") across the relationship lines in the top left corner of Figure 2.2b indicate that the **party id** and **marital status type id** are part of the MARITAL STATUS entity primary

Table 2.2 Person Data

PERSON ID	LAST NAME	FIRST NAME	GENDER	BIRTH DATE	HEIGHT	WEIGHT
5000	Smith	John	Male	1/5/49	6′	190
5100	Smith	Judy	Female			
5200	Barry	Nancy	Female			
5300	Martinez	Marc	Male			
5400	Jones	William	Male			
5500	Jones	Shirley	Female	4/12/59	5′2″	100
5600	Cunningham	Bobby	Male	3/14/65	5′11″	170
5700	Johnson	Harry	Male	12/9/37	5′8″	178
5800	Goldstein	Barry				
5900	Schmoe	Joe	Male			
6000	Red	Jerry	Male			

key. This convention allows a shorthand notation, providing for the primary key to be identified as a combination of the primary key attributes (identified with a "#") as well as the primary keys of the entity to which the relationship with a tilde is referencing.

The PHYSICAL CHARACTERISTICs entity provides a means to store the history of a person's physical characteristics such as height and weight. This history is also useful in health-related fields. The details of each characteristic is stored in the PHYSICAL CHARACTERISTIC TYPE entity, which could have values of "height," "weight," "blood pressure," and so on. The **value** attribute in the PHYSICAL CHARACTERISTIC maintains the characteristic's measurement such as a height of 6′1″ and is an alphanumeric attribute to accommodate different characteristics.

A person may have many PERSON NAMEs either at the same time (name aliases) or over time as his or her name changes. This may be important information in many applications. An example of this is in a prison or correctional facility where the enterprise would want to maintain a history of names and aliases. In these cases, the PERSON NAME entity can be used to store all the names and aliases. The **current last name, current first name, current middle initial, current prefix, current suffix,** and **current nickname** attributes are now maintained in the PERSON NAME and PERSON NAME TYPE entities. The PERSON NAME entity stores the name and the time period during which it is valid, and the PERSON NAME TYPE entity maintains the type of name it is in

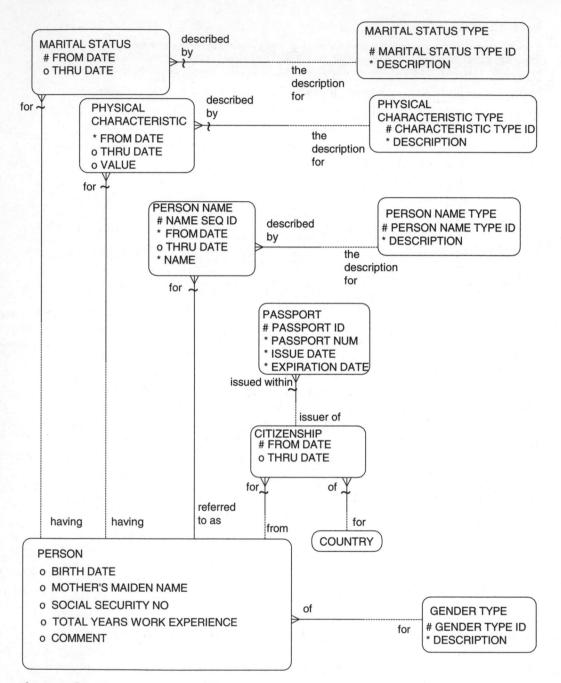

Figure 2.2b Person—alternate model.

the **description** attribute. For instance, the PERSON NAME TYPE **description** may be "first" or "last." This data model provides much more flexibility because many names can now be stored. Some cultures have more than one middle or last name, and this structure handles diverse needs. Because the current name has great applicability in many circumstances, the current last name, current first name, current middle name, current personal title (i.e., Mr., Mrs., Dr., Ms.), current suffix (i.e., Jr., Senior, III) and any nicknames or aliases could be stored in the PERSON entity as in the previous diagram, and the PERSON NAME could be used to store a history of names.

Also shown in Figure 2.2b are entities to show the CITIZENSHIP and PASS-PORTs that a person has had instead of the simple **current passport number** and **passport expiration date** attributes in the first model. This could be useful in travel applications.

The GENDER TYPE entity stores common descriptions for gender classifications and may contain instances such as "male," "female," "male to female," "female to male," and "not provided." If a history is needed, for instance, in specialized medical enterprises, there could be an associative entity of PERSON GENDER that may be between PERSON and GENDER TYPE.

As the model illustrates, a great deal of demographic information is maintained about people and organizations. By maintaining information about people and organizations once in a single place, the enterprise can capture much more consistent data and be able to apply this information in many contexts.

Party

Organizations and people are similar in many respects. They both have common characteristics that describe them, such as their credit rating, address, phone number, fax number, or e-mail address. Organizations and people can also serve in similar roles as parties to contracts, buyers, sellers, responsible parties, or members of other organizations. For example, membership organizations (like a computer users group) may keep similar information on their corporate members and their individual members. Contracts can usually specify an organization or a person as a contracted party. The customer for a sales order may be either an organization or a person.

If person and organization were modeled as completely separate entities, the data model would be more complex. Each contract, sales order, membership, or transaction that involved either a person or an organization would need two relationships: one to the person entity and one to the organization entity. Furthermore, these relationships are mutually exclusive and thus would require an exclusive arc (see Chapter 1 for a discussion on exclusive arcs). For instance, a sales order could be placed by a person or an organization, but a single sales order cannot be placed by both a person and an organization at the same time.

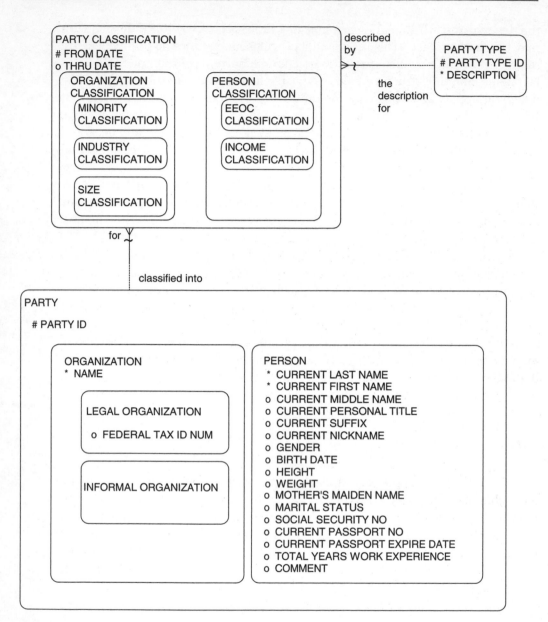

Figure 2.3   Party.

Therefore, Figure 2.3 shows a superentity named PARTY that has as its two subtypes PERSON and ORGANIZATION. This PARTY entity will enable storage of some of the common characteristics and relationships that people and organizations share.

Parties are classified into various categories using the entity PARTY CLASSI-FICATION, which stores each category into which parties may belong. There are subtypes for ORGANIZATION CLASSIFICATION such as INDUSTRY CLASSIFICATION, SIZE CLASSIFICATION, and MINORITY CLASSIFICATION as well as subtypes to categorize people such as EEOC (Equal Employment Opportunity Commission) CLASSIFICATION and INCOME CLASSIFICATION. The ORGANIZATION CLASSIFICATION and PERSON CLASSIFICATION could be related to ORGANIZATION and PERSON, respectively, if one wanted to model them more specifically. For simplicity purposes, however, this model shows them as subtypes of PARTY CLASSIFICATION, which is related to PARTY. These represent only a few possible types for illustration purposes, and other possible values for categories are maintained in the PARTY TYPE entity.

Examples for MINORITY CLASSIFICATION include "minority-owned business," "8A business," or "woman-owned business." INDUSTRY CLASSIFI-CATION may include "telecommunications," "government institute," or "manufacturer." SIZE CLASSIFICATION may be "small," "medium," "large," and "national account" and may also be defined by a range of number of employees. For people, the EEOC CLASSIFICATION instances may include values such as "african american," "native american," "asian or pacific islander," "hispanic," and "white non-hispanic." The instance "women" is another EEOC classification; however, it is covered using the **gender** attribute within the PERSON entity. INCOME CLASSIFICATIONs may include values to indicate yearly income such as "less than $20,000," "$20,001 to 50,000," "$50,001 to 250,000," and "over $250,000."

These categorizations of parties can be used to determine if there are any special business considerations for parties, special pricing arrangements, or special terms based on the type of party. It is also a mechanism for classifying businesses into types of industries for market segmentation and to target marketing efforts. A **from date** and **thru date** are included so history can be tracked because it is possible for the definition to change over time [e.g., businesses may "graduate" from the 8A (minority startup) program].

Table 2.3 shows several party occurrences that are merely consolidations from the person and organization examples. This single entity allows the data models to refer to either a person or an organization as a party to a transaction. The table shows our previous examples of organizations and people along with the PARTY TYPEs that serve to classify them according to various demographic categories. Organizations and people may be classified several ways, thus the need for the many-to-many relationship between PARTY and PARTY TYPE. "ABC Corporation" is classified as a "minority owned business" and a "manufacturer." "ACME Corporation" is classified as a "woman-owned business," "mail order firm," and a "large organization." People may be classified into various categories such as EEOC CLASSIFICATION types as well as other personal classifications such as INCOME CLASSIFICATION. Table 2.3 shows

Table 2.3 Party Data

PARTY ID	PARTY NAME (ORGANIZATION NAME OR FIRST NAME/LAST NAME)	PARTY TYPE
100	ABC Corporation	Minority-owned business Manufacturer
200	ABC Subsidiary	Minority-owned business Manufacturer
300	Accounting Division	
400	Information Systems Department	
500	Customer Service Division	
600	Customer support team	
700	ACME Corporation	Woman-owned business Mail order firm Large organization
800	Fantastic Supplies	Janitorial service organization Small organization
900	Hughs Cargo	8A organization Service organization Small organization
1000	Sellers Assistance Corporation	Marketing service provider Medium-sized organization
1100	Smith Family	
5000	John Smith	
5100	Judy Smith	
5200	Nancy Barry	
5300	Marc Martinez	Hispanic Income classification $50,000–250,000
5400	William Jones	African American
5500	Shirley Jones	
5600	Barry Cunningham	
5700	Harry Johnson	
5800	Barry Goldstein	
5900	Joe Schmoe	
6000	Jerry Red	

that Marc Martinez is classified as a "Hispanic" with an income classification of "$50,000–250,000" and that William Jones is classified as an "African American." Many of the people do not have classifications, which illustrates that this information is totally optionally and may not be available from many of the parties.

Party Roles

As noted previously, a person or organization may play any number of roles such as a customer, supplier, employee, or internal organization. Because the same PARTY may play many roles over time or at the same time, the need to define the information about each role arises. The PARTY entity defines the nature of the party, which will not change over time. The PARTY TYPE classifies the party into certain categories. The PARTY ROLE entity defines *how a party* acts or, in other words, what roles the party plays in the context of the enterprise's environment. There may be certain information related to a party that applies only to a specific role. For instance, credit information may be applicable only to customers and thus be a relationship or attribute of this role only. Specific relationships may be applicable only to certain roles. For instance, the relationship from the entity EMPLOYMENT with a "from date" and "start date" is specifically related to a role of employee.

Are these roles just subtypes of the party entity, or is there a PARTY ROLE entity to indicate that each PARTY may act in one or more PARTY ROLEs? For example, are the entities CUSTOMER and SUPPLIER subtypes of the PARTY entity, or should they be subtypes of a PARTY ROLE entity to show that the same PARTY can be both a CUSTOMER and a SUPPLIER? One can argue the data model either way (which has happened innumerable times during the course of this writing).

With either of these approaches, it is important to establish that these roles such as CUSTOMER, SUPPLIER, EMPLOYEE, and INTERNAL ORGANIZATION are entities that need to be tracked in addition to the PARTY entity. The PARTY entity allows the enterprise to track consistent information about the person or organization once. The PARTY ROLE allows the enterprise to maintain information (attributes or relationships) about each party within the context of their specific roles. For example, a certain party may have various contact information (home address, office address, home phone, cell phone, and so on) regardless of how many roles he or she may play within the enterprise (the party may be a customer, a supplier, and an agent). For the party's role as a customer, and only for that role, it may be important to store credit rating information.

Figure 2.4 provides a data model to illustrate how to model specific roles within an enterprise. It contains many common roles that are widely applicable to many enterprises. The **Party Role id** primary key attribute allows the same

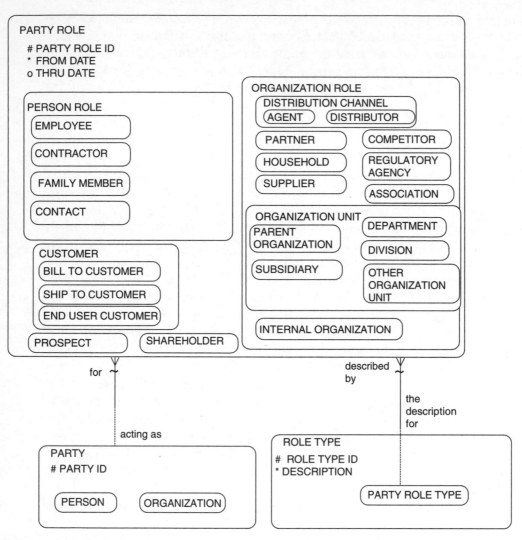

Figure 2.4 Party roles.

party to play the same role at different points in time. Roles are subtyped into PERSON ROLEs, ORGANIZATION ROLEs, and roles that may be either. PERSON ROLEs include EMPLOYEE for legal employees of the enterprise, CONTRACTOR for a person who is or has performed a contract with the enterprise, FAMILY MEMBER to indicate that this person is part of a biological family, and CONTACT to indicate someone who is acting as a representative with an organization (this may be a sales contact, support contact, customer contact, supplier contact, or any other type of representative). .

Common roles that may be for either people or organizations are CUSTOMER, which is a party that has purchased (BILL TO CUSTOMER), been shipped (SHIP TO CUSTOMER), or used (END USER CUSTOMER) products (either goods or services) from the enterprise. A SHAREHOLDER may also be either a person or an organization and is therefore not a person role or organization role. The same applies to a PROSPECT, which is a person or organization that the enterprise thinks will purchase, be shipped, or use their products.

Organization Roles

The ORGANIZATION roles include DISTRIBUTION CHANNEL (which typically is an AGENT or a DISTRIBUTOR), COMPETITOR, PARTNER, REGULATORY AGENCY, HOUSEHOLD, ASSOCIATION, SUPPLIER, various ORGANIZATION UNITs such as a PARENT ORGANIZATION, SUBSIDIARY, DEPARTMENT, DIVISION, and OTHER ORGANIZATION UNIT as well as INTERNAL ORGANIZATION, which indicates if the organization is part of the enterprise or is an external organization.

A DISTRIBUTION CHANNEL is an organization that markets the enterprise's products. An AGENT markets these products without buying or carrying goods while a DISTRIBUTOR generally markets the goods by first buying them and then selling them. A COMPETITOR carries similar products and is tracking performance for comparative analysis. A PARTNER is an organization that is identified as an ally and with whom mutually beneficially relationships are established. A REGULATORY AGENCY is an organization that regulates or governs the activities of the enterprise. A HOUSEHOLD is an informal organization of people that live within the same residence and is typically a family. This information is helpful to establish customer demographics for personal products. An ASSOCIATION is an organization that provides services such as networking and sharing of information within particular fields of interest or industries. A SUPPLIER is an enterprise that may or does provide products (goods and/or services) to the enterprise. An ORGANIZATION UNIT identifies the form of this organization and is useful to identify parts of organizations as well as maintenance of organizational structures. This role may be further subtyped as a PARENT ORGANIZATION, SUBSIDIARY, DEPARTMENT, DIVISION, or OTHER ORGANIZATION UNIT to cover more unique types of organizations that are specific to the enterprise. A PARENT ORGANIZATION is a role whereby this enterprise encompasses other enterprises. A SUBSIDIARY organization is a role whereby this organization is encompassed by another enterprise and is partially or wholly owned by the parent organization. A DIVISION is a portion of an organization dedicated to a specific purpose within the enterprise. A DEPARTMENT is also a portion of an organization dedicated to a more specific purpose within the enterprise and is sometimes within a division of the enterprise. An INTERNAL ORGANIZATION is an organization that is part of the enterprise for whom the data model is developed.

Common Party Role Subtypes

These subtypes are intended in order to provide a list of common subtypes used in most enterprises, and it should be understood that each enterprise may modify this list of subtypes to suit its own specific needs. Therefore, each PARTY ROLE may be described by one and only one PARTY ROLE TYPE. The PARTY ROLE TYPE is a subtype of ROLE TYPE that has a **description** attribute that stores available values of role types. Roles may be defined declaratively such as this person is a "prospect" or roles may be associated with specific transactions such as orders, agreements, requirements, and so on. Therefore, this book will use the ROLE TYPE entity to show additional role types showing how parties are involved in the enterprise. Other ROLE TYPE subtypes that will be discussed later in this book will be an ORDER ROLE TYPE, AGREEMENT ROLE TYPE, REQUIREMENT ROLE TYPE, and specific role types for many other types of transactions.

Examples of PARTY ROLE TYPEs include all the subtypes previously mentioned such as "employee," "contact," "customer," "supplier," "internal organization," and so on, plus more specific role types such as "placing customer," "bill to customer," "installation customer," "customer contact," "supplier contact," and any other roles not specified in the PARTY ROLE subtypes. As a reminder, for illustrative purposes, the notation of this book shows subtypes within an entity such as PARTY ROLE and then also shows a relationship to a "TYPE" entity to cover all the other possible types.

Some PARTY ROLEs are dependent on the context of another party in order to fully define them, and some roles can stand on their own. For instance, a PARENT ORGANIZATION role is useful to identify companies that own other companies. This role is usually dependent on the other organization that is the SUBSIDIARY ORGANIZATION. These roles are therefore dependent on having a PARTY RELATIONSHIP instance, which will be defined in the next section. PARTY ROLES such as "notary" or "doctor" can stand on their own, and parties may have these roles, even without an associated PARTY RELATIONSHIP.

Each PARTY ROLE may be valid for certain time frames, and therefore the attributes **from date** and **thru date** are part of the PARTY ROLE. These attributes are optional because many of the time frames for the roles will be dependent on (and can be derived from) the PARTY RELATIONSHIP entity, which will be discussed in the next section. These attributes are particularly useful for relationship-independent roles such as "notary" or "doctor."

Should Roles Be Defined at the Time of the Transaction?

One may make the point that the enterprise doesn't really know the role of the party until certain transactions take place and therefore this role information is derived and unneeded. For instance, if CUSTOMER is defined as a party that has purchased, been shipped, or used products, the ORDER, INVOICE, DEPLOYMENT USAGE (from Volume 2) or SHIPMENT entities will dictate who is a customer; this information will be available from relationships between these entities and the PARTY entity. As a practical matter, it is important to be able to declaratively state the role of certain parties. The enterprise may declaratively state that "XYZ company" is a prospect, although there aren't any transactions that the enterprise maintains about the event of becoming a prospect. Similarly, the enterprise may want to declaratively state a certain party is a customer even though there aren't any associated transactions. Additionally, even though this is a technical consideration, the enterprise, as a practical matter, would want to know who was a customer, supplier, employee, and so on without having to search for the related transactions. The relationship-independent roles such as "notary" and "doctor" need to be declaratively stated without necessarily being related to transactions that the enterprise is interested in storing.

Another point about the argument of these roles being defined when the transactions occur is that, in some circumstances, the enterprise could instantiate these roles at the time of the transactions. The roles do not necessarily have to be instantiated before any transactions occur. For instance, when a party places an order, the party could then be set up as an instance of a PARTY ROLE of a CUSTOMER (and the enterprise may specifically have them in several customer roles such as BILL TO CUSTOMER, SHIP TO CUSTOMER, END USER CUSTOMER) and then the ORDER could be related to these instances.

Party Role Example

Table 2.4 illustrates examples of possible roles. Notice that most parties will have at least one role because they are maintained for some reason, and they often have more than one role. It is possible for a party to not have even a single role, for instance, in maintaining census data for people (although one could argue that the role is "census participant").

Role Types Throughout This Book

The previous section illustrated that parties may play many roles. Roles may be defined "declaratively" for a party without a transaction involved, such as the person is a "doctor." Roles may also be defined for any type of transactions involved in the data model. There may be roles for orders, shipments, invoices, and any other types of transactions occurring in the data model.

All of these roles will have a standard structure and will be associated with a PARTY, be of a ROLE TYPE, and be associated with the transaction. For example, each ORDER may have many ORDER ROLEs of certain ORDER ROLES

Table 2.4   Party Role Data

PARTY ID	PARTY	PARTY ROLE
100	ABC Corporation	Internal organization Parent organization
200	ABC Subsidiary	Internal organization Subsidiary organization
300	Accounting Division	Internal organization Division
400	Information Systems Department	Internal organization Department
500	Customer Service Division	Internal organization Department
600	Customer support team	Internal organization Team
700	ACME Corporation	Customer Supplier
800	Fantastic Supplies	Supplier Prospect
900	Hughs Cargo	Supplier
1000	Sellers Assistance Corporation	Agent
1100	Smith Family	Prospect
5000	John Smith	Employee Supplier coordinator Parent Team leader Mentor
5100	Judy Smith	Child
5200	Nancy Barry	Supplier service contact
5300	Marc Martinez	Customer contact
5400	William Jones	Employee Account manager (internal sales representative)
5500	Shirley Jones	Project manager Employee QA representative
5600	Barry Cunningham	Contractor
5700	Harry Johnson	Notary
5800	Barry Goldstein	Employee Apprentice
5900	Joe Schmoe	Customer contact
6000	Jerry Red	Employee Customer service representative

TYPEs (party taking order, party giving order, party paying for the order) associated with PARTYs. Each of these ROLE TYPEs (ORDER ROLE TYPE, PARTY ROLE TYPE, SHIPMENT ROLE TYPE, INVOICE ROLE TYPE, and so on) will be considered subtypes of ROLE TYPE and will therefore inherit the attributes of ROLE TYPE such as **role type id** and **description**. This subtype notation for role is shown in Figure 2.6 (a PARTY ROLE TYPE is a subtype of ROLE TYPE); however, the rest of the book will show only the specific role type, for example, ORDER ROLE TYPE without its supertype for simplification reasons.

Party Relationship

As noted previously, a person or organization may play any number of roles such as a customer, supplier, employer, or subsidiary. Many roles that a party plays make sense only in relation to another party. If ACME Company is a customer, is it a customer of ABC Subsidiary or a customer of the parent company, ABC Corporation? Maybe it is a customer of the widgets division or the gadgets division.

Customer relationship management is a hot field in our industry. An amazing fact is that many customer relationship management systems fail to include an entity to track each relationship between parties. These systems will frequently have a "contact" entity (and table) to track information about parties (if they even implement the concept of parties). Then they will associate statuses, priorities and notes, and various dates about these contacts.

The problem is that a great deal of information such as statuses, priorities, notes, and certain dates are *not* related to a "contact"; they are related to a relationship between two parties. For example, picture three salespeople selling different product lines who all have a relationship to the same "contact" of Marc Martinez at ACME Company. Is it possible that each salesperson may want to assign his or her own status, priority, notes, and relationship start date? Each salesperson has a unique relationship to Marc and one salesperson who has sold a great deal to Marc may record a relationship status of "very active" while another salesperson records a status of "inactive" because they don't do much business for the time being. If a **status** attribute is related to just the contact (Marc), these sales representatives will probably override each other's information depending on their relationship and perspective. Each salesperson will also have conversations and want to record notes about their relationships, some of which may be private to their relationship. Of course, the enterprise would also want to be able to access the entire information about the "contact" but they should also want to maintain the unique information about each relationship. *In other words, if relationships are so important, why not maintain information about each relationship?*

Therefore, in addition to modeling the roles of the party, there is a need to model the relationship between parties. For example, there is a need to know not only that Marc Martinez is a customer contact, but to maintain the details of Marc's relationship with each of the sales representatives. Similarly, there is a need to know not only that ACME Company is a customer, but that ACME Company is a customer of ABC Subsidiary (as opposed to another internal organization of the enterprise).

A relationship is defined by the two parties and their respective roles. For example, Figure 2.5 shows CUSTOMER RELATIONSHIP, EMPLOYMENT, and ORGANIZATION ROLLUP as subtypes and examples of PARTY RELATION-SHIPs. The PARTY RELATIONSHIP entity allows parties to be related to other parties and maintains the respective roles in the relationship. The PARTY RELATIONSHIP entity has attributes of **from date** and **thru date** in order to show when the relationship started and optionally when (and if) it ended.

The PARTY RELATIONSHIP entity shown in Figure 2.5 allows parties to be related to other parties and maintains the respective roles in the relationship.

While there are many subtypes of party relationships, a few subtypes are shown, namely, EMPLOYMENT, CUSTOMER RELATIONSHIP, and ORGANI-ZATION ROLLUP. For example, the PARTY RELATIONSHIP TYPE subtype of CUSTOMER RELATIONSHIP may be related to the PARTY ROLE subtype of CUSTOMER and a PARTY ROLE subtype of INTERNAL ORGANIZATION. The PARTY RELATIONSHIP entity has attributes of **from date** and **thru date** in order to show the valid time frames of the relationship. For the CUSTOMER RELATIONSHIP, this would indicate when the party formed a customer relationship and when (and if) it ended.

The CUSTOMER RELATIONSHIP subtype shows that a CUSTOMER may be involved as a customer in several INTERNAL ORGANZATIONS and vice versa—hence, this associative, many-to-many entity. If there was a need not only to store customers of the enterprise but also to track who is a customer of what organization (i.e., who are our partners' and competitors' customers) then CUSTOMER RELATIONSHIP subtype could be related to the CUSTOMER and SUPPLIER role subtypes instead of the CUSTOMER and INTERNAL ORGANI-ZATION roles. This would enable relating customers to any organization and showing who are the customers and suppliers of any organization.

The EMPLOYMENT subtype of PARTY RELATIONSHIP provides a means for relating people who are employees of each of the enterprise's internal organizations—hence, the relationships to EMPLOYEE and INTERNAL ORGANI-ZATION. This is also a many-to-many relationship because, over time, a person may be an employee of several internal organizations and an INTERNAL ORGANIZATION may have several EMPLOYEEs.

The ORGANIZATION ROLLUP associative entity shows that each ORGANI-ZATION UNIT may be within one or more ORGANIZATION UNITs, over time. One may argue that a DEPARTMENT is always within one and only one DIVI-

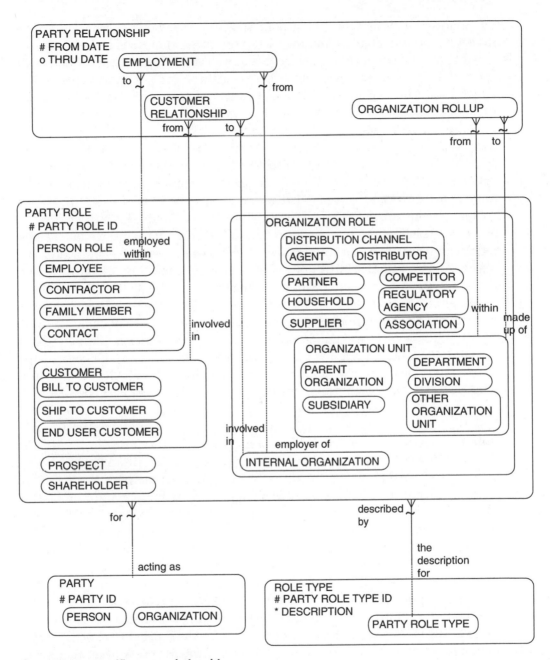

Figure 2.5 Specific party relationships.

SION; however, what if the organization structure changes over time and at first it was within one division and then it moved to another division? If there are known one-to-many relationships between two PARTY ROLES, the modeler can show the one-to-many relationship between these roles instead of using the PARTY RELATIONSHIP entity. Most relationships between two PARTY ROLES, though, tend to be of a many-to-many nature.

These examples illustrate that there is some commonality between various party relationships. Figure 2.6a shows many more examples of party relationships and generalizes the model instead of showing the specific relationships between each pair of roles. When customizing or applying this model, it is recommended to draw relationship lines for each specific PARTY RELATIONSHIP subtype to the two PARTY ROLEs to which it is related. This will clarify the nature of each relationship, and this is crucial because each of these relationships represents very important information. Figure 2.6a shows the general nature of these PARTY RELATIONSHIPs being related to and from PARTY ROLEs.

Figure 2.6a also shows the corresponding PARTY RELATIONSHIP TYPE and its relationship to PARTY ROLE TYPE entity. The PARTY RELATIONSHIP TYPE **description** attribute describes in more detail the meaning behind this type of relationship. An example is that a "customer relationship" (which would be the **name** value) has a **description** of "where the customer has purchased or used purchasing products from an internal organization." (Substitute "supplier" for internal organization if a larger scope for customer is needed.).

Each relationship type is valid only for a specific role pair. For example the "customer relationship" party relationship type is only valid for the "customer"/ "internal organization" role pair. The application of the PARTY RELATIONSHIP TYPE of "customer relationship" would yield a PARTY RELATIONSHIP instance with PARTY ROLEs for the actual parties that play the roles of "customer" and "internal organization." The **name** attribute in the PARTY RELATIONSHIP TYPE describes the nature of a specific relationship. For example, a "customer relationship" **name** may define the relationship between the "customer" PARTY ROLE and the "internal organization" PARTY ROLE identifying where this party is a customer to each internal organization.

The PARTY ROLE TYPE entity is a list of possible roles that can be played by the parties within a PARTY RELATIONSHIP TYPE. The two relationships from PARTY ROLE TYPE to PARTY RELATIONSHIP TYPE define the nature of the relationship. To form a "customer relationship" PARTY RELATIONSHIP TYPE, there would be two lines to the PARTY ROLE entity: one to the "customer" instance in the PARTY ROLE TYPE entity and another to the "internal organization" PARTY ROLE instance.

Is the **party relationship type id** part of the key to the PARTY RELATIONSHIP entity? If roles are defined in such a way that each pair of roles forms a unique PARTY RELATIONSHIP instance, then it is not necessary to define the party relationship id as part of the key. In this scenario, the PARTY RELA-

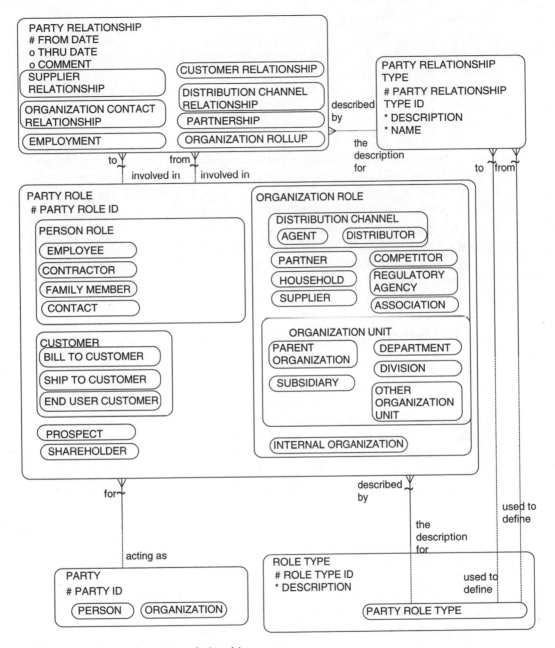

Figure 2.6a   Common party relationships.

TIONSHIP TYPE entity has as part of its key, two **party role ids** and hence the foreign key inheritance lines (the small horizontal tildes "~" across the relationship line) shown in the relationship between PARTY RELATIONSHIP TYPE and PARTY ROLE TYPE.

One could also argue that different pairs of roles types could be related to the same relationship. For instance, there could be a "person client" role and an "organization client" role, each of which could be used in the party relationship "client relationship," which links either of these roles to an "internal organization" in order to fully define the relationship. Instead of defining these roles, one could just define a "client role" and the PARTY entity will define if it is a person or an organization. Alternatively, one could define two party relationships: a person client relationship and an organization client relationship. Still, if the enterprise wants to have the flexibility to model different combinations of roles for the same party relationship, then include the **party relationship type id** as part of the unique identifier of the PARTY RELATIONSHIP entity and form many-to-many relationships between PARTY ROLE TYPE and PARTY RELATIONSHIP TYPE.

Party Relationship Examples

Whereas Table 2.3 identified the roles that parties played, the following tables show their relationships to other parties to complete the information needed. Table 2.5 shows the examples of data maintained in the PARTY RELATIONSHIP to represent organization to organization relationships and Figure 2.6b graphically illustrates these relationships.

The internal organizations illustrated within Table 2.5 are ABC Corporation, ABC Subsidiary, XYZ Subsidiary, and ABC's Customer Service Division. The first 2 rows show that ABC Subsidiary and XYZ subsidiary are subsidiaries of the parent corporation, ABC Corporation. The third row shows that the Customer Service Division is a division of ABC Subsidiary. The fourth row shows that ACME Company is a customer of ABC Subsidiary. The fifth row shows that Sellers Assistance Corporation has a relationship with ABC Subsidiary as its agent and can sell products for ABC Corporation. Notice that the sixth row shows that Fantastic Supplies is a supplier for ABC Subsidiary. If Fantastic Supplies was a supplier for all of ABC Corporation, there would be a relationship to the parent company, ABC Corporation, instead of to the subsidiary.

Table 2.6 shows examples of people's relationships within their respective organizations. Table 2.4 identified that John Smith and William Jones were employees, and this table further identifies that they are employees of ABC Subsidiary (as opposed to the parent company, ABC Corporation). Nancy Barry is a supplier representative for Fantastic Supplies; therefore, people can contact her to purchase items from Fantastic Supplies. Marc Martinez is the customer representative for ACME Company and is the person to contact for getting in touch

Table 2.5 Organization-to-Organization Party Relationships

PARTY RELATIONSHIP TYPE NAME	FROM PARTY	FROM ROLE	TO PARTY	TO ROLE	FROM DATE	THRU DATE
Organization rollup	ABC Subsidiary	Subsidiary	ABC Corporation	Parent corporation	3/4/ 1998	
Organization rollup	XYZ Subsidiary	Subsidiary	ABC Corporation	Parent corporation	7/7/ 1999	
Organization rollup	Customer Service Division	Division	ABC Subsidiary	Subsidiary	1/2/ 2000	
Customer relationship	ACME Company	Customer	ABC Subsidiary	Internal organization	1/1/ 1999	
Agent relationship	Sellers Assistance Corporation	Sales agent	ABC Subsidiary	Internal organization	6/1/ 1999	12/31/ 2001
Supplier relationship	Fantastic Supplies	Supplier	ABC Subsidiary	Internal organization	4/5/ 2001	

with this customer. Barry Cunningham is a contractor for the parent company, ABC Corporation. Table 2.6 shows person-to-person relationship examples. These relationships are stored in the same entity (PARTY RELATIONSHIP) as organization-to-organization relationships; however, Table 2.6 shows only person-to-person relationships for ease of understanding.

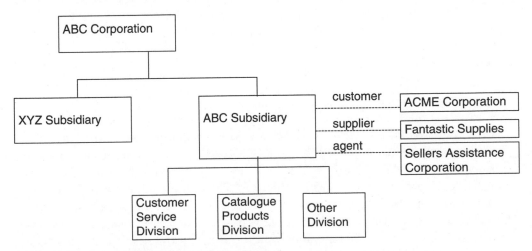

Figure 2.6b Party relationship hierarchy example.

Table 2.6   Person-to-Organization Party Relationships

PARTY RELATIONSHIP TYPE NAME	FROM PARTY	FROM ROLE	TO PARTY	TO ROLE	FROM DATE	THRU DATE
Employment	John Smith	Employee	ABC Subsidiary	Employer	12/31/ 1989	12/01/ 1999
Employment	William Jones	Employee	ABC Subsidiary	Employer	5/07/ 1990	
Organization contact relationship (supplier contact)	Nancy Barry	Supplier representative	Fantastic Supplies	Supplier	2/28/ 1999	
Organization contact relationship (customer contact)	Marc Martinez	Customer representative	ACME Company	Customer	8/30/ 2001	
Contractor relationship	Barry Cunningham	Contractor	ABC Corporation	Internal organization	1/31/ 2001	12/31/ 2001

To complete the examples of party relationships, Table 2.7 provides examples of people who have relationships with other people. Examples of person-to-person relationships include customer contact relationships, supplier contact relationships, people's mentors, and people's family structures. John Smith is the supplier coordinator for ABC and has a relationship with Nancy Barry, who is the supplier service contact (and is the supplier representative for Fantastic Supplies, as shown in the previous table). William Jones is an account manager and has a relationship with Marc Martinez, who is the customer representative for ACME Company. John Smith is the mentor for Barry Goldstein, and the last row shows that Judy Smith is John Smith's daughter.

Party Relationship Information

PARTY RELATIONSHIPs have other information associated with them, as shown in Figure 2.7. Each PARTY RELATIONSHIP may have a PRIORITY TYPE, a PARTY RELATIONSHIP STATUS TYPE, and several COMMUNICATION EVENTs associated with it. The PRIORITY TYPE entity establishes the relative importance of the relationship to the enterprise. Examples may include "very high," "high," "medium," and "low." Alternatively, an enterprise may choose to use "first," "second," "third," and so on to prioritize the importance of various relationships. The PARTY RELATIONSHIP STATUS TYPE entity defines the

Table 2.7   Person-to-Person Party Relationships

PARTY RELATIONSHIP TYPE NAME	FROM PARTY	FROM ROLE	TO PARTY	TO ROLE	FROM DATE	THRU DATE
Supplier contact relationship	John Smith	Supplier coordinator	Nancy Barry	Supplier service contact	3/15/1999	
Customer contact relationship	William Jones	Account manager (for ABC Subsidiary)	Marc Martinez	Customer contact	5/10/1999	
Mentoring relationship	John Smith	Mentor	Barry Goldstein	Apprentice	9/2/2001	
Parent-child relationship	John Smith	Parent	Judy Smith	Child	4/5/1979	

current state of the relationship. Examples include "active," "inactive," or "pursuing more involvement." Each COMMUNICATION EVENT records any type of contact between parties within a relationship—for example, phone calls, meetings, e-mails, and so on. This entity will be further described later in this chapter. Table 2.8 provides examples of information that may be maintained for party relationships. The table shows that the customer relationship with ACME is regarded as high and the relationship is active. The agent relationship with Sellers Assistance Corporation is currently inactive. The supplier relationship with Fantastic Supplies is active, and the priority is regarded as medium. John Smith and Nancy Barry's supplier coordinator relationship is active, and so is the customer contact relationship between William Jones and Marc Martinez.

Status Types

Similar to ROLE TYPEs, there will be many statuses for many entities throughout the data models—for example, ORDER STATUS, SHIPMENT STATUS, WORK EFFORT STATUS, and so on. The PARTY RELATIONSHIP STATUS TYPE is shown as a subtype of STATUS TYPE. Other STATUS TYPEs throughout this book will also be subtypes of STATUS TYPE; however, again for simplicity purposes (and to make best use of room on the paper), the subtype relationship will not always be explicitly shown as it is in Figure 2.7).

Party Contact Information

People and organizations may be contacted many different ways; by mail, phone, fax, e-mail, cell phone, pager. This section describes three very flexible

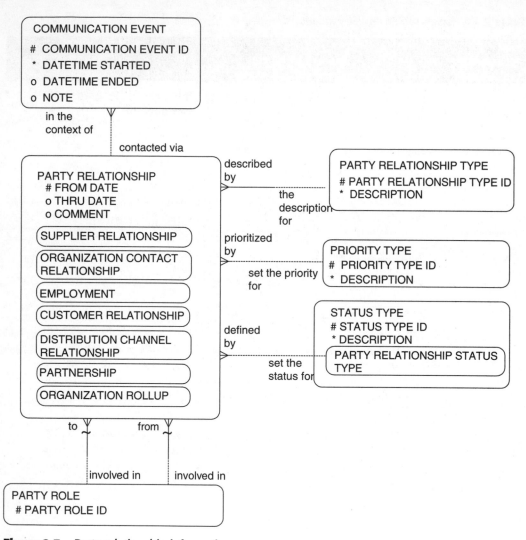

Figure 2.7   Party relationship information.

data models for storing information about addresses, phone numbers, fax numbers, and any other type of mechanism used for contacting parties.

Most data models will portray contact information in separate attributes such address line 1, address line 2, home phone, office phone, office fax, and so on. There are two main issues with modeling information this way. First of all, how does one know how many contact numbers to allow for and what types? What if someone has two or three home addresses or home phones? What if new mechanisms arise for contacting people? In practice, when the database

Table 2.8 Party Relationship Information

PARTY RELATIONSHIP TYPE NAME	FROM PARTY	FROM ROLE	TO PARTY	TO ROLE	STATUS	PRIORITY
Customer relationship	ACME Company	Customer	ABC Subsidiary	Internal organization	Active	High
Agent relationship	Sellers Assistance Corporation	Sales agent	ABC Subsidiary	Internal organization	Inactive	
Supplier relationship	Fantastic Supplies	Supplier	ABC Subsidiary	Internal organization	Active	Medium
Supplier contact relationship	John Smith	Supplier coordinator	Nancy Barry	Supplier service contact	Active	
Customer contact relationship	William Jones	Account manager (for ABC Subsidiary)	Marc Martinez	Customer contact	Active	

doesn't allow for all possibilities, the user just adds this information into the "comment" field which makes searching much more difficult!

The other issue with modeling contact information as individual attributes is that each contact address, number, or string may have its own information. For instance, addresses may have directions, and contact numbers may have information associated with them such as indications not to solicit or information about the best times to call. If these contact mechanisms are not modeled on their own, a great deal of redundancy can occur. For instance, if the address of the headquarters of a large company is stored as an attribute, the directions may be stored inconsistently a number of times in the database.

Postal Address Information

One way to contact a person or organization is by either visiting them at their address or mailing them at their postal address. Figure 2.8 provides a data model to capture postal address and geographic boundary information. The POSTAL ADDRESS entity maintains all addresses used by the enterprise in a central place. The PARTY POSTAL ADDRESS entity shows which POSTAL ADDRESSes are related to which PARTYs. The GEOGRAPHIC BOUNDARY entity maintains any type of encompassing area such as a COUNTY, CITY, STATE, COUNTRY, POSTAL CODE, PROVINCE, or TERRITORY, and it is

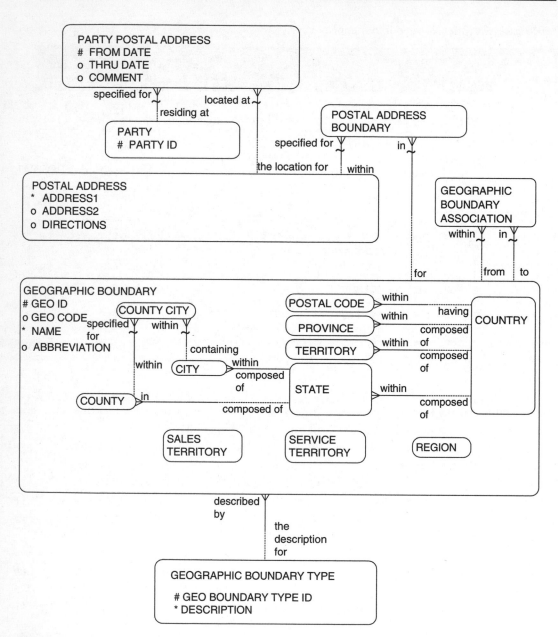

Figure 2.8   Postal address information.

related back to the POSTAL ADDRESSes as well as recursively to other GEO-GRAPHIC BOUNDARY.

An organization may have many addresses or locations. For instance, a retailer might have several outlets at different addresses. In this instance, there is only one organization but many locations or addresses. Additionally, the same postal address might be used by many organizations. For instance, many subsidiaries of an organization might share the same address. Also, different organizations might share the same address if they are in a shared office facility.

There is also a many-to-many relationship between PERSON and POSTAL ADDRESS. A particular address may have many people residing there, such as many employees who work at the same facility. And, of course, people generally have many addresses: their home address, work address, vacation address, and so forth. Therefore, there is a many-to-many relationship between PARTY and POSTAL ADDRESS.

Instead of two separate relationships for people and organizations, the model shows a many-to-many relationship between PARTY and POSTAL ADDRESS that is resolved via an intersection entity (sometimes referred to as an associative or cross-reference entity) named PARTY POSTAL ADDRESS, as shown in Figure 2.8. Notice that PARTY ADDRESS has a **from date** and **thru date** that allow tracking of the address history of parties.

Tables 2.9 and 2.10 give examples of party addresses. Table 2.9 lists the individual address records, while Table 2.10 cross-references parties to addresses. With this model, addresses are stored only once—thus eliminating redundant data problems—and can be reused many times in relationship to many parties. For instance, in Tables 2.9 and 2.10, the same address, address ID 2300, is used by ABC Corporation and ABC Subsidiary. Additionally, ABC Subsidiary has more than one address, as illustrated by its two entries in Table 2.10.

The POSTAL ADDRESS entity stores attributes to identify the specific location for either visiting or sending mail to a party. The **address1** and **address2** attributes provide a mechanism for two text lines of an address. There may be a need for more address line attributes depending on the needs of the enterprise. The **directions** attribute provides instructions on what roads to travel and what turns to take in order to arrive at that address. Often this direction information is repeated in databases where the address is not treated as a separate entity on its own.

Geographic Boundaries

Each address may have many other GEOGRAPHIC BOUNDARYs. For example, each POSTAL ADDRESS may have a CITY, PROVINCE, TERRITORY, or other GEOGRAPHIC BOUNDARY, depending on its location within the world. POSTAL ADDRESSES may also be identified within other boundaries such as a SALES TERRITORY, SERVICE TERRITORY, or REGION. Each POSTAL

Table 2.9   Postal Address Data

ADDRESS ID	ADDRESS1	ADDRESS2	CITY
2300	100 Main Street	Suite 101	New York
2400	255 Fetch Street		Portland
2500	234 Stretch Street		Minneapolis

Table 2.10   Party Postal Address Data

PARTY	ADDRESS ID
ABC Corporation	2300
ABC Subsidiary	2300
ABC Subsidiary	2400
ACME Company	2500

ADDRESS may also have a POSTAL CODE. The POSTAL CODE identifies the mailing code that is used for sorting addresses and delivery within postal services. In the United States, the postal code is referred to as the zip code.

An alternate data model for this structure could be to tie the POSTAL ADDRESS to the specific GEOGRAPHIC BOUNDARYs that apply, instead of using the associative entity, POSTAL ADDRESS BOUNDARY. For instance, there could be a one-to-many relationship from POSTAL ADDRESS to CITY and another one-to-many relationship from POSTAL ADDRESS to POSTAL CODE. If there is a need for worldwide applicability—perhaps some addresses use territories (Australia), provinces (Canada), prefectures (Japan)—there would need to be a supertype for all of these or individual relationships. If a more specific application of this model is needed, the reader is encouraged to modify this model with more specific relationships.

GEOGRAPHIC BOUNDARYs are recursively related to other GEOGRAPHIC BOUNDARYs. For instance, each SALES TERRITORY, SERVICE TERRITORY, or REGION may be defined by relating it to a number of CITYs, STATEs, or COUNTRYs.

In many data models, phone numbers are shown as attributes of the organization or person. Usually, there are also fields for fax numbers, modem numbers, pager numbers, cellular numbers, and electronic mail addresses. This often leads to limitations in the systems built. For instance, if someone has two or three business phone numbers and there is only one business phone number field for a person, where are the other business phone number entered? In this new world, where there are many methods for contacting parties, more flexible data structures are needed.

Party Contact Mechanism—Telecommunications Numbers and Electronic Addresses

The CONTACT MECHANISM entity in Figure 2.9 stores access mechanisms for parties. Each CONTACT MECHANISM may be the way to contact a particular PARTY. The intersection entity PARTY CONTACT MECHANISM shows which contact mechanisms are related to which parties. The CONTACT MECHANISM TYPE entity maintains allowable values for different types of contact mechanisms, for example, "phone," "mobile phone," "fax number," "e-mail address," and so on.

CONTACT MECHANISMs are subtyped to include TELECOMMUNICATIONS NUMBER and ELECTRONIC ADDRESS. TELECOMMUNICATIONS NUMBER includes any access via telecommunications lines such as phones, faxes, modems, pagers, and cellular numbers. ELECTRONIC ADDRESS includes any access via services like the Internet or other electronic mail services.

The CONTACT MECHANISM TYPE entity shows all the possible values for types of contact mechanism. Examples include "phone," "fax," "modem,"

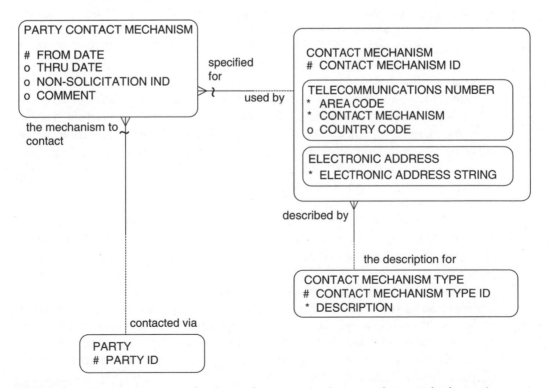

Figure 2.9 Party contact mechanism—telecommunications numbers and electronic addresses.

"mobile phone," "Internet address," and "Web URL." With technology growing so quickly, it is very likely that there will be other ways to get in touch with someone. The data structure in Figure 2.9 provides an easy method for adding any new contact mechanisms by simply inserting and using new CONTACT MECHANISM TYPEs.

The attribute **non-solicitation ind** on PARTY CONTACT MECHANISM provides a mechanism to indicate that that the mechanism is not to be called for solicitation purposes. If someone indicated that he or she did not want to be solicited on a particular number, it would be important to record this from a consideration point of view as well as a legal point of view.

Party Contact Mechanism (Expanded)

If CONTACT MECHANISMs are a means of reaching a person or organization, why not include POSTAL ADDRESSes as a subtype of CONTACT MECHANISM? Postal addresses are merely another mechanism for reaching someone. Imagine contact management systems that could provide flexible, scroll-down lists showing all the different ways of getting ahold of a party showing all the phone numbers, fax numbers, e-mail and postal addresses and categorized by their purpose (i.e., "primary home address," "summer home address," "main office number," "secondary fax number," "billing inquiries," "headquarters number," "emergency only," and so on.). This could greatly facilitate how we contact parties and allow for very flexible and easily accessible contact information.

Another advantage of including POSTAL ADDRESSES as a subtype of CONTACT MECHANISM is that many business processes need a contact mechanism to complete a transaction and that contact mechanism may be a postal address, telecommunications number, or electronic address. For example, an order may be secured with either a POSTAL ADDRESS or an ELECTRONIC ADDRESS (i.e., an e-mail address).

Figure 2.10 provides a standard data model with this flexible structure. The CONTACT MECHANISM entity contains the subtypes POSTAL ADDRESS, TELECOMMUNICATIONS NUMBER, and ELECTRONIC ADDRESS. Because it has already been established that there is a many-to-many relationship between each of these subtypes and PARTY, this diagram shows a many-to-many relationship between CONTACT MECHANISM and PARTYs.

Also PARTY CONTACT MECHANISMs are optionally related to PARTY ROLE TYPE to indicate that each party's contact mechanism may be specified for a particular roles only. For instance, an organization may provide address information only in their role as a customer, and this may not be applicable to any other role.

Contact mechanisms may be related to each other and hence the recursive entity, CONTACT MECHANISM LINK. For example, certain phone numbers,

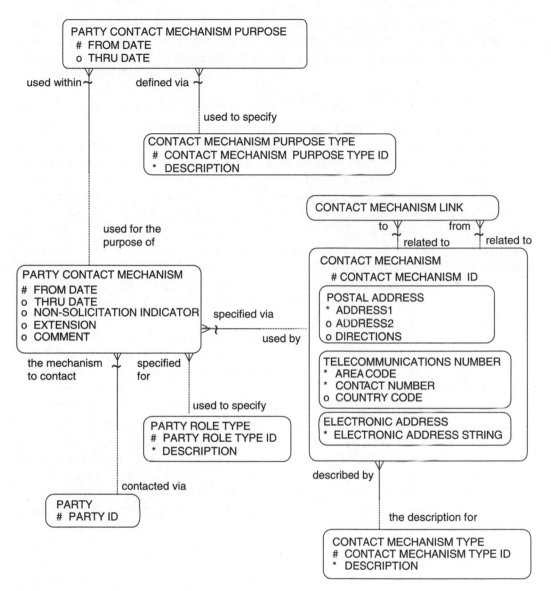

Figure 2.10   Party contact mechanism (expanded).

when busy, may be automatically routed to pagers or cellular numbers. Fax numbers may be automatically connected to e-mail addresses. This may be important information to know when contacting parties.

Contact Mechanism Purpose

Each contact mechanism for each party may have many purposes. For instance, an address might be used as a mailing address, a headquarters address, a service address, and so on. Most systems have a separate record for the mailing address, headquarters address, and service address, even though the address information may be exactly the same. Furthermore, just as addresses are intended for specific purposes, so are other contact mechanisms. A single contact mechanism may have more than one purpose. For example, business people sometimes have a single number for both their phone and fax needs.

Therefore, the data model in Figure 2.10 shows that each PARTY CONTACT MECHANISM may have one or more PARTY CONTACT MECHANISM PURPOSEs, each of which is described by a CONTACT MECHANISM PURPOSE TYPE.

Because the purposes of various contact mechanisms change over time, the **from date** and **thru date** identify when the purposes are valid. The CONTACT MECHANISM PURPOSE TYPE maintains the possible list of purposes that can be applied.

An alternate way this could be modeled is to relate the CONTACT MECHANISM PURPOSE TYPE directly to the PARTY CONTACT MECHANISM and include the **contact mechanism purpose type id** as part of the key to the PARTY CONTACT MECHANISM entity. This would be a simpler design, but it would lead to redundancy in many cases. For example, if the same party's address served as a mailing, headquarters, and service address, it would be stored as three instances in the PARTY CONTACT MECHANISM entity. Each instance would have the same party and contact mechanism id but would have a different purpose. Therefore information related to just the party and contact mechanism, such as the **non-solication ind**, would be repeated. In other words, the PARTY CONTACT MECHANISM entity has significance on its own and may have its own attributes or relationships, independent of the purpose(s). For this reason, our model shows separate PARTY CONTACT MECHANISM and PARTY CONTACT MECHANISM PURPOSE entities.

Table 2.11 gives examples of party contact mechanisms. The first seven entries show that there are many contact mechanisms for ABC Corporation. The first contact mechanism is a phone number and serves as the general phone number for the organization. The main fax number shows on the second row. ABC Corporation has a secondary fax number, shown as (212) 356-4898. The next rows show that 100 Main Street has more than one purpose; it is both the headquarters and the address for billing inquiries. ABC Corporation has another address where it has a sales office at 500 Jerry Street. ABC Corporation has its Web address at abccorporation.com. ABC Subsidiary, which is part of ABC Corporation, has two addresses listed: one at 100 Main Street for a service address and one at a sales address at 255 Fetch Street. As another example, John Smith has several contact mechanisms listed such as his main office number, main home number, his cellular or mobile number, and his home and work addresses. Barry Goldstein's contact numbers show two work numbers, a primary number and a secondary number, along with a work e-mail, personal e-mail, and home address.

Table 2.11 shows the flexibility and maintainability of correct contact information for all types of current contact mechanisms as well as new contact mechanisms that could potentially emerge as telecommunications evolves.

Table 2.11 Party Contact Mechanisms

PARTY	CONTACT MECHANISM	CONTACT MECHANISM TYPE	CONTACT MECHANISM PURPOSE
ABC Corporation	(212) 234 0958	Phone	General phone number
ABC Corporation	(212) 334 5896	Fax	Main fax number
ABC Corporation	(212) 356 4898	Fax	Secondary fax number
ABC Corporation	100 Main Street	Postal address	Headquarters
ABC Corporation	100 Main Street	Postal address	Billing inquiries
ABC Corporation	500 Jerry Street	Postal address	Sales office
ABC Corporation	Abccorporation.com	Web address	Central Internet address
ABC Subsidiary	100 Main Street	Postal address	Service address
ABC Subsidiary	255 Fetch Street	Postal address	Sales office
John Smith	(212) 234 9856	Phone	Main office number
John Smith	(212) 748 5893	Phone	Main home number
John Smith	(212) 384 4387	Cellular	
John Smith	345 Hamlet Place	Postal address	Main home address
John Smith	245 Main Street	Postal address	Main work address
Barry Goldstein	(212) 234 0045	Phone	Main office number
Barry Goldstein	(212) 234 0046	Phone	Secondary office number
Barry Goldstein	Bgoldstein@abc.com	E-mail address	Work e-mail address
Barry Goldstein	Barry@barrypersonal.com	E-mail address	Personal e-mail address
Barry Goldstein	2985 Cordova Road	Postal address	Main home address

Facility Versus Contact Mechanism

A contact mechanism could be tied to a particular PARTY, such as a person's cellular telephone number, or it may be tied to a physical location, for example, the telephone number for a manufacturing plant or the telephone number for a tower facility. These physical facilities are not postal addresses or parties (although they are associated with postal addresses and parties), and another entity is needed to describe them. The CONTACT MECHANISM entity maintains information about a label or identifier for contacting a party; the FACILITY stores the attributes or relationships associated with physical structures.

Figure 2.11 provides a structure to record information about physical facilities. FACILITY subtypes include WAREHOUSE, PLANT, BUILDING, ROOM, OFFICE, and the FACILITY TYPE allows for other types. Each FACILITY may be made up of other FACILTIES. For example, a BUILDING may be made up of ROOMs; if there is a more specific need to track floors, a BUILDING may be made up of FLOORs that are made up of ROOMS. An attribute that may be of interest to the physical facility is **square footage.**

Each **FACLITY** may involve one or more parties, thus the FACILITY ROLE entity maintains what PARTYs are playing what FACILITY ROLE TYPEs for what FACILITYs. For instance, certain parties may use the facility, lease the facility, rent the facility, or own the facility—hence, the FACILITY ROLE TYPE entity stores these possible values. Also, each FACILITY may be contacted via one or more CONTACT MECHANISM. A PLANT facility may be contacted using several of the previously mentioned contact mechanisms such as phone, fax, e-mail, postal address, and so on. The FACILITY could have more than one of each of these CONTACT MECHANISMs; for example, it may have a street postal address of 100 Smith Street and another address of PO Box 1234.

Depending on the environment, a CONTACT MECHANISM may be the mechanism to contact more than one FACILITY. For example, perhaps the same postal address may be the contact mechanism for more than one plant that is grouped together within the same postal address. Since this may be possible, the FACILTIY CONTACT MECHANISM associative entity provides for a many-to-many relationship between CONTACT MECHANISM and FACILITY.

Party Communication Event

It is important in many applications to track information regarding with whom and when contact or communication was made within relationships between parties. For instance, sales or account representatives often need to know who was called for what purpose and when in order to properly follow up with their customers. The contact or communication might have been via a telephone

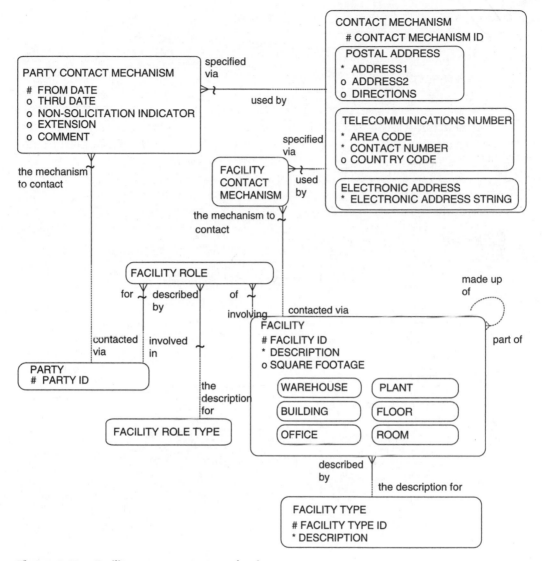

Figure 2.11   Facility versus contact mechanism.

call, an in-person sales meeting, a conference call, a letter, or any other method of encounter.

In Figure 2.12, the entity COMMUNICATION EVENT provides a history of the various communications that have been made or will be made between parties. A COMMUNICATIONS EVENT is defined as the interchange of information between parties via some type of contact such as a phone call, meeting, videoconference, and so on. The COMMUNICATION EVENT may be within the context of a particular PARTY RELATIONSHIP, or it may be between many par-

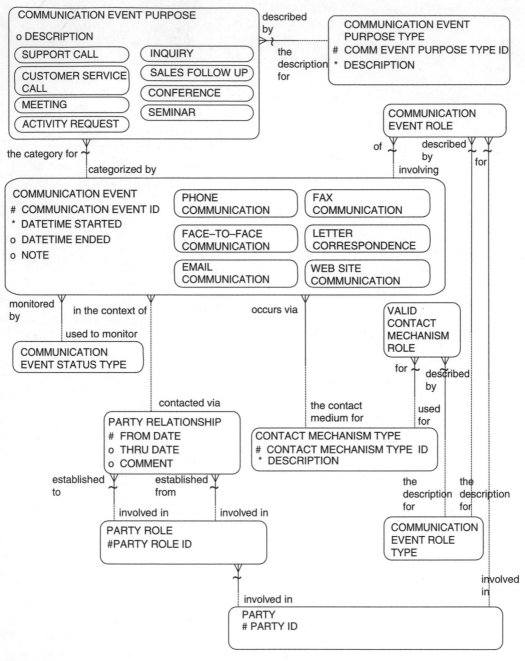

Figure 2.12 Communication event.

ties and therefore use the COMMUNICATION EVENT ROLE to describe the roles of parties. For contact events that involved more than two parties (for instance, a meeting or seminar), the COMMUNICATION EVENT ROLE may define the parties and the roles they play with the event (facilitator, participant, note taker, and so on).

The COMMUNICATION EVENT will usually be within the context of a PARTY RELATIONSHIP and not the COMMUNICATION EVENT ROLE because it is within a relationship that communications usually make sense. It is possible to have several relationships between two parties. For instance, Marc Martinez might be the customer contact for John Smith in one relationship. At a later date, Marc Martinez might decide to work for John Smith's company (ABC Subsidiary) and report to him. It would be appropriate to track the communication events for these relationships separately.

COMMUNICATION EVENTs may be categorized two main ways: what contact mechanism was used to conduct the event (phone, fax, letter, e-mail, face to face, and so on) and what was the purpose of the contact event (support call, sales follow-up, customer service call, conference, seminar). A COMMUNICATION EVENT occurs via one and only one CONTACT MECHANISM TYPE; however, it may have many COMMUNICATIONs EVENT PURPOSEs. For instance, a particular meeting may be a customer service support call as well as a request to deliver an additional item. Figure 2.12 provides the subtypes of INQUIRY, SUPPORT CALL, CUSTOMER SERVICE CALL, MEETING, SALES FOLLOW-UP, CONFERENCE, SEMINAR, ACTIVITY REQUEST as well as the COMMUNICATION EVENT PURPOSE TYPE to indicate that there may be additional COMMUNICATION EVENT PURPOSEs. Other possible purposes include "initial sales call," "service repair call," "demonstration," "sales lunch appointment," or "telephone solicitation." The description attribute provides for storing additional information about the purpose such as "This is a critical sales call that must turn client around".

The VALID CONTACT MECHANISM ROLE provides a mechanism to identify what types of COMMUNICATION EVENT ROLES TYPEs are valid for what types of CONTACT MECHANISM TYPEs. For instance, a "caller" and "receiver" may be valid for a "phone" contact mechanism type, while "facilitator," "participant," and "note taker" are valid roles for a "face-to-face communication." The COMMUNICATION EVENT STATUS TYPE maintains the state of the event. Example statuses include "scheduled," "in progress," and "completed."

The COMMUNICATION EVENT maintains the **datetime started**, **datetime ended,** and a **note** describing the contact. An example note may be "initial sales call went well and customer seemed interested in moving forward quickly with a demonstration of the Thingamajig product". Table 2.12 gives other examples of types of communication events.

Table 2.12 gives examples of possible communication events. William Jones, an account manager for ABC Corporation, has made several sales contacts with

Table 2.12 Communication Events

COMMUNICATION EVENT ID	FROM PARTY	TO PARTY	START DATETIME	COMMUNICATION EVENT PURPOSE	CONTACT MECHANISM TYPE	COMMUNICATION EVENT STATUS TYPE
1010	William Jones	Marc Martinez	Jan 12, 2001, 3 PM	Initial sales call Initial product demonstration	Face to face	Completed
1300	William Jones	Marc Martinez	Jan 30, 2001, 2PM	Demo of product	Web-based interaction	Completed
1450	William Jones	Marc Martinez	Feb 12, 2002, 10AM	Sales close Gather order details	Face to face	Completed
1900	William Jones	Marc Martinez	June 1, 2002, 1PM	Customer service follow-up Customer satisfaction survey	Phone	Scheduled
3010	John Smith	Nancy Barry	Sept 12, 2001, 3PM	Purchasing follow-up (to find out status of pending purchase order)	E-mail	Completed
3011	Joe Schmoe	Jerry Red	Sept 19, 2001, 3PM	Technical support call Request for a software patch	Phone	Pending resolution

Marc Martinez, the customer contact for ACME Corporation. The first four entries in Table 2.12 show the date, time, purpose, and type of contact mechanism used as well as the status of the event. The status is used to indicate if the activity has been completed or if it is just scheduled. William Jones started with a face-to-face initial sales meeting on January 12 and then proceeded with a more detailed product demonstration using the company's Web site, which has the capabilities to do a product demonstration and includes chatting capabilities. The fifth entry shows an email contact initiated by John Smith to Nancy Barry who is a supplier representative. The sixth entry shows that Joe Schmoe has made a call to Jerry Red regarding a problem and illustrates that communication event tracking is important not only in sales but in other areas of the business such as purchasing relationships. This data structure provides a mechanism for tracking communication events for all types of relationships and circumstances and is a very powerful business tool.

Communication Event Follow-Up

Very often, communication events require follow-ups and management in order to ensure proper service, sales coverage, or support. Many times, cases are opened to manage related communication events involving the same issue. For instance, if a customer calls up about a technical support problem, an action may need to be taken—for instance, sending the latest patch to correct the problem.

Figure 2.13 shows the data model that both supports grouping communication events into cases and relates each event to some work that may be required as a result of the communication event. A CASE may be set up for a series of related COMMUNICATION EVENTs regarding a particular issue. Each CASE may have several CASE ROLEs that identify who is responsible for the CASE, who checks the quality of service within the CASE, who is the customer for the CASE, and so on.

Each COMMUNICATION EVENT may be related to one or more WORK EFFORTS because in a single event one of the parties may have more than one follow-up action. WORK EFFORTS will be further defined and explained later in this book in Chapter 6, Work Efforts. Also each WORK EFFORT may be related to one or more COMMUNICATION EVENTs because a caller may request a WORK EFFORT, follow up on the progress of the WORK EFFORT, and have several other communications about the WORK EFFORT.

Table 2.13 provides sample data for the WORK EFFORTs that stem from communication events. All the communication events listed are related to a technical issue of a customer's software crashing and calling in on a support line to establish the first communication event. Jerry Reed is the person handling the call; he opens case "105." Joe Schmoe is the customer calling in, and Larry Assure is his manager, who is monitoring this case. The first call is taken

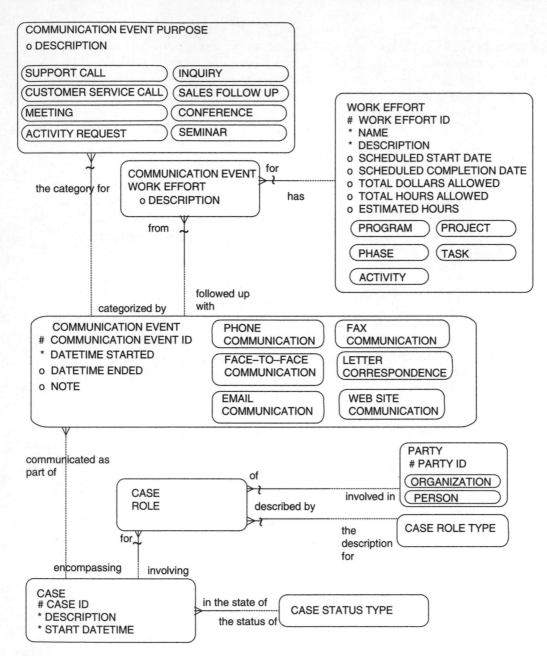

Figure 2.13   Communication event follow up.

Table 2.13 Communication Event Follow-Up

CASE	CASE DESCRIPTION	CASE ROLE	COMMUNICATION EVENT ID	START DATETIME	COMMUNICATION EVENT PURPOSE	CONTACT MECHANISM TYPE	COMMUNICATION EVENT WORK EFFORT	WORK EFFORT
105	Technical support issue with customer—software keeps crashing	Jerry Red—technical resolution lead Joe Schmoe—case customer Larry Assure—quality assurance manager	3010	Sept 19, 2001, 3PM	Technical support call Activity request	Phone	Request for a software patch	Work effort id 1029—Send software patch out to customer to correct problem
			3098	Sept 20, 2001, 2PM	Send software patch	E-mail		Work effort id 1029—Send software patch out to customer to correct problem
			3120	Sept 19, 2001, 3PM	Technical support follow-up Call. resolution	Phone		

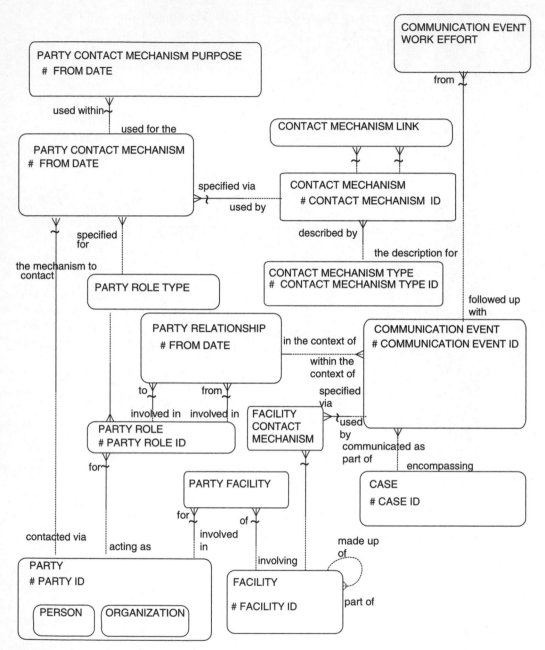

Figure 2.14   Overall party model.

on Sept 19 at 3 p.m. Jerry realized that he needs to send out a software patch so he sets up a work effort "1029" to make sure this gets done. On Sept 20 he follows up on this outstanding work effort and sends out the software patch with another communication effort, namely an e-mail. The example illustrates that a work effort to send a software patch in order to correct the problem may be related to two communication events; it is related to the request to send the software as well as to the communication event in which the software patch was sent. It also could have been related to follow-up calls from the customer about the sending of the patch. The third communication event shows that he followed up to make sure the patch worked and to close the case.

Summary

Most data models and database designs unnecessarily duplicate information regarding people and organizations. As a result, many organizations have a difficult time maintaining accurate information. This chapter has illustrated how to build a very flexible and normalized data model for people, organizations, party relationships, addresses, contact mechanisms, and contacts made between parties. Figure 2.14 shows the key entities discussed in this chapter and their relationships.

Please refer to Appendix A for a listing of entities and attributes. SQL scripts to build tables and columns derived from the logical models in this book can be found on the full-blown CD-ROM, which is licensed separately.

CHAPTER 3

Products

Having established the models for parties and party roles and their relationships, this chapter focuses on the products that parties produce and use. Products are defined as goods or services that were, are, or will be sold by the enterprise. *Goods* are products that are more tangible in nature and generally created in advance for sale. *Services* are products that involve the use of parties' time and are less tangible in nature. Every organization needs to know a great deal of product information on a regular basis, such as the following issues:

- How do the enterprise's services or goods compare in quality and price to those of its competitors?

- What inventory is needed at each location to meet the needs of customers?

- What are the prices, costs, and profitability for the services or goods that are offered?

- Where can the enterprise purchase the best services and goods at the best prices?

Just as the party model stores common information about parties independent of their roles, the product model stores common product information regardless of whose products they are. This product model is therefore more flexible, stable, and understandable because product information is modeled only one time, regardless of whether it is the enterprise's products, competitors' products, or suppliers' products. This chapter models information on the following areas of product:

- Product definition
- Product category
- Product identification
- Product feature
- Suppliers and manufacturers of products
- Inventory item storage
- Product pricing
- Product costing
- Product to product associations (alternate model also provided)
- Product and parts (alternate model also provided)

Product Definition

Just as parties include both internal and external parties, the product model includes products that the enterprise provides, products from suppliers, and products that competitors provide. Some of the information may be independent of the supplier, such as the description, category, and features of the product. Some of the information about the products, such as the availability and pricing of products, may depend on the supplier of the product.

Figure 3.1 shows an entity called PRODUCT that models all products including the products the enterprise sells, products from suppliers, and competitors' products. The model shows that the key is **product id**, which is an identifier for the product. The attributes of PRODUCT are **name,** which uniquely describes a product; **introduction date,** stating when the product was first available to be sold; **sales discontinuation date,** which documents when the product will not be sold any more by the manufacturer; **support discontinuation date,** which states when the product will no longer be supported by the manufacturer; and a **comment,** which documents particular descriptions or notes relating to the product.

Products include *both* tangible goods, which are called GOODs, and nontangible offerings, which are called SERVICEs. For example, a GOOD may include specific types of pens, furniture, equipment, or anything that can be physically stored. (Even a software program, which is a GOOD, can be physically stored.) The alternate subtype, SERVICE, is for products that involve sell-

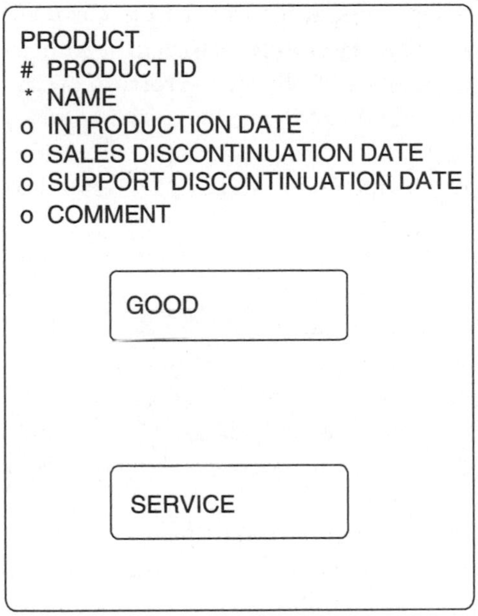

Figure 3.1   Product definition.

Table 3.1   Products

PRODUCT ID	PRODUCT DESCRIPTION	PRODUCT SUBTYPE
PAP192	Johnson fine grade 8½ by 11 inch bond paper	Good
PEN202	Goldstein Elite pen	Good
DSK401	Jerry's box of 3½-inch diskettes	Good
FRMCHFA1500	Preprinted forms for insurance claims	Good
CNS109	Office supply inventory management consulting service	Service

ing people's time and expertise such as consulting services, legal services, or any other services that provide time and/or expertise. (See Table 3.1.)

Product Category

The classification of products is a key aspect of maintaining product information. Products are often classified many ways—by product line, by model, by product grade, by industry segments, and by various other product categories.

Often, these classifications are shown as separate entities in the data model. The issue of showing these product categories separately is that other information may be based on any of these categories and should be related to the supertype of PRODUCT CATEGORY to provide more flexibility. For instance, targeting market interest in products may be based on several product categories. Another example is that product pricing may be based on and related to many product categories.

Figure 3.2 illustrates that a PRODUCT may be classified in one or more PRODUCT CATEGORYs to group products together that may be useful for several purposes, such as catalog organization, sales analysis, listings, or other types of product analysis. The PRODUCT CATEGORY can include more that one PRODUCT, and therefore the associative entity, PRODUCT CATEGORY CLASSIFICATION describes which products are in which category. For example, all pens, pencils, paper, notebooks, desk sets, and diskettes are classified into the category of office supplies.

Product categories may change over time; therefore, the PRODUCT CATEGORY CLASSIFICATION has the attributes **from date** and **thru date,** which state when the product was classified into its grouping.

PRODUCT CATEGORYs may be made up of other PRODUCT CATEGORYs and hence the recursive entity PRODUCT CATEGORY ROLLUP that allows each product category to be made up of many other categories as well as a subcategory to be in a different parent category. An example of this is that the product, "Johnson fine grade 8½ by 11 bond paper," is classified as a paper product, which is a subcategory of the office supplies category and may also be a subcategory of the computer supplies category.

To assist in sales forecasting and prospecting, the entity MARKET INTEREST is included in this model. It is an intersection entity linking information about PARTY TYPE and PRODUCT CATEGORY that allows an enterprise to record the category of products for which particular types of parties may be interested. If the PARTY TYPE includes specific industries or industry segments as types and these have been associated with actual parties, then an enterprise can easily identify organizations within segments of a target industry that may be interested in types of products or services. These organizations could then be the focus of a new sales campaign for those types of products. Because interests change over time, the attributes **from date** and **thru date** are also included.

Table 3.2 illustrates examples of product categories. Notice that diskettes are categorized as both office supplies and computer supplies. This categorization may be useful for showing different types of products under various product catalogs. The enterprise needs to be careful when classifying a product into multiple categories, as it can result in misleading results when performing certain queries. For instance, if products were grouped into multiple categories and there was a sales analysis report by category, the total sales amount for the

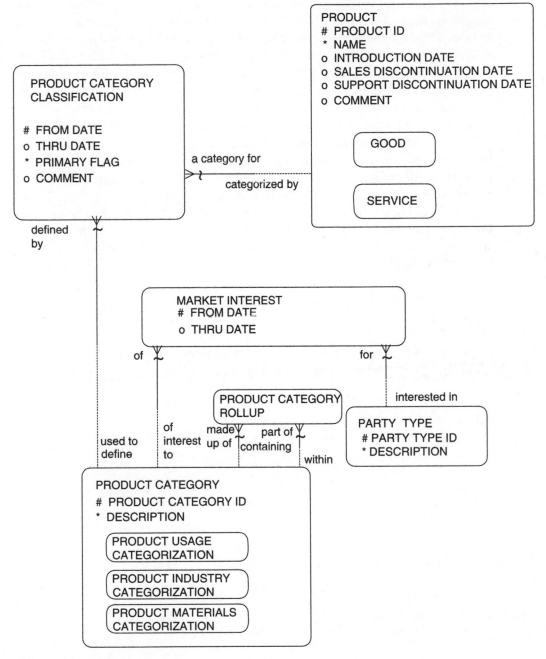

Figure 3.2 Product category.

report would be overstated because some product sales would be counted numerous times for each of their categories. The model has a **primary flag** to indicate which is the primary category for the product to avoid this situation.

Notice that in Table 3.2 the diskettes are classified in two categories; however, one category is flagged as the primary category to avoid duplication of results when analyzing sales. The enterprise needs to enforce a business rule that only one category for the product may be primary. The last row shows a preprinted claims insurance forms product that falls into two product categories, a forms product and an insurance product. The types of parties that have been identified as possibly having an interest in the insurance category of products are insurance companies, insurance brokers, and health care provider organizations such as doctors' offices, hospitals, and so on.

If the category that is primary varies depending on the application, then instead of the **primary flag** attribute, another entity would need to be added such as PRODUCT CLASSIFICATION TYPE which would be related to the PRODUCT CATEGORY CLASSIFICATION, to allow for more flexibility. In-

Table 3.2   Product Categories

PRODUCT ID	PRODUCT DESCRIPTION	PRODUCT CATEGORY	PRIMARY FLAG	PARTY TYPE MARKET INTEREST
PAP192	Johnson fine grade 8½ by 11 bond paper	Office supplies	Yes	
		Paper	No	
PEN202	Goldstein Elite pen	Office supplies	Yes	
		Pens	Yes	
DSK401	Jerry's box of 3½ inch diskettes	Office supplies	No	
		Computer supplies	Yes	
CNS109	Office supply inventory management consulting service	Consulting services	Yes	
FRMCHFA1500	Preprinted forms for insurance claims	Forms	Yes	
		Insurance	No	Insurance companies Insurance brokers Health care provider organizations

stances within this entity could be "primary category for catalogues," "primary category for sales analysis" and so on.

Product Identification Codes

Goods may have various ids that are used as a standard means of identifying the goods. Figure 3.3 provides a data model to identify the various code or id values that a good may have. A single code may uniquely identify goods and/or services, however, some goods may have more than identification value. The GOOD IDENTIFICATION entity has an attribute of **ID value** to store the various identification codes that the good may have. The subtypes of GOOD IDENTIFICATION designate the types of ids that may be given to a good. The MANUFACTURER'S ID NO is a good id designated by the manufacturer. The **SKU** (stock-keeping unit) is a standard product id that distinctly identities various products. The subtype **UPCA** stands for Universal Product Code—American and is a mechanism for identifying products within America. **UPCE**

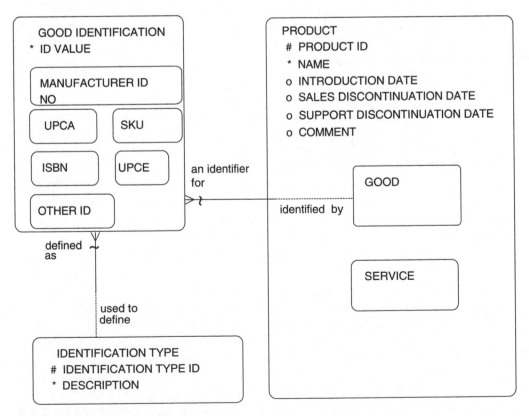

Figure 3.3   Product identification.

(Universal Product Code—European) is a mechanism for identifying products in Europe. **ISBN** (International Standard Book Number) is a mechanism to identify specific books throughout the world. A single good may have more than one standard id. For instance, a certain office supply product may have a manufacturer ID number designated by the manufacturer and a UPCA number identified by the industry.

Product Features

Products may have features that could also be called characteristics, options, variations, or modifiers, allowing either customization of a product or describing the characteristics of a product. One may think that these should be two separate entities, one to describe the features included in the product and another to record the available options. The issue with having two separate entities is that the same feature may be part of one product and be an option in another product. For example, a "copier paper" product offering may be defined using white paper as a part of the product definition, while another product, "colored stationery," may have the color "white" as an option. Additionally, the same product variation may be part of the product and later in time be considered an optional feature.

Therefore, the data model will maintain product features that may be required as part of the product, may come standard with a product (meaning that this feature may be deselected), or may be selected as an option for a product. Examples of features include the product quality, brand name (which may be different from the manufacturer), color, size, dimension, style, hardware features, software features, or billing options.

In Figure 3.4, a PRODUCT FEATURE entity is used to define these ways in which the product may be modified or tweaked. Because a PRODUCT FEATURE may be used in many products and each product may have many features, the PRODUCT FEATURE APPLICABILITY maintains which PRODUCTs may be available with which PRODUCT FEATUREs. The PRODUCT FEATURE CATEGORY entity allows for the classification of PRODUCT FEATUREs such as "quality", "color", or "size". The subtypes, STANDARD FEATURE, REQUIRED FEATURE, SELECTABLE FEATURE, and OPTIONAL FEATURE allow the capability to specify if the features come as part of the standard configuration of the product, if the feature is mandatory as part of the product, if the feature needs to be selected (e.g., color), or if the feature is an optional component.

The UNIT OF MEASURE entity helps define the product in terms of the type of measurement for the product. It also helps further define the DIMENSION subtype of PRODUCT FEATURE. The UNIT OF MEASURE CONVERSION allows different units of measures to be converted to a common unit in order to assess inventory levels of a type of good.

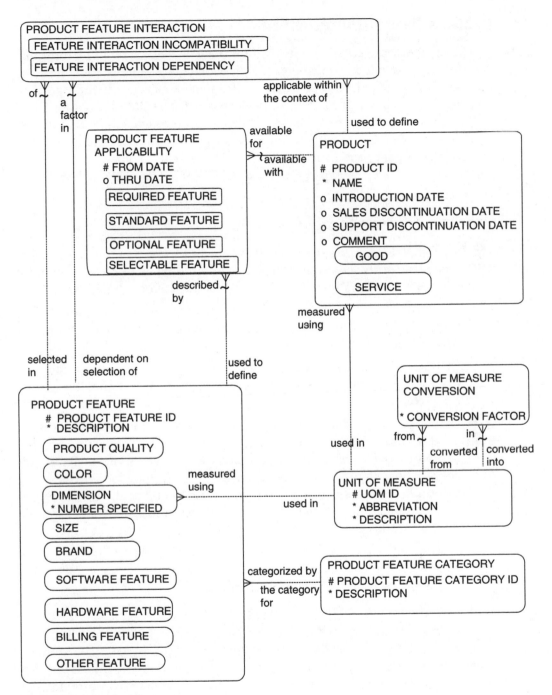

Figure 3.4   Product feature.

Product Feature Interaction

The applicability of certain product features may depend on other features that have been selected. For example, if one is buying a laptop computer, the optional feature of selecting an internal DVD may be possible if and only if an internal rewritable CD-ROM has not been selected. The PRODUCT FEATURE INTERACTION entity provides the capability to store which features are incompatible with other features (they will be subtyped SELECTION INTERACTION INCOMPATIBILITY) and which features are dependent on other features being selected (they will be subtyped FEATURE INTERACTION DEPENDENCY).

Product Feature Subtypes

The PRODUCT FEATURE entity may have many subtypes and will invariably be customized for the enterprise, depending on the types of features that are applicable. Subtypes of PRODUCT FEATURE may include the following:

- PRODUCT QUALITY classifies the product by value such as "grade A" or "grade B." For service products, such as a consultant, this may represent "expert" or "junior."

- COLOR describes the color(s) of the good. A good may have more than one COLOR option, but a different color may also denote that it is a separate good.

- DIMENSION describes the various numeric descriptions of the good such as "8½-inch width," "11-inch length," or "10 pound." The DIMENSION is related to UNIT OF MEASURE, which has a description attribute that defines how the feature is being measured. The unit of measure may determine how the product can be inventoried and sold, such as by the "box" or "each." For service products, the unit of measure values may be "hours" or "days."

- SIZE specifies how large or small a product is in more general terms than dimension such as "extra large," "large," "medium," or "small." This feature could be useful in the garment industry.

- BRAND NAME describes the marketing name tied to the good, such as "Buick" for a General Motors vehicle. Note that the brand name may be different from the manufacturer's name.

- SOFTWARE FEATURE allows additional software to be added to products or allows certain software settings to be specified for a product. For instance, software dollar limits could be set for products that are based on usage, such as meters. Another example could be the setting of software preferences for a software package or hardware purchase.

- HARDWARE FEATUREs allow for the specification of certain components that are included or that may be added to a product—for example, a cover for a printer.
- A BILLING FEATURE is an example of a product feature that specifies the standard types of terms that may be associated with a product, such as recording that an Internet access service may be available with either monthly or quarterly billing.

Product Feature Examples

An example of a sample product with features is a "Johnson fine grade 8 ½ by 11 gray bond paper" where Johnson is the brand name, 8½ inches wide and 11 inches long are the dimensions, gray is the color, fine grade is the quality, and bond paper is the product type. In this example, these features would all be maintained as REQUIRED FEATUREs.

This product may be further defined by specifying the particular colors in which the product is available. This is done by associating the available optional features that could be associated with this product. This product may come in two colors, and therefore there is a need to relate two optional product features that could be selected: "blue" and "gray" bond paper. These optional features allow pricing to be related at the base product and the ability to specify optional features to a particular product that may or may not affect other information about the product such as pricing. In the example, a customer may order the product with different colors; however, the prices associated with the product need be stored only once, at the product level. Alternatively, pricing may be based on the product features also. (There will be more discussion on product pricing later in this chapter.)

Products may be defined at multiple levels of specificity. For example, an enterprise may want to define a product known as "Johnson fine grade 8½ by 11 bond paper" as well as another product offering that is more specific, such as "Johnson fine grade 8½ by 11 *gray* bond paper". This data model will allow a great deal of flexibility to define required features that help determine the product or as optional features that could be available for the product.

Table 3.3 shows examples of possible products and different types of features. Notice that the product name may describe many of the features of a product so that it may be ordered by name, while the feature allows products to be correctly defined and categorized and allows for customization of the product without necessarily having to store a product for each product variation. The details behind the product are stored in PRODUCT FEATURE APPLICABILITY entity and are shown in this table to clarify the definition of the product.

There are other possible types of features of products, many of which are dependent on the enterprise's type of business. Shoe manufacturers may be

Table 3.3 Product Features

PRODUCT ID	NAME	QUALITY	COLOR	DIMENSION AND UNIT OF MEASURE	BRAND NAME	UNIT OF MEASURE
PAP192	Johnson fine grade 8½ by 11 paper	Fine grade, Required feature Extra glossy finish, Optional feature	Blue Gray Cream White Selectable feature	8½" width 11" length Required feature	Johnson, Required feature	Ream
PEN202	Goldstein Elite pen	Fine point, Required feature	Black, Standard Feature Blue, Optional feature		Goldstein, Required feature	Each
DSK401	Jerry's box of 3½" diskettes		Red, Required feature	3½", Required feature	Jerry's, Required feature	Box
CNS109	Office supply inventory management consulting service	Expert, Required feature			ABC Corporation, Required feature	

interested in styles, clothing organizations characterize products by lines, commodities organizations have varieties, and so on. This model is useful as the baseline model, but the subtypes of the PRODUCT FEATURE may need to be customized for the enterprise.

Unit of Measure

Is a unit of measure another example of a product feature? If the same product may be sold in different units of measure, then perhaps a unit of measure may be another variable or feature of the product. Most organizations will conclude that if the same type of product is sold in different units of measure, then it really is a different product. For instance, a ream of paper is quite different from a piece of paper and would be regarded as a separate product.

The UNIT OF MEASURE entity is therefore not a subtype of PRODUCT FEATURE in this model. This entity allows products to be further defined in terms of the product measurement. It is important for enterprises to be able to determine inventory for products that are identical except for the unit of measure.

The associative entity UNIT OF MEASURE CONVERSION provides the capability to use a common unit of measure to calculate how much inventory the enterprise has of a product. The attribute **conversion factor** in UNIT OF MEASURE CONVERSION is provided for this purpose. For example, there may be several products for Henry #2 pencils that have different units of measure such as "each," "small box," and "large box." In many cases, organizations need to show total inventories, costs, and sales for all of a product regardless of its unit of measure. By defining a common unit of measure, such as "each," and including a conversion factor (e.g., 12 for "small box" and 24 for "large box"), it is possible to determine the total amount of Henry #2 pencils there are in inventory and how many have been sold.

Another example is process manufacturers that are often dealing with liters, gallons, tons, and other metric conversion factors. It is often necessary to provide a common unit of measure to determine inventory levels. If this type of unit of measure conversion is required, then the UNIT OF MEASURE CONVERSION entity could be used. This would show the many-to-many recursion between different units of measures. The **conversion factor** attribute is required in the UNIT OF MEASURE CONVERSION entity to provide for a conversion to common units of measure. For example, the **conversion factor** would be "**4**" in the relationship between quarts and gallons.

Suppliers and Manufacturers of Products

Figure 3.5 shows which suppliers and manufacturers are associated with each product. Because products may be sold by more than one organization and organizations sell more than one product, the entity SUPPLIER PRODUCT shows which products are offered by which organizations. The **available from date** and **available thru date** state when the product is offered by that supplier. This information is important because it provides the capability to find out where and when specific products may be purchased, what products competitors sell, and which products the enterprise sells. Another important consideration for SUPPLIER PRODUCTs is lead time, which indicates the average amount of time it takes for a supplier to deliver the product to the customer location from the time of order. While the actual average lead time can be derived from information stored in orders and shipments (this will be covered in later chapters), the **standard lead time** is provided because some suppliers quote a standard amount for delivery of each product.

Because there may be many suppliers from which the enterprise can order products, the PREFERENCE TYPE entity provides information to track the priority of whom to order from first, second, third, and so on. This priority is the information that would be stored in the **description** attribute and related back to the SUPPLIER PRODUCT entity. In addition to preferences that rank the pre-

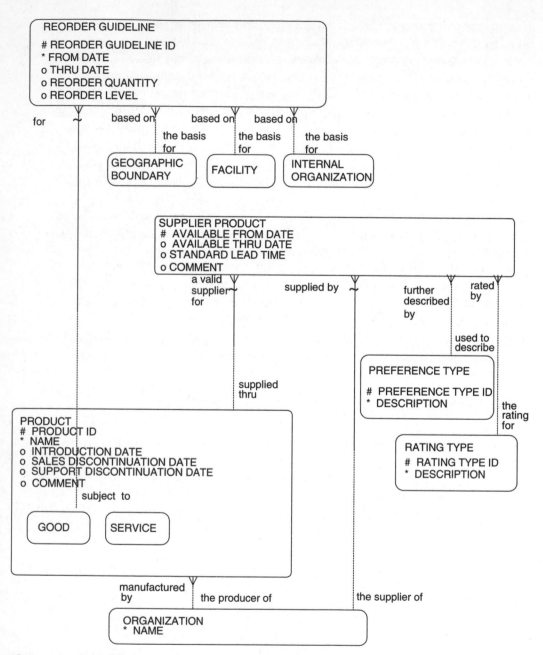

Figure 3.5   Suppliers and manufacturers of products.

ferred SUPPLIER PRODUCTs in order, each SUPPLIER PRODUCT also has a RATING TYPE that is used to rate overall performance for each product.

The REORDER GUIDELINE entity provides information on how to best reorder products. The REORDER GUIDELINE for a product is defined for each GOOD because services do not generally get reordered based on this type of guideline. The attribute of **reorder level** states the quantity at which the good needs to be reordered or reproduced. The attribute **reorder quantity** states the recommended amount of the good to order. This may have been derived by analysis to determine the most efficient quantity. This reorder level and quantity may be for goods that the enterprise is buying or for goods that the enterprise is selling because some firms let the vendor monitor the stock levels of inventory and do the appropriate ordering. The reorder guidelines may vary based on whether the product need is for a particular GEOGRAPHIC BOUNDARY, such as for a certain state, FACILITY, such as for a specific plant, and/or for a particular INTERNAL ORGANIZATION, such as a division.

Table 3.4 provides examples of the suppliers that provide "Johnson fine grade 8½ by 11 bond paper." Notice that the enterprise, ABC Corporation, sells this product; and if the enterprise does not have this product in stock, there are two other sources for obtaining this product. The pallets are a product that the enterprise needs to purchase for its own use. The table illustrates representative data that would be stored in SUPPLIER PRODUCT.

Products may be manufactured by only one organization. Of course, it is possible for an organization to subcontract with another organization to produce a product. The organization that hired the subcontractor is still the manufacturer. For example, a car manufacturer often hires another organization to produce

Table 3.4   Supplier Products

PRODUCT	SUPPLIER	PREFERENCE TYPE	RATING TYPE	STANDARD LEAD TIME
Johnson fine grade 8½ by 11 bond paper	ABC Corporation	First	Outstanding	2 days
Johnson fine grade 8½ by 11 bond paper	Joe's Stationery	Second	Outstanding	3 days
Johnson fine grade 8½ by 11 bond paper	Mike's Office Supply	Third	Good	4 days
6' by 6' warehouse pallets	Gregg's Pallet Shop	First	Outstanding	2 days
6' by 6' warehouse pallets	Pallets Incorporated	Second	Good	3 days
6' by 6' warehouse pallets	The Warehouse Company	Third	Fair	5 days

its cars. Because the original car manufacturer is still responsible for the product, it is considered the manufacturer.

Inventory Item Storage

Figure 3.6 shows how inventory items are modeled. While a GOOD represents a cataloged item or a standard product that can be purchased, an INVENTORY ITEM represents the physical occurrence of a good at a location. The GOOD may be "Johnson fine grade, 8½ by 11 bond paper," while the INVENTORY ITEM is the 100 reams of this good sitting in the central warehouse.

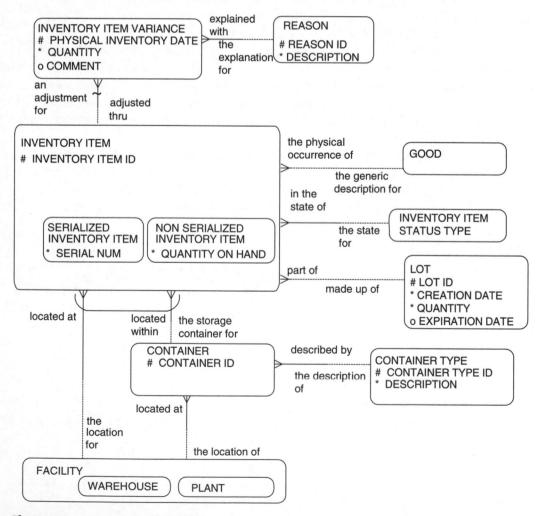

Figure 3.6   Inventory item storage.

The INVENTORY ITEM may be either a SERIALIZED INVENTORY ITEM, which means each item's **serial num(ber)** is tracked, or a NON-SERIALIZED INVENTORY ITEM, which means a group of items is tracked together and the **quantity on hand** for these is maintained by their location. The **quantity on hand** attribute is updated based on incoming and outgoing shipments of this good (shipments will be covered in Chapter 5). The model does not include attributes for **ordered quantity expected in** or **committed quantity going out** as this information can be derived from order information (orders will be covered in Chapter 4).

A concept found in some production-oriented industries is that of the LOT. A lot is simply a grouping of items of the same type generally used to track inventory items back to their source; it is often the result of a production run. Another source of lot information may be from the shipment from suppliers, which could determine the lot. This information is very important in the event a recall of items is required.

Inventory items can be separately identified by lots because an INVENTORY ITEM may be made up of one and only one LOT. This implies that there may be more than one inventory item of the same item type at a specific location, if there is more than one lot involved. Lot identification numbers, **lot ids**, are tracked so that if there is a customer complaint at a later time, it will be possible to identify where the items came from.

The inventory item may be tracked at a facility level, such as a warehouse, or it may be tracked at a more detailed level within a facility such as a container or a bin. The FACILITY entity is related to the INVENTORY ITEM and maintains the physical structure, building, warehouse, plant, or office where inventory items are located. A more detailed location is referred to as a CONTAINER, which resides within a facility. The CONTAINER TYPE entity specifies the type of container such as a "shelf," "file drawer," "bin," "barrel," "room," or any other detailed location.

The INVENTORY ITEM STATUS TYPE maintains the current condition of the items, for example, "good," "being repaired," "slightly damaged," "defective," or "scrap." If a history of the status of inventory items is needed for serialized items, then the enterprise may need an additional intersection entity of INVENTORY ITEM STATUS with a status date. This entity would be between the INVENTORY ITEM and INVENTORY ITEM STATUS TYPE.

Table 3.5 provides examples of INVENTORY ITEM. ABC Corporation stores most of its office supplies in bins within each facility. The first four rows show how much inventory of various serialized goods is located in various bins within different facilities. Notice that there are two records for "Johnson fine grade 8½ by 11 bond paper": the inventory of 156 reams (the product record defines the unit of measure in reams) stored at 100 Main Street with ABC Corporation and the inventory of 300 reams stored at 255 Fetch Street with ABC Subsidiary. The last row shows a serialized item of a copier, a large item that

may be stored at a facility level, instead of a container within a facility. Therefore, the container type is left blank.

The INVENTORY ITEM VARIANCE entity keeps a history of inventory item
shrinkage or overages that were noticed during physical inventories or inspec-
tions of the item. The **physical inventory date** specifies the date that the item
variance was discovered. The **quantity** is the difference between quantity of
items within INVENTORY ITEM (which is 1 for serialized items and the quantity on hand for non-serialized items) and the physical inventory at the time of
the **physical inventory date.** The information within the INVENTORY ITEM
VARIANCE could be used to adjust the INVENTORY ITEM quantities. When
this adjustment occurs, the **on-hand amount** of the INVENTORY ITEM should
be reduced if the **quantity** in ITEM VARIANCE is negative, and it should be
increased if the **quantity** is positive.

Table 3.5   Inventory Item

GOOD	FACILITY	CONTAINER TYPE	INVENTORY ITEM ID	INVENTORY ITEM TYPE	QUANTITY ON HAND	SERIAL NUMBER
Johnson fine grade 8½ by 11 bond paper	Warehouse at ABC Corporation 100 Main Street	Bin 200	1	Non-serialized	156	
Johnson fine grade 8½ by 11 bond paper	Warehouse at ABC Subsidiary 255 Fetch Street	Bin 400	2	Non-serialized	300	
Goldstein Elite Pen	Warehouse at ABC Corporation 100 Main Street	Bin 125	1	Non-serialized	200	
Jerry's box of 3½ inch diskettes	Warehouse at ABC Corporation 100 Main Street	Bin 250	1	Non-serialized	500	
Action 250 Quality Copier	Warehouse at ABC Corporation 100 Main Street		1	Serialized	1	1094853

The REASON entity provides standard explanations of the variance to the inventory item's on-hand amount. Possible values may be "theft," "shrinkage," "unknown variance," and "ruined goods." The comment attribute in the INVENTORY ITEM VARIANCE allows additional non-standard explanations. For example, if the enterprise discovered that there was a loss of inventory items due to theft, it can record the date the theft was discovered, the amount of the product that was stolen, and the specific details behind the theft. This serves as an audit trail to account for any changes to the product's **on-hand quantity** resulting from transactions other than incoming and outgoing shipments.

Product Pricing

Every organization seems to have different mechanisms for pricing its products. There are some common principles behind pricing that are captured in the data model in Figure 3.7.

In most organizations, there are several aspects to pricing a product: the base price for which the organization sells the product, various discounts applied against the base price such as quantity breaks, surcharges such as freight and handling charges, and the manufacturer's suggested price. The PRICE COMPONENT stores these aspects of prices for each supplier's products.

Notice the entity is named PRICE COMPONENT to allow the entity to be reused in other circumstances such as in agreement pricing, which will be covered in Chapter 4.

Pricing Subtypes

This entity is broken down into two non-mutually exclusive sets of subtypes (see explanation in Chapter 1, Non-Mutually Exclusive Sets of Subtypes, describing this notation). One subtyping that occurs is the subtypes of BASE PRICE, which has the starting price for the product, DISCOUNT COMPONENT, which stores valid reductions to the base price, SURCHARGE COMPONENT, which adds on possible charges, and MANUFACTURERS SUGGESTED PRICE. Another subtyping that categorizes types of prices is that the PRICE COMPONENT may be a ONE TIME CHARGE (such as for buying a good), a RECURRING CHARGE (an ongoing charge such as a monthly fee for a standard type of service), or a UTILIZATION CHARGE, which is a price component based on billing for usage of a product. The RECURRING CHARGE is based on per TIME FREQUENCY MEASURE (per hour, per day, per month), which is a type of UNIT OF MEASURE. The UTILIZATION CHARGE is based on a UNIT OF MEASURE, such as per a certain **quantity** of "internet hits" to describe the charge for Web hosting services.

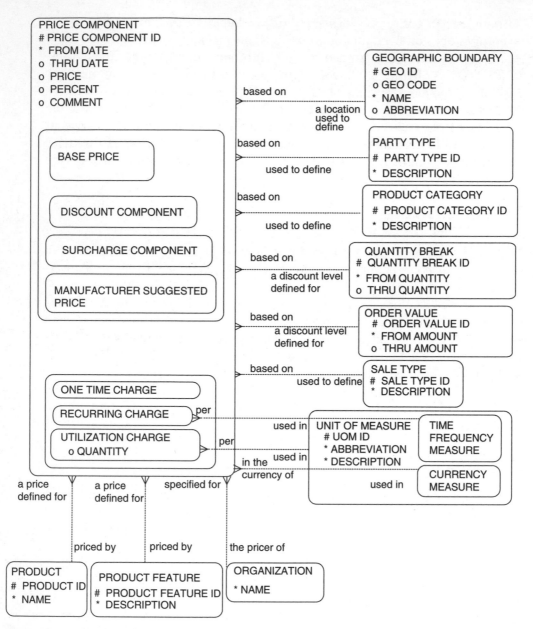

Figure 3.7   Standard product pricing.

Price Component Attributes and Relationship to Product or Product Feature

The PRICE COMPONENT stores a **from date** and **thru date** to indicate the starting and ending dates for which the price component is valid.

The **price** attribute maintains a dollar amount and a **percent** attribute that can be used to record discounts or quantity breaks. Each PRICE COMPONENT stores a value in either the **price** attribute or the **percent** attribute but not both. The **comment** allows each price component to be annotated, for example, "special discount provided to increase sales."

The PRICE COMPONENT entity is related to either the PRODUCT or PRODUCT FEATURE entity or both of them because product features may be priced independently or in conjunction with the price. For example, a product feature of the color blue may be priced with the product Goldstein elite pen. The PRICE COMPONENT may be specified for different ORGANIZATIONs because it is possible for multiple organizations to supply the same product. For instance, it may be important to maintain the various prices for all alternate suppliers of the enterprises product Johnson fine grade 8½ by 11 bond paper, including, of course, the price that the enterprise charges.

Pricing Factors

Each PRICE COMPONENT may be based on many variables or combinations of these variables. Pricing variables include GEOGRAPHIC BOUNDARY, PARTY TYPE, PRODUCT CATEGORY, QUANTITY BREAK, ORDER VALUE, and SALE TYPE. These represent common variables for pricing; however, the enterprise needs to determine if these variables are applicable or if there are other pricing variables for the enterprise. The GEOGRAPHIC BOUNDARY relationship allows pricing to be dependent on geographical regions such as countries, states, cities, or any other geographic boundaries. The PARTY TYPE relationship allows pricing to be dependent on the classifications of the party buying the goods such as special pricing for minority parties or governmental organizations. The PRODUCT CATEGORY relationship allows pricing to be associated with any classifications of products such as by product family, product model, product type, product function, and so on. The QUANTITY BREAK relationship allows special pricing for different quantity levels of purchasing. The ORDER VALUE allows different pricing levels based on total amounts of orders. The SALE TYPE allows different prices based on different methods of selling; for instance, Internet-based sales may have a different price than retail-based sales or catalog-based sales. It is important to provide a very flexible data model because pricing is very likely to change over time within organizations.

The optional relationship to these various pricing variables provides for a very flexible design since any combination of these factors may be used to determine a price component.

Each subtype of the PRICE COMPONENT may have values that are based on these pricing factors. For example, the BASE PRICE may be dependent on the type of enterprise that purchases the product, which is why there is an optional relationship to the PARTY TYPE entity. Another example is that there may be a lower price for minority-owned businesses. The base price may be dependent on the geographic area of the delivery, so there is also an optional relationship to the GEOGRAPHIC BOUNDARY entity. For instance, there may be a higher base product price if the good(s) are delivered to an area outside the enterprise's normal geographic boundaries. The base product price may also be based on quantities of products ordered. The QUANTITY BREAK entity stores various ranges of quantity breaks in the **from quantity** and **thru quantity** attributes. The enterprise needs to enforce business rules to determine which base price component takes priority over another component. For instance, there may be a base product price for a minority-owned business and a different base product price for customers in the eastern region. If a buyer fits both criteria, then the enterprise needs to build business rules to determine which price takes precedence.

The DISCOUNT COMPONENT may be dependent on the PARTY TYPE, GEOGRAPHIC BOUNDARY, QUANTITY BREAK, or certain PRODUCT CATEGORYs. For instance, there may be a 2 percent standard discount for all organizations with a PARTY TYPE of "minority-owned business." The enterprise may specify a discount for any delivery to a customer within the same city or GEOGRAPHIC BOUNDARY as the enterprise because the delivery charges would be less. Another discount may be based on the number of products purchased and therefore be dependent on the QUANTITY BREAK. Perhaps if the customer purchases more than 100 reams of a certain type of paper, there could be either an amount or percentage discount per good. There may also be a discount based on a PRODUCT CATEGORY such as 5 percent off for all paper products during the month of September as part of an advertising campaign. Notice that this discount does not even specify a PRODUCT or PRODUCT FEATURE, which is why both of these have optional relationships to PRICE COMPONENT. Finally, there may be combinations of pricing discounts such as a special on furniture within a certain geographic area. Another example of a pricing combination occurs when a quantity break applies exclusively to a specific party type, such as a minority-owned business.

A SURCHARGE COMPONENT is a PRICE COMPONENT that adds to the base price of the product. Examples of surcharges include freight costs and additional mileage costs. Product price surcharges are generally based on the GEOGRAPHIC BOUNDARY, such as additional freight charges being assessed based on the distance of the customer from the enterprise's nearest warehouse.

ONE TIME CHARGEs, RECURRING CHARGEs, and UTILIZATION CHARGEs may also be specified for different combinations of the various pricing factors.

International Pricing

Sometimes pricing is specified in different currencies for products that are sold internationally. The relationship to CURRENCY MEASURE allows a PRICE COMPONENT for each CURRENCY MEASURE such as "US dollars," "yen," "marks," and so on. These would be stored in the CURRENCY MEASURE description and used to define each PRODUCT COMPONENT **price**.

Units of measures are related to other units of measure as shown in the Product Feature model, Figure 3.4, in the UNIT OF MEASURE CONVERSION entity. In this case, the enterprise could store the monetary conversions from currency to currency if the enterprise had the will and means to capture this information.

Example of Product Pricing

Table 3.5 illustrates an example of price components for the product "Johnson fine grade 8½ by 11 bond paper." In this example, ABC Corporation has established standard base prices for certain geographical regions and for certain volumes of quantity ordered. The first four rows show the standard prices for the eastern and western regions and depend on the quantity being ordered. In addition, ABC Corporation has established a 2 percent discount if the purchasing party is a government agency. There is a 5 percent discount on all paper products (i.e., products with a product category of "paper") that is applicable in September 2001. The dates for this promotion would actually be entered in the PRICE COMPONENT attributes of **from date** and **thru date.** A surcharge of $2.00 is added to the product price for all deliveries to Hawaii.

In this model, products may have different price components for each organization, so the same model can be used to store competitors' prices to determine how competitive the enterprise's price is. Notice that the third to last row of Table 3.5 shows the standard price of the product for its competitor, Joe's Stationery. This model can maintain product prices for each product purchased from the enterprise's suppliers.

This model can also store the product prices for product features. Features may have prices that are within context of a product, or they may just have a price independent of the product. The second to last row records that the "cream color" feature for Johnson fine grade 8½ by 11 bond paper is priced at an additional $1.00. This means that the "cream color" feature could have a different price if applied to another product. The last row shows that the feature "extra glossy finish" has a base price of $2.00 and is independent of the product to which it is applied.

There are many different variations on the way each enterprise prices its products. When it comes to negotiating deals, it is amazing how creative people

Table 3.5 Standard Product Pricing

PRODUCT DESCRIPTION	PRODUCT FEATURE	ORGANIZATION	PRICE COMPONENT TYPE	PRICE COMP ID	PARTY TYPE	GEOGRAPHIC BOUNDARY	QUANTITY BREAK	PRICE	PERCENTAGE
Johnson fine grade 8½ by 11 bond paper		ABC Corporation	Base	1		Eastern region	0–100	$9.75	
Johnson fine grade 8½ by 11 bond paper		ABC Corporation	Base	2		Eastern region	101–	$9.00	
Johnson fine grade 8½ by 11 bond paper		ABC Corporation	Base	3		Western region	0–100	$8.75	
Johnson fine grade 8½ by 11 bond paper		ABC Corporation	Base	4		Western region	101–	$8.50	
Johnson fine grade 8½ by 11 bond paper		ABC Corporation	Discount	5	Govt				2
Johnson fine grade 8½ by 11 bond paper		ABC Corporation	Discount	6	Paper products (special offer in Sept. 2001)				5
Johnson fine grade 8½ by 11 bond paper		ABC Corporation	Surcharge	7		Hawaii		$2.00	
Johnson fine grade 8½ by 11 bond paper		Joe's Stationery	Base	8				$11.00	
Johnson fine grade 8½ by 11 bond paper	Cream color	ABC Corporation	Base	9				$1.00	
	Extra glossy finish	ABC Corporation	Base	10				$2.00	

and organizations can get! Therefore, this pricing model is very flexible and can handle many different pricing scenarios. It is important that the enterprise determine its business rules in order to avoid confusion. For example, does the enterprise have a business rule that certain discounts override other discounts? Does the enterprise allow the sales representative to choose which discount applies if several discounts are applicable? Does the organization include quantity breaks as part of its base price, or does it consider quantity breaks a discount to the base price? These types of questions need to be answered in order to use this model effectively and store the right type of information within the attributes.

Product Costing

It is important for organizations to have good information on product costs in order to ensure that the products are priced profitably. Having appropriate product cost information may also help to determine appropriate commissions, if they are based on profitability.

Some data modelers might have the insight to realize that the actual product costs are in many aspects of a data model and derivable from data in various entities. For instance, purchase orders hold information about the cost of the raw materials. The shipment to the customer will have freight charges, which are a cost component of the product. Time sheets and payroll records hold information about the labor costs involved in the manufacturing or delivery of products. For manufactured goods, the cost of scheduling equipment in production runs is stored in equipment assignment records. Overhead such as rent, office supplies, and other administrative goods can be factored into the product cost as well.

Instead of using actual product costs to figure out the cost of various products, this model uses estimated costs that product analysts will typically enter for each product. The advantage to using estimated costs is that product analysts can predict future trends of how much they think the product will cost instead of simply using historical information. For example, the freight charges might have historically been $1.00 from destination A to destination B. Data on current freight charges may be more appropriate for figuring out the real cost of a product. The enterprise can use the actual product costs combined with its understanding of the marketplace and future trends to enter what it believes will be the best estimate of the costs of selling its products.

Of course, the only product costs that are worthwhile tracking are usually those for the enterprise's own products. Supplier and competitor cost information is usually not available. An exception is that some government organizations need to track the costs of their suppliers' products to ensure that profit margins are not excessive.

Figure 3.8 is a data model for storing estimated product costs. Many cost components figure into the overall costs of a product. Therefore, either a PRODUCT or a PRODUCT FEATURE may be costed by many ESTIMATED COST COMPONENTs. The ESTIMATED PRODUCT COST entity maintains information on each product and its many costs. The COST COMPONENT TYPE entity specifies what type of cost it is. COST COMPONENT TYPEs include ESTIMATED MATERIALS COSTs, ESTIMATED LABOR COSTs, and ESTIMATED OTHER COSTs such as manufacturing costs (i.e., the use of machinery and equipment), shrinkage costs (i.e., theft or perishable good losses), shipping costs, costs in selling

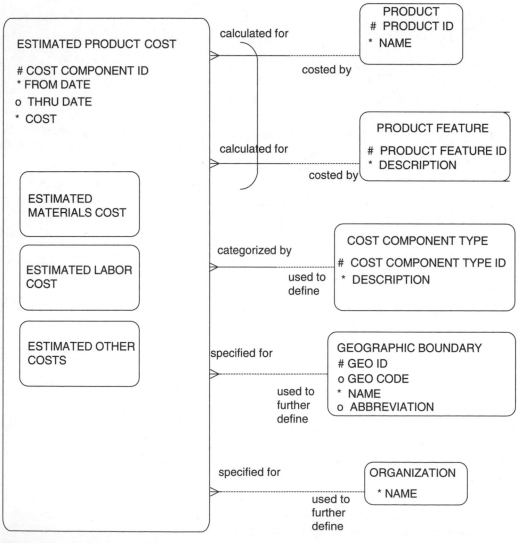

Figure 3.8 Estimated product cost.

the product (i.e., commissions or brokerage charges), and administrative costs of running an office. Additionally, product costs may vary by season or over time, so the attributes **from date** and **thru dates** are included to show the time period that the cost is valid.

The cost component may vary based on where the costs are incurred and hence the optional relationship to GEOGRAPHIC BOUNDARY. For instance, manufacturing costs may be less expensive in a plant located in one country versus another country. Delivery costs may be less expensive if the shipment is located in a nearby location versus an overseas shipment. Shrinkage costs due to theft may be higher in certain cities.

The estimated costs may, in some cases, vary by ORGANIZATION. If the organization is tracking and comparing the costs for multiple suppliers, then the enterprise may want to be able to record separate costs for each organization and hence this optional relationship to ORGANIZATION.

Product cost component may vary depending on the type of business. For instance, a distributor may track the cost of buying the goods, shipping and handling charges, selling costs, and administrative overhead. A manufacturer may track the cost of the materials used, labor used to produce the goods, the cost of running manufacturing equipment, selling costs, and administrative overhead. The costs for a service organization generally include the cost of labor, selling costs, and administrative costs.

Table 3.6 shows examples of product cost information that would be stored in ESTIMATED PRODUCT COST. The table shows that while the anticipated purchase cost of the product "Johnson fine grade 8½ by 11 bond paper" is the

Table 3.6   Estimated Product Costs

PRODUCT	COST TYPE	GEOGRAPHIC BOUNDARY	COST	FROM DATE	THRU DATE
Johnson fine grade 8½ by 11 bond paper	Anticipated purchase cost	N.Y.	$2.00	Jan 9, 2001	
Johnson fine grade 8½ by 11 bond paper	Administrative overhead	N.Y.	$1.90	Jan 9, 2001	
Johnson fine grade 8½ by 11 bond paper	Freight	N.Y.	$1.50	Jan 9, 2001	
Johnson fine grade 8½ by 11 bond paper	Anticipated purchase cost	Idaho	$2.00	Jan 9, 2001	
Johnson fine grade 8½ by 11 bond paper	Administrative overhead	Idaho	$1.10	Jan 9, 2001	
Johnson fine grade 8½ by 11 bond paper	Freight	Idaho	$1.10	Jan 9, 2001	

same for New York as it is in Idaho, the administrative overhead and freight costs are less if this product is sold in Idaho.

Product to Product Associations

Products have many different types of relationships to other products. This section will provide models to handle product componentization, product substitution, product obsolescence, product complement, and product incompatibility. Figure 3.9a illustrates a data model that provides for these common information requirements of products, and Figure 3.9b represents an alternative model for maintaining this type of information.

Let's first address the need to store what products are made up of other products or product components. Most people view the combining of components into a saleable product as a function limited to manufacturing organizations. Other types of organizations package together components to make a product offering. Some distribution companies assemble kits that include individual goods that could also be sold. For instance, a beauty supply distributor may combine combs, scissors, and makeup into a beauty kit that the customer can purchase. Service organizations often bundle together services that are sold as a single product. For instance, there may be a single price for a software application package that consists of the documentation, the software stored on a CD-ROM, introductory training, and a certain number of hours of initial consulting.

The PRODUCT COMPONENT entity shows which products are made up of other products. A product can be made up of more than one other product; alternatively, a product may be used in several other products. For example, an office desk set may consist of a pen, pencil, calendar, clock, and wood base. Any one of these components may be used in the assembly of another product. Service organizations may also assemble one or more of their services into a product and, alternatively, use the same service in many product offerings.

The PRODUCT COMPONENT has attributes of **from date** and **thru date** to signify the time periods that certain product components are made of other product components. This implies that the components of a product may change. At one point in time, an office desk set may include a certain type of pen; at a later time it may include a different type of pen.

Another attribute of PRODUCT COMPONENT is the **quantity used.** This attribute indicates how many of a certain product are used in the assembly of another product. For example, in some office desk sets two pens may be included in the set. The **instruction** attribute explains how to assemble the products. If a comprehensive set of instructions is needed, then a new entity named INSTRUCTION should be added and related to the PRODUCT COMPONENT. The **comment** attribute is used to describe any other note about the

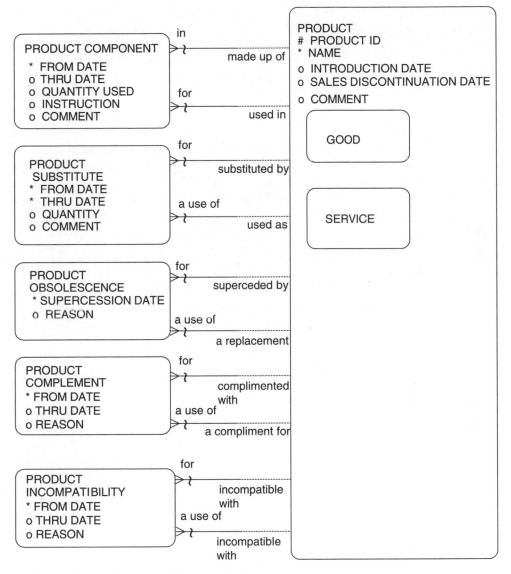

Figure 3.9a   Product to product associations.

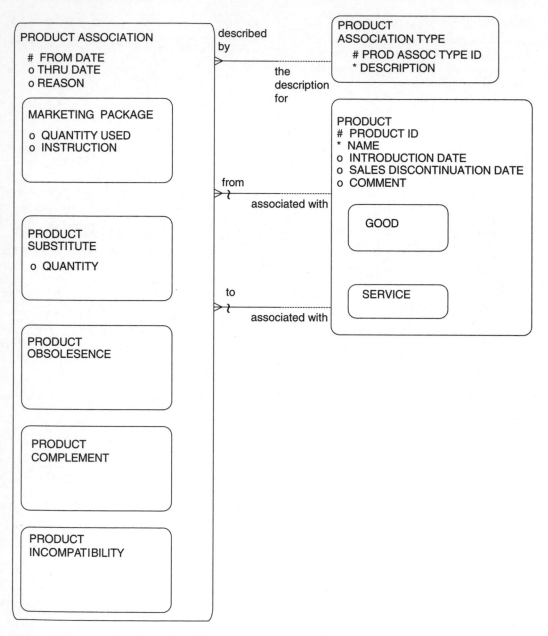

Figure 3.9b Product to product associations—alternate model.

Table 3.7 Product Components

PARENT PRODUCT TYPE	CHILD PRODUCT TYPE	QUANTITY
Office supply kit	Johnson fine grade 8½ by 11 bond paper	5
Office supply kit	Pennie's 8½ by 11 binders	5
Office supply kit	Shwinger black ball point pen	6

assembly of products. Table 3.7 shows an example of a product that is made up of other products.

Some enterprises need to know the makeup of their products. For instance, some laboratories need to know how their research apparatus is put together. Organizations that repair the equipment they sell need to know how the product is assembled even though they might not have manufactured it themselves.

The PRODUCT SUBSTITUTE entity shows which products may be substituted by other products. A PRODUCT may be substituted by many other PRODUCTs. For example, perhaps a certain pen within an office desk set may be substituted by a few other pens of similar quality. Alternatively, a PRODUCT can also be used as a substitute for many PRODUCTs. Perhaps a specific pen is used as a substitute in many circumstances. The **from date** and **thru date** attributes specify the time frames that products may be substituted for each other. The **quantity** attribute allows a product to be substituted for a certain quantity of another product. For example, Table 3.8 provides an example of a small box of pencils being substituted for 12 individual pencils of the same type. The **comment** attribute provides additional information regarding the substitution of a product; for example, "try not to substitute with this product if it can be avoided as the product is of a lower quality than the standard product."

The PRODUCT OBSOLESCENCE entity shows which products are about to be or have already been superseded by other products. There is a many-to-many recursive relationship from the PRODUCT entity to show that a product can be superseded by numerous new products and that a new product may supersede many old products. For example, the next release of a software package may combine several separate pieces of software into a single piece of software or vice versa.

The PRODUCT COMPLEMENT entity provides the capability of showing products that are well suited to function with other products. For example, the

Table 3.8 Substitute Products

PRODUCT	SUBSTITUTE PRODUCT	QUANTITY
Small box of Henry #2 pencils	Individual Henry #2 pencil	12
Goldstein Elite pen	George's Elite pen	

product "Jerry's desk blotter refill paper" may be a complementary product to "Jerry's desk blotter" because it could be suggested as a desirable accessory product when buying the desk blotter.

The PRODUCT INCOMPATIBILITY entity provides the capability to maintain which product may not be used with other products. For instance, a "Barry's pen refill" may not be compatible with the product "Goldstein Elite Pen"; it would be good to let customers know this by maintaining this PRODUCT INCOMPATIBLE information and using it at the time of an order. If a great many of the combinations of product lead to product incompatibilities, the model could alternatively have a PRODUCT COMPATIBILITY recursive entity to show which products are compatible with other products.

Figure 3.9b shows an alternate model for maintaining these products associations. Because there are many common attributes and because the relationship structures of these product associations are identical, the former product associations are now supertyped into a PRODUCT ASSOCIATON entity. The PRODUCT ASSOCIATION TYPE entity provides an entity that could store additional types of product associations should the need arise, hence yielding a more flexible data structure.

Products and Parts

How should the data model handle the modeling of parts, raw materials, supplies, and product components? Are office supplies, spare part supplies, or pieces that are part of a product also considered products? In one sense, they must have been attained from somewhere and are a product of some organization. On the other hand, the parts that may be used to repair products or bought for office supplies are substantially different from the mainstream products that are the key offerings for the enterprise.

One method of handling this is to simply subtype the GOOD entity into FINISHED GOOD, RAW MATERIAL, and SUBASSEMBLY, as shown in Figure 3.10a. A FINISHED GOOD is a product that is ready to be shipped, and some work may have been performed to get the product to its current state. A RAW MATERIAL is a component used in making a product in which no work on it has been performed by the enterprise and it is the lowest level component that makes up a product. A RAW MATERIAL may be sold as a good or used in another good. A SUBASSEMBLY good is a product that is in a state of partial completion and is not generally sold to a customer or purchased from a supplier. If the enterprise purchased the subassembly from a supplier, it would be considered a RAW MATERIAL because the enterprise did not perform any additional work on the product.

Another method for data modeling this structure is to consider a PART something separate from a PRODUCT. This really depends on one's perspective as well as the enterprise's needs. If the enterprise buys screws for use in assem-

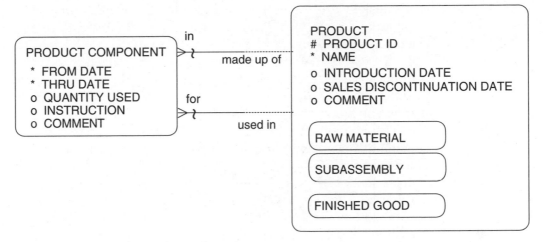

Figure 3.10a Products and parts.

bling its product, it is buying someone else's product. If one wanted to be more specific and create a separate entity for the individual pieces or parts that make up a product offering, then the model in Figure 3.10b may be better suited. Additionally, if the nature of the enterprise regards parts as a very significant piece of information, for instance, in an assembly line manufacturing enterprise, then it may be appropriate to model the PART entity separately.

In Figure 3.10b, the PART entity represents a physical item that exists, as opposed to a PRODUCT that is what is marketed. A PART, and specifically a FINISHED GOOD, may be used to produce one or more PRODUCTs. How can this be? Sometimes, the same physical item can be sold as two different products depending on circumstance of the sale such as to whom the product is sold. A telecommunications company may sell the same finished good, for example, a telephone line, as two products: a residential line or a business line, depending on whether the customer is an individual or a business. Therefore, the PRODUCT represents the marketing offering, which could vary from the actual item, which is the PART.

The PART is subtyped into RAW MATERIAL, SUBASSEMBLY, and FINISHED GOOD, which have the same definitions as stated previously. Instead of using the PRODUCT COMPONENT entity to show how RAW MATERIALS and SUBASSEMBLYs are combined into FINISHED GOODS, the PART BOM (bill of materials) entity maintains which parts are made up of other parts. The PRODUCT COMPONENT entity would now maintain packages of products together. An alternative name for the PRODUCT COMPONENT could be MARKETING PACKAGE because in this model it represents packaging of products and not parts.

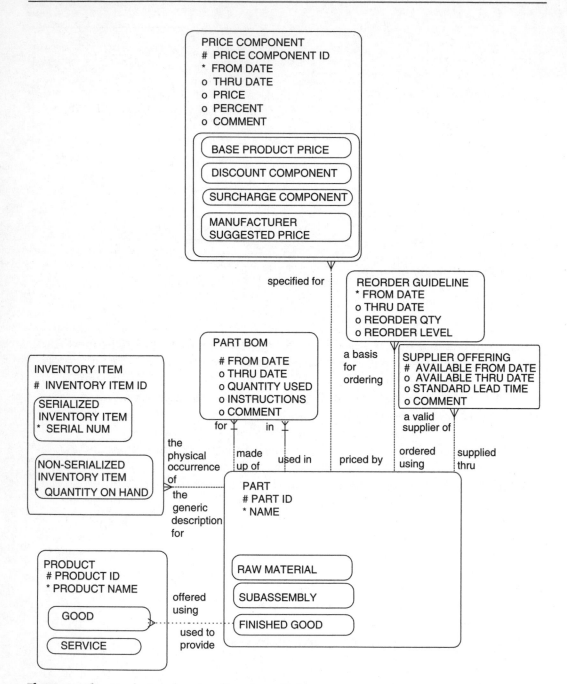

Figure 3.10b   Product and parts—alternate model.

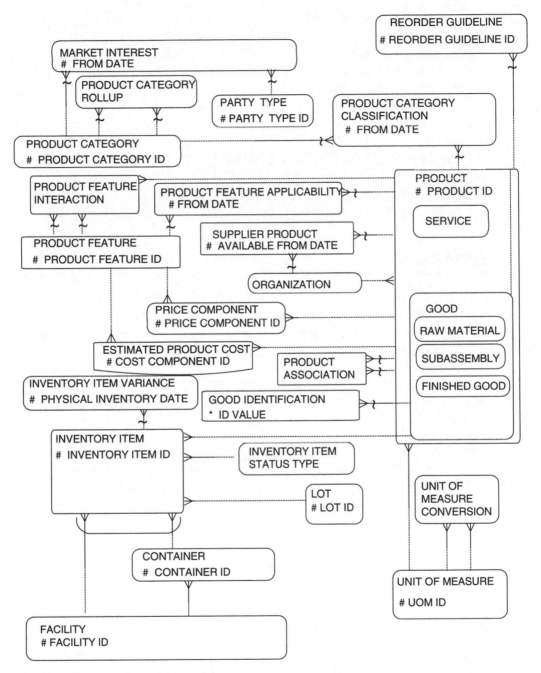

Figure 3.11   Overall product model.

The model shows that if PARTs are modeled they need to be related to INVENTORY ITEMs, PRICE COMPONENT, REORDER GUIDELINE, and SUP-PLIER PRODUCT. Parts need to be inventoried in addition to products, and this relationship could also be shown as a mutually exclusive arc to either PARTs or PRODUCTs. Parts may be priced using the PRICE COMPONENT relationship, and these may include parts the enterprise is selling or parts the enterprise is buying. Parts may need reordering information as well as information on which party supplies the parts, hence the relationships to REORDER GUIDELINE and SUPPLIER OFFERING (formerly SUPPLIER PRODUCT). If the enterprise manages parts separately from products, then the entity SUPPLIER PRODUCT should be changed to SUPPLIER OFFERING because this entity now repre-sents parties that offer either parts or products.

Summary

This chapter has focused on the data model for products, which include both goods and services. Goods are tangible, physical goods whereas services are the selling of professionals' time to accomplish some function. The data models in this chapter incorporate the information needs for the enterprise's own prod-ucts, suppliers' products, and competitors' products. Product information cov-ered in this chapter includes the definition of products, supplier products and manufacturers, product storage, product pricing, product costing, and product to product association information. Figure 3.11 provides an overview of the product models covered in this chapter.

Please refer to Appendix A for a listing of entities and attributes. SQL scripts to build tables and columns derived from the logical models in this book can be found on the full-blown CD-ROM, which is licensed separately.

CHAPTER 4

Ordering Products

The previous chapters focused on information about the parties that conduct business and what products they need. This chapter focuses on how parties obtain these products—in other words, the ordering of products.

Businesses need information to answer many questions about orders; they need to know the terms associated with each order. For instance:

- When is the expected delivery time, and are there consequences for late delivery?
- Who is responsible for paying for the order?
- What is the negotiated price for each product that is ordered?
- What people and organizations are involved in the order?
- Who placed the order? To whom is the order being shipped?
- Was there an approved requirement for the order?
- Were there previous quotes for the order?
- Were there requests to many vendors to bid for the order?
- Are there general agreements in place that govern the terms of the order such as special pricing arrangements?

This chapter discusses the following models:

- Standard order model
- Order and order items
- Order parties and contact mechanisms
- Order adjustments
- Order status and terms
- Order Item Associations
- Requirements
- Requests
- Quotes
- Agreements
- Agreement items
- Agreement terms
- Agreement pricing
- Agreement to orders

Standard Order Model

Most organizations model orders using the standard data model that is shown throughout many textbooks on data modeling. Figure 4.1 illustrates this standard data model. A SUPPLIER is related to one or more PURCHASE ORDERs, which have PURCHASE ORDER LINE ITEMs that relate to PRODUCT. This model is similar for sales. A CUSTOMER can be related to one or more SALES ORDERs, which have SALES ORDER LINE ITEMs that relate to specific PRODUCTs. Table 4.1 shows the example of a typical sales order. A customer, ACME Company, placed a sales order on June 8, 2001, for several items (or items), each of which is defined in the PRODUCT entity. The sales order stores information such as the date the order was given, the customer placing the order, shipping instructions, and payment terms.

Table 4.1   Standard Order Model

ORDER ID	CUSTOMER	ORDER DATE	SHIPPING INSTRUCTIONS	PAYMENT TERMS
12560	ACME Company	June 8, 2001	Via truck	Net 30
23000	Jones Corporation	Sept 5, 2001	UPS	Net 30

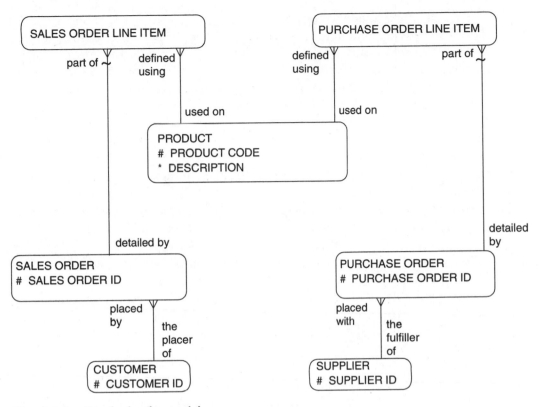

Figure 4.1 Standard order model.

Order line items show the individual products or services that were purchased. Table 4.2 shows examples of ORDER LINE ITEMs. In this example, three items are being ordered: 10 reams of paper, 4 pens, and 6 boxes of diskettes.

When a purchase order is given to a supplier, the same types of relationships exist. A supplier is given many purchase orders, each of which has line items that correspond to a specific product type.

Table 4.2 Order Item

ORDER ID	ITEM ID	PRODUCT	QUANTITY	UNIT PRICE
12560	1	Johnson fine grade 8½ by 11 bond paper	10	$8.00
12560	2	Goldstein Elite pen	4	$12.00
12560	3	Jerry's box of 3½-inch diskettes	6	$7.00

The attributes of sales orders and purchase orders are very similar, if not the same. An order is an order; the only real difference between a sales order and a purchase order is a matter of perspective. In other words, the information on the seller's sales order should, for the most part, correspond to the information on the purchaser's purchase order. The only reason that the attributes may be different is that the two parties may require different information depending on whether one is the seller or the buyer. For example, the enterprise taking the sales order may need to know the commissions for the salespeople involved in the order, whereas when a purchase order is given to a vendor, the purchaser is usually not privileged enough to know what the commission is for the salespeople.

As Figure 4.1 shows, the relationships and data structures between sales and purchase orders are very similar. By having two separate models for both of these types of orders, the model does not recognize the similar properties of sales and purchase orders and developers cannot take advantage of common applications to handle both sales and purchases. For instance, if the structures are the same, developers can create common routines against the same data structures. There could be common routines to look up the terms of an order, to monitor the status of the order against the expected delivery date, or to calculate line-item price extensions.

There is another embedded assumption in this standard order data model: Only one organization is involved in the sales order model, namely the customer, and only one organization is involved in the order in the purchase order model, namely the supplier. Most systems model information from an "I" perspective. This perspective states that the model doesn't have to indicate the party receiving sales orders or placing purchase orders; it's obviously us (meaning the enterprise building the system)! The problem with this perspective is that there may be several internal organizations within the enterprise that may receive a sales order or place a purchase order and this information needs to be recorded for each order. Even if an organization is a small business, there may be a broker who takes a sales order or the organization may grow later on to include subsidiaries, divisions, or other related internal organizations.

There are actually many parties involved in the order who could be involved in many roles. There could be a placing customer, delivery customer, bill-to customer, installation customer, person taking the order, organization that books the order, and similar roles for purchase orders.

Additionally, there are many contact mechanisms involved in sales and purchase orders. Where should the order be billed? Where should the order be shipped? From what contact mechanism did the order originate; for example, did it come from a specific e-mail or phone number? What was the location or contact mechanism that received the order? A model that maintains these various contact mechanisms for the order is needed.

The following order model addresses these previous issues and provides a more flexible structure to maintain purchase and sales order information.

Order and Order Items

The data model in Figure 4.2 is more flexible, modular, and maintainable than the data model in the previous section and is the one that will be built on throughout the remainder of this book. This model portrays a broader perspec-

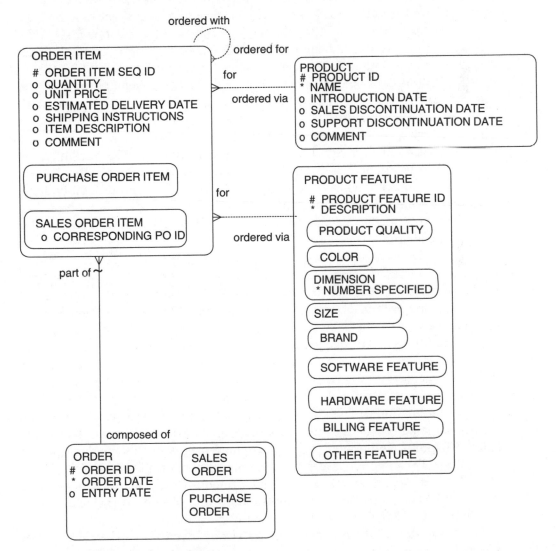

Figure 4.2   Orders and order items.

tive than the "I" model of the previous section and has a more stable, object-oriented approach where orders are related to parties that may play several roles, depending on the circumstances. The following models also provide flexible order data structures for maintaining contact mechanism information, adjustments, statuses, terms and order item associations.

Figure 4.2 shows that the ORDER entity is subtyped into SALES ORDER and PURCHASE ORDER to cover both sales and purchase orders. Orders are composed of ORDER ITEMs that specify the product(s) that are to be ordered, hence the relationship to PRODUCT. The ORDER ITEM is also subtyped into PURCHASE ORDER ITEM and SALES ORDER ITEM to accommodate information about the ORDER ITEM that is just for a purchase order item or for a sales order item. Each ORDER ITEM may be for one and only one PRODUCT or may be for one and only one PRODUCT FEATURE. PRODUCT FEATUREs may be ordered via an ORDER ITEM such as a certain COLOR, SIZE, SOFTWARE FEATURE, or other product variation that may be included in the order. These features can be specified via the recursive relationship **ordered with** from an ORDER ITEM that is for a product to an ORDER ITEM that is for a product feature, which is **ordered for** the former.

The attribute on ORDER named **order date** specifies the date on which the enterprise received or gave the order. The attribute **entry date** is the date on which the order was entered into the enterprise's system. The ORDER entity is subtyped into a SALES ORDER and a PURCHASE ORDER entity in order to accommodate specific attributes or relationships related to either a sales order or a purchase order.

ORDER ITEMs represent the ordering of specific goods or services. Therefore, each ORDER ITEM is defined using one and only one PRODUCT. ORDER ITEMs have a **quantity** attribute. For goods, this represents the number of goods that are ordered. For services, this represents the amount of hours, days, or other measurement being billed. The unit of measure for this quantity is determined by the unit of measure that is associated with the product (see Chapter 3, Figure 3.4). The **unit price** attribute stores the charge for an item or the rate for a service. The **estimated delivery date** is the date that the good is expected to be shipped to the customer or the expected date of service fulfillment to the customer. The **shipping instructions** attribute stores directions for transporting products to their destination, for example, "do not leave outside," "fragile—handle with care," or "requires signature by customer when delivering." The **comments** attribute allows additional explanation of the order item. The **item description** attribute provides a mechanism for storing descriptions for items that are non-standard and would not be maintained within the PRODUCT or PRODUCT FEATURE entities.

This **item description** attribute could also account for orders that are not product specific such as order items to perform work efforts or to order time for professional services. It will be shown in Chapter 6, Figure 6.3, that order items may also be related to one or more WORK EFFORTs—for example, when a customer places an order for a job to be done.

In Chapter 3, the data model shows that the price for each product can be stored as PRICE COMPONENTs and based on many variables such as geographic location, quantity breaks, the type of party, and outstanding promotions on certain types of products. So why is the **unit price** not a derived field? The **unit price** is important as this attribute allows the user to override the calculated price with the negotiated price for this order. Base, discount, and surcharge product price components can all appear as order items associated with a particular product.

Many models will portray orders having "order line items." The reason that this model does not call them "order line items" is that this term connotes physical lines on an order form. The physical lines on an order form often encompass many other things aside from the items that have been ordered. For instance, there may be notes to records adjustments, taxes, estimated freight costs, explanations, and other descriptive detail for the order. Rather than portray the entity as capturing each of the documented lines on an order form, the ORDER ITEM entity represents a major information need for the order, namely the items or products that have been ordered.

Table 4.3 illustrates the ORDER ITEM entity. The major difference in this entity from the standard order line item entity in Table 4.2 is that both sales and purchase order items are included in this entity. Notice that the purchase order has two items: one for a service ("hourly office cleaning service") and one for an item ("basic cleaning supplies kit"). This is one reason that orders are not subtyped as service and good orders because one order can include both services and goods.

Table 4.3 Sales and Purchase Orders

ORDER ID	ORDER SUBTYPE	ORDER DATE	ORDER ITEM SEQ ID	PRODUCT	QUANTITY	UNIT PRICE
12560	Sales order	June 8, 2001	1	Johnson fine grade 8½ by 11 bond paper	10	$8.00
			2	Goldstein Elite pen	4	$12.00
			3	Jerry's box of 3½-inch diskettes	6	$7.00
23000	Sales Order	Sept 5, 2001	1	George's Elite pen	10	$11.00
A2395	Purchase order	July 9, 2001	1	Hourly office cleaning service	12	$15.00
			2	Basic cleaning supplies kit	1	$10.00

ORDER ITEMs may be selected with certain product features that allow customization of the order. This is becoming more and more common in business as the need for customized products rises. Table 4.4 shows examples of product features that may be selected with sales order 12560 or with purchase order A2395. Only features that are optional or selectable are shown as standard, and required features can be derived through the product model. The feature of choosing the color "gray" is a selectable feature for that product, and "extra glossy paper" is a product quality feature that is optional and has a charge. Notice that more than one feature may be recorded for an order item, as has been done for the "Johnson fine grade 8½ by 11 bond paper" item. Each of these features is related to the first item in the order, namely the Johnson paper. Purchase orders may also record features that have been selected such as a billing feature of automatically charging the amounts to a credit card.

There are two ways that features for ordered products could conceivably be modeled. Ordered features could be modeled as a recursive relationship from a feature-related ORDER ITEM to a product-related ORDER ITEM. Alternatively, ordered features could be handled by maintaining the relationships to both the ordered feature with its related product recorded in the same order item. One issue with the latter approach is that the same product may be ordered on two

Table 4.4   Sales and Purchase Orders

ORDER ID	ORDER SUBTYPE	ORDER ITEM SEQ ID	PRODUCT	ORDER ITEM FEATURE SELECTED	FEATURE PRICE	ORDERED FOR (RECURSIVE RELATIONSHIP)
12560	Sales order	1	Johnson fine grade 8½ by 11 bond paper			
		2		Color—gray		Order 12560, Item Seq ID 1
		3		Product quality, Extra glossy finish	$2.00	Order 12560, Item Seq ID 1
		4	Goldstein Elite pen	Color—blue		
		5	Jerry's box of 3½-inch diskettes			
A2395	Purchase order	1	Hourly office cleaning service	Billing feature, automatically charged to credit card		
		2	Basic cleaning supplies kit			

different order items, and each product may have a different set of features associated with it. For this reason, a recursive relationship is used, relating an order item specifying a feature to another order item for the ordered product.

Order Parties and Contact Mechanisms

As said previously, many parties are involved in an order. The standard order model at the beginning of this chapter shows a simplistic model where there is a CUSTOMER for sales orders and a SUPPLIER for purchase orders. Who is the customer? Is it the party placing the order? The party receiving delivery? The party paying for the order? The party that is located at the point of installation (if there is an installation involved)? The party that uses the product? The same questions need to be addressed with regard to purchase orders, although the roles for the order may be named differently.

Each of these facts may be important. It is therefore essential to record each of these roles in association with the order. The key parties involved in an order are the following:

- The party placing the order
- The party taking the order
- The parties that will receive the delivery of the order
- The party that will pay for the order
- The party for whom the product is installed and/or set up
- The people who were involved in various roles regarding the order such as the person entering the order, quality assuring the order, managing the order, and so on

Figure 4.3 illustrates a data model for these order roles and associated contact mechanisms for sales orders. The next section will address a similar data model for purchase orders (Figure 4.4), and then a model will be presented that can handle either sales or purchase orders (Figure 4.5).

Sales Order Parties and Contact Mechanisms

Figure 4.3 provides a specific data model showing the roles and the contact mechanisms involved in a sales order. Each SALES ORDER and SALES ORDER ITEM have many PARTY ROLE subtypes as well as many CONTACT MECHANISMs associated with them. A SALES ORDER may be **placed by** a PLACING CUSTOMER, **taken by** an INTERNAL ORGANIZATION CONTACT, and **with a**

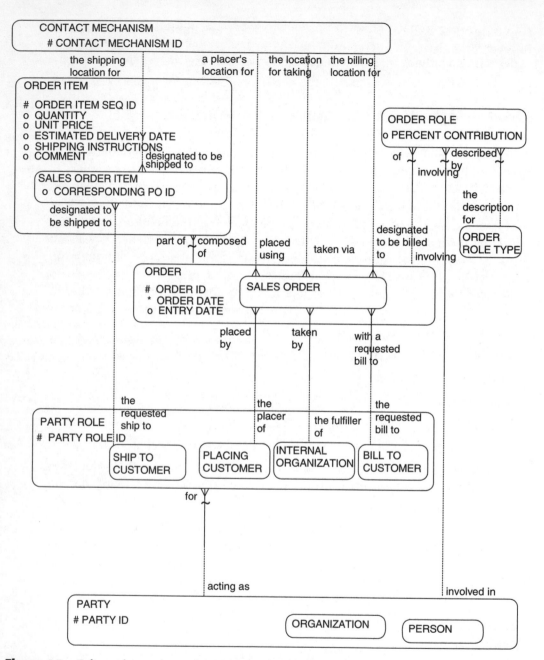

Figure 4.3 Sales order parties and contact mechanisms.

requested bill to a BILL TO CUSTOMER. This clearly represents the business rules of most standard sales orders.

The SALES ORDER may be **placed using** a CONTACT MECHANISM, which may be an address or phone number, and this number may also be used for confirmation of the order (or alternatively another **confirmation number** relationship could be added). The ORDER may be **designated to be billed to** a certain CONTACT MECHANISM, which may be a specific postal address or e-mail address. The order is also **taken via** a CONTACT MECHANISM that helps establish the phone number or email server that handled the order.

The ORDER ITEM may be **designated to be shipped to** a SHIP TO CUSTOMER and **designated to be shipped to** a specific CONTACT MECHANISM, which could be a postal address or e-mail address. The SHIP TO CUSTOMER is not related to the SALES ORDER entity but to the SALES ORDER ITEM because different SALES ORDER ITEMs may be designated to go to different parties. The **designated to be shipped to** CONTACT MECHANISM may also vary by ORDER ITEM within the same ORDER. For example, the customer may order one item to be delivered to one address and a different item delivered to another address.

If installation is needed, the enterprise may want to consider adding another relationship to record the installation address, which may be different from the shipping address. If this is needed, then the modeler can add the relationship: the SALES ORDER ITEM may be **designated to be installed at** an INSTALLATION CUSTOMER and be **designated to be installed at** a CONTACT MECHANISM, which would probably be a postal address.

Are the relationships from ORDER to PARTY and CONTACT MECHANISM independent relationships, or should an ORDER be related to a PARTY CONTACT MECHANISM that provides for both of these together? For example, instead of having two separate relationships to show the **placed by** PARTY ROLE and the **placed using** CONTACT MECHANISM, should the sales order be tied to a PARTY CONTACT MECHANISM that stores the party placing the order at their associated contact mechanism? The issue with doing the latter is that one may have one fact without the other. The enterprise may know who the placing party is and may not know its contact mechanism. In some cases, such as Internet-based orders, the enterprise may know the contact mechanism and not know who the party is! Therefore, these are modeled as independent facts of the order.

Note also that the PARTY CONTACT MECHANISM represents the addresses, phone numbers, fax numbers, and other contact mechanisms associated with the party for ongoing contact purposes. The relationship to CONTACT MECHANISM in this model represents the specific contact information to be used for the order and may or may not also belong in the master contact information that is in PARTY CONTACT MECHANISM. For example, the customer may want to specify a contact mechanism that is solely for use for that order.

Party Placing Order and Related Contact Mechanism

Orders may be placed by an individual or an organization depending on the business requirements of the organization for whom the system is built. In mail-order catalog businesses, the order is usually placed by a person. In manufacturing firms, the order is usually placed by an organization. The order may also be placed by an agent or a broker of a party. The PARTY RELATIONSHIP entity can identify if certain types of parties are allowed to place an order for the enterprise, such as checking to see if a valid broker relationship exists.

The SALES ORDER is related to the CONTACT MECHANISM to maintain order confirmation or follow-up information. This information may or may not be different from the party's contact information that is stored in the PARTY CONTACT MECHANISM, which stores all the default contact information for a party. The PARTY CONTACT MECHANISM information could serve to warn if a new contact mechanism is used for an order. A party could elect to designate the contact mechanism that placed the order for order confirmation purposes that they do not want in their contact information. An example of this could be a temporary location that is only for the purpose of the order and not for ongoing contact information purposes.

Party Taking Order and Related Contact Mechanism

The order is always taken by a party whether it is taken at the enterprise for a sales order or taken by the supplier for purchase orders. Figure 4.3 shows that an ORDER must be taken by a PARTY ROLE or INTERNAL ORGANIZATION and may be taken via a particular CONTACT MECHANISM. The order may be taken by a particular subsidiary, division, or department. A particular store may take an order, or the corporate headquarters may take the order. The order may also be taken through the World Wide Web; therefore, the order would be associated with a contact mechanism of the URL and the internal organization that received the order would also be recorded.

Ship-to Party and Contact Mechanism

In certain circumstances, orders are placed by one party and delivered to other parties. It is possible for someone to order a gift that is to be shipped to another party. It is also possible for an authorized agent of an organization to place an order that may be delivered to its client's address or addresses.

Figure 4.3 shows that each ORDER ITEM may be **with a requested bill to** a BILL TO CUSTOMER and **designated to be shipped to** one and only one CONTACT MECHANISM. Physical items will always require a destination where the items need to be shipped. Orders for service are also generally delivered to a specific location. The **designated to be shipped to** relationship is at the item level because one order could have many destinations. For example, a large department store chain may order 5,000 cases of cola with instructions to deliver 1,000 cases to each of its five regional stores. With this model it is possible to then record five items of 1,000 cases each, then specify a different delivery address for each item. If this relationship was to the ORDER entity, it would be necessary to record five different orders, which would result in storing redundant information and increase the margin for error during data entry.

It may seem as though the shipping information should be specified as part of the SHIPMENT model, for instance as a scheduled shipment, but there is a reason why it is not. As will be seen in the next chapter, a SHIPMENT can be made up of order items from many orders. That is, if several order items from *different* orders are to be sent to the same location, these can be consolidated into one delivery. Therefore, it is important to record the requested ship-to information on the order because it may affect how shipments are delivered. In other words, the information on **designated to be shipped to** parties cannot be specified by a SHIPMENT because it has not yet been determined which orders will be combined together in which shipments.

Note that this relationship is optional because there are cases where the location of the delivery is immaterial. For example, an order to provide cleaning services for a corporation may be provided across the entire enterprise, so there may not be a need for a **designated to be shipped to** relationship because there is not a single delivery address for the work.

The **shipped from** relationship is not specified in this chapter because this will most likely be determined after the order is created, when the SHIPMENT is determined. This relationship is included in the data model in Chapter 5, which covers shipments.

Bill-to Party and Contact Mechanism

The order needs to specify the party responsible for paying for the order as well as the contact mechanism that serves as the billing location for the order (generally where the invoices are sent). The relationship from SALES ORDER **with a requested bill to** a BILL TO CUSTOMER identifies the party responsible for paying for the invoice. The relationship from SALES ORDER **designated to be billed to** a CONTACT MECHANISM identifies where to send the bill and where to follow up for payment.

Table 4.5 gives examples of orders and the associated party addresses or contact mechanisms. Note that the **order item seq id** 3 order 12560 has a different ship-to than the other order items and is allowable because the ship-to is determined at the order item level. Order 23000 has a different ship-to party and contact mechanism than bill-to. Furthermore, this was an Internet-based order,

Table 4.5 Order Roles

ORDER ID	PLACING CUSTOMER AND CONTACT MECHANISM	TAKEN BY INTERNAL ORGANIZATION AND CONTACT MECHANISM	BILL TO CUSTOMER AND CONTACT MECHANISM	ORDER ITEM SEQ	SHIP TO CUSTOMER AND CONTACT MECHANISM
12560	ACME Company 234 Stretch Street	ABC Subsidiary 100 Main Street	ACME Company 234 Stretch Street	1	ACME Company 2300 Drident Avenue
				2	ACME Company 2300 Drident Avenue
				3	ACME Company 234 Stretch Street
23000	Jones Corporation 900 Washington Blvd	ABC Subsidiary supplies@ABC.com	Smith Corporation 900 Washington Blvd	1	Jones Corporation 2300 Drident Avenue
24830	Bford@person.com	ABC Subsidiary supplies@ABC.com	Bob Ford 2930 Briarwood Avenue	1	Bob Ford 2930 Briarwood Avenue
A2395	ABC Subsidiary 100 Main Street	Ace Cleaning Service 3590 Cottage Avenue	ABC Corporation 100 Main Street	1	ABC Retail Store 2345 Johnson Blvd
				2	ABC Retail Store 2345 Johnson Blvd

taken via a contact mechanism that is a web URL. Order 24830 was placed by an e-mail address as the contact mechanism that placed the order.

Person Roles for Orders

In addition to the key order relationships named previously, many other parties could be involved in the order process. Examples include the person giving the order, the person processing the order, the person approving the order, the parties that are scheduled to coordinate installation, and the parties responsible for fulfilling the order. Therefore, other parties may play various roles in an order. Figure 4.3 includes a data model structure that maintains the other roles parties play in orders.

Each ORDER may be involving one or more ORDER ROLEs, which are described by an ORDER ROLE TYPE. Each ORDER ROLE must be involving one and only one PARTY. While many times these roles will involve people, organizations may also play some of these roles, such as a service team that is responsible for ensuring fulfillment of an order.

Table 4.6 gives examples of the various roles that parties could play in an order. In order 23000, John Jones and Nancy Barker were the salespeople involved in closing the sale. Because they are both equally involved, the **percent contribution** attribute stores the fact that they were both given 50 percent of the credit for the sale. This information could be used in a commissions system. Frank Parks is responsible for processing the order or, in other words, entering the data into the system. Joe Williams is the party responsible for reviewing the information in the order. The order needs to be authorized or approved as a valid commitment by John Smith. Notice that the roles dictate the party responsible for accomplishing these functions so even if the function has not been performed yet, a party can still be slotted to play a role.

The roles described are just a sample of possible roles, and parties could play many other roles in the order. For instance, in some cases, the product needs to be set up or installed, and therefore installation parties are needed. These relationships identify the party that is responsible from the customer for coordi-

Table 4.6   Party Order Roles

ORDER ID	PERSON	ROLE	PERCENT CONTRIBUTION
12560	John Jones	Salesperson	50
12560	Nancy Barker	Salesperson	50
12560	Frank Parks	Processor	
12560	Joe Williams	Reviewer	
12560	John Smith	Authorizer	

nating the setup and repair of the order as well as the place. For instance, if a customer orders a personal computer, either the end user or the customer PC support person may be the installation contact, and the address or phone number of that person could be given. The model could be expanded to allow for a many-to-many relationship of PARTYs as well as CONTACT MECHANISMs to store numerous parties and contact information if necessary.

Purchase Order Parties and Contact Mechanisms

As discussed earlier, the data contained in purchase orders is very similar to the data in sales orders because they both represent the same type of transaction, only from different points of view.

Figure 4.4 provides a data model with purchase order roles and contact mechanisms. Not surprisingly, the data structures are very similar to those of the previous model. Because either a sales order or a purchase order represents a commitment between parties, regardless of whether one is on the buying or selling side, each party has a need to track the details of the order. The only difference is the name of the roles involved. For instance, instead of the INTERNAL ORGANIZATION taking the sales order, the SUPPLIER is that party that takes the purchase order. Instead of the PLACING CUSTOMER, the PLACING PARTY is shown to account for the party that gives the order, which may be an internal organization or an agent of the enterprise. Instead of a BILL TO CUSTOMER, the BILL TO PURCHASER role is used, and instead of a SHIP TO CUSTOMER, the SHIP TO BUYER maintains the party to whom the order is shipped.

Table 4.7 provides an example of the roles involved in purchase order A2395. In addition to these roles there would be additional ORDER ROLEs for the people involved in the purchase order, similar to the sales order model.

Generic Order Roles and Contact Mechanisms

Should the sales order and purchase order models be combined to take advantage of similar data constructs that could simplify the systems design? Should the data model show relationships from the order to specific party role entities (SHIP TO CUSTOMER, BILL TO CUSTOMER, and so on), or leave the model flexible and relate the order to many ORDER ROLEs of ORDER ROLE TYPEs, thus facilitating easier database changes over time? Should the model show specific relationships to order role entities as well as flexible role types that could be changed easily?

This is really not just an issue limited to orders. Any transaction type entity will have many parties associated with it. This may be modeled more generi-

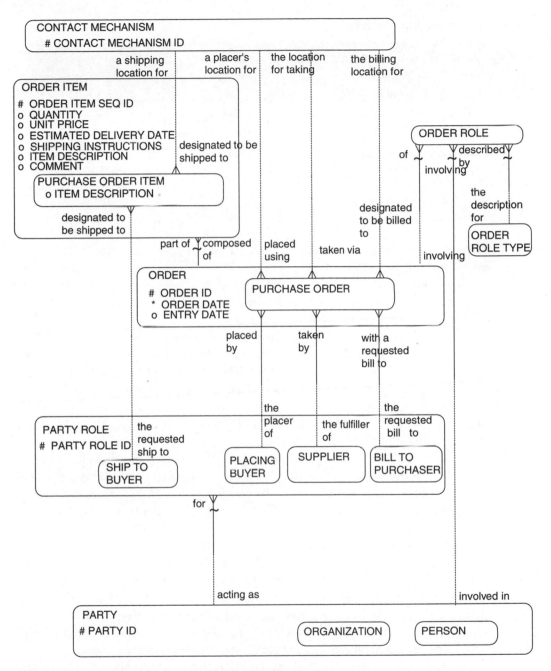

Figure 4.4 Purchase order parties and contact mechanisms.

Table 4.7 Purchase Order Roles

ORDER ID	PLACING PARTY AND CONTACT MECHANISM	SUPPLIER AND CONTACT MECHANISM	BILL TO PURCHASER AND CONTACT MECHANISM	ORDER ITEM SEQ	SHIP-TO BUYER AND CONTACT MECHANISM
A2395	ABC Subsidiary 100 Main Street	Ace Cleaning Service 3590 Cottage Avenue	ABC Corporation 100 Main Street	1	ABC Retail Store 2345 Johnson Blvd
				2	ABC Retail Store 2345 Johnson Blvd

cally by showing a relationship to a transaction role (ORDER ROLE, SHIPMENT ROLE, INVOICE ROLE) of a ROLE TYPE and then associated with a PARTY. Alternatively, specific PARTY ROLE subtypes could be related to the transaction. For example, an ORDER may be related to the party role, BILL TO CUSTOMER, SHIP TO CUSTOMER, and so on.

The advantage of showing specific relationships to party roles such as BILL TO CUSTOMER and SHIP TO CUSTOMER is that the model can show and enforce business rules. For instance, perhaps there is a business rule that says there is one and only one BILL TO CUSTOMER associated with an order. Or perhaps the enterprise allows more than one BILL TO CUSTOMER, and this can be shown as well. The point is that the business rule of the enterprise is explicitly stated in the data model.

The other advantage of showing specific relationships is that the model is less abstract and easier to read. It is easier to comprehend that an order is associated with a BILL TO CUSTOMER instead of that orders are associated with many ORDER ROLEs of ROLE TYPEs and one of the instances of ROLE TYPE is "bill-to customer."

The advantage of developing the data model with the transaction (i.e., ORDER, SHIPMENT, INVOICE) associated with more than one ROLE (ORDER ROLE, SHIPMENT ROLE, INVOICE ROLE) is that the data model, and the ensuing database design, is then much more flexible. The business rule could change from one bill-to customer to the allowance of many bill-to customers over time. If this flexible model is used, the underlying data structure does not have to be changed (although there may be a change needed to some code or a stored procedure). This structure would also allow additional roles to be added without changing the underlying data model or data structure.

Therefore, if the business rule is stable and not expected to change over time, then using the more specific data modeling method is preferable. Be careful, as it is common for one to think a data structure will not need to be changed and then invariably things change! If it is anticipated that the data model structure may need to change over time, then the more flexible way of modeling roles should be used.

Figure 4.3 and 4.4 showed specific data models for modeling the sales and purchase order roles; Figure 4.5 shows an alternate, more flexible data model for modeling these roles and contact mechanisms.

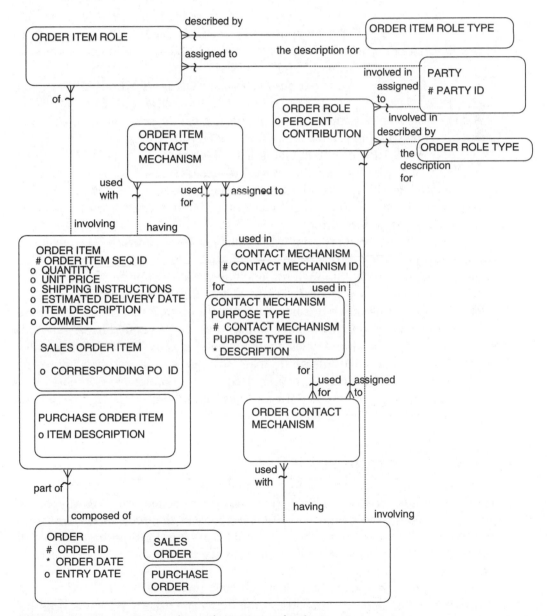

Figure 4.5   Generic order roles and contact mechanisms.

Figures 4.5 shows that each ORDER may involve one or more ORDER ROLEs, each of which is assigned to a PARTY and is described by an ORDER ROLE TYPE. This structure accommodates handling any number of roles for either sales orders or purchase orders by storing the possible roles in ORDER ROLE TYPE and then relating them to the ORDER ROLE. Possible ORDER ROLE TYPES include "placing party," "bill-to customer," "internal organization taking order," "placing customer," "placing buyer," "supplier," "bill to purchaser," "order entry person," "order salesperson," and "order authorizer." Each ORDER ITEM may also have ORDER ITEM ROLEs of ORDER ITEM ROLE TYPEs, which could include "ship-to buyer," "ship-to customer," "installation customer contact," and "installer."

Each ORDER may have one or more ORDER CONTACT MECHANISMs, and each ORDER ITEM may have one or more ORDER ITEM CONTACT MECHANISMs in order to record the address, phone, fax, e-mail, or other contact mechanism to confirm, ship, bill, take, or install the order. The CONTACT MECHANISM PURPOSE TYPE maintains values such as "ship to," "bill to," "confirmation," "placing," or "taken via" to describe the role of the contact mechanism. The CONTACT MECHANISM entity stores the actual address, phone number, fax number, e-mail address, or other contact mechanism that was used in conjunction with the order.

As the business rules of the enterprise change, the organization may want to track additional roles or there may be changes to the cardinality rules. This generic model is flexible enough to handle new data requirements easily. For example, a new order entry process may dictate that there may be at least two contact mechanisms that can serve to confirm orders. This structure accommodates as many contact mechanisms and roles as are needed in any circumstance. Restrictive business rules such as allowing only one bill-to customer could be accommodated outside the data structures in stored procedures or common routines. This rule, for example, could also change over time to allow more than one party to be billed for an order, and the model would be able to easily handle this requirement.

Order Adjustments

There are other parts of the order that do not reflect the ordering of specific products or features. Examples include discounts, surcharges, processing fees, and shipping and handling charges. Should these be considered subtypes of ORDER ITEMs or be considered their own entity and related to ORDER ITEMs?

If these adjustments are portrayed as subtypes of ORDER ITEM, then a recursive relationship would need to exist between ORDER ITEMs in order to relate the adjustments to the appropriate other ORDER ITEM. This data model is somewhat complicated because many of these adjustments may affect either or both the ORDER and ORDER ITEM. Is an adjustment really a similar enough thing to the ORDER ITEM, which represents the product being ordered? Another way of looking at this is that the item being ordered is an ORDER ITEM and an ORDER ADJUSTMENT is a separate entity since an adjustment doesn't really represent something that is "ordered."

For these reasons, the ORDER ADJUSTMENT is shown in Figure 4.6 as a separate entity. The subtypes are DISCOUNT ADJUSTMENT, SURCHARGE ADJUSTMENT, SALES TAX, SHIPPING AND HANDLING CHARGES, FEE, and MISCELLANEOUS CHARGE. The DISCOUNT ADJUSTMENT and SURCHARGE ADJUSTMENT are subtypes that store price adjustments to either the complete ORDER or to each ORDER ITEM. These price adjustments may be either an amount or a percentage.

The first three items in Table 4.8 are examples of discounts and a surcharge. The first shows that there is a $1.00 discount off each unit of a certain item (the next section will cover how to relate it to the item to which it refers). The second item shows that there is a 10 percent discount off the entire order, and the third item shows that there is a $10.00 surcharge for delivery outside the normal area.

The SALES TAX provides information on the sales tax charged either on the whole order or on a particular order item. SHIPPING AND HANDLING CHARGE would add an order adjustment to the ORDER or ORDER ITEM. FEE could store adjustments for charges such an "order processing fee," "handling fee" for covering the arrangements of the shipment of an order, or a "management fee."

The MISCELLANEOUS CHARGE subtype provides a mechanism to store information about any other charges that could occur on an order. An example of this could be "adjustment error" to correct a prior order. The ORDER ADJUSTMENT TYPE entity provides the ability to classify the various types of adjustments into detailed categories. The **description** attribute defines the possible values that may be related to adjustments.

An additional data structure is provided in Figure 4.6, which provides information on how much sales tax to charge. The SALES TAX LOOKUP entity stores a sales tax percentage that could vary by GEOGRAPHIC BOUNDARY such as COUNTY, CITY, or STATE and also may vary by PRODUCT CATEGORY. For instance, food products may have different tax implications than non-perishable products. Some types of products may be tax-exempt and could be classified this way by relating them to a "tax exempt" PRODUCT CATEGORY.

Table 4.8 provides examples of adjustments that could be stored in the model. The first row shows that the third order item, "Jerry's box of 3½-inch diskettes," has an order adjustment of a discount of $1.00 applied to it. The next three rows are adjustments that were applied to the whole order because no order item is signified. There was a 10 percent discount off the entire order, a

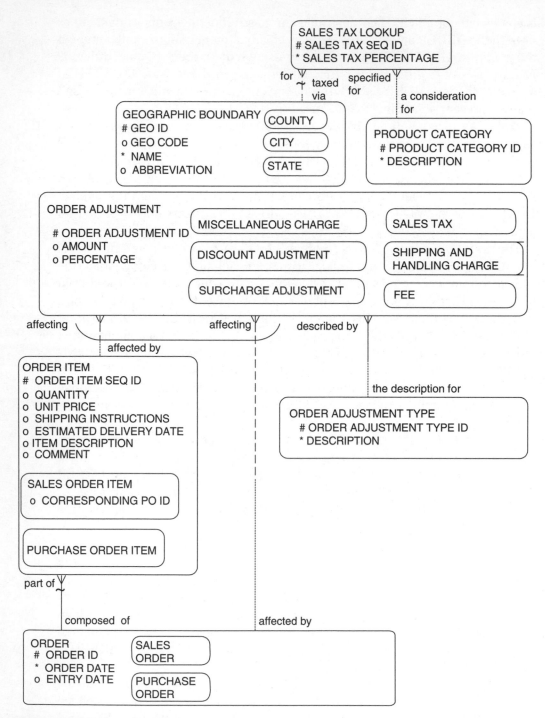

Figure 4.6 Order adjustments.

Table 4.8 Order and Order Item Adjustments

ORDER ID	ORDER ITEM SEQ ID	PRODUCT	ADJUSTMENT TYPE	AMOUNT	PERCENTAGE
12560	3	Jerry's box of 3½-inch diskettes	Discount	$1.00	
12560			Discount		10
12560			Surcharge—Delivery outside normal geographic area	$10.00	
12560			Fee—order processing fee	$1.50	

surcharge of $10.00 applied because the delivery location was outside the acceptable geographic area, and a fee associated with it of $1.50 for order processing charges.

Order Status and Terms

Figure 4.7 builds on the order model by illustrating information needs for the status and terms of the ORDER and ORDER ITEMs. This figure includes an ORDER STATUS entity to track the progress as well as to know the current state of an ORDER or ORDER ITEM. The ORDER STATUS TYPE maintains the status of possible order. The ORDER TERM entity tracks the conditions of business associated with the ORDER or ORDER ITEM. The TERM TYPE entity maintains the possible terms available to use.

Order Status

Because an order may be in many different states at different points in time, the model in Figure 4.7 shows that the order may have more than one status over a period of time. The **status datetime** attribute of ORDER STATUS provides for the tracking of when each status of the order occurred. For example, this model will allow the tracking of when the order was received, when it was approved, and when and if it was canceled. The description attribute of the ORDER STATUS TYPE entity stores the possible statuses such as "received," "approved," and "canceled." If it is necessary to know only the current status of the order and not a history of when each status occurred, then there could simply be a many-to-one relationship from ORDER to ORDER STATUS TYPE (and ORDER ITEM to ORDER STATUS TYPE).

Why not have "shipped," "completed," "backordered," or "invoiced" as order statuses? As will be discussed in later chapters, because shipments and

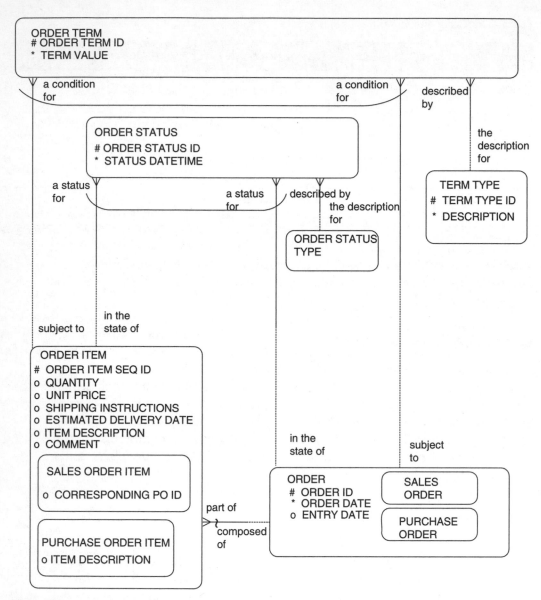

Figure 4.7 Order status and terms.

invoices are tied to orders, "shipped," "completed," and "invoiced" can be derived through the relationships to shipment items and invoice items. "Back-ordered" can be derived through the ORDER ITEM ASSOCIATION entity discussed later in this chapter. Although these statuses are derivable values in the logical model, the physical database design may have these statuses available in the ORDER STATUS TYPE table for easy access.

Order Terms

The parties involved may agree on many arrangements or terms. Delivery terms, exchange or refund policies, and penalties for non-performance are some examples. Each ORDER or ORDER ITEM may have one or more ORDER TERMs, each of which is categorized by a TERM TYPE. The **term value** attribute is applicable only to some of the order terms, and its meaning is dependent on the type of term.

Table 4.9 shows examples of order terms. Order 12560 has three terms defined to it. The first two terms document that if the purchaser cancels the order 10 days after placing it, there is a 25 percent cancellation charge. The third term says there are no refunds or exchanges after this item has been delivered.

While one may think that that terms are associated with only the order header, in some cases the individual order items also have terms associated with them. Table 4.9 shows several examples of terms that are associated with the order item. The "Goldstein Elite pen" order item has a term that it cannot be exchanged or refunded once delivered.

On the purchase order A2395, for the order item "hourly office cleaning service" there is a 5 percent non-performance penalty if the order is delivered more than 30 days past the **estimated delivery date**.

Order Item Association

Sometimes there is a relationship from one order item to another order item. The ORDER ITEM ASSOCATION entity in Figure 4.8 relates sales order items to purchase order items.

Table 4.9 Order Term

ORDER ID	ORDER ITEM SEQ ID	PRODUCT	VALUE	TERM TYPE
12560			25	Percentage cancellation charge
			10	Days within which one may cancel order without a penalty
	2	Goldstein Elite pen		No exchanges or refunds once delivered
A2395	1	Hourly office cleaning service	5	Percentage penalty paid by supplier for nonperformance
	1	Hourly office cleaning service	30	Number of days within which delivery must occur

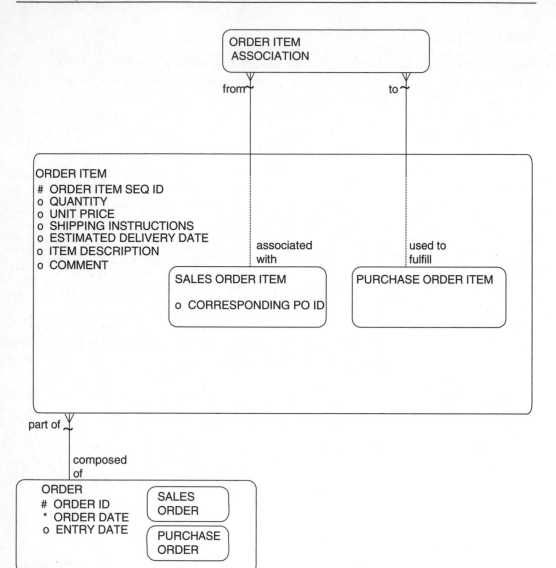

Figure 4.8 Order item association.

An example of this association occurs when a sales order item is dependent on a purchase order item. For example, a distributor may receive a sales order but may not have enough inventory in stock to cover one of the items on it. In turn, the distributor may place a purchase order to one of its suppliers (or many purchase orders to many suppliers) to fulfill the item that was short. In other words, the sales order item was "backordered" and covered by a purchase order item.

Table 4.10 Order Item Association

ORDER ID	ORDER ITEM SEQ ID	ORDER ID	ORDER ITEM SEQ ID
13480	1	23490	1

A single item on a purchase order may be used to fulfill several items on sales orders. Alternatively, a sales order item may be fulfilled by many purchase orders items because the additional inventory may be ordered from many different suppliers. The ORDER ITEM ASSOCIATION handles this many-to-many relationship.

The example shown in Table 4.10 illustrates the data that would occur from a purchase order item tied to a sales order item. Order 23490 is a purchase order that has an item that will provide the items needed for sales order 13480, item 1.

Another situation where sales and purchase orders are linked is when a sales order requires the corresponding purchase order number from the buyer. Because the seller may want to track the buyer's corresponding purchase order ID, the attribute **corresponding PO ID** is on the SALES ORDER ITEM entity. This attribute is defined at the order item level and not the order header because each order item of the sales order may be related to a different purchase order. The ORDER ITEM ASSOCIATION entity is not used to relate the purchase order to a sales order in this case because the seller is generally not interested in recording the full details behind the purchase order—the seller usually needs only the purchase order number.

In the latter case, one sales order item is generally not related to multiple purchase orders. If an item on a sales order is placed due to two or more purchase order items, the sales order item may be split into separate sales order items to be able to trace the exact amount of the item that corresponded to each purchase order.

Optional Order Models

The data models and information about orders covered thus far in this chapter are very common to most enterprises. The remainder of this chapter will illustrate data models that may or may not be applicable to an enterprise, depending on the information requirements of each specific enterprise. The data models already presented may represent a complete ORDER data model for some enterprises.

The next sections illustrate additional aspects around the order subject data area. These include: REQUIREMENTs to identify either customer or internal needs, which could lead to either sales or purchase orders, REQUESTs, which represent the solicitation of suppliers or solicitation to the enterprise to bid on orders, QUOTEs, which are the responses to requests to bid, and AGREE-MENTs, which define terms and conditions that may govern orders. Each enterprise needs to evaluate which of these data models are applicable to its business and should be incorporated into its design.

Requirements

An order occurs because a party has a need for something. Some enterprises will track these needs, and some may not. The enterprise may track its customer needs as well as its own needs. An example of a customer need is capturing a requirement of a customer to help build a system for him or her. An example of an internal need is a requirement to purchase certain office supplies.

The organization may be interested in tracking either customer or internal needs, or both, depending on the type of enterprise. In some enterprises, such as professional service organizations, it is very important to capture the needs of customers. In other organizations, such as mail-order catalog enterprises, the enterprise may not track its customer needs and track only needs for their internal requirements.

Figure 4.9 provides a very flexible data model that handles the capturing of both customer and internal requirements.

A REQUIREMENT is an organization's need for *anything*. The REQUIRE-MENT entity represents a need that may be either a CUSTOMER REQUIRE-MENT or an INTERNAL REQUIREMENT. Similarly, each REQUIREMENT could be either a PRODUCT REQUIREMENT or a WORK REQUIREMENT. A PRODUCT REQUIREMENT may be related to a specified PRODUCT and/or several DESIRED FEATUREs because the need may be expressed as either a need for a product or a need for something with certain types of characteristics.

REQUIREMENTs may be made up of other REQUIREMENTs and hence the recursive relationship around REQUIREMENT. For instance, there may be a WORK REQUIREMENT to buy office supplies. This requirement may be further broken down into more specific requirements to buy paper, pencils, pens, and CD-ROMs. Similarly, a WORK REQUIREMENT to "develop a new sales analysis system" may be further broken down into more specific requirements to "conduct needs analysis," "select application packages," "select hardware and software," and "implement system." With this recursive structure, the enterprise may define multiple levels of requirements.

Many people may be associated with the REQUIREMENT in various REQUIREMENT ROLEs of REQUIREMENT ROLE TYPEs such as "owner," "originator," "manager," "authorizer," or "implementer." The REQUIREMENT may have several REQUIREMENT STATUSes over time such as "active," "on

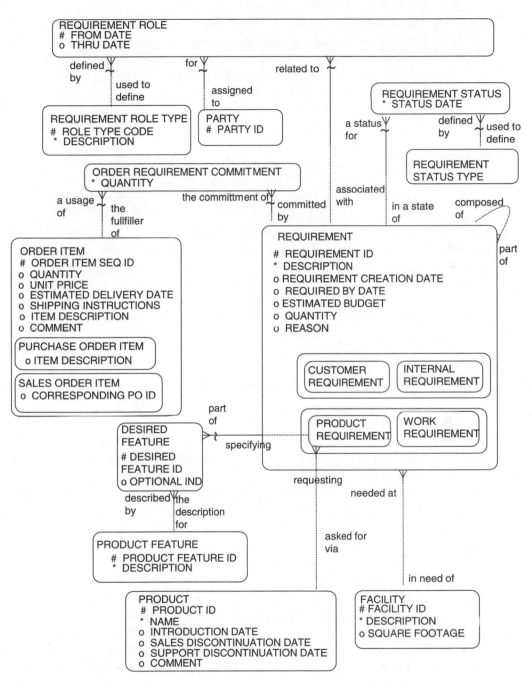

Figure 4.9 Requirements.

hold," or "inactive." Each REQUIREMENT may be needed at a certain FACIL-ITY such as a particular plant, warehouse, office, or room of a building.

The REQUIREMENT may be related to one or more ORDER ITEMs via the associative entity ORDER REQUIREMENT COMMITMENT. This entity would maintain which SALES ORDER ITEMs fulfilled which REQUIREMENT from CUSTOMER REQUIREMENTs. It would also maintain which PURCHASE ORDER ITEMs are fulfilled by the REQUIREMENT from INTERNAL REQUIREMENTs.

REQUIREMENTs have a **description** attribute that defines the need of the requirement. The **requirement creation date** specifies when the requirement was first created, and the **required by date** within the REQUIREMENT entity specifies the date by which the requirement item is needed. The **estimated budget** attribute identifies how much money is allocated for fulfilling this requirement. The **description** allows a full explanation and comments for the requirement. The attribute **quantity** determines the number of items needed in the requirement and allows the requirement to specify that several products or things are needed. For instance, there may be a requirement to hire three programmers. The **reason** attribute explains why there is a need for the requirement.

Requirement Roles

Similar to orders, requirements may have many people involved in them. For instance, one person may be responsible for creating the requirement, and another person may be responsible for approving the requirement. The REQUIREMENT ROLE entity maintains which people play which roles in the requirement. Therefore, the relationship to PARTY identifies the person or organization that is responsible for playing the role. The **from date** and **thru date** attributes on REQUIREMENT ROLE define the time period for which the party is responsible for playing the role. The REQUIREMENT ROLE TYPE entity maintains the possible values for these role types.

Some example roles that parties could play in a requirement are "owner," "originator," "manager," "authorizer," or "implementor." The owner is the party for whom the requirement is created. The originator is the person or organization that identified the need or requirement. The manager is the person responsible for monitoring the requirement and seeing that it is fulfilled. The authorizer is the person who approves or denies the requirement. The implementor is the party who makes sure that once authorized, the requirement is fulfilled.

Requirements Status

Requirements also have a status such as "active," "on-hold," or "inactive." The REQUIREMENT STATUS entity stores a history of the various statuses of the requirement and the date each status occurred. The REQUIREMENT STATUS TYPE entity maintains the types of statuses that could occur. If the history of the requirement statuses is unimportant and the enterprise is interested only in the current status, then an alternate data model would reflect a many-to-one relationship from REQUIREMENT to REQUIREMENT STATUS TYPE.

Product Requirements

Notice that the relationship to PRODUCT is optional and only applies to PRODUCT REQUIREMENTs. Chapter 6 more fully describes the work requirement and work effort data models.

PRODUCT REQUIREMENTs may specify the need for certain features as illustrated in the relationship to DESIRED FEATURE. The **optional ind** (indicator) attribute in the DESIRED FEATURE indicates that the feature is desired and not required if the value is "yes." For example, the "Goldstein Elite pen" could be specified together with a DESIRED FEATURE of color "blue" with an optional ind of "yes" stating that this is nice to have but not absolutely required.

Order Requirement Commitments

A requirement or a need to obtain products can naturally result in orders. One REQUIREMENT may lead to many ORDER ITEMs. For example, the need for 1500 #2 pencils may be fulfilled by several purchase order items. Alternatively, there may be several outstanding requirements for #2 pencils that may all be ordered in a single order item. Figure 4.9 therefore shows a many-to-many relationship between REQUIREMENT and ORDER ITEM.

The ORDER REQUIREMENT COMMITMENT determines how many items are allocated from an order item to a requirement. For instance, suppose there are two requirements, each with items for 1500 #2 pencils (3000 total pencils needed), and one order item for 2000 of these items that partially fills the requirements. Then it is necessary to specify how many of the order items were used to fulfill each requirement. The **quantity** attribute in ORDER REQUIREMENT COMMITMENT serves this purpose.

Requirement Example

Table 4.11 shows some examples of requirements. The first two requirements are internal requirements, one for the parent company, ABC Corporation, and one for the subsidiary, ABC Subsidiary. Requirement 24905 is a requirement to have PCs repaired. The requirement specifies a request to fix 14 PCs. This work requirement may be fulfilled by one or more order items.

Requirement 43005 shows a requirement with related sub-requirements. The requirement to have the office cleaned on a regular basis involves the two sub-requirements of hiring a cleaning service and procuring cleaning supplies.

Table 4.11 Requirements

REQUIREMENT ID	REQUIREMENT CREATION DATE	REQUIREMENT OWNER	DESCRIPTION	RELATED REQUIREMENT	QTY	PRODUCT	DESIRED FEATURE
24905	Apr. 13, 2001	ABC Corporation	Repair 14 PCs		14		
43005	May 16 2002	ABC Subsidiary	Requirement to have office cleaned on a regular basis				
43006	May 16 2002	ABC Subsidiary	Cleaning service	43005			
43007	May 16 2002	ABC Subsidiary	Cleaning supplies	43005			
30003	May 15, 2001	ACME Corporation	Requirement for office supplies				
30004	May 16 2002	ABC Subsidiary	Reams of bond paper	30003	50		8½ by 11-inch, Fine Grade
30005	May 16 2002	ABC Subsidiary	Goldstein Elite pen	30003	40		Blue
30006	May 16 2002	ABC Subsidiary	Reams of copier paper	30003	20		8½ by 11-inch, white
30007	May 16 2002	ABC Subsidiary	Diskettes	30003	200		3½", High density, Formatted
34988	Jun. 20, 2001	ABC Corporation	Repair 15 PCs	30003	15		

The next requirement, requirement 30003, is a customer requirement from ACME Corporation, which is need of office supplies to run its own office. The overall requirement is linked (through the recursive relationship) to several lower level requirements of 50 reams of bond paper, 40 Goldstein Elite Pens, 20 reams of copier paper, and 200 diskettes.

The 50 reams of bond paper is specified though the free-form **description** attribute in the REQUIRMENT entity and further specified by relating the DESIRED FEATUREs of "8½ by 11-inch" dimension and quality of "Fine Grade." The second lower level requirement shows that the specific product of "Goldstein Elite pen" is desired in the color "blue." The third and fourth lower level requirements for "reams of copy paper" and "diskettes" are specified with a combination of the REQUIREMENT **description** and DESIRED FEATUREs. The example illustrates that each REQUIREMENT may be specified by relating it to a specific PRODUCT, describing it with a **description**, and/or **specifying** DESIRED FEATUREs.

The last requirement in the table shows a similar requirement to fix PCs that may have been generated from another part of ABC Corporation.

Requests

Instead of immediately ordering the products on a requirement, sometimes a process of requesting and receiving quotes is used. A request is a means of asking vendors for bids, quotes, or responses to the requirement. The request could be sent to the enterprise, or it could be sent out from the enterprise to solicit responses from suppliers.

Figure 4.10 shows the key entities associated with requests. The REQUEST may have many REQUEST ROLEs, each of which is of a REQUEST ROLE TYPE and is related to a PARTY. Examples of roles include "originator" (the party that the request is from), "preparer," "manager," and "quality assurer." The RESPONDING PARTY maintains information about the parties that may be responding. The CONTACT MECHANISM records what contact mechanism will be used or was used to send the request to the responding party. Each REQUEST may be composed of one or more REQUEST ITEMs. Each REQUEST ITEM represents one or more REQUIREMENT ITEMs that may be combined in the request. Because REQUIREMENTs may be related to multiple REQUEST ITEMs, the associative entity, REQUIREMENT REQUEST, resolves the many-to-many relationship.

Request

There are several types of requests. The REQUEST entity has three subtypes that are the most common forms of requests. The **RFP** subtype stands for

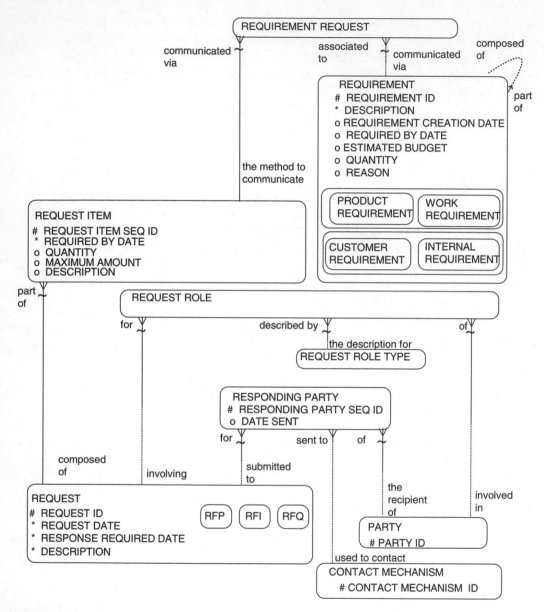

Figure 4.10 Requests.

"request for proposal" and asks vendors to propose a solution to the needs specified in the details of the request. The **RFQ** subtype stands for "request for quote" and asks for bids from vendors on specific products. The **RFI** subtype stands for "request for information" and is generally sent out before an RFP or RFQ in order to determine preliminary information about the qualification of vendors. This is often used as a mechanism to screen the vendors that will be allowed to respond to an RFP or RFQ.

The REQUEST entity maintains the **request date,** which is when the request was created, a **request required date,** which is the deadline when vendors need to respond to the request, and a **description,** which details the nature of the request.

Table 4.12 illustrates the information contained in a REQUEST. The first row is a request for information to determine which vendors are qualified to bid on repairing PCs. The second row is a request for proposal that follows the RFI and asks vendors to bid on solutions to the PC repair maintenance needs. The third row illustrates an RFQ, which is an incoming request that asks the enterprise to quote prices and terms for specific office supply products.

Requests are sent by a certain party and to certain parties. The party that it is sent by is stored at the REQUEST ROLE of "originator." The party(s) that it is sent to is stored in the RESPONDING PARTY entity. A RESPONDING PARTY is one that is asked to respond to a request with information or a bid, quote, or proposal for the request. The RESPONDING PARTY entity is principally used for outgoing requests because incoming requests will usually have only one responding party, namely the part of the enterprise that received the request and will respond to it. The **date sent** attribute indicates when the enterprise sent the request to the responding party.

Table 4.12   Requests

REQUEST ID	REQUEST ORIGINATOR	REQUEST TYPE	REQUEST DATE	RESPONSE REQUIRED DATE	DESCRIPTION
23498	ABC Corporation	RFI	Jan 12, 2001	Feb 10, 2002	To request information concerning PC repair vendors
38967	ABC Corporation	RFP	Mar 13, 2002	Apr 23, 2002	To request a quote from vendors on repairing PCs
38948	ACME Corporation	RFQ	Mar 13, 2002	Mar 21, 2002	To request a quote on office supplies

Request Items

Requests have items describing the various things they need in the request. The REQUEST ITEM has an attribute of **quantity** stating how many of the items are needed. The **required by date** indicates when the items need to be delivered to the requesting organization. The **maximum amount** attribute describes an upper limit price for the item, beyond which the enterprise will not even consider.

The request may be for a specific product, as in an RFQ, or it may be a request asking vendors to provide solutions to a specific problem. If the request is for a product, then the relationship to PRODUCT accommodates these types of request items. If the request is for a proposal to specific problems as in an RFP, then the **description** attribute maintains a description of the problem.

REQUIREMENTs are related to REQUEST ITEMs. One REQUIREMENT may be related to more than one REQUEST ITEM. For example, the first two rows of Table 4.13 show that requirement 24905 had two requests associated with it. A request for information was sent out first, then a request for quote followed.

Table 4.13   Request Items

REQUEST ID	REQUEST ORIGINATOR	REQUEST TYPE	DESCRIPTION	REQUEST ITEM SEQ ID	QUANTITY	REQUIREMENT ID, DESCRIPTION
23498	ABC Corporation	RFI	To request information concerning PC repair vendors	1	29	24905, Repair 14 PCs, 34988, Repair 15 PCs
38967	ABC Corporation	RFQ	To request a quote from vendors on repairing PCs	1	29	24905, Repair 14 PCs, 34988, Repair 15 PCs
38948	ACME Corporation	RFQ	To request a quote on office supplies	1	50	30004, Reams of bond paper
				2	40	30005, Goldstein Elite pen
				3	20	30006, Reams of copier paper
				4	200	30007, Diskettes

One REQUEST ITEM may be associated with more than one REQUIRE-MENT. Table 4.13 shows that the request for information 23498 combined the need for items in requirements 24905 and 34988, resulting in a request to fix 29 PCs, 14 from one requirement and 15 from another. Also note that more than one request was sent out for these same requirements. One request was for an informal RFI (request for information) and one for an RFQ (a more formal request for quotation). This is an example of the need for the intersection entity REQUIREMENT REQUEST, as shown on Figure 4.10.

Request id 38948 provides an example where each REQUEST ITEM within it corresponds directly to an associated REQUIREMENT in a 1:1 fashion. **Request item seq ID** "1" corresponds to REQUIREMENT "30004," **request item seq ID** "2" corresponds to REQUIREMENT "30005" and so on. However, the many-to-many associative entity, REQUIREMENT REQUEST, still accommodates this information.

The data model in Figure 4.10 provides the flexibility to have the same REQUIREMENT requested many times in several REQUEST ITEMs. The latter example showed that, for the same requirement, there may be a request for information and then a request for proposal.

A simpler, alternate model that may meet the needs of many organizations could be to relate REQUESTs directly to REQUIREMENTs. This only makes sense if the enterprise knows that there will not be multiple REQUEST ITEMs for the same REQUIREMENT and also if REQUIREMENTs may not be combined into a single REQUEST ITEM.

Quote Definition

A *quote* is a response to a request; it is synonymous with a bid or proposal. The quote provides the pricing and terms associated with products that fill the need for the request.

Figure 4.11 shows the data model associated with quotes. QUOTEs are issued by a PARTY and given to a PARTY. The enterprise, or a part of the enterprise, may be the receiver or giver of a QUOTE. Other roles are associated with the quote that are stored in the QUOTE ROLE entity, and allowable values for roles are maintained in the QUOTE ROLE TYPE entity. The entity QUOTE stores the basic information related to the quote and is composed of QUOTE ITEMs that describe the specific PRODUCT or WORK EFFORT being quoted. QUOTE ITEMs must be related to a single REQUEST ITEM because quote items are defined as responses to these request items. Each QUOTE ITEM may, in turn, lead to one or more ORDER ITEMs because the quoted item may be ordered more than once. Similar to orders, each QUOTE or QUOTE ITEM may have terms associated with it that create the need for the relationships to QUOTE TERM and to TERM TYPE.

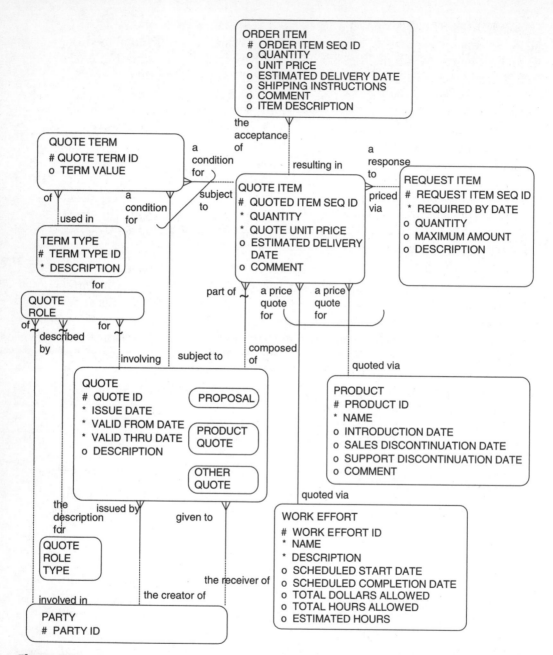

Figure 4.11 Quotes.

Quote Roles

Similar to requests, two very significant relationships are explicitly stated, namely, what party issued the quote and the party to whom the quote was given. Just as orders, requirements, and requests have other various roles, quotes also have people playing various roles. Examples of roles for a quote might be "quoted by," "reviewed by," and "approved by."

Quote

The QUOTE entity stores header information about the quote. For example, the **issue date** maintains when the quote was communicated to the intended party. The **valid from date** and **valid thru date** maintain when the quote can first be acted on and when the quote expires. The **description** attribute describes the nature of the quote.

A QUOTE has a subtype of PROPOSAL that is generally more elaborate and includes many sections, such as statements of need, proposal descriptions, benefits, cost justifications, resources required, and so forth. Another subtype is a PRODUCT QUOTE, which is simpler and just tracks the terms and prices behind the products being quoted. There may be other types of quotes, such as bids or offers, depending on the enterprise and its terminology. Table 4.14 gives some examples of quotes.

The first quote is a proposal because within the quote there may be a description of the approach to repairing the PCs. The second quote is a product quote because it is simply quoting prices for specific pens and pencils.

Quote Items

The QUOTE ITEM entity contains information for specific products and is therefore related to PRODUCT. The QUOTE ITEM is also associated with a REQUEST ITEM. One may conclude from looking at this model that the relationship to PRODUCT is unnecessary because it is possible to derive the product that a quote item references. This may be done by traversing the model from QUOTE ITEM to REQUEST ITEM to PRODUCT. The product from the quote, however, may be different from the product requested. For instance, the prod-

Table 4.14 Quotes

QUOTE ID	QUOTE TYPE	ISSUE DATE	DESCRIPTION	VALID FROM	VALID THRU
35678	Proposal	Feb 19, 2002	Proposal to support the repair of PCs	Feb 19, 2002	Mar 19, 2002
36908	Product Quote	Mar 12, 2001	Bid on pens and pencils	Mar 12, 2002	Mar 30, 2002

uct requested may be a "#2 pencil." The product quoted may be more specific, such as a "Johnson Red Striped #2 pencil."

QUOTE ITEM has a many-to-one relationship with REQUEST ITEM. When a request is sent out, the quote, bid, or proposal should correspond to only one specific request from an organization, whether it is verbal or written. A request, such as an RFP, though, may have many quotes associated with it because many suppliers may respond.

Table 4.15 shows examples of quotes that correspond to the requests of Table 4.12. Each quote item corresponds to a request item. The original request ("38967") called for a quote to fix 14 PCs. The corresponding quote in the first row of Table 4.14 ("35678") was for 70 hours of service, which is the estimate for fixing the PCs.

The quoted items for paper and pens in rows 2 and 3 shows more specific products than were asked for in the corresponding request items from Request id "38948" from Table 4.12. Only two of the four items that were requested in request "38948" were quoted.

The QUOTE ITEM may also be associated with an ORDER if the quote is accepted. An ORDER ITEM will generally not have more than one QUOTE ITEM associated with it. The quote item may be the basis for the pricing on several orders; therefore, several ORDER ITEMs may be associated with one QUOTE ITEM.

Quote Terms

Similar to orders, both quotes and quote items may have terms associated with them. A quote to fix PCs may have a term stating that someone within the organization needing the repair must act as a central point of contact. The term may specify that if this central point of contact does not exist, the quoted price may be raised. A term of a particular quote item on furniture items may be that the receiving party needs to pay the actual freight costs incurred.

The relationship from QUOTE to QUOTE TERM allows many terms to be associated with the quote. The QUOTE ITEM may also have many terms associated with it via the relationship to QUOTE TERM. The TERM TYPE identifies

Table 4.15   Quote Item

QUOTE ID	QUOTE ITEM SEQ ID	QUANTITY	PRODUCT	QUOTE UNIT PRICE	REQUEST ID	REQUEST ITEM SEQ ID
35678	1	70	PC Repair	$75	38967	1
36908	1	50	Johnson fine grade 8½ by 11 bond paper	$3.75	38948	1
	2	40	Johnson Black pens	$1.25	38948	2

the possible terms that can be applied. This entity is also used for other types of transactions such as orders.

Agreement Definition

An *agreement* is a set of terms and conditions that govern the relationship between two parties—for example, a customer and a supplier. A key difference between an order and an agreement is that an order is a one-time commitment to buy products while an agreement specifies how the two parties will conduct business over time.

Figure 4.12 shows the data model associated with agreements. Agreements are classified into AGREEMENT TYPE—for instance, PRODUCT AGREEMENTs, EMPLOYMENT AGREEMENTs, or OTHER AGREEMENTs, depending on the needs of the enterprise. The AGREEMENT TYPE allows maintenance of many more specific types of agreements. AGREEMENTs may involve many AGREEMENT ROLEs of PARTYs such as AGREEMENT ROLES TYPEs of "seller," "buyer," "licensee," "licensor," "contracting firm," and "employer," and the roles will depend on the type of agreement involved. The AGREEMENT may be associated with a specific PARTY RELATIONSHIP such as a sales agreement that is associated with a customer relationship.

ADDENDUMs (see Figure 4.13) modify the agreement to which they may be attached. Each AGREEMENT may be composed of one or more AGREEMENT ITEMs that, in turn, may be related to a specific PRODUCT. Both AGREEMENT and AGREEMENT ITEM may have terms associated with them and are thus further defined by one or more AGREEMENT TERMs or AGREEMENT ITEM TERMs.

The agreement roles may be defined using either the relationship to PARTY RELATIONSHIP or the AGREEMENT ROLEs or both. For example, there may exist a customer relationship that, when formalized, is done so through an agreement. Each PARTY RELATIONSHIP may be involved in one or more AGREEMENTs. There also may be more than two parties involved in the agreement, such as in a three-way partnership agreement. The AGREEMENT ROLE entity would be used to store the roles associated with the agreement in this circumstance. The AGREEMENT ROLE may also store many other roles such as "legal council," "approver," "guarantor," "entered by," and any other role involving parties in the agreement.

There are many different types of agreements, and these will vary substantially depending on the nature of the organization. Often many types of agreements are involved in the enterprise, and most of the chapters in Volume 2 illustrate various standard types of agreements that are used in different industries.

Figure 4.12 provides a few standard types of agreements, and Table 4.16 provides sample data for some of these agreements. PRODUCT AGREEMENTs

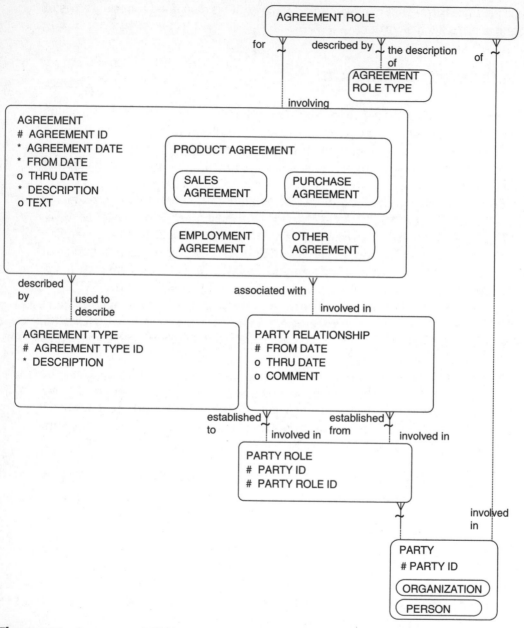

Figure 4.12 Agreement definition.

define the terms and conditions of the buying and selling of products. A PROD-UCT AGREEMENT may be subtyped as either a SALES AGREEMENT or a PURCHASE AGREEMENT. Agreement 10002 in Table 4.16 is a SALES AGREE-MENT. ABC Corporation acts in the "supplier" agreement role and ACME Company acts in the "customer" agreement role. The agreement represents a contractual commitment and is associated with their party relationship of customer relationship, which was an informal relationship.

The EMPLOYMENT AGREEMENT subtype defines the arrangement behind an employee and employer relationship. Agreement 86749 in Table 4.16 is an employment agreement. Over time there could be several employment agreements; this represents just one of them.

The third agreement shown is a PARTNERSHIP AGREEMENT and is between three parties all playing the same role as a "partner." The data model supports as many roles necessary for any agreement and allows new role types to be added and hence is a very flexible model.

Table 4.16 Agreement

AGREEMENT ID	AGREEMENT TYPE	DESCRIPTION	AGREEMENT ROLES	ASSOCIATED PARTY RELATIONSHIP	STARTING DATE	ENDING DATE
10002	Sales agreement (associated with customer relationship)	Agreement regarding the pricing and terms of buying inventory items	ABC Corporation (supplier) ACME Company (customer)	Customer relationship	Jan 1, 2002	Dec 30, 2002
86749	Employment agreement	Hired William as an entry-level information systems programmer	William Jones (employee) ABC Corporation (employer)	Employment relationship	May 7, 1990	
489589	Partnership agreement	Agreement to form an informal partnership with terms designer to compensate partners	ABC Corporation (partner), Sellers Assistance Corporation (partner) XYZ Corporation (partner)		June 1, 2000	June 1, 2001

There may be other types of agreements depending on the enterprise involved. For example, there may be ownership agreements, real estate agreements, franchising agreements, licensing agreements, and so on. The AGREEMENT TYPE maintains the various types of agreements that are valid for the enterprise.

One may argue that redundant data is stored in this data model because the roles are stored in the PARTY RELATIONSHIP as well as the AGREEMENT. For instance, in the CUSTOMER RELATIONSHIP, which is a subtype of PARTY RELATIONSHIP, ABC Corporation has a role of internal organization and ACME Corporation has a role of customer. When a formal agreement is established between these parties and a contract is drawn stipulating certain terms of this agreement, an AGREEMENT instance is created, and the AGREEMENT ROLE entity stores ABC Corporation as a supplier and ACME Corporation as a customer.

Doesn't the model already have ACME Corporation as a customer? One answer to this is that there is a difference between a party's role in an informal relationship and in a formal agreement or contract. The informal relationship may exist, or the agreement may exist, or both may exist. Therefore, this model provides a mechanism to store roles involved in any of these cases.

One may also argue that the AGREEMENT can inherit the roles from the associated PARTY RELATIONSHIP. This could work in many circumstances and is perhaps a valid alternative. Agreements may involve more than two parties, though, and it is probably cleaner to store all the roles for agreements in the same place, namely, the AGREEMENT ROLE entity.

Agreement Item

An agreement defines a formal contract between two or more parties whereby they both make a commitment to terms for a certain length of time. Each AGREEMENT may have AGREEMENT ITEMs that allow for either subagreements or portions of the agreement. These portions may be particular sections or clauses and may allow the agreement to be subdivided and referred to by section. Alternatively, the agreement may have portions that apply to certain geographic areas, certain types of products, or certain parts of the organization involved in the agreement.

Figure 4.13 shows a data model that shows the information requirements needed for AGREEMENT ITEMs. Each AGREEMENT ITEM represents a component of an agreement and has agreement text and optionally an agreement image that could represent a graphic component. For simple agreements, such as a one-page agreement between parties, there may not be a need to store AGREEMENT ITEMs because the text of the agreement may be stored in the AGREEMENT entity **text** attribute. Standard terms could be attached to the agreement that will be shown in the next figure, which stores the text and

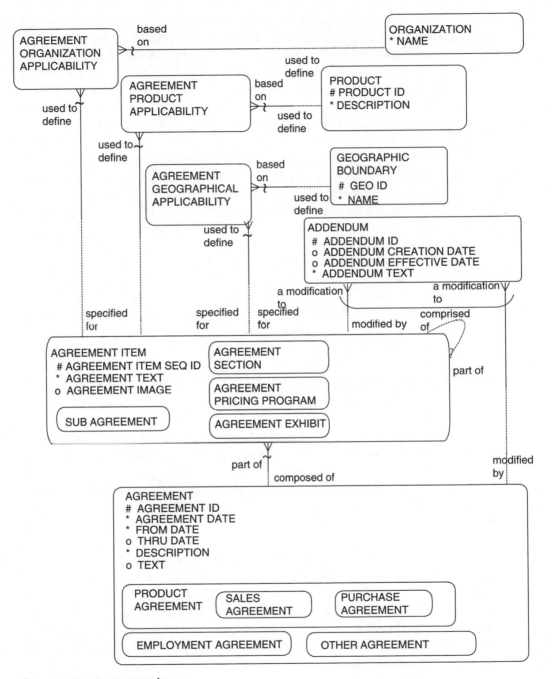

Figure 4.13 Agreement item.

terms of the agreement. For more complex agreements, there may be many AGREEMENT ITEMs that represent portions of the agreement.

The AGREEMENT ITEM has subtypes of SUB AGREEMENT, AGREEMENT SECTION, AGREEMENT PRICING PROGRAM, and AGREEMENT EXHIBIT. A SUB AGREEMENT represents an agreement within an agreement, such as a confidentiality agreement that forms part of an overall professional services agreement or several subagreements for different parts of an organization. An AGREEMENT SECTION represents a portion of an agreement that is split out as an AGREEMENT ITEM, allowing it to be related to a specific organization, product, or geographic area if needed. The AGREEMENT PRICING PRO-GRAM represents information about agreed-on prices for products or features based on different criteria. An AGREEMENT EXHIBIT is a portion of an agreement that is attached to an agreement and usually referred to throughout the agreement.

Each AGREEMENT ITEM may be comprised of other AGREEMENT ITEMs, as shown by the recursive relationship on AGREEMENT ITEM. Subagreements may be broken down into agreement sections, which may be further broken down into agreement clauses. The recursive relationship allows agreement items to be composed in as many levels of detail as necessary.

Either an AGREEMENT or an AGREEMENT ITEM may be **modified by** an ADDENDUM that could modify the text of the AGREEMENT or AGREEMENT ITEM with the **addendum text** attribute within the ADDENDUM. The ADDEN-DUM entity maintains the **addendum creation date**, which is when the adden-dum was created, and an **addendum effective date,** which is when the addendum goes into effect. The **addendum text** describes the addendum. An example of an addendum is a time extension to the thru date of a customer-ven-dor agreement. In this case, the **thru date** would be updated in the AGREE-MENT entity, and an ADDENDUM would be added to show the history of changes to the applicable agreement item. Each AGREEMENT may be modi-fied by one or more ADDENDUMs.

Each AGREEMENT ITEM may be specified for certain geographic bound-aries, products, and/or organizations. The AGREEMENT GEOGRAPHICAL APPLICABILITY, AGREEMENT PRODUCT APPLICABILITY, and AGREE-MENT ORGANIZATION APPLICABILITY allow AGREEMENT ITEMs to be customized for certain geographic boundaries, products, or organizations. For instance, perhaps different subsidiaries within an enterprise may have specific parts of the agreement that apply to each subsidiary. This structure allows sep-arate sections, which can be applied to each subsidiary. Similarly, certain sec-tions of an agreement may be applicable only to certain products or geographic areas.. There may be other factors that define the AGREEMENT ITEM, such as the applicability for specific types of product, and therefore other "applicabil-ity" entities could be added, such as, in this case, an AGREEMENT PRODUCT CATEGORY APPLICABILITY.

Table 4.17   Agreement Items

AGREEMENT ID	AGREEMENT ITEM SEQ ID	PRODUCT
10002	1	Johnson fine grade 8½ by 11 blue bond paper
	2	Jerry's box of 3½ inch diskettes

Table 4.17 shows a simple example that agreement 10002 is an agreement that has two agreement items governing the terms for buying two products: "Johnson fine grade 8½ by 11 blue bond paper" and "Jerry's box of 3½-inch diskettes."

Agreement Terms

An agreement and its items may each have terms associated with them. The AGREEMENT TERM entity stores the valid terms of the agreement as well as the effective dates of the terms. Different types of terms can be referenced from the TERM TYPE entity. The AGREEMENT TERM entity provides a structure to maintain various types of terms that could either be applied to the AGREEMENT (for simpler agreements without items) or to the AGREEMENT ITEM. Terms and conditions can include legal terms, financial terms, incentives, thresholds, clauses for renewals, agreement termination, indemnification, non-competition, and provisions for exclusive relationships.

For example, a product agreement between a supplier and its customer may call for an exclusive arrangement preventing the supplier from selling its products to the customer's competitors. An example of this exclusive arrangement is found when a consulting firm performs services for its client that involve sensitive proprietary information that needs to be safeguarded from the competition. Therefore, the customer may request that the supplier not do business with the customer's competitors for a specified time in order to protect its confidentiality. In Table 4.18, the first row of data gives an example of an AGREEMENT TERM that is associated with agreement 23884. The term is that the agreement calls for an exclusive arrangement prohibiting the supplier from supplying similar services to the customer's competitors for up to 60 days after the contract ends.

Each agreement item may have terms associated with it. The AGREEMENT TERM entity may also maintain the valid terms of an agreement item. The second, third, and fourth rows of Table 4.18 show examples of agreement items and the terms associated with them. The second and third rows (agreement ID #10002, item #1) represent the same AGREEMENT ITEM for the product "Johnson fine grade 8½ by 11 blue bond paper." There is more than one term

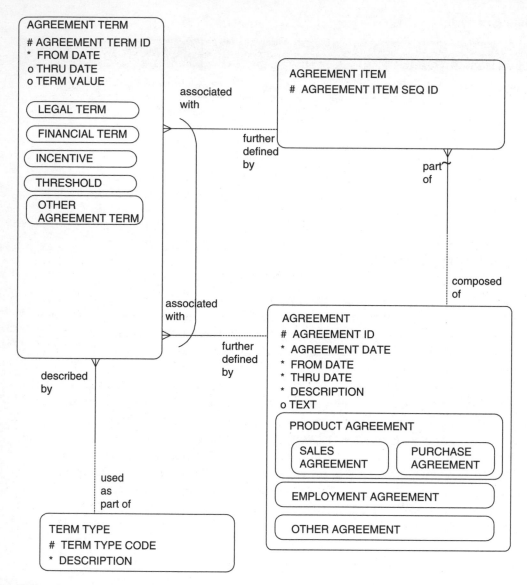

Figure 4.14   Agreement terms.

associated with this agreement item. The two terms specify that the agreement item is valid only for up to 1,000 of these items between January 1, 2002 and December 31, 2002. The agreement also has a term that the dollars expended cannot exceed $10,000 from January 1, 2002 through June 30, 2002. The fourth row (agreement ID #10002, item #2) specifies that the customer is agreeing to buy these types of products exclusively from the supplier.

Table 4.18 Agreement Terms

AGREEMENT ID	AGREEMENT ITEM SEQ ID	PRODUCT	TERM TYPE	TERM VALUE	FROM DATE	THRU DATE
23884			Exclusive arrangement prohibiting supplier from supplying similar services to customer's competitors for specified number of days after contract ends	60		
10002	1	Johnson fine grade 8½ by 11 blue bond paper	Quantity not to exceed	1000	Jan 1, 2002	Dec 31, 2002
		Johnson fine grade 8½ by 11 blue bond paper	Dollars not to exceed	$10,000	Jan 1, 2002	June 30, 2002
	2	Jerry's box of 3½ inch diskettes	Customer will exclusively buy from supplier		Jan 1, 2002	Dec 30, 2002

Agreement Pricing

The entity AGREEMENT ITEM relates to an entity that maintains agreed-on product prices between parties. The prices may vary by time periods, quantities, party addresses, and geographic regions.

Figure 4.15 illustrates the use of the pricing model discussed in Chapter 3 (see Figure 3.7) for agreements. In order to handle the needs of agreement pricing, the PRICE COMPONENTs are now additionally related to an AGREEMENT PRICING PROGRAM (subtype of AGREEMENT ITEM). Each AGREEMENT PRICING PROGRAM may have many PRICE COMPONENTs.

As already discussed, these PRICE COMPONENTs may be a base price (BASE PRICE), a discount (DISCOUNT COMPONENT), a surcharge (SURCHARGE COMPONENT), or a MANUFACTURER SUGGESTED PRICE. The attribute **price** is used to record base prices, flat discounts, or flat surcharges. The attribute **percent** is used to record percentages for discounts or surcharges to certain agreement items. The relationships to GEOGRAPHIC BOUNDARY, PRODUCT CATEGORY, QUANTITY BREAK, ORDER VALUE, and/or SALE TYPE allow different prices based on different combinations of these factors.

An alternative data model is to have a PRODUCT PRICE COMPONENT entity and a separate AGREEMENT PRICE COMPONENT entity. The disad-

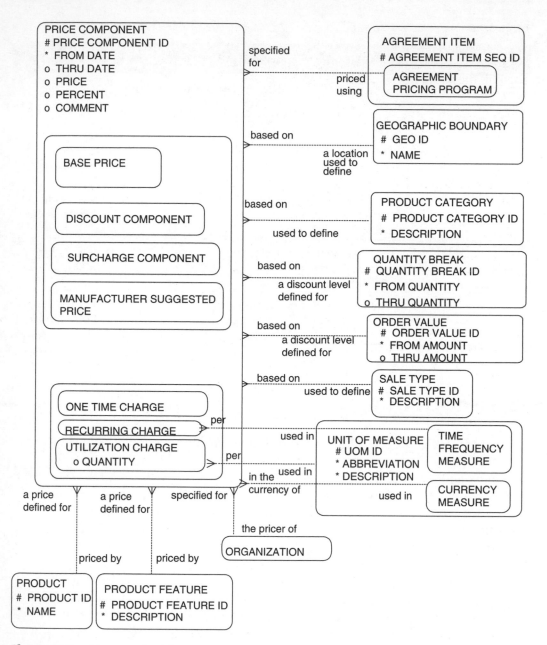

Figure 4.15 Agreement pricing.

vantage to this alternate model is that there is reuse of a very similar entity with similar attributes. The advantage is that the data structures to price products and agreements are slightly different and that the information in these data structures will probably be used in very different circumstances. One slight difference in these structures is that product pricing may be based on the PARTY TYPE entity (this relationship is shown in Figure 3.7 Product pricing) ; this is not necessary in agreement pricing because the pricing is for a particular party and will therefore not vary by the type of party.

Table 4.19 gives some examples of the pricing components used within agreements. The three rows are the pricing arrangement for agreement 10002 item 1, which refers to the product "Johnson fine grade 8½ by 11 blue bond paper." The agreement says that the price in the eastern region for this product is $7.00 and in the western region the price is $7.50. If more than 1,000 reams are ordered in the same order, then a 2 percent discount is applied to this product.

With the addition of this pricing model application, pricing may be determined by three different means: through the standard price associated with a product, through an agreement made in advance, or through a specific negotiation of an order. It is important to specify the business rules that govern when to use which price. Most enterprises have business rules in place that an agreement will override the standard product price and that specific negotiation on an order will overrule standard product prices or agreements.

Agreement to Order

In most cases, there is no direct relationship between ORDER and AGREEMENT because the terms and pricing of an agreement will dictate business rules that govern the processing of an order.

The data model in Figure 4.16 shows ORDER and AGREEMENT data structures regarding pricing. These data structures have already been shown in separate diagrams and Figure 4.16 provides another view to these structures to provide insight about the relationship from ORDER to AGREEMENT.

Table 4.19 Agreement Item Price

AGREEMENT ID	AGREEMENT ITEM SEQ	PRODUCT	PRICE COMPONEN SUBTYPE	GEOGRAPHIC BOUNDARY	QTY BREAK FROM	QTY BREAK THRU	PRICE	PERCENT
10002	1	Johnson fine grade 8½ × 11 blue bond paper	Base	Eastern region			$7.00	
			Base	Western region			$7.50	
			Discount		1000			2

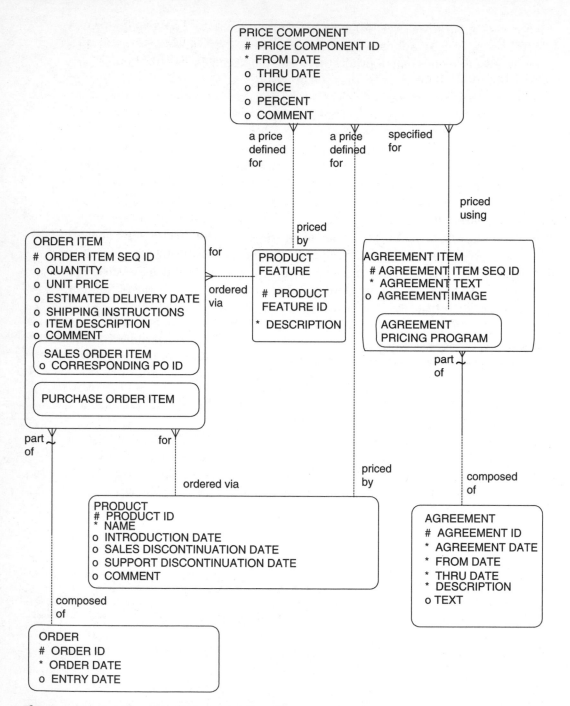

Figure 4.16 Relationship of agreement to order.

As illustrated in Figure 4.16, each ORDER has ORDER ITEMs with an associated PRODUCT and optionally with PRODUCT FEATUREs specified. The AGREEMENT has AGREEMENT ITEMs, which may be an AGREEMENT PRICING PROGRAM that has PRICE COMPONENTs dictating the pricing of the PRODUCTs and PRODUCT FEATUREs. The order processing routines would check to see if one or more agreements were in effect by comparing the **order date** to the agreement **from date** and **thru date** as well as seeing if the party ordering the products is the same as the party that had this agreement in place. The ORDER ROLEs and AGREEMENT ROLEs (not shown in the diagram) would need be compared to accomplish this. The AGREEMENT or AGREEMENT ITEM may also have terms associated with it that may be checked at the time of order processing.

The fact that orders are governed by agreements means that the order is subject to the pricing and terms of the agreement. Of course, it is possible for an order to override the pricing and terms of an agreement in some circumstances. For example, perhaps there is an agreement between a customer and a supplier that a certain type of pen will cost $2.00 each. All orders generally follow the terms of this agreement; however, the supplier might make an exception and discount the price of pens by $.50 for a specific order due to a complaint about the late delivery of a previous order. This may be a gesture on the part of the supplier, even though there are no terms or conditions to give this discount.

Summary

The data model from this chapter provides a way to maintain information about orders, requirements, requests, quotes, and agreements (see Figure 4.17). These models incorporate both sales and purchase order perspectives and cover services as well as goods.

Orders go through a process, beginning with a requirement or a need for a product(s). The requirement may be directly fulfilled by an order, or it may lead to a request to suppliers, a quote, then an order. Agreements may be established in advance that govern relationships and transactions between parties and influence terms and pricing. This chapter models most of the information that many enterprises need to establish commitments between parties.

Models for delivering these commitments are covered in Chapters 5 and 6. The delivery of commitments of goods is usually accomplished through shipments, which are covered in Chapter 5. The delivery of services is usually accomplished through work efforts, which are covered in Chapter 6.

Please refer to Appendix A for a listing of entities and attributes. SQL scripts to build tables and columns derived from the logical models in this book can be found on the full-blown CD-ROM, which is licensed separately.

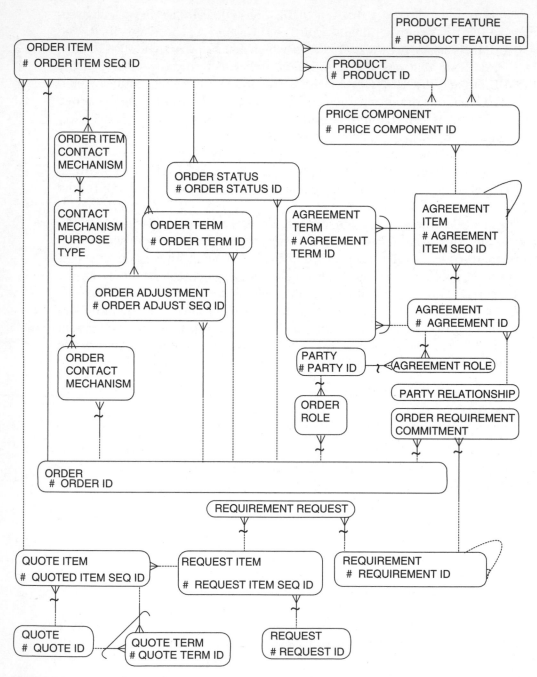

Figure 4.17   Overall order model.

CHAPTER

5

Shipments

Now that orders have been taken, how do they get to their destinations and, once there, how are they paid for? Other questions to answer are these:

- What is being shipped?
- When will it ship?
- To and from where is it shipped?
- What is the current status of the shipment?
- What inventory receipts and issuances occurred during what times at what locations?
- What is the volume and nature of incoming and outgoing shipments?
- Was the entire order shipped or only part of it?
- What shipping documents have been completed and maintained?
- What carrier was used in the shipment and what routes did the shipment take?

This chapter will deal with the shipment of items that are scheduled to be or have been delivered. As will be shown, the information to support these functions does not, at first glance, seem very complex; however, the data interrelationships in a real-world environment can be complicated.

Models discussed in this chapter are the following:

- Shipments
- Shipping detail
- Shipment-to-order relationship
- Shipment receipt for incoming shipments
- Item issuance for outgoing shipments
- Shipping documents
- Shipment method

Shipments

The basic data model for shipments is shown in Figure 5.1. There is the SHIPMENT entity, which can have many types. The relationships from SHIPMENT to PARTY are to record the **shipped-from** PARTY and the **shipped-to** PARTY. The relationship from SHIPMENT to POSTAL ADDRESS is to track where the shipment began and where the shipment was delivered. The model also shows that additional CONTACT MECHANISMs can be maintained to record where queries can be made to inquire about the shipment from the sender as well as a contact number for the receiver to facilitate delivery just in case the carrier cannot easily access or find the postal address.

An enterprise may need to know many things about a shipment. Some are critical; some are not so critical. The first thing to record in the SHIPMENT entity is the **estimated ship date**, which indicates when the shipment is expected to begin its journey to the client. This will be critical to customer service personnel when an irate client calls to see what happened to his or her order. The **estimated ready date** documents when the item is expected to be ready for shipment (perhaps packaging or other preparation is needed for the item). Other bits of information to know include **estimated arrival date**, **estimated ship cost**, **actual ship cost** (may be important for billing), and any special **handling instructions** (i.e., "fragile," "requires signature upon delivery," etc.). In the case of a cancellation, there is a need to know the latest date the shipment could be canceled. The **last updated** attribute provides a way to determine when this information was last changed because the estimated dates may change frequently, although the enterprise would hope not. The actual dates of all these events are recorded in SHIPMENT STATUS, which is discussed in a later section.

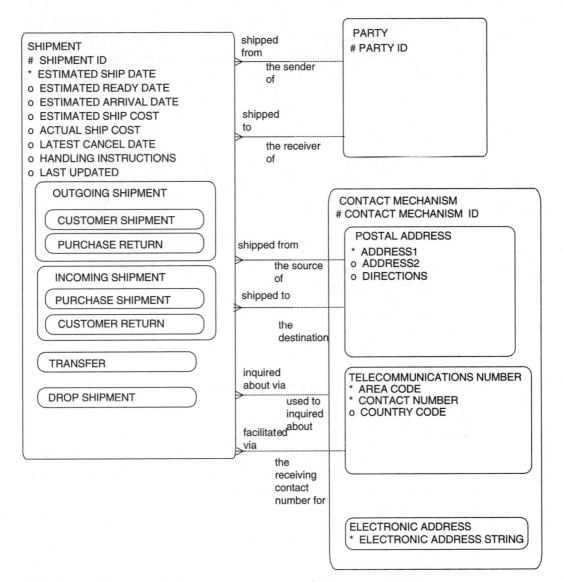

Figure 5.1   Shipment definition.

Shipment Types

As can be seen in Figure 5.1, several subtypes on the SHIPMENT entity are included in the model to distinguish between some basic types of shipments. These types could be inferred based on the organizations involved in the shipment, but they have been included for clarity. If the shipment is from an internal organization to an external organization, then it is an OUTGOING SHIPMENT, which may be either a CUSTOMER SHIPMENT or a PURCHASE RETURN. A CUSTOMER SHIPMENT defines shipments sent out to customers. A PURCHASE RETURN defines shipments that were returned to the supplier. If it is an external organization shipping to an internal organization, then it is referred to as an INCOMING SHIPMENT and may be a PURCHASE SHIPMENT or a CUSTOMER RETURN. A PURCHASE SHIPMENT is an incoming shipment of purchased items from a supplier. A CUSTOMER RETURN is an incoming shipment from a customer that has returned the products bought from the enterprise. A shipment from an internal organization to another internal organization (e.g., from department A to department B) is called a TRANSFER. If the shipment moves from an external organization to a different external organization, then it is a DROP SHIPMENT. Typically, a drop shipment is a mechanism for a distributor to ship products directly from its supplier to its customer.

Shipments Parties and Contact Mechanisms

The shipment would not be a shipment if the enterprise wasn't sending something somewhere—but where? Shipments must be delivered to and from a location. Therefore, there are two relationships to POSTAL ADDRESS. One shows the location that is the ultimate destination of the shipment; the other shows the source or starting point of the shipment. A shipment, once scheduled, will need to show both **shipped to** and **shipped from** even prior to actual shipment.

The shipment is related to parties in addition to contact mechanisms. The **shipped to** party is needed as well as the **shipped from** party. The **shipped to** party will most likely be the same as **the designated to be shipped to** PARTY of the ORDER, and similarly the **shipped to** CONTACT MECHANISM relationship will likely be the **designated to be shipped to** relationship from ORDER to CONTACT MECHANISM. Therefore, it is possible to use these pieces of information as a default in order to determine the **shipped to** party and **shipped to** contact mechanism.

This may appear to be a duplication of data (PARTY and CONTACT MECHANISM information tied to both SHIPMENT and ORDER), but the information needs to appear in both places because the shipment record may not be created until much later than the order. If the shipment record was created during order entry, then the information could be stored only in the shipment record. This, of course, could also be controlled through business rules and processes. It is also possible that the shipment information may change and be overridden during the shipment process.

The model shows additional relationships from SHIPMENT to CONTACT MECHANISM to provide information about how to trace the shipment. There may be a **receiving contact number for** the receiver of the SHIPMENT, which would be a TELECOMMUNICATIONS NUMBER such as a phone number. This could be used to contact the receiver should the postal address of the shipment be in question. The **used to inquire about** relationship from CONTACT MECHANISM to SHIPMENT provides a way for any party to inquire about the shipment.

Table 5.1 shows some sample data regarding SHIPMENT and related CONTACT MECHANISM information. The first three rows show customer shipments that are shipped to the customer, ACME Corporation, from the internal organization, ABC Subsidiary. Shipments #1146 and #1149 represent incoming shipments, specifically purchase shipments from the supplier, General Goods Corporation. Shipment #1578 represents the return of a purchase, specifically, the return of goods to the supplier, General Goods Corporation. Shipment #3485 represents a transfer of goods from ABC Subsidiary to ABC Corporation. Finally, shipment #4800 represents a drop shipment from ABC's sales agent, Sellers Assistant Corporation, to its customer, ACME Corporation.

Shipping Detail

What items are being shipped, and what is the status of the shipment? This is what is reflected in the data model in Figure 5.2. Each SHIPMENT may be detailed by many SHIPMENT ITEMs. This provides a mechanism to track what was shipped or received and how many of each item was shipped via the **quantity** attribute.

Now that one can tell where a shipment is going to and coming from, and when it is being shipped, it is necessary to know what is being shipped and how many items are being shipped. The SHIPMENT ITEM entity will provide information on how many items will be shipped or are scheduled to be shipped. Details about what was shipped may be found in either the GOOD entity if it is a standard product or in the **shipment contents description**, if the item is not a standard item that is kept on file. For example, there could be a one-time incoming shipment from a supplier that is not maintained in the GOOD entity because it is not a standard product. Because shipments may change state during their life cycle (i.e., from "in transit" to "delivered"), the SHIPMENT STATUS entity is needed to describe the state of the shipment at various points in time. The recursive relationship around the SHIPMENT ITEMs accounts for the fact that shipment items may be in response to other shipment items, for example, when an organization receives the item, determines that the item is defective, and sends it back (which is another shipment item that is related to the original shipment item).

Why is a SHIPMENT ITEM related to GOOD and not INVENTORY ITEM? After all, the shipment item is involved in the process of taking something out of inventory and/or receiving into inventory. One reason is that the particular

Table 5.1 Shipment Data and Contact Mechanisms

SHIPMENT ID	SHIPMENT TYPE	ESTIMATED SHIP DATE	ESTIMATED ARRIVAL DATE	SHIPPED-TO PARTY AND POSTAL ADDRESS	SHIPPED-FROM PARTY AND POSTAL ADDRESS
9000	Customer shipment	Mar 6, 2001	Mar 8, 2001	ACME Corporation 234 Stretch Street	ABC Subsidiary 300 Main Street
9200	Customer shipment	Mar 12, 2001	Mar 14, 2001	ACME Corporation 234 Stretch Street	ABC Subsidiary 300 Main Street
9400	Customer shipment	Mar 22, 2001	Mar 25, 2001	ACME Corporation 234 Stretch Street	ABC Subsidiary 300 Main Street
1146	Purchase shipment	Mar. 19, 2001	Mar. 20, 2001	ABC Corporation 100 Main Street	General Goods Corporation 300 Jennifer Street
1149	Purchase shipment	Mar. 25, 2001	Mar. 31, 2001	ABC Corporation 100 Main Street	General Goods Corporation 300 Jennifer Street
1578	Purchase return	Apr 9, 2001	Apr 12, 2001	General Goods Corporation 300 Jennifer Street	ABC Corporation 100 Main Street
3485	Transfer	Jun 23, 2001	Jun 25, 2001	ABC Subsidiary 300 Main Street	ABC Corporation 100 Main Street
4800	Drop shipment	July 12, 2001	July 13, 2001	Sellers Assistance Corporation 400 Benny Street	ACME Company 234 Stretch Street

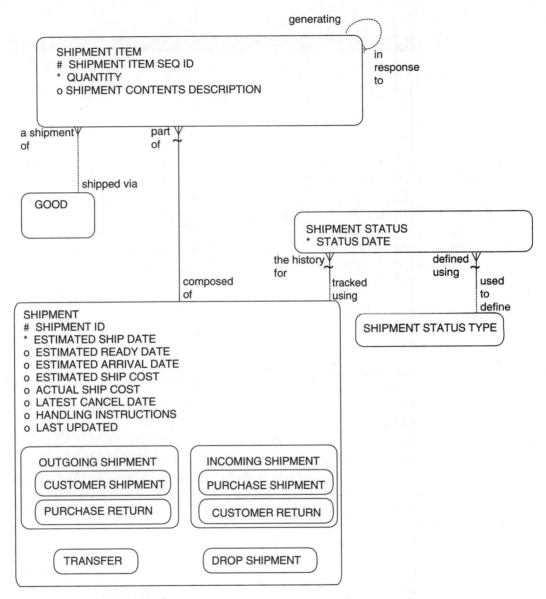

Figure 5.2 Shipping detail.

Table 5.2 Shipment Items

SHIPMENT ID	ITEM SEQ	QUANTITY	INVENTORY ITEM
9000	1	1000	Jones #2 pencils
	2	1000	Goldstein Elite pens
	3	100	Boxes of HD diskettes

inventory item(s) may not be known when scheduling the shipment. Another reason is that the inventory items are related indirectly to the SHIPMENT ITEM through other entities such as SHIPMENT RECEIPT and ITEM ISSUANCE of inventory items that will be shown later in this chapter.

Table 5.2 highlights possible data for SHIPMENT ITEM. Shipment #9000 details the previously described customer shipment to ACME Corporation, and Table 5.2 shows that three items are being shipped.

Shipment Status

The entity SHIPMENT STATUS in Figure 5.2 allows for the accurate tracking of the status of the shipment over its life. The status (from SHIPMENT STATUS TYPE) identifies the state of the shipment at a point in time. Possible statuses include "scheduled," "shipped," "in route," "delivered," and "canceled." This model will allow the storage of any and all statuses of interest to the enterprise.

Table 5.3 shows sample data that could be stored with this entity. While the **estimated ship date** and **estimated arrival date** are stored as attributes in the SHIPMENT entity, the SHIPMENT STATUS stores the dates (and times, if needed) that activities actually occurred on the shipment. Customer shipment #9000 was scheduled for shipment March 4 (meaning that the shipment was first recorded) and actually shipped out on Mar 7 and received on Mar 7. Drop shipment #4800 was scheduled for shipment on July 9 and then canceled on July 10.

Table 5.3 Shipment Status Data

SHIPMENT ID	SHIPMENT STATUS	STATUS DATE
9000	Scheduled	Mar 4, 2001
	Shipped	Mar 7, 2001
	Received	Mar 7, 2001
4800	Scheduled	July 9, 2002
	Canceled	July 10, 2002

Shipment-to-Order Relationship

For the data model to be truly integrated and functional, there is a need to link orders taken to the shipments made. This will be handled through the entity ORDER SHIPMENT in Figure 5.3. This entity is the resolution of a many-to-many

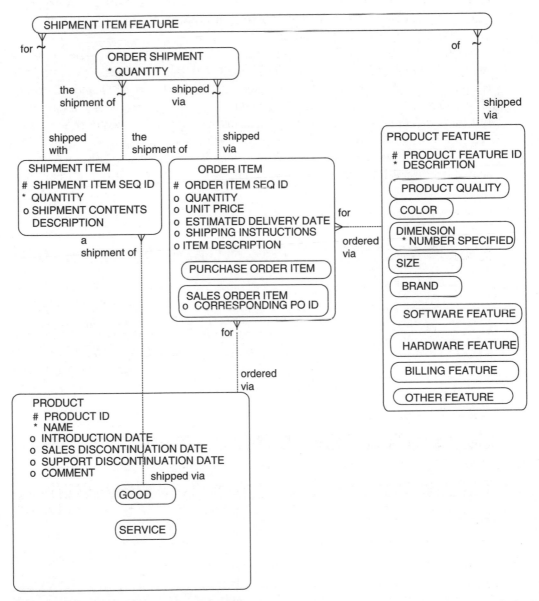

Figure 5.3 Shipment-to-order relationship.

relationship between SHIPMENT ITEM and ORDER ITEM. The many-to-many relationship is required to handle partial shipments and combined shipments.

Each SHIPMENT ITEM may be a shipment of one and only one GOOD and/or one or more SHIPMENT ITEM FEATUREs; alternatively it may be described only via a **shipment contents description** for non-standard items. Why is it necessary to record the goods and product features for a shipment if they are already included in the order? First of all, shipments and shipment items may exist independently of an order—for instance, with transfers of inventory. Second, it is possible that the good shipped is different from the ordered item. For example, perhaps a substitution occurred.

Tables 5.4, 5.5, and 5.6 give some sample data to demonstrate the many-to-many relationship from ORDER ITEMs to SHIPMENT ITEMs. For simplicity purposes, the data represents customer orders #100 and #200 and customer shipments #9000, #9200, and #9400. The data in these tables may seem complex, but there is a very good explanation behind this: In the real world, the relationship between orders and shipments is a complex one.

Table 5.4 shows that there are two orders, #100 and #200. Table 5.5 shows that there are three shipments, #9000, #9200, and #9400. Table 5.6 illustrates

Table 5.4   Order Item Data

ORDER ID	ORDER ITEM SEQ ID	QUANTITY	PRODUCT
100	1	1500	Jones #2 pencils
	2	2500	Goldstein Elite pens
	3	350	Standard erasers
200	1	300	Goldstein Elite pens
	2	200	Boxes of HD diskettes

Table 5.5   Shipment Item Data

SHIPMENT ID	SHIPMENT ITEM SEQ ID	QUANTITY	PRODUCT
9000	1	1000	Jones #2 pencils
	2	1000	Goldstein Elite pens
	3	100	Boxes of HD diskettes
9200	1	350	Standard erasers
	2	100	Boxes of HD diskettes
	3	1500	Jones #2 pencils
9400	1	500	Jones #2 pencils

Table 5.6 Order Shipment Cross-Reference Data

ORDER ID	ORDER ITEM SEQ ID	SHIPMENT ID	SHIPMENT ITEM SEQ ID	QUANTITY (SHIPPED)
100	1	9000	1	1000
	1	9400	1	500
	2	9000	2	700
	3	9200	1	350
200	1	9000	2	300
	2	9000	3	100
	2	9200	2	100

how one order item could be distributed across multiple shipments. The first two lines of Table 5.6 show the relationship of one order item to two shipment items. Order ID #100, item #1 (from Table 5.4) was partially delivered by shipment #9000, item #1, then completed in a later delivery of shipment #9400, item #1, with a quantity of 1,000 to the first and 500 to the second. In this way, the entire order of 1,500 Jones #2 pencils was delivered.

Conversely, one shipment item could be used to deliver items from more than one order. The third and fifth rows of Table 5.6 illustrate this point. Shipment ID #9000, seq id #2, shown in Table, 5.5, is a shipment to deliver 1000 Goldstein Elite pens. It combines a partial shipment of order #100, item #2 (700 out of 2,500 Elite pens ordered), with order #200, item #1 (300 Elite pens). The partial shipment could be due to a lack of inventory at the time the shipment was made. This scenario assumes that business rules and processes are in place to ensure that both orders (i.e., #100 and #200) are intended to go to the same location and are for the same product. Note that the relationship is not between ORDER (as opposed to ORDER ITEM) and SHIPMENT because it is usually necessary to track the actual items being ordered and shipped.

Is it possible to ship an item with different features than were ordered? Certainly it is possible to do this by mistake. Another possibility is that the customer agreed to accept a different feature than what was ordered. In this case, the order could be changed, or the enterprise may want to reflect that the customer ordered an item with a specific feature, but he or she agreed to accept something else in the delivery.

To handle these cases, one can relate the PRODUCT FEATUREs to SHIPMENT ITEMs using the associative entity, SHIPMENT ITEM FEATURE to show which features the shipments had or were scheduled to have. The relationship from SHIPMENT ITEM through the associative entity SHIPMENT ITEM FEATURE to PRODUCT FEATURE in Figure 5.3 allows the enterprise to maintain SHIPMENT ITEMs as well as the PRODUCT FEATUREs that are to be shipped.

Table 5.7   Order Shipment Cross-Reference of Product Features

ORDER ID	ORDER ITEM SEQ ID	ORDER ITEM FEATURE	QUANTITY	SHIPMENT ID	SHIPMENT ITEM SEQ ID	QUANTITY (SHIPPED)	SHIPMENT ITEM FEATURE
100	2	Color blue	2500	9000	2	1000	Color black
200	1	Color blue	300				

An alternative to the model shown is to store which ordered features are being shipped in the associative entity between order item and shipment item, ORDER SHIPMENT. When there is a difference in what is being shipped versus what is being ordered, this can be derived because each SHIPMENT ITEM is ultimately tied to an INVENTORY ITEM (this will be shown in later sections of this chapter), which is an actual instance of the good and has a configuration that includes the features included on it. The issue with this alternative is that there is still no mechanism for storing the features for a *scheduled* shipment (specific inventory is not yet tied to it) when the shipment features are different from the ordered features.

Table 5.7 provides an example whereby blue pens were ordered and then black pens were delivered in response to the orders. The shipment combines 700 pens from one order and 300 pens from another order, as in the previous example. This table also shows that the order item feature was blue; however, the shipment item feature was black. This could mean that either there was a mistake or the shipment was intentionally shipped with a different feature, perhaps because there were no blue pens in stock and the customer indicated that he or she would accept the color black as a substitute.

This example has involved only customer shipments to simplify the explanation of the data model. The data structures in these data models will also support the many-to-many relationships that occur with all types of shipments, including purchase shipment, drop shipments, and transfers. All of these types of shipments may combine the need to move items and involve partial shipments, which is why many-to-many relationships are necessary in any type of shipment.

Shipment Receipts

Incoming shipments may be received at a formal dock or informally at a desk. Either way, information about the receipt of these items needs to be recorded. There is a need for information about how many items of what types were accepted or rejected; this information includes the contents of packages, the roles involved in the receipt, the date and time of the receipt, and where it was accepted into inventory.

Figure 5.4 provides a data model for shipment receipts. Each SHIPMENT ITEM may be packaged within one or more SHIPMENT PACKAGEs and vice versa, hence the associative entity, PACKAGING CONTENT with a **quantity** attribute to determine how many items are in which package. The **shipment package id** could very well be a bar-coded number in order to track shipment packages more easily. Each SHIPMENT PACKAGE may be received via one or more SHIPMENT RECEIPTs that store the details of the receipt. However, the SHIPMENT PACKAGE may exist without having a SHIPMENT RECEIPT, for instance on outgoing shipments when the organization assembles something into a package. So there is only a mandatory relationship from SHIPMENT RECEIPT to SHIPMENT PACKAGE and not vice versa. There could be many SHIPMENT RECEIPT ROLEs involved in each receipt, such as the person signing for the receipt, the inspector of the goods, the person responsible for storing the receipt within inventory, the receiving manager, and the organization that is receiving the item. Each SHIPMENT RECEIPT may be verified against and applied to an ORDER ITEM to record if the receipt was what was expected. Each SHIPMENT RECEIPT may be stored in an INVENTORY ITEM, allowing these received goods' physical storage place to be recorded.

The SHIPMENT RECEIPT maintains the record of each item and how many items are actually within a received package. The SHIPMENT RECEIPT will store the **datetime received,** which indicates exactly when the receipt occurred. The **item description** maintains what was received for non-standard items that would not be maintained as goods within the data model—for instance, for one-time purchases. The relationship to GOOD maintains what was received for standard goods. The **quantity accepted** represents the quantity of that item that the organization determined to be acceptable to receive. The **quantity rejected** represents the quantity of the item that the organization determined to be unacceptable to receive. The REJECTION REASON stores an explanation of why certain items may not be accepted. The recursion around the SHIPMENT ITEM handles related shipment items to each other, allowing the enterprise to track shipments that were sent back.

The model assumes that all SHIPMENT ITEMs are packaged in one form or another. Therefore, the SHIPMENT RECEIPT is always within a SHIPMENT PACKAGE, even if there is a single SHIPMENT ITEM that is in the SHIPMENT PACKAGE. There does not necessarily have to be packaging for the shipment, although usually items have some form of packaging such as a box, carton, or container.

Should the shipment receipt be related to the SHIPMENT PACKAGE or the SHIPMENT ITEM? In other words, is it a receipt for a shipment item or for a package? Suppose you received a package that had many different shipment items and some of them represented only partial amounts of the shipment items because perhaps the shipment box wasn't big enough for the full quantities. The model relates the receipt to the package because that is what was physically

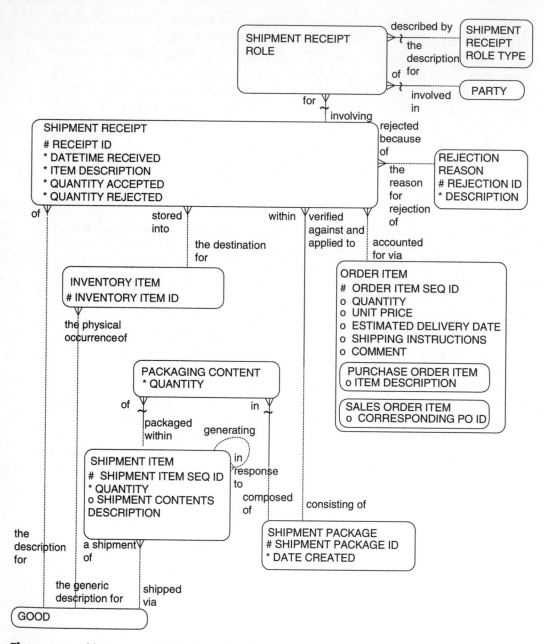

Figure 5.4 Shipment receipt for incoming shipments.

received. A reconciliation from the SHIPMENT RECEIPT to the SHIPMENT ITEM is needed, and this can be accomplished by traversing the data model through SHIPMENT PACKAGE to PACKAGING CONTENT to SHIPMENT ITEM in order to compare received items against what was expected.

Table 5.8 provides examples of receipts for shipments that are being received. These could represent the stocking of inventory items from suppliers so that ABC Corporation can sell them to its customers. Purchase shipment #1146 illustrates that a single shipment item could have multiple packages. The first two rows show that the first item of Jones #2 pencils was shipped using two packages. Package #52000 stored 1,000 pencils in its package, and shipment package #52001 stored the other 1,000 pencils. These may have been received at the same time, or the receipts may have occurred at different times because the boxes could have been separated. Shipment items seq id 2 and 3 each fit neatly into their own respective packages.

Multiple shipment items may also be delivered in the same package. All three shipment items within shipment #1149 were delivered in a single shipment package #53100. All the items were accepted. This shows that a single SHIPMENT PACKAGE could contain many SHIPMENT ITEMS.

The transfer shipment #4800 shipped one item in one package; however, only 300 of the 500 items were accepted. A rejection reason, such as "damaged goods," "wrong amount," and so on, could have been recorded, depending on the reason for rejecting the other 200 items.

Item Issuance for Outgoing Shipments

Outgoing items being shipped need to issued, or in other words pulled, from inventory. A process takes place that may involve generating a pick list to determine which items need to be extracted from inventory, based on the current shipment needs. Different people are involved in the issuance of inventory in various roles to pick the items and quality assure the process.

Figure 5.5 provides a data model to handle the information requirements of the item issuance process. Based on the shipment needs, which could be obtained by reviewing the outstanding SHIPMENTs and SHIPMENT ITEMs, a PICKLIST is generated, identifying the plan for picking from inventory. Each PICKLIST will have a PICKLIST ITEM that stores the **quantity** of goods needed and are to be picked from each INVENTORY ITEM in order to meet the shipment needs. Various algorithms may have been used to generate this picklist, and once it is generated it is important to record because it represents the plan of action for issuing items out of inventory. Each SHIPMENT ITEM may be **obtained via** one or more ITEM ISSUANCEs, which are each **issued from** an INVENTORY ITEM. Each ITEM ISSUANCE may have many people involved in

Table 5.8 Shipment Receipts

SHIPMENT ID	SHIPMENT ITEM SEQ ID	QUANTITY	PRODUCT	PACKAGING CONTENT QUANTITY	SHIPMENT PACKAGE ID	RECEIPT ID	QUANTITY ACCEPTED
1146 (incoming shipment from a supplier)	1	2000	Jones #2 pencils	1000	52000	12900	1000
				1000	52001	12901	1000
	2	1000	Goldstein Elite pens	1000	52002	12901	1000
	3	1000	Boxes of HD diskettes	100	52003	13902	100
1149 (incoming shipment from a supplier)	1	200	Standard erasers	200	53100	13903	200
	2	200	Boxes of HD diskettes	200	53100	13904	200
	3	100	Jones #2 pencils	100	53100	13905	100
4800 (transfer)	1	500	Jones #2 pencils	500	52004	13804	300

this process and therefore may have many ITEM ISSUANCE ROLEs for each PARTY involved; each role is **described by** the ITEM ISSUANCE ROLE TYPE.

Notice that the relationship between ITEM ISSUANCE and SHIPMENT ITEM is optional because items may be issued from inventory for other reasons other than from shipments. For instance, an item may be issued for use within the enterprise at the same location that the inventory is stored.

Table 5.9 provides examples of item issuances. Shipment ID #9000 represents a customer shipment of three items. A thousand Jones #2 pencils are needed, and item issuance #12900 issues these 1,000 items out of inventory. For the second item, 1,000 Goldstein Elite pens, only 800 were available in the inventory location. A replenishment was expected soon, so the other 200 were issued out of inventory shortly afterward to accommodate the shipment item. This illustrates that multiple ITEM ISSUANCEs may be associated with a SHIPMENT ITEM. The last two rows in the table show a similar circumstance of two item issuances for the same shipment item, only in this case the items are packaged in separate packages.

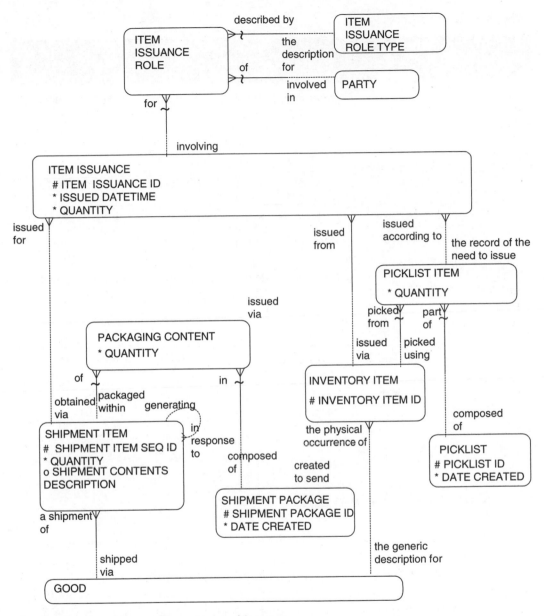

Figure 5.5 Item issuance for outgoing shipments.

Table 5.9   Item Issuances

SHIPMENT ID	SHIPMENT ITEM SEQ ID	QUANTITY	PRODUCT	PACKAGING CONTENT QUANTITY	SHIPMENT PACKAGE ID	ITEM ISSUANCE ID	QUANTITY ISSUED
9000 (outgoing shipment to a customer)	1	1000	Jones #2 pencils	1000	62000	12900	1000
	2	1000	Goldstein Elite pens	1000	62000	12901	800
						13100	200
	3	100	Boxes of HD diskettes	100	62000	12902	100
9200 (outgoing shipment to a customer)	1	350	Standard erasers	350	62001	13800	350
	2	100	Boxes of HD diskettes	100	62002	13801	100
	3	1500	Jones #2 pencils	1500	62002	13802	1000
				500	62003	13803	500

Shipment Documents

Shipments often are required to carry shipment documents for various reasons. Some reasons are practical in nature, such as to easily identify the contents of packages with a packing slip or bills of lading to identify the contents of shipments. Some reasons are regulated, such as tax, tariff, or export documentation.

To which shipment entity are shipping documents related? The SHIPMENT? SHIPMENT ITEM? SHIPMENT PACKAGE? Depending on the shipment document, the document may be related to either the entire shipment or a specific package.

Figure 5.6 provides a data model for the information requirements of shipment documents. SHIPMENT DOCUMENT is a subtype of DOCUMENT since there may be many other documents that the enterprise maintains. Each SHIPMENT DOCUMENT may be for a SHIPMENT ITEM, a SHIPMENT PACKAGE,

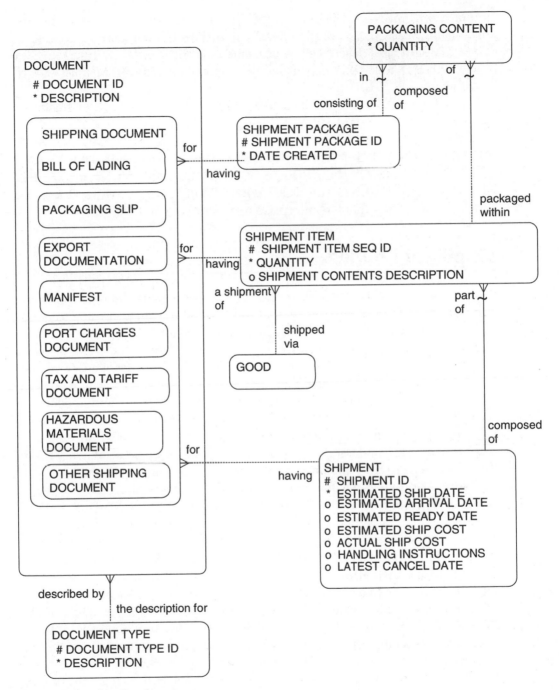

Figure 5.6 Shipping documents.

and/or a SHIPMENT, depending on the type and nature of the document. For instance, a PACKAGING SLIP generally describes the contents of a package while a MANIFEST describes the contents of a SHIPMENT. A HAZARDOUS MATERIALS DOCUMENT may describe the contents of a SHIPMENT ITEM or possibly a whole SHIPMENT.

The shipment documents used may vary based on the type of business; however, some standard subtypes are provided in this model. SHIPMENT DOCUMENTs are subtyped into BILL OF LADING, PACKAGING SLIP, EXPORT DOCUMENT, MANIFEST, PORT CHARGES DOCUMENT, TAX AND TARIFF DOCUMENT, HAZARDOUS MATERIALS DOCUMENT, or OTHER SHIPPING DOCUMENT. The DOCUMENT TYPE entity provides for other types of documents that the enterprise may want to maintain.

Shipment Routing

There is often a need to track the routes that the shipments and their items and packages travel in order to ensure that items are delivered according to needs and expectations. Enterprises need information about the various paths or shipment route segments to determine the status of the shipment and possibly expedite it. Some packages may have only one path that is tracked, for example, from a warehouse to a customer address. Some packages may have several shipment route segments, such as from a warehouse to a distribution center to an airline route, then to a local truck route, and finally to the customer's receiving dock. Depending on the nature of the enterprise, it may be important to track the progress of the shipment package as it moves along the delivery route. There is a need to track incoming as well as outgoing shipment packages.

Figure 5.7 provides a data model to track the packages along their routes in order to deliver them to their desired destination. Each SHIPMENT ROUTE SEGMENT maintains information about each leg of the journey for a SHIPMENT. In other words, it identifies the particular portions of the journey along which a shipment travels. The SHIPMENT ROUTE SEGMENT must be shipped via a particular SHIPMENT METHOD TYPE, such as by ground, cargo ship, or air. It must be shipped by a particular CARRIER, even if that carrier is part of the enterprise itself. Optionally, the enterprise may want to track the particular VEHICLE involved used in the segment as well as the from and to FACILITYs that maintain each location through which the shipment route segment travels.

The relationship to VEHICLE would usually be tracked in circumstances where the enterprise maintains its own fleet. If the enterprise uses external carriers, the enterprise would probably not need this relationship within its data model. Could more than one vehicle be used in a particular SHIPMENT ROUTE SEGMENT? For instance, could truck #100 be used and then truck #120 take over the route at midpoint? This data model will define this circumstance as

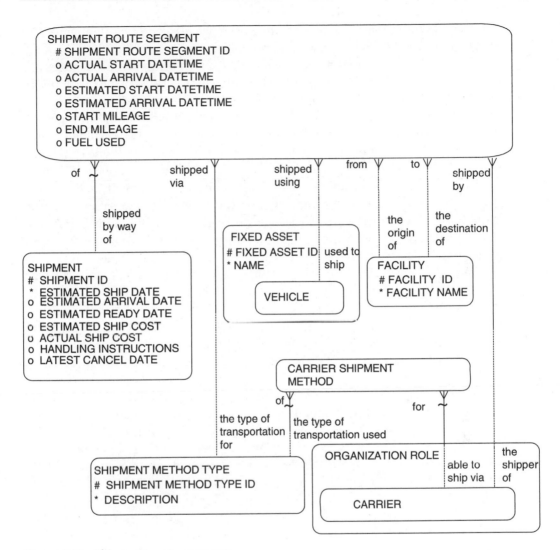

Figure 5.7 Shipment route segments.

two shipment route segments; therefore, each route would have one and only one vehicle.

The relationships to FACILITY are optional because the enterprise may not have the will and means to track each physical location to and from which the shipment travels. This relationship would probably not be needed for enterprises that always use external carriers to ship their goods.

One question that arises is whether a SHIPMENT ROUTE SEGMENT should be related to a SHIPMENT, SHIPMENT ITEM, and/or a SHIPMENT PACKAGE. Does the organization need to trace the routes of entire shipments, individual items within the shipments, or the path of each package within a shipment? The routes of each shipment item would probably not need to be traced separately because these items will be stored together as part of a shipment. Packages are also maintained as part of a shipment (through their relationships to SHIPMENT ITEM). Could the packages within a shipment be combined and intermixed with packages from different shipments to provide optimal routings of goods? Another question is whether different packages within the same shipment can take two different routes, and would this actually constitute the same shipment? For instance, could the shipment of an office desk and some supplies, which are packaged separately, be shipped through two different shipment methods and still be considered the same shipment? For the purposes of the data model presented, these would be considered two different shipments, and therefore it would probably be wise to track and monitor these as two separate shipment transactions, even though they may be applicable to the same order.

Another scenario is that one of the shipment packages got lost along the way and there was a need to track the routes of the shipment packages separately. If the enterprise had the will and means to track the routes for each package, then instead of a relationship from SHIPMENT ROUTE SEGMENT to SHIPMENT, there could be a many-to-many relationship set up from SHIPMENT ROUTE SEGMENT to SHIPMENT PACKAGE (with an associative entity in between these entities).

The SHIPMENT METHOD TYPE entity contains information about the way the item or items were shipped. The various types of shipment methods described in SHIPMENT METHOD TYPE may include records such as "ground," "rail," "first class air," or "cargo ship." These values may differ depending on the enterprise's needs. Each SHIPMENT may be shipped via one or more SHIPMENT METHODS. For example, a shipment may require transportation by train, then by truck.

Table 5.10 contains examples of what might be stored in the SHIPMENT ROUTE SEGMENT entity. Notice that shipment #9000 is shipped in two shipment route segments that are all controlled by ABC Subsidiary. The first segment is by one truck, and then the shipment to the final destination is completed by a second truck. The other shipments are more straightforward and involve only one shipment route segment. Shipment #9200 is outsourced to the organization Very Reliable Parcel Service, and only one segment of the shipment journey is tracked because they pick up the shipment and delivery it straight to the customer. Shipment 1146 represents an incoming shipment whose route may also need to be tracked in order to know when to expect the goods.

Shipment Vehicle

If an enterprise does its own shipping and owns the method of shipment, then it may need to track the actual vehicle being used. Thus, the entity VEHICLE is

Table 5.10 Shipment Route Segment

SHIPMENT ID	SHIPMENT TYPE	SHIPMENT ROUTE SEGMENT ID	SHIPMENT METHOD TYPE	CARRIER	ESTIMATED START DATETIME	ESTIMATED ARRIVAL DATETIME
9000	Customer shipment	1	Truck	ABC Subsidiary	Mar 7 2001 10AM	Mar 7 2001 1PM
		2	Truck	ABC Subsidiary	Mar 7 2001 2PM	Mar 7 2001 4 PM
9200	Customer shipment	1	Ground	Very Reliable Parcel Service	Mar 12 2001 1PM	Mar 14 2001 1PM
1146	Purchase shipment	1	Air	Air Goods Delivery Express	Mar 19 2001 4PM	Mar 20 2001 12 noon

needed to record this information. The entity VEHICLE is a subtype of FIXED ASSET (further explained in Chapter 8, Figure 8.5). There is a one-to-many relationship from VEHICLE to SHIPMENT ROUTE SEGMENT because one truck could be used to deliver many shipments. Notice in Table 5.10 that shipment #9000, which had two segments within the shipment, is now broken down further into the actual trucks being used

Information that enterprises may want to keep about the VEHICLE would be the statistics behind the use of the vehicle, such as the **start mileage** and **end mileage** (if appropriate) and amount of **fuel used**. For detailed tracking one may also want to track the date and time a particular vehicle picked up a shipment and when it unloaded it. With this information it can easily be determined in what order multiple vehicles were used to deliver a single shipment and how long it took, including transfers. See Table 5.11 for examples.

In the example given, one shipment (#9000) is delivered using two vehicles (Truck #1 and Truck #25). Looking at the appropriate start and end times, it is possible to determine that there was a 30-minute delay in the delivery of shipment #9000 while it was being transferred from the first vehicle to the second. Also, notice in the data that the vehicle "Truck #1" was used to deliver a second shipment (#9002). The reason the start time is the same as that of the previous shipment is that the truck contained two shipments that were loaded at the same time.

The data shown also provides information for calculating the real cost of the delivery. It shows the mileage and amount of fuel used. Knowing the cost of fuel, it would be possible to determine this part of the cost of delivery for each shipment. Additionally, mileage could be used to determine wear and tear on the vehicles used.

Table 5.11 Shipment Vehicle Data

SHIPMENT ID	SHIPMENT METHOD	VEHICLE NAME	ACTUAL START DATETIME	ACTUAL END DATETIME	START MILEAGE	END MILEAGE	FUEL USED
9000	Truck	Truck #1	Mar 7, 2001 10:00 A.M.	Mar 7, 2001 11:35 A.M.	52,000	52,061	2 gallons
		Truck #25	Mar 7, 2001 12:05 P.M.	Mar 7, 2001 8:16 P.M.	73,525	74,006	25 gallons
9002	Truck	Truck #1	Mar 7, 2001 10:00 A.M.	Mar 7, 2001 11:35 A.M.	52,000	52,061	2 gallons

An enterprise may also need to track estimated and actual dates and times for each shipment route segment and for each vehicle to determine if the shipment is running behind schedule. The **estimated start datetime** and **estimated arrival datetime** attributes as well as the **actual start datetime** and **actual arrival datetime** on SHIPMENT ROUTE SEGMENT provide this additional functionality, if it is needed.

Summary

In this chapter there has been discussion of the details of shipments and how they relate to orders and to each other. The chapter provided models for shipments, shipment items, relationships of shipment items to order items, shipment receipts, item issuances, shipping documents, and shipment route segments. The key entities and relationships are shown in an overall model in Figure 5.8. These data structures, combined with the interrelationships with other aspects of the models, will allow for the development of robust, integrated systems. These models should, once implemented, minimize the occurrence of redundant data and make the maintenance of referential integrity simpler.

Please refer to Appendix A for a listing of entities and attributes. SQL scripts to build tables and columns derived from the logical models in this book can be found on the full-blown CD-ROM, which is licensed separately. Note that there are some differences in the way service is delivered versus items. Inventory items are things that can be shipped. Service cannot really be shipped by any conventional means; instead, it is delivered to a customer through an entity called WORK EFFORT, which will be explained in the next chapter.

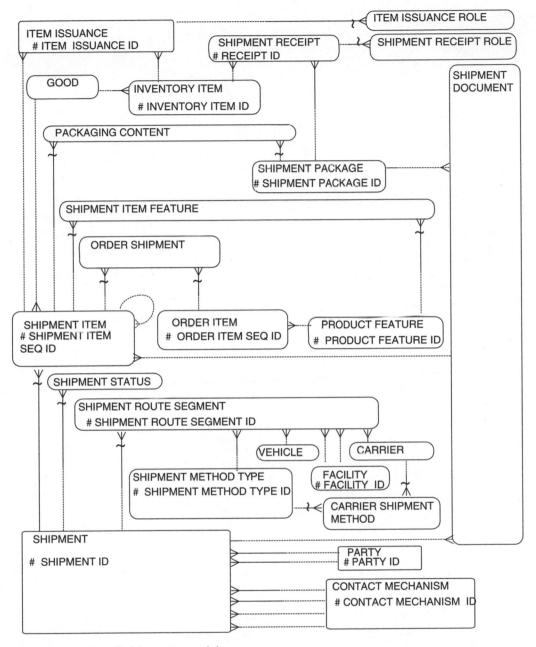

Figure 5.8 Overall shipments model.

6

Work Effort

A key component of conducting business is the act of providing various types of services to various parties. As previously noted, businesses generally provide two types of product offerings: They sell either goods or services. When businesses sell services, they have a responsibility to perform those services, and then they need to bill for them. This often involves the completion of some type of work effort. Businesses also perform work efforts within their internal organizations to accomplish tasks, such as completing a project, producing inventory for sale, or maintaining some corporate asset.

Some questions that enterprises need to answer in the course of doing business include the following:

- What type of work effort is required?
- What items need to be produced, or what services need to be delivered?
- Who will be involved, and what are their roles?
- Where will the work take place?
- How long will it take?
- What is the current status of the effort?
- Are the appropriate resources (people, inventory, equipment) available? If not, when will they be?

- What standards and metrics are in place to measure work effort effectiveness?
- What results are work efforts producing and how efficient are they?

This chapter will illustrate the following models that help answer those questions:

- Work requirements
- Work requirement roles
- Work effort generation (alternate model also provided)
- Work effort associations
- Work effort party assignment
- Work effort time tracking
- Work effort rates
- Inventory item assignment
- Fixed asset assignment
- Party fixed asset assignment
- Work effort type standards
- Work effort results

Work Requirement and Work Efforts

A WORK REQUIREMENT and a WORK EFFORT are two different but related entities. A work requirement represents the *need* to perform some type of work. This could be a requirement stemming from a decision to manufacture inventory items, deliver services, conduct a project, or repair an asset of the enterprise such as a piece of equipment or a piece of software.

A work effort is the *fulfillment* of the work requirement. This includes setting up and planning for the actual work that will be performed, as well as recording the status and information related to the efforts and tasks that are taking place.

Work Requirement Definition

Where does a work requirement come from? A work requirement is created when there is a need to perform some type of work by the enterprise, either for the enterprise or for an external organization, most likely a customer. Examples of work requirements include the following:

- The need to manufacture a particular item because market research indicates an increased demand for that item beyond previous projections

- The need for a piece of equipment within the enterprise to be repaired

- The need for an internal project such as an analysis of existing operations, development of a plan, or creation of a new product or service

Figure 6.1 shows the key entities used to define a work requirement. First, the WORK REQUIREMENT is a subtype of the previously modeled REQUIRE-

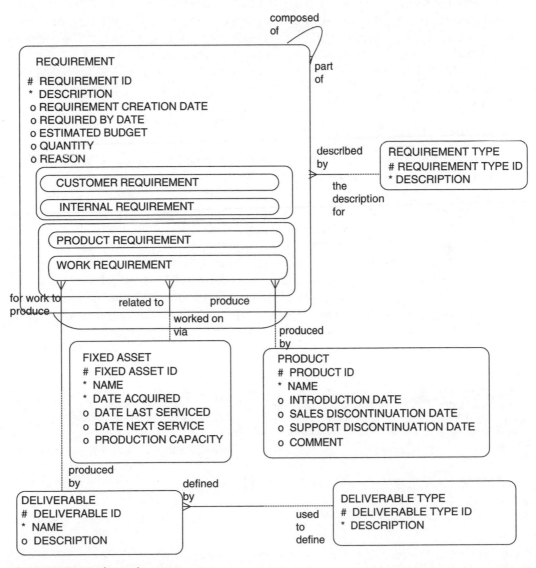

Figure 6.1   Work requirement.

MENT entity. The REQUIREMENT TYPE defines the possible categories for requirements, which, of course, includes categorizations for WORK REQUIRE-MENTs. Possible values for REQUIREMENT TYPE include "project," "maintenance," and "production run." The WORK REQUIREMENT may be for work to be delivered of either a DELIVERABLE, FIXED ASSET, or a PRODUCT.

Several key pieces of information need to be kept in the WORK REQUIRE-MENT entity. The **description** attribute defines the need of the requirement. The **requirement creation date** is a date by which the work is required. The **required by date** within the REQUIREMENT entity specifies the date by which the requirement is needed. The **estimated budget** attribute identifies how much money is allocated for fulfilling this requirement. The attribute **quantity** determines the number of items needed in the requirement. The **reason** attribute explains why there is a need for the requirement.

Table 6.1 shows some data that could appear in the WORK REQUIREMENT entity.

Requirement Types

In addition, other information is needed depending on the REQUIREMENT TYPE. If the type is "production run," then information about what is to be produced and how many is of critical importance. This is why the model includes an optional attribute for **quantity** and a possible relationship to PRODUCT.

If the type is "maintenance" or "repair," then there is a definite need to know what piece of equipment needs to be worked on. To accommodate this need, the model also includes an optional relationship to FIXED ASSET.

Finally, if the type is "internal project," then WORK REQUIREMENT may be associated with a DELIVERABLE. This would include such things as a management report, analysis document, or the creation of a particular business method

Table 6.1   Work Requirement Data

WORK REQUIREMENT ID	REQUIREMENT TYPE	REQUIREMENT CREATION DATE	REQUIRED BY DATE	DESCRIPTION
50985	Production run	Jul 5, 2000	Aug 5, 2000	Anticipated demand of 2,000 custom engraved black pens with gold trim
60102	Internal project	Oct 15, 2000	Dec 15, 2000	Develop sales and marketing plan for 2002
70485	Maintenance	June 16, 2000	June 18, 2000	Fix engraving machine

or tool. The DELIVERABLE TYPE entity would contain a list of the possible types of deliverables an enterprise may produce for itself, such as "management report," "project plan," "presentation," or "market analysis."

Note that there is an exclusive arc across DELIVERABLE, FIXED ASSET, and PRODUCT because a single WORK REQUIREMENT can be related to one PRODUCT or one DELIVERABLE or for work on one FIXED ASSET, but not all three. Table 6.2 shows examples of various types of work requirements.

The data shown indicates that work requirement #50985 is a "production run." Because of this, the product to be produced, "engraved black pen with gold trim," and the required quantity to produce, 2,000 of these items, are also included. Requirement #51245 and #51285 are also requirements to produce certain amounts of the same pen. Requirement #60102 is an "internal project" related to the deliverable "2001 Sales/Marketing Plan." Work requirement #70485 is a "maintenance" task that requires a particular piece of equipment to be repaired, so the asset ID for this machine is also included. As discussed with previous examples, appropriate business rules need to be in place to ensure that work requirements of certain types are appropriately related to the entities describing what the work requirement produces.

This data model does not include relationships from WORK EFFORT to SHIPMENT to handle the work requirements or corresponding work efforts of

Table 6.2   Work Requirement Types

WORK REQUIREMENT ID	WORK REQUIREMENT TYPE	DESCRIPTION	PRODUCT	QUANTITY REQUIRED	DELIVERABLE	FIXED ASSET ID
50985	Production run	Anticipated demand of 2,000 custom-engraved black pens with gold trim	Engraved black pen with gold trim	2,000		
51245	Production run	Anticipated demand of 1,500 custom-engraved black pens with gold trim	Engraved black pen with gold trim	1,500		
51285	Production run	Anticipated demand of 3,000 custom-engraved black pens with gold trim	Engraved black pen with gold trim	3,000		
60102	Internal project	Develop sales and marketing plan for 2001			2001 Sales/ Marketing Plan	
70485	Maintenance	Fix engraving machine				5025

managing the delivering of inventory items. Usually, the sales order and shipping entities covered in Chapters 4 and 5 provide enough information to help the enterprise manage the delivery of items. The enterprise generally doesn't need to track the work efforts involved in delivering a product because they are usually quite simple and consist of loading, shipping, and unloading the items. This model, however, can be easily modified to provide for tracking work requirements and work efforts associated with delivery of items by creating a relationship from WORK EFFORT to SHIPMENT ITEM (work efforts will be discussed later in this chapter).

Anticipated Demand

Anticipated demand is a situation where WORK REQUIREMENTs may be needed, and it warrants special consideration. Not only do specific customer or internal requirements generate the need to schedule a production run, but so can anticipated or forecasted demand (as shown in Tables 6.1 and 6.2). Anticipated demand from a corporate forecaster can result in an internal work requirement to produce certain inventory items. For example, a forecast based on the trend analysis in a sales data warehouse could show that there should be a spike in future sales of a particular item. Rather than wait for the actual sales orders to start coming in, a work requirement to produce the expected increase is entered so that when orders do come in the enterprise will have an ample supply on hand to meet the demand.

Anticipated demand applies only to inventory items, not services, because it is not really possible to prefabricate a service. It is not possible to fix something or provide accounting, legal, or professional services to a client before a contract or order for this is in place. It is, however, possible to prepare for anticipated service orders by preparing standard work products to be used as templates, but those would be treated as internal projects. For instance, an enterprise may initiate a work requirement for an infrastructure project to prepare an outline project plan in anticipation of an accounting audit review or other consulting-type engagement.

Work Requirement Compared to Order

Is a work requirement a special type of ORDER because it describes a requirement to complete some type of work? As shown in Figure 4.9 in Chapter 4, each REQUIREMENT has a many-to-many relationship with each ORDER ITEM; however they are different entities because the REQUIREMENT represents the need and the ORDER represents a commitment to have the need fulfilled.

A REQUIREMENT also has major differences in structure and attributes from a standard order item. For instance, for internal work requirements, there is generally no need to track the terms of the work order, relate it to agreements, or include pricing structures. It is possible, though, that companies may need this information for internal monitoring of intercompany transactions because different parts of the company may perform these work effort functions.

Is a WORK REQUIREMENT then related to a subtype of ORDER ITEM, namely a WORK ORDER ITEM? This is a valid construct and one that is adopted within these models because order items represent commitments, including items for completing work. Both sales and purchase order items may be related to work orders, and therefore the data model would need another type of classification for PRODUCT ORDER ITEMs and WORK ORDER ITEMs. For example, a professional services firm may record several requirements for a customer that lead to an engagement (a type of order), which is then associated with several work efforts (projects). The section on work efforts will show how to model this.

Another question that arises is where a requisition falls into the model. Depending on the definition for requisition, it is either a synonym for a requirement or an order. If a requisition describes a request for getting something done or ordering something, then a requisition is really a requirement. If a requisition describes a commitment to having work done or having something ordered, then the requisition is synonymous with an order item.

Work Requirement Roles

Just as there are many roles that parties play in a purchase or sales order (refer to Chapter 4), there are many roles that organizations and people play in the work requirement. Among these roles, several could be important to an enterprise including: the internal organization for which the work requirement is created, the person requesting the work, people involved in the authorization of the work requirement, and the person responsible for ensuring the work requirement is completed. Figure 6.2 depicts the entities needed to maintain this information.

The WORK REQUIREMENT ROLE TYPE entity is used to store all the valid roles defined by an enterprise that could be related to a WORK REQUIREMENT. The PARTY WORK REQUIREMENT ROLE entity contains the intersection of PARTY, WORK REQUIREMENT, and WORK REQUIREMENT ROLE TYPE. In this case, the primary key will be a combination of the **work requirement ID**, **party ID**, and **role type id**. This, however, is not enough because it is possible (though not likely) that one party may be assigned the same role at different times over the life of a work requirement. Because of this, the model includes a date (or alternatively one could add an additional sequence ID) as part of the primary key in order to ensure uniqueness. Table 6.3 contains sample data to demonstrate some of these possibilities.

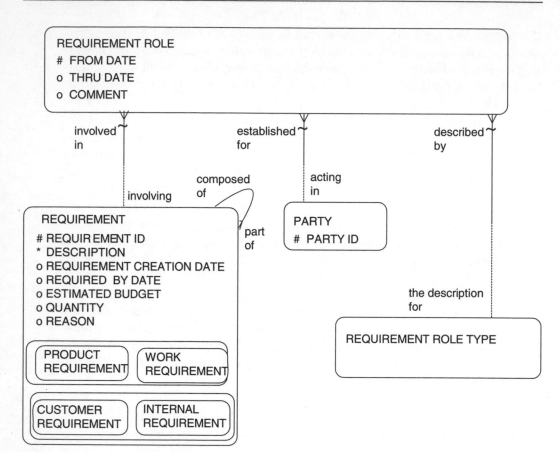

Figure 6.2 Work requirement roles.

Table 6.3 Party Work Requirement Role Data

WORK REQUIREMENT ID	PARTY	WORK REQUIREMENT ROLE TYPE	FROM DATE	THRU DATE
50985	ABC Manufacturing, Inc.	Created for	Jul 5, 2000	
	John Smith	Created by	Jul 5, 2000	
	John Smith	Responsible for	Jul 5, 2000	Dec 15, 2000
	Sam Bossman	Authorized by	Jul 8, 2000	
	Dick Jones	Responsible for	Dec 16, 2001	Feb 20, 2001
	John Smith	Responsible for	Feb 21, 2000	
60102	Sam Bossman	Created for	Jun 10, 2000	
	Dick Jones	Responsible for	Jun 15, 2000	Jan 1, 2001

As the example data shows for work requirement ID #50985, John Smith has two roles. He created the work requirement, and he is responsible for tracking the work requirement through its cycle from start through fulfillment. At one point he is replaced by Dick Jones, but later he is reassigned his original role. Notice, too, that Dick Jones has the role "responsible for" on two work requirements during overlapping time periods. As with the model for role assignments in orders, this model is flexible enough to allow for a variety of options.

Work Effort Generation

Enterprises need to track requirements to perform work, commitments to do work, and the actual work that is being performed. Requirements have been addressed in the last section and it was established that the commitment to do work is a type of order item. The remainder of this chapter will focus on managing the work effort, which is the tracking of the work being performed.

Figure 6.3a shows a data model that tracks work from the REQUIREMENT to one or more committed WORK ORDER ITEMs to the fulfillment of one or more WORK EFFORTs. The WORK REQUIREMENT represents the need to do something, the WORK ORDER ITEM represents the commitment to complete some work, and the WORK EFFORT entity tracks the fulfillment and performance of work that results from a WORK ORDER ITEM. There is a many-to-many relationship between each of these, allowing requirements to be flexibly combined into commitments and commitments to be grouped into manageable work efforts. The ORDER REQUIREMENT COMMITMENT associative entity was explained in Chapter 4, and the WORK ORDER ITEM FULFILLMENT associative entity is introduced in this chapter.

The WORK ORDER ITEM will usually result from WORK REQUIREMENTs; however, it could result from certain PRODUCT REQUIREMENTs such as for products that need to be manufactured. The work effort may be fulfilling an internal commitment to do work, or it may be fulfilling an external requirement such as a SALES ORDER ITEM. The work effort may result from scenarios such as these:

- A work requirement (as defined in the previous section).
- A customer orders an item that needs to be manufactured.
- A service that was sold now needs to be performed.
- A customer places an order to repair or service an item that was previously sold to him or her.

In addition to defining the basic information for a WORK EFFORT, the model also keeps track of WORK EFFORT TYPE, WORK EFFORT PURPOSE TYPE, and the FACILITY where the work takes place.

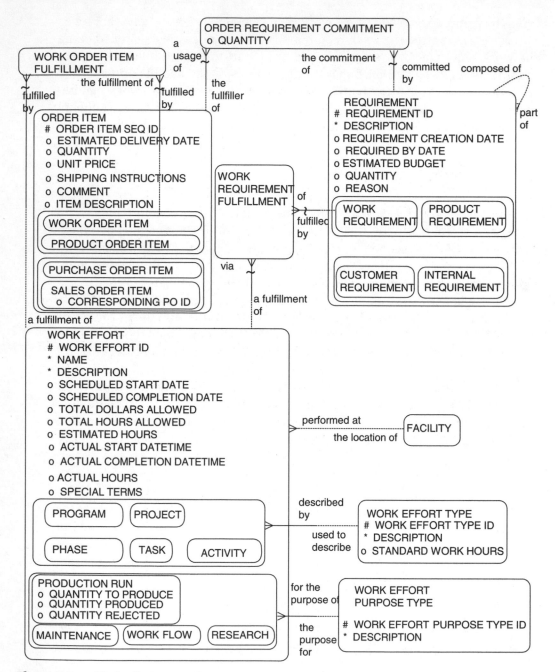

Figure 6.3a Work effort generation.

Work Effort Type and Work Effort Purpose Type

In order to fulfill the requirement of either a work requirement or a work order item, the WORK EFFORT entity is used. The WORK EFFORT is subtyped according to its level of detail. Possible subtypes include PROGRAM, PROJECT, PHASE, ACTIVITY, and TASK. The WORK EFFORT TYPE entity is used to include more types if necessary. The standard work hours attribute in WORK EFFORT TYPE is used to record the estimate of how many hours it would normally take to complete this effort.

A WORK EFFORT tracks the work to fix or produce something for manufacturing and involves the allocation of resources: people (labor), parts (inventory), and fixed assets (equipment). Therefore each WORK EFFORT may be for the purpose of a WORK EFFORT PURPOSE TYPE. Subtypes for WORK EFFORT PURPOSE TYPE include MAINTENANCE, PRODUCTION RUN, WORK FLOW, and RESEARCH. The work effort may be a MAINTENANCE effort, such as performing preventive maintenance on various pieces of equipment. It could be a PRODUCTION RUN to fulfill an immediate or anticipated request. The **quantity to produce** maintains the expected quantity for the production run, and the **quantity produced** records the actual production from that production run. Another purpose for a work effort is a WORK FLOW, which indicates that there is a task or effort that was assigned in the process of doing business, perhaps by a work flow system. RESEARCH would indicate that the work effort is needed to track the researching of some type of question—for example, the reason why a customer had a certain credit status.

Work Effort Attributes

Other information that an enterprise may want to record about the WORK EFFORT could include a **name** for the overall effort (such as a project name) and a detailed **description** of the effort. To facilitate project tracking, the enterprise may also want to list a **scheduled start date, scheduled completion date**, and **estimated hours** for the effort. The **actual start datetime, actual completion datetime**, and **actual hours** are stored to track efficiency of efforts. If there is a need for any **special terms** that anyone needs to know about, those can be recorded as well.

Some institutions have other considerations that need to be considered. Funding or time limits may be imposed under certain circumstances by various agencies, so the model includes attributes to store **total dollars allowed** and **total hours allowed**. An example of this would be IRS regulations restricting the amount of time a contractor can work for an enterprise without being considered an employee. Also, many government-funded organizations have spending limits set by budget appropriations or even by law.

Fulfillment of Work Requirements

Each requirement to do work may be fulfilled by work efforts. Depending on the nature of the work requirement and how much data the enterprise has the will and means to capture, the work requirement may be either directly related to the work effort or related to an order item that, in turn, is related to a work effort.

For example, if there is a requirement from a customer to have certain work performed—for instance, the customer may have specified a need to build a specific application system—the enterprise would want to record the REQUIREMENT, relate it to the ORDER ITEM (which it obtained, we hope), and then track the corresponding work effort(s). The many-to-many relationships from REQUIREMENT to ORDER ITEM and then from ORDER ITEM to WORK EFFORT provide a very flexible structure to map requirements, to commitments (orders), and then to the corresponding projects (work efforts).

If there was an internal need to complete work—for instance, a repair to a piece of machinery—then the enterprise may want only to capture the WORK REQUIREMENT and corresponding WORK EFFORTs. The associative entity, WORK REQUIREMENT FULFILLMENT, between WORK REQUIRMENT and WORK EFFORT, allows work requirements to be combined into a single effort or a single requirement to be managed in several work efforts.

As indicated by the data in Table 6.4, a single work effort may have originated from one or more work requirements, or the corresponding work effort may be originated from an ORDER ITEM or a WORK REQUIREMENT. The ORDER ITEM will typically be from a sales order and not a purchase order because sales orders, especially for services, more typically create a need to track a work effort. The enterprise usually will not track work efforts for items that they have purchased, although it may happen if the work effort is large enough and it is important for the purchaser to track the progress of the delivery.

The model shows a many-to-many relationship from REQUIREMENT to ORDER ITEM. There may be a sales order that has an item for 1,000 items. Management may decide to manage this as three separate work efforts and perhaps create three production runs in separate plants in order to generate the inventory needed to fulfill this one order. Likewise, an internal work requirement to revamp an enterprise's computer systems could be divided into multiple projects in order to phase the development effort.

Table 6.4 contains data samples for some scenarios of how a work effort originated. Several requirements may be combined into a single work effort, as shown in the first two rows of Table 6.4. Requirement items #50985 and #51245, which may have come from different managers, are combined into a single production run. Conversely, a single requirement, for example #51285, may be fulfilled with two work efforts in order to better manage each of these production runs. This scenario may occur with other types of requirements being fulfilled by a single work effort or multiple work efforts originating from a single require-

Table 6.4 Work Efforts from Work Requirement

WORK EFFORT ID	NAME	DESCRIPTION	SCHEDULED START DATE	WORK REQUIREMENT
28045	Production run	Production run of 3,500 pencils	June 1, 2000	Work Requirement Item #50985 Anticipated demand of 2,000 custom-engraved black pens with gold trim
				Work Requirement Item #51245 Anticipated demand of 1,500 custom-engraved black pens with gold trim
51285	Production run	Production run of 1,500 pencils	Dec 5, 2000	Work Requirement Item #51285 Anticipated demand of 3,000 custom-engraved black pens with gold trim
51298	Production run	Production run of 1,500 pencils	Dec 6, 2000	
32898	Fix engraving machine	Repair engraving machine #12 because it may not be powered up	Dec 12, 2000	Repair of engraving machine
39409	Sales and marketing plan development	Develop a sales and marketing plan for 2002 including sales projections, channel distribution strategy, and competitive analysis	Dec 15, 2000	Work Requirement #60102 Develop sales and marketing plan for 2002

ment. Thus, the associative entity WORK REQUIREMENT FULFILLMENT handles this many-to-many relationship. The last two rows show the requirements and the corresponding work effort for fixing an engraving machine and developing a sales and marketing plan.

Table 6.5 provides an example of the data when a REQUIREMENT is mapped to an ORDER ITEM and then fulfilled with a WORK EFFORT. The requirement was from a customer who had a need for customized pens. This need was converted into a sales order item to produce 2,500 customized pens. The order item was fulfilled using two work efforts, namely production run #1 and production run #2.

Table 6.5 Work Efforts Originated from Order Items

WORK EFFORT ID	NAME	DESCRIPTION	SCHEDULED START DATE	ORDER ITEM	REQUIREMENT ITEM
29534	Production run #1 of pens	Production of 1,500 customized engraved pens with gold lettering	Feb 23, 2001	Sales Order Item to produce 2,500 customized engraved pens	Need for customized pens
29874	Production run #2 of pens	Production of 1,000 customized engraved pens with gold lettering	Mar 23, 2001	Sales Order Item to produce 2,500 customized engraved pens	Need for customized pens

Work Effort and Facility

A final question to ask is: Where is the WORK EFFORT going to take place? As shown in Figure 6.3a, the WORK EFFORT may be performed at or associated with one and only one FACILITY.

As stated in the discussion of WORK EFFORT, some parts of the work effort may not happen at the main site. Take for example a project to develop a sales and marketing plan for the enterprise. The effort is associated with a main office where the headquarters are located. Various tasks associated with this effort, such as interviews, may happen at a branch office, while others, such as writing up the report, happen at the main office. For the tasks that do not occur in the main office, there may be a desire to record that secondary work location. The optional relationship to FACILITY from WORK EFFORT may occur at any level in the WORK EFFORT breakdown (because work efforts are defined recursively). For those efforts that have no facility association, it is assumed that they occur at the main facility associated with the parent WORK EFFORT (or that location is immaterial in this case).

The FACILITY is used because these work efforts may happen at an actual physical structure such as a particular building, room, or floor. The enterprise may need another relationship (which is not shown here), from WORK EFFORT to POSTAL ADDRESS, just in case the facility is not stored and there is simply an address that is known.

Work Effort Generation—Alternate Model

Some organizations do not have a need to maintain which requirements are fulfilled by which order items. They may, however, have internal requirements and associated work efforts that fulfill these work requirements. Figure 6.3b

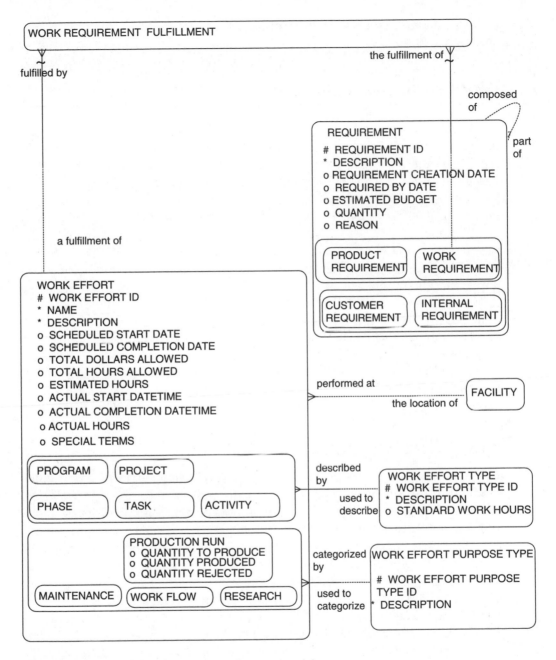

Figure 6.3b Work effort generation—alternate model.

provides an alternate model for work effort generation to handle this type of situation.

Work Effort Associations

Work efforts may be defined at various levels of detail and broken down in different ways. Each subtype of WORK EFFORT may be related to different subtypes depending on the circumstances. For instance, to manage programs within an enterprise and associated internal projects PROGRAMs may be broken down into PROJECTs, which may be broken down into ACTIVITYs, which may be broken down into TASKs. For a production run, a JOB may be broken down into ACTIVITYs—for instance, as in a production run. Tasks are the activities or steps that need to occur to accomplish a work effort. For any WORK EFFORT there may be any number of WORK EFFORTs that may be broken down into any number of other WORK EFFORTs. In addition, for some tasks there may also be a WORK EFFORT DEPENDENCY, meaning that one effort may need to be performed before another task, which is maintained in the WORK EFFORT PRECEDENCY. Another type of dependency is that one effort may need to be done concurrently with the other effort that is maintained in the WORK EFFORT CONCURRENCY. The one-to-many recursion around WORK EFFORT provides for work efforts to be redone by other work efforts and to capture this relationship (see Figure 6.4).

Work Effort Association Definition

Table 6.6 shows the work efforts for a job of producing pencils on a particular production run. Included in the data are the attributes for **scheduled start date** and **scheduled completion date** and the **estimated hours**. These tasks will be useful for planning staff and equipment assignments (discussed in a later section). Included are scheduled work efforts and the sub-efforts that make up each work effort. Job #28045, which is a production run of pens, has four activities related to it. Notice that the first activity of setting up a production line is an activity not only of this production run but also of the next production run. Hence, each work effort may be made up of many other work efforts, and conversely each work effort may be used within one or more other work efforts. This many-to-many recursion is handled by the WORK EFFORT ASSOCIATION entity in the model, and Table 6.6 shows how work efforts are related to other work efforts. The WORK EFFORT TYPE carried out by the enterprise may track the **standard work hours** usually spent on this type of effort. Notice that the **estimated hours** of the WORK EFFORT may be different from the **standard work hours** because particular circumstances are

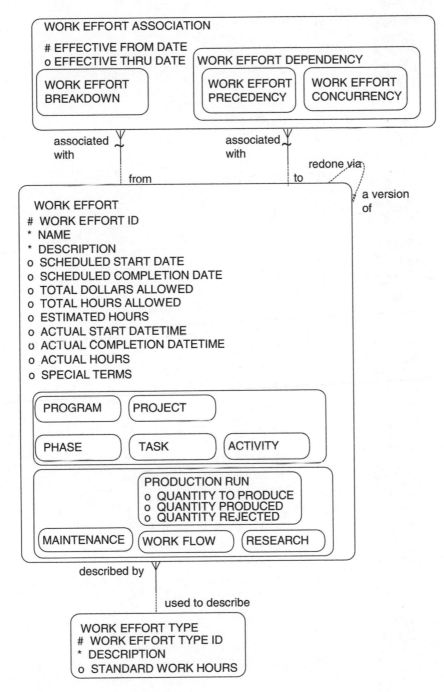

Figure 6.4 Work effort breakdown.

Table 6.6 Work Effort Breakdown Data

WORK EFFORT ID (JOB)	WORK EFFORT SUB-TYPE	WORK EFFORT DESCRIPTION	ASSOCIATED WORK EFFORT(S) ID AND DESCRIPTION	STANDARD WORK HOURS	SCHEDULED START DATE	SCHEDULED COMPLETION DATE	ESTIMATED HOURS
28045	Job	Production run #1			Jun 1, 2000	Jun 4, 2000	
120001	Activity	Set up production line	28045 Production run #1 51245 Production run #2	20	Jun 1, 2000	Jun 2, 2000	20
120002	Activity	Operate machinery	28045 Production run #1	10	Jun 3, 2000	Jun 3, 2000	10
120003	Activity	Clean up machinery	28045 Production run #1	5	Jun 4, 2000	Jun 4, 2000	5
120004	Activity	Quality assure goods produced	28045 Production run #1	10	Jun 3, 2000	Jun 4, 2000	10
3454587	Task	Move pen manufacturing machinery in place	1200 Set up production line	5	Jun 1, 2000	Jun 1, 2000	4
3454588	Task	Move raw materials in place for production run	1200 Set up production line	8	Jun 1, 2000	Jun 1, 2000	7
3454589	Task	Set up assembly line rollers	1200 Set up production line	7	Jun 1, 2000	Jun 1, 2000	6

involved in the execution of the task (perhaps the project manager knows that very efficient workers will be assigned and will therefore lower the estimate).

Work Effort Dependency

The WORK EFFORT DEPENDENCY entity allows the enterprise to track the fact that some efforts may not be a *breakdown* of other efforts but may actually be *dependent* on other efforts. For example, the task "operate machinery" cannot be executed until the task "set up production line" is completed. The WORK EFFORT DEPENDENCY entity provides a method for relating work efforts with other work efforts. Work efforts may be dependent on each other in different ways. In the example regarding "operate machinery" and "set up production line," the second effort must be preceded by the completion of the first task and is a WORK EFFORT PRECEDENCY subtype. Other situations may occur where two tasks need to be executed in parallel. In that case, the WORK EFFORT CONCURRENCY subtype would be used.

Work Efforts and Work Tasks

An alternative to using the WORK EFFORT ASSOCIATION could be to show a WORK EFFORT with a one-to-many relationship to a separate entity, WORK TASK (with a recursion around WORK TASK) in order to distinguish the whole project from its individual phases, activities, tasks, and so on. The issue with this model is that there are usually many similarities between the whole work effort and its parts. For instance, parties, inventory, and fixed assets may be assigned to a whole project (a work effort) or an individual task. The benefit of having a WORK EFFORT that is recursively associated with other WORK EFFORTs, is that work efforts may be dynamically linked to other work efforts as needed.

Work Effort Party Assignment

In order for the WORK EFFORT to be completed, certain resources need to be made available. Parties, inventory, and equipment may need to be assigned to WORK EFFORTs at different levels of detail. For instance, people may need to be assigned roles at a high level, such as a program or project, and roles may also be assigned at more detailed levels of activity. This section discusses the assignment of parties to WORK EFFORTs. It includes the entities WORK EFFORT PARTY ASSIGNMENT, WORK EFFORT ROLE TYPE, PARTY SKILL, SKILL TYPE, WORK EFFORT STATUS, and WORK EFFORT STATUS TYPE (see Figure 6.5).

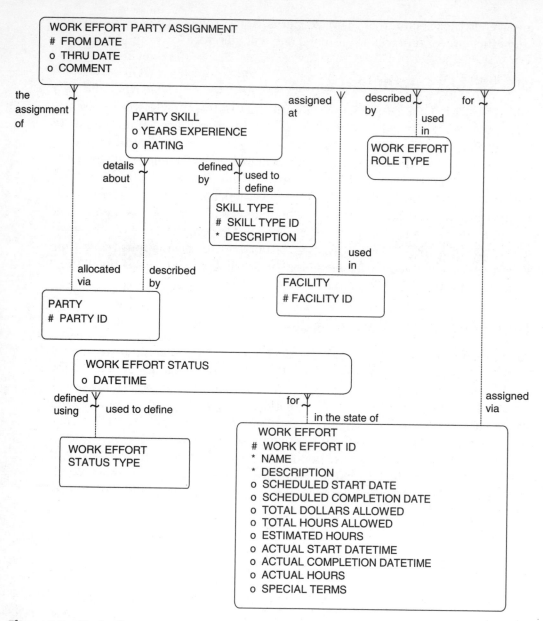

Figure 6.5 Work effort party assignment.

Work Effort Party Assignment

For planning and scheduling purposes, the model includes a means by which people, or groups of people, can be assigned or allocated to a WORK EFFORT. This is accomplished through the WORK EFFORT PARTY ASSIGNMENT entity (refer to Figure 6.5). With this it is possible to assign parties to work efforts in various roles as well as at various levels of the work effort. Table 6.7 gives examples of the data available when the relationships are resolved.

Dick Jones is shown as being assigned as the project manager to the sales and marketing plan development work effort, with Bob Jenkins being the pro-

Table 6.7 Work Effort Party Assignment Data

WORK EFFORT ID AND DESCRIPTION	PARTY	WORK EFFORT ROLE TYPE	FROM DATE	THRU DATE	COMMENT
39409 Develop a sales and marketing plan	Dick Jones	Project manager	Jan 2, 2001	Sept 15, 2001	
	Bob Jenkins	Project administrator			
	John Smith	Team member	Mar 5, 2001	Aug 6, 2001	Leaving for three-week vacation on Aug 7, 2001
	John Smith	Team member	Sept 1, 2001	Dec 2, 2001	
	Jane Smith	Team member	Aug 6, 2000	Sept 15, 2001	Very excited about assignment
29000 Develop project plan (part of effort 39409)	Dick Jones	Creator	Jan 2, 2001	Jan 4, 2001	
29000 Develop project plan (part of effort 39409)	Bob Jenkins	Data entry in system	Jan 4, 2001	Jan 4, 2001	
29003 Conduct initial interviews (part of effort 39409)	John Smith	Performer	Jan 5, 2001	Feb 5, 2001	
29005 Conduct market research (part of effort 39409)	USA Consulting	Outsourcing responsibility	Mar 1, 2001	Jul 1, 2001	Contracted outside

ject administrator. John Smith is assigned to the project from March 5, 2001 to August 6, 2001 and then not assigned for a good part of August due to a vacation, then assigned again from September 1, 2001 through December 2, 2001. Dick, the project manager, can see that there will be a three-week period when John Smith is not assigned to this effort (between August 6 and September 1) and has assigned an employee, Jane Smith, with a lot of interest in this work effort, to be scheduled for this effort during this time period. With this information the manager will know not to assign John to any critical tasks that must be completed in August.

Additionally, the data indicates that for work effort #39409 there are additional work efforts within the overall work effort. One work effort is to develop a project plan that has two parties assigned to it. Dick Jones, the project manager, is responsible for developing the plan, and his assistant, Bob Jenkins, is responsible for entering it into the project management system. John Smith is assigned the effort of conducting initial interviews. An outside contracting firm is allocated to the project for four months; its responsibility is to do market research. Thus the data structure allows for efforts to be completely outsourced with no internal employee actually assigned to the work, only a particular organization. In this case, the internal manager is not concerned with who does the work, only that it be well managed and tracked with this outside firm. This illustrates the reason why parties are assigned to work efforts and not just persons.

Party Skill and Skill Type

When scheduling these assignments, managers need to know the qualifications of prospective parties. This can be handled using the PARTY SKILL and SKILL TYPE entities. PARTY SKILL contains a list of parties, skill types, years of experience, and a skill rating. Table 6.8 contains sample data.

As indicated by the data, skills are associated not only with people but with companies as well (this is why the entity is PARTY SKILL, not PERSON SKILL).

Table 6.8   Party Skill Data

PARTY	SKILL TYPE	YEARS OF EXPERIENCE	RATING
John Smith	Project management	20	10
	Marketing	5	6
Dick Jones	Project management	12	8
USA Consulting	Market research	25	10
	Sales analysis	15	7
	Data warehousing	5	5

This information could be vital to project managers who are staffing new efforts. If no people within the enterprise are available for use, the manager can evaluate outside agencies for their ability to support the effort in question. Additionally, for people who have not already been allocated, this information can be used to determine appropriate work effort assignments. **Years experience** tells how many years that the person or organization has been involved in this skill. It may seem that this is derivable data from the start date that one started using a skill; however, skills are often used on and off within a time frame, and often the data in this attribute is subjective. The **rating** indicates how proficient the party is in the skill, and this may also be subjective.

Work Effort Status

Another required piece of information is the status of the work effort. It is through the association to WORK EFFORT STATUS that the status for WORK EFFORT is maintained. The status of the work effort may have an effect on the REQUIREMENT STATUS (see Figure 4.9); however, they may also be independent of each other. For instance, a status of "completed" on the work efforts required to implement a requirement may lead to the requirement having a status of "fulfilled." They, however, may have different unrelated statuses, such as the requirement having a status of "approved" and the work effort having a status of "in progress."

Some example data for work effort statuses is provided in Table 6.9.

Based on this data, the status for any level of the work effort may be available. A manager could see that the work effort is still in progress, that three of the four activities have been completed, and that the last activity of quality assuring the goods has not yet been completed. Because there are many statuses for any work effort, the data can also show when work efforts were started, completed, or underwent any other status at any point in time.

Work Effort Party Assignment

This entity allows a WORK EFFORT to be assigned to one or more PARTYs in order to allow different roles or just allow many people to be assigned in order to accomplish the effort faster. If desired, an enterprise could put in place business rules that require parties to be assigned at the top level of the effort—for example, the overall project—in order to be assigned to lower levels of responsibility. For this reason, a **scheduled start date** and **scheduled completion date** are included as attributes of the work effort in order to schedule parties or record what actually occurred in terms of their assignment. For instance, a person may be assigned to a work effort, and then the dates of the scheduled assignment may change until the person is actually working on the effort. The **scheduled completion date** is optional to handle such things as ongoing ser-

Table 6.9 Work Effort Statuses

WORK EFFORT ID	WORK EFFORT SUBTYPE	WORK EFFORT DESCRIPTION	ASSOCIATED WORK EFFORT(S) ID AND DESCRIPTION	SCHEDULED START DATE	SCHEDULED END DATE	WORK EFFORT STATUS
28045	Job	Production run #1		Jun 1, 2000	Jun 4, 2000	In progress
120001	Activity	Set up production line	28045 Production run #1 51245 Production run #2	Jun 1, 2000	Jun 2, 2000	Started Jun 2 2000, 1PM Completed June 2, 2000 2PM
120002	Activity	Operate machinery	28045 Production run #1	Jun 3, 2000	Jun 3, 2000	Started Jun 3 2000 1 PM Completed Jun 3 2000 4PM
120003	Activity	Clean up machinery	28045 Production Run #1	Jun 4, 2000	Jun 4, 2000	Started Jun 4, 9AM Completed June 4 10AM
120004	Activity	Quality assure goods produced	28045 Production run #1	Jun 3, 2000	Jun 4, 2000	Pending

vice contracts or people who are assigned indefinitely to an effort until they are notified otherwise. Because an enterprise may also wish to track such things as assignment extensions, the **from date** is also included in the primary key of WORK EFFORT PARTY ASSIGNMENT, allowing more than one assignment for the same PARTY and WORK EFFORT.

Work Effort Role Type

Because many parties could be assigned to a single effort, some other information that may be important to track would be the role a particular party plays in a work effort. This is tracked by selecting the appropriate WORK EFFORT ROLE from the entity WORK EFFORT ROLE TYPE and assigning this role to a particular PARTY. This information is especially useful when one party fills multiple roles, as is often the case, or for identifying who does what on a task that requires a team of people. Possible roles could be "supervisor," "analyst," "laborer," "quality assurer," or "contractor."

Work Effort Assignment Facility

The relationship from WORK EFFORT PARTY ASSIGNMENT to FACILITY appears even though each work effort (and their sub-work efforts) may also be related to a facility. Why is that? This optional relationship is there to handle efforts that must be completed in what is now a very mobile society. With the increase in telecommuting, there is no longer any assurance, or requirement, that a particular work effort or part of a work effort must always be in a particular location. Take, for example, the task of building a complex data warehouse model for a large corporation. This task could involve many data modelers as well as business analysts. It is entirely conceivable that they could all work remotely from home offices, communicating with each other and the client via fax, e-mail, and voice mail. In this case, the facility that each individual is using is associated with the individuals assigned to the work effort.

Instead of a relationship to FACILITY, should the CONTACT MECHANISM for that party be used as the location for the WORK EFFORT PARTY ASSIGN-MENT? It may very well be that only a postal address or e-mail address is known for that party. If the FACILITY of the assignment is sometimes not known, the CONTACT MECHANISM could be added as another relationship to the WORK EFFORT PARTY ASSIGNMENT.

For WORK EFFORTs that have no location recorded for them, it is assumed that they occur at the facility associated with the parent WORK EFFORT or that the location is immaterial.

Work Effort Time Tracking

Tracking time entries is critical to many organizations, and a model for this is shown in Figure 6.6. The TIME ENTRY entity is, of course, very important for payroll, but it is also important for task tracking, cost determination, and perhaps client billing. This entity quite simply holds information about how much time was spent during a given period on various WORK EFFORTs. Included in this information are the **from datetime**, **thru datetime**, and the **hours** worked in order to capture the time frame and amount of hours worked. Each TIME ENTRY may be part of a TIMESHEET that may record many time entries. Each TIME ENTRY may be for a particular WORKER, which is a PARTY ROLE, namely anyone who performs work, and may be an EMPLOYEE or a CONTRAC-TOR. Each TIMESHEET may have several other PARTYs in various TIME-SHEET ROLEs categorized by TIMESHEET ROLE TYPEs such as "approver," "manager," "enterer."

The model shows that each WORKER may be **submitting** many TIME-SHEETs over time, which are each **composed of** TIME ENTRYs for a particular

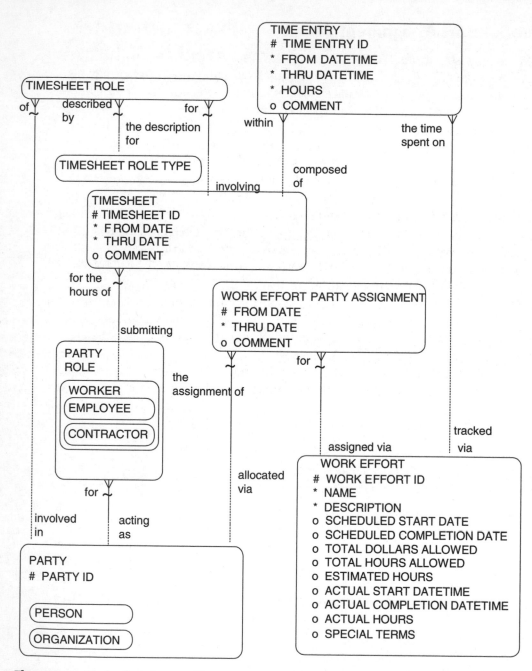

Figure 6.6 Work effort time tracking.

period of time. Each TIME ENTRY is **within** a TIMESHEET and also tied back to a WORK EFFORT, which determines the effort to which time is charged.

Why not relate the TIME ENTRY to a WORK EFFORT PARTY ASSIGNMENT, as the time entry must be attributed to a PARTY that is assigned to a WORK EFFORT? The reason that TIME ENTRYs are not directly related to WORK EFFORT PARTY ASSIGNMENTs is that this would result in redundantly storing the PARTY of the time entry. The PARTY of the time entry is already identified, as a TIME ENTRY is **within** a TIMESHEET **for the hours of** a WORKER, which must be **for** a PARTY.

If other units of measures are needed for time entries aside from **hours**, such as the number of days, then instead of an **hours** attribute, the attribute should be **quantity** with a relationship to UNIT OF MEASURE.

Table 6.10 contains sample time entry data. Dick Jones submitted a timesheet covering the period of January 1, 2001 to January 15, 2001. He had two time entries to develop a plan and to identify potential team members. The first task was worked on from January 2 to January 4, and 13 hours were worked; the second was from January 5 to January 6, and 7 hours were used. John Smith had two time entries totaling 36 hours on one timesheet, consisting of two time entries for the February 1–February 16 period and another 45 hours for the next time period for one of the same tasks, "Conduct Initial Interviews." Depending on how granular time entries are, there may be several time entries for the same work effort and even within the same time period. For instance, if time entries were recorded each day, there may have been several time entries for "Conduct Initial Interviews" for John Smith, one time entry for each day.

Work Effort Rates

In addition to tracking time, many applications need to track the rate and/or cost of the work effort. If the work effort is for professional services that will be billed, then it is very important to track the rate that will be charged for the effort. Alternatively, there may be a cost of doing work, for instance, to establish the cost of performing various business operations.

Figure 6.7 shows a model to capture the rates and/or costs associated with work efforts. Rates and costs may be based on three factors: the rate/cost established for a particular party, the rate/cost established for a certain type of position (the position of "assembly line worker" may have a standard rate), or the rate/cost established for the work effort assignment.

There may be more than one rate/cost for each of these factors because the rates/costs may change over time. Therefore, each WORK EFFORT PARTY ASSIGNMENT may have many WORK EFFORT ASSIGNMENT RATEs (over time). Also, because sometimes rates are established by the person or organization conducting the effort (John Smith's rate is $180 per hour), each PARTY

Table 6.10 Timesheet and Time Entry Data

TIMESHEET ID	TIME SHEET FROM DATE	TIME SHEET THRU DATE	PARTY	WORK EFFORT ID	TIME ENTRY FROM DATETIME	TIME ENTRY THRU DATETIME	HOURS
1390	Jan 1, 2001	Jan 15, 2001	Dick Jones	29000 Develop project plan (part of effort 39409)	Jan 2, 2001	Jan 4, 2001	13
				29005 Identify potential team members for project	Jan 5, 2001	Jan 6, 2001	7
1200	Feb 1, 2001	Feb 15, 2001	John Smith	29003 Conduct initial interviews	Feb 1, 2001	Feb 5, 2001	30
				294395 Facilitate monthly goals Session	Feb 6, 2001	Feb 6, 2001	6
1450	Feb 16, 2001	Mar 1, 2001	John Smith	29003 Conduct initial interviews	Feb 16, 2001	Mar 1, 2001	45

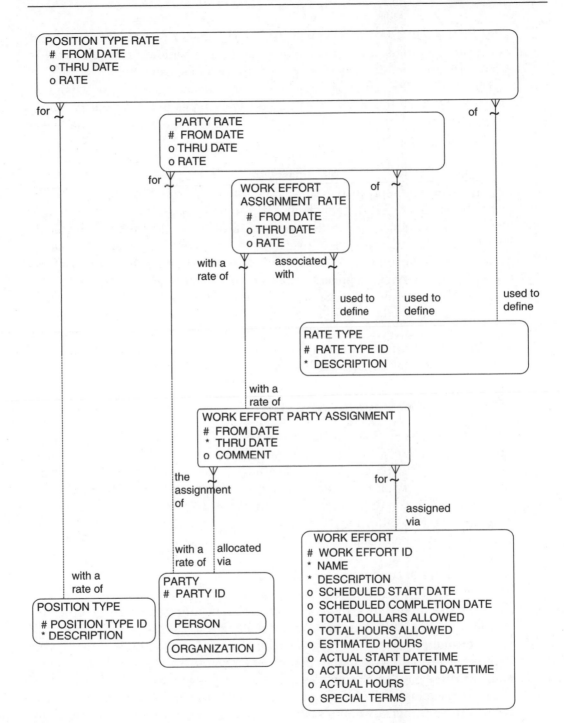

Figure 6.7 Work effort rates.

(PERSON or ORGANIZATION) may have many PARTY RATEs over time. And because many times a position dictates the rate (a senior consultant's rate is $250 per hour) each POSITION may have several rates over time.

The RATE TYPE entity provides the ability to classify the various types of rates to allow the flexibility to capture different types of rates such as billing rates, payroll rates (amount that needs to be paid to the worker), costs, overtime rates, and so on.

Each RATE entity may store a rate, overtime rate, cost, or other type of rate depending on the needs of the organization. The RATE TYPE would indicate which rate is being specified. A RATE TYPE **description** of "billing rate" establishes how much is billed and whether it is to be billed to an external or internal organization. A RATE TYPE **description** of "cost" determines how much will be used as the cost basis to calculate how much the work is costing. Depending on the application, either or both of these are needed. For instance, a professional services application may store both because it needs to know its cost for the professional as well as the rate charges to the client. A manufacturing firm may need to store the cost of the people who are assembling a product, and it may or may not need the rate attribute. For instance it may want to track rates to establish how much to charge another part of the organization (this would be an internal transaction for accounting purposes).

Work Effort Assignment Rate

The entity WORK EFFORT ASSIGNMENT RATE is used to record the rates and/or costs charged to a particular party working on a work effort (WORK EFFORT PARTY ASSIGNMENT). The rate or cost may come from the rate assigned to a party or a position, or it may be maintained for the specific work effort, depending on the enterprise's business rules. The entity has a **from date** and **thru date** to allow for the recording of multiple rates for an assignment over time. The relationship to RATE TYPE provides the ability to record various kinds of rates against an assignment such as for billing rates, costs, regular time, overtime, second shift, third shift, and so on.

Table 6.11 shows examples of rate data.

As the example shows, there are four different rate types recorded for Mr. Smith: "regular billing" rate, an "overtime billing" rate, a "regular pay" rate, and an "overtime pay" rate. The "regular billing" and "overtime billing" rate types determine how much to charge clients for Gary Smith's time. The "regular pay" and "overtime pay" determine how much to pay Gary Smith.

These rates may have been determined for that work effort, they may have been derived from Gary Smith's normal rate,they may have been derived from Gary Smith's position in the organization, or they may have been derived from a combination of these factors. Using the information for the billing rates, it would be easy to calculate how much to charge the client for Gary Smith's time,

Table 6.11   Work Effort Rate Data

WORK TASK	PARTY	RATE TYPE	FROM DATE	THRU DATE	RATE
Develop Gary Smith accounting program		Regular billing	May 15, 2000	May 14, 2001	$65.00
		Overtime billing	May 15, 2000	May 14, 2001	$70.00
		Regular pay	May 15, 2000	May 14, 2001	$40.00
		Overtime pay	May 15, 2000	May 14, 2001	$43.00
		Regular pay	May 15, 2001		$45.00
		Overtime pay	May 15, 2001		$45.00

or pay Gary Smith, by multiplying his hours from the TIME ENTRY times the appropriate rate type.

Note that business rules need to be in place to ensure that the rates used are for the same time period as the hours being charged for. There are also business rules needed to determine what rate should be used if more than one rate applies—for example, if Gary Smith has rates for his position, for him and for his work effort party assignment. Also there is a need to put business rules in place to determine what constitutes overtime work.

Notice also in the table that Mr. Smith has an increase in pay rate recorded to be effective on May 15, 2001. There is no **thru date.** This indicates that the rate will be good until the end of the assignment. Also, note that the "overtime pay" is the same as the "regular pay" after the increase occurs. This would indicate that the enterprise may have automated rules on when to pay overtime, but in this case Mr. Smith no longer gets a higher rate. By recording the second rate, the payroll process that calculates his check does not need to be changed; it will simply calculate his overtime pay as always, but it effectively is at the same rate.

Inventory Assignments

In order to complete certain work efforts, raw materials or other items may be required. Figure 6.8 shows the intersection entity WORK EFFORT INVENTORY ASSIGNMENT between WORK EFFORT and INVENTORY ITEM. This tracks the actual use of inventory during the execution of a work effort. Table 6.12 shows the data that might be associated with assembling pencil components, which is a task (a type of work effort) within a larger work effort to produce 100 pencils.

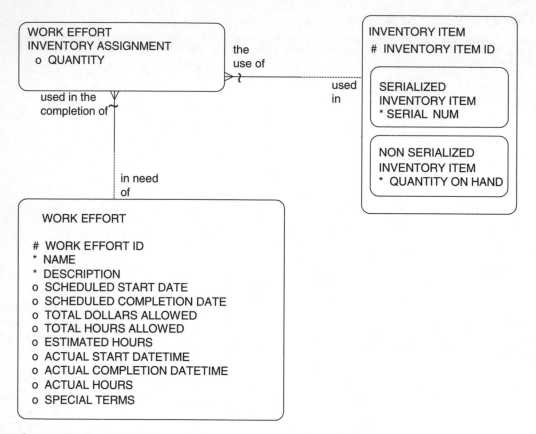

Figure 6.8 Inventory assignments.

As indicated by the data shown, this one task (assemble pencil components) used three different items from inventory to be completed. For each item used, a quantity of 100 was used. When this work effort uses inventory, business processes need to be in place to ensure that the inventory information is updated to reflect the depletion from inventory.

Table 6.12 Inventory Assignment

WORK EFFORT	INVENTORY ITEM	QUANTITY
Assemble pencil components	Pencil cartridges	100
Assemble pencil components	Erasers	100
Assemble pencil components	Labels	100

Fixed Asset Assignments

As with inventory, some work efforts will require various pieces of equipment, machinery, vehicles, or property in order to be completed. These are called FIXED ASSETS in this model (see Figure 6.9). This entity shows several subtypes of interest: PROPERTY, VEHICLE, EQUIPMENT, and OTHER FIXED ASSETs. In addition, other asset types may be identified within the entity FIXED ASSET TYPE. In order to track when and for what an asset is being used, the

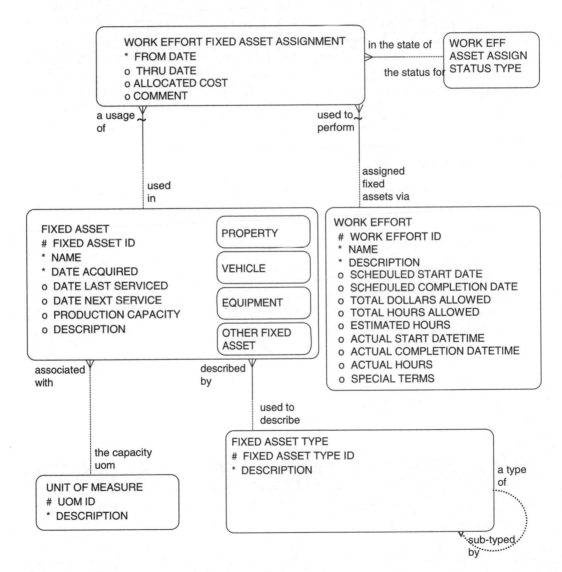

Figure 6.9 Fixed asset assignments.

model includes the entity WORK EFFORT FIXED ASSET ASSIGNMENT. To further establish the state of the assignment, a reference to WORK EFF ASSET ASSIGNSTATUS TYPE is used.

Fixed Asset

Other information stored in FIXED ASSET that may be of interest to an enterprise includes the **asset ID**, a **name** for identification, **date acquired,** which was established when the asset was acquired (important for depreciation, which is discussed in Chapter 8, Figure 8.5), **date last serviced,** which may not be needed if this can be derived from maintenance records (which are work efforts), and **date next service,** which is when the next service is scheduled. The **production capacity** maintains a value for the asset's production capabilities and a relationship to UNIT OF MEASURE, that allows this capacity to be maintained in various measurements such as the number of units that can be produced per day. Examples of data that could be found in FIXED ASSET are shown in Table 6.13.

Fixed Asset Type

Of course, many kinds of assets may be important to an enterprise for various reasons. These can be listed using the FIXED ASSET TYPE entity. Notice that there is a recursive relationship on this entity. This relationship allows for the detailed breakdown of the various asset types. As an example, take the fixed asset type of "equipment." The information that a given asset is a piece of equipment is probably not enough in some cases. It would be nice to know what kind of equipment it is, should it be needed for a work effort. In the same manner, it might be good to know that a "vehicle" is a "minivan" and that the "minivan" is actually a "Ford Aerostar." Table 6.14 shows sample data for this entity.

In the examples, there arc three asset types ("pencil making machine," "pen making machine," "paper making machine") that roll up to a type of "equipment." In addition, there are several types of vehicles, "truck," "fork lift," "jet," and "car," that roll up to "vehicle." Then there is the type "Mac Truck-18

Table 6.13 Fixed Asset Data

FIXED ASSET ID	ASSET TYPE	NAME	DATE ACQUIRED	DATE LAST SERVICED	DATE NEXT SERVICE	PRODUCTION CAPACITY	UOM
1000	Pencil-making machine	Pencil labeler #1	Jun 12, 2000	Jun 12, 2000	Jun 12, 2001	1,000,000	Pens/day
2266	Fork lift	Fork lift #25	Mar 1, 1999	Mar 15, 2001	Aug 1, 2001	5	People

Table 6.14 Fixed Asset Type Data

FIXED ASSET TYPE ID	DESCRIPTION	PARENT ASSET TYPE
1000	Equipment	
1390	Pencil-making machine	Equipment
1458	Pen-making machine	Equipment
1532	Paper-making machine	Equipment
2000	Vehicle	
2019	Truck	Vehicle
2188	Mac truck-18 wheels	Truck
2266	Fork lift	Vehicle
2356	Jet airplane	Vehicle
2567	Car	Vehicle

wheels," which is a type of "truck," which is a type of "vehicle." All of these are asset types. This model is flexible enough to allow as much detail as needed.

Fixed Asset Assignment and Status

Because a machine or piece of equipment can usually be used only for one effort at a time, it is necessary to tell what is being used and when it is in use. Figure 6.9 shows the model for tracking this information. In it there is the WORK EFFORT FIXED ASSET ASSIGNMENT entity, which is at the intersection of WORK EFFORT and FIXED ASSET. In this entity are attributes for storing the start and end date for the assignment, which are the **from date** and **thru dates**. These will be very important for task scheduling purposes. In addition, there is a relationship to WORK EFF ASSET ASSIGN STATUS TYPE. The status type will indicate such things as whether the assignment is "requested" or "assigned." The **allocated cost** attribute provides a record of how much cost was recorded to that work effort for the usage of that fixed asset. This information would be important to capture the costs incurred during any work efforts for usage of fixed assets.

Table 6.15 gives some examples.

Note that the from and thru dates for the assignment may not be the same as the **scheduled start date** and **scheduled completion date** on the WORK EFFORT. A certain machine may be needed only for part of the work effort's life cycle. Business rules (or database constraints) need to be in place, however, to ensure that the equipment assignment is at least within the scheduled date range for the associated effort.

Table 6.15 Fixed Asset Assignment Data

WORK EFFORT	FIXED ASSET	FROM DATE	THRU DATE	COMMENT
Label pencils	Pencil labeler #1	Jun 12, 2000	Jun 15, 2000	
Move raw materials in place for production run	Fork lift #25	Apr 15, 2000	May 15, 2000	May need for longer time
Test database tool	Office laptop #2	Jul 1, 2000		Ongoing effort

Party Fixed Asset Assignments

Besides being assigned to work efforts, assets can be assigned or *checked out* to a PARTY. During this time, it is not uncommon to hold the party responsible for the safekeeping or use of the asset in question. This association is depicted in Figure 6.9. Again, an intersection called PARTY FIXED ASSET ASSIGNMENT joins information from PARTY and FIXED ASSET (see Figure 6.10). Also related to this entity is PARTY ASSET ASSIGN STATUS TYPE, which provides additional information about the assignment. Sample data is provided in Table 6.16.

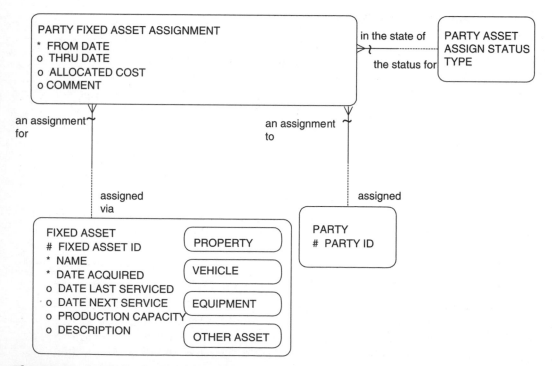

Figure 6.10 Party fixed asset assignments.

Table 6.16   Party Fixed Asset Assignment Data

PARTY	FIXED ASSET	START DATE	END DATE	STATUS
John Smith	Car#25	Jan 1, 2000	Jan 1, 2001	Active
Dick Jones	Tool set #5	Mar 15, 2000	Mar 15, 2000	Lost

Assignment data like this provides the enterprise with vital information for tracking the condition and whereabouts of its assets. In this case, the enterprise knows that John Smith has the truck known as "Truck #25" until January 1, 2001, so if they need to give someone else a car, they know that this car is not available. The data also shows that Dick Jones was assigned a particular tool set and that he lost it.

Work Effort Type Standards

In order to facilitate planning, this model includes additional entities to record various standards regarding different *types* of work efforts for the purposes of planning (see Figure 6.11). This data model provides information about what types of skills, what goods, and what types of fixed assets are needed for various types of work efforts. These metrics can be used to predict the resources needed for the scheduled work efforts, so that the organization can properly prepare.

Figure 6.11 shows the standards that apply to each WORK EFFORT TYPE. Each WORK EFFORT TYPE may have standards regarding the types of skills that are generally needed to accomplish the effort (WORK EFFORT SKILL STANDARD), the type of goods or parts that are needed within the work effort (WORK EFFORT GOOD STANDARD), and the types of fixed assets needed to accomplish the work effort (WORK EFFORT FIXED ASSET STANDARD). These standards would need to be determined by the enterprise and entered using these structures. This information can then be used for scheduling resources and estimating time and costs for each work effort. Additionally it can be used to compare actual skills, goods, and fixed asset usage against the standards.

Each of these standards entities has attributes that define expected needs for that type of work effort. The WORK EFFORT SKILL STANDARD maintains the **estimated num people,** which records how many people of that skill type are typically needed for that type of work effort. The **estimated duration** records how long the skill is needed for the work effort type. The **estimated cost** is an estimation of how much this type of skill will cost for the associated work effort type.

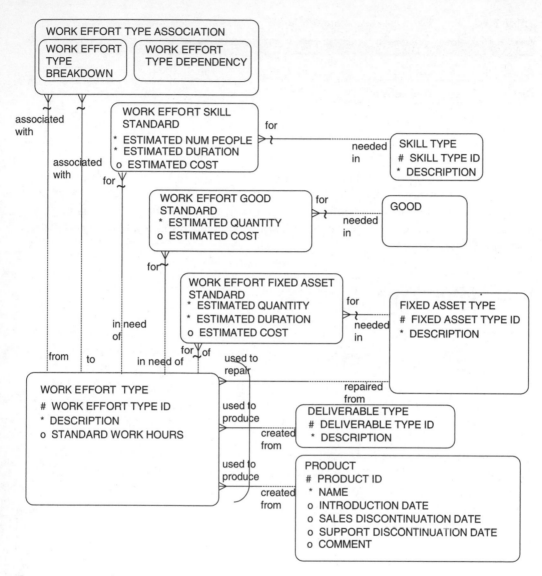

Figure 6.11 Work effort type standards.

The WORK EFFORT GOOD STANDARD maintains an **estimated quantity** attribute, maintaining how many of each GOOD is typically needed, and an **estimated cost** attribute, maintaining the estimated cost that is expected for that type of work effort.

The WORK EFFORT FIXED ASSET STANDARD maintains an **estimated quantity** attribute to determine how many of the fixed assets are needed for the work effort type. The **estimated duration** maintains how long that fixed asset is typically needed for the work effort type. The **estimated cost** maintains the anticipated cost for that type of work effort.

Similarly to WORK EFFORTs, each WORK EFFORT TYPE has associated WORK EFFORT TYPEs that represent the standard WORK EFFORT TYPE BREAKDOWNs and WORK EFFORT TYPE DEPENDENCYs. These represent the standard types of efforts that normally make up a larger type of work effort as well as the standard dependencies that occur.

Figure 6.10 also shows that each WORK EFFORT TYPE may be characterized by the fact that it is used to repair a FIXED ASSET TYPE or to produce a certain DELIVERABLE or a certain PRODUCT.

Work Effort Skill Standards

The WORK EFFORT SKILL STANDARD entity provides the enterprise with information on how many people are needed with what skills, for how long, and what are the estimated costs. For a "large production run of pencils" there may be a skill of "foreman" for three hours with a cost of $100 as well as a skill of "assembly line worker" for three people for three hours each with a cost of $200.

Work Effort Good Standards

The WORK EFFORT GOOD STANDARD entity relates WORK EFFORT TYPEs to the GOODs that are typically needed for that work effort. If the PARTs model is used (Figure 2.10b), the entity PART would be substituted for GOOD. The entity includes an attribute for the **estimated quantity** required and an attribute for **estimated cost**. This information can be used for ensuring that enough of those goods exist in inventory to execute a particular work effort. Table 6.17 contains sample data for this entity.

Note that the relationship is to GOOD, not INVENTORY ITEM. Because this information is for planning, it is necessary to know only the *type* of GOOD needed. There is no need to locate an actual inventory item in stock. If, in examining this information, it is determined that for a planned WORK EFFORT, the WORK EFFORT TYPE will require more of a GOOD than is currently in inven-

Table 6.17 Work Effort Good Standard Data

WORK EFFORT TYPE	ITEM	ESTIMATED QUANTITY	ESTIMATED COST
Large production run of pencils	Erasers	1,000	$2,500
	Labels	1,000	$2,000
Large production run of pens	Ink cartridges	2,000	$3,000

tory, then the enterprise will know that it needs to reorder that good in order to complete the planned effort.

Another point to note is that not all WORK EFFORT TYPES will have inventory requirements. For example, a work effort type of "prepare project plan," which is a work effort associated with providing service as opposed to creating products, would not have any inventory requirements.

An alternative to this model for manufacturing firms and other firms that deal heavily with bill of materials, is to change the relationship to PART instead of GOOD and distinguish PARTs from GOODs. This is an option in many parts of the data models, and it is discussed in more detail in Volume 2, Chapter 2.

Work Effort Fixed Asset Standard

In a similar manner, WORK EFFORT FIXED ASSET REQUIREMENT will provide information for the scheduling and assignment of types of fixed assets. Other information carried by this entity includes the **estimated quantity** of the type of fixed asset needed, the **estimated duration** amount of time the fixed assets will be used in the execution of this WORK EFFORT TYPE and the **estimated cost**. Examples of this data are given in Table 6.18.

Work Effort Results

Finally, it is important to document the results of the work effort. The data model in Figure 6.12 shows the entities and relationships needed to maintain this information. While the WORK EFFORT TYPE maintained what the WORK EFFORT standards showing what should have been produced, it is important to capture what was actually produced as a result of the WORK EFFORT.

The model in Figure 6.12 shows that each WORK EFFORT may result in the production of one or more DELIVERABLEs via the WORK EFFORT DELIVERABLE PRODUCED; it may result in the repair of a FIXED ASSET; or it may result in production of one or more INVENTORY ITEMs via the WORK EFFORT INVENTORY PRODUCED entity.

Keep in mind that the relationships to these entities should be maintained at lower levels of the WORK EFFORT instances. This allows the deliverables,

Table 6.18 Work Effort Fixed Asset Requirement Data

WORK EFFORT TYPE	FIXED ASSET TYPE	ESTIMATED QUANTITY	ESTIMATED DURATION
Large production run of pencils	Pencil labeler	1	10 days
	Fork lift	2	5 days

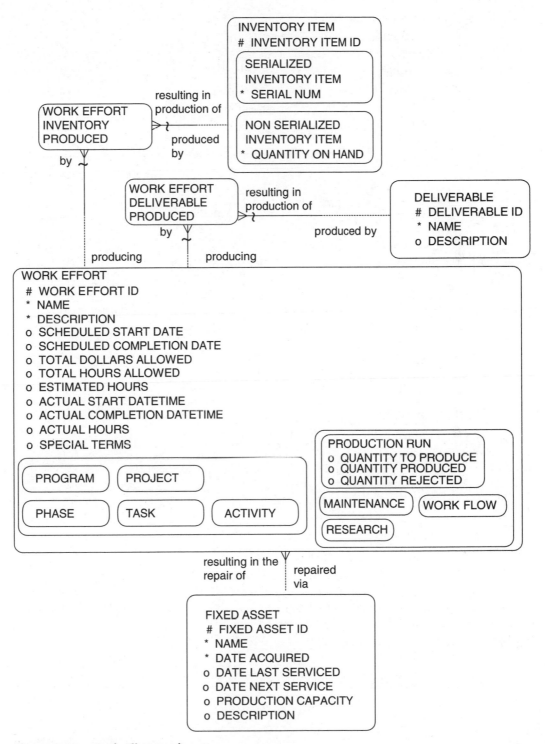

Figure 6.12 Work effort results.

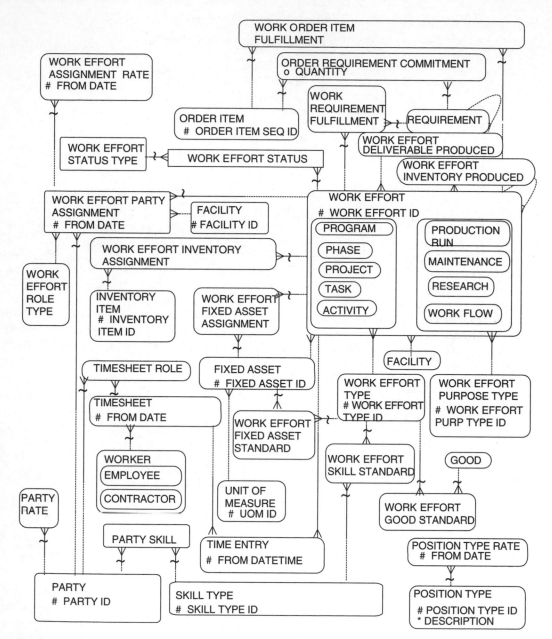

Figure 6.13   Overall work effort model.

inventory items produced, and fixed assets repaired to be rolled up to see the total results for an overall work effort such as an entire project.

Summary

The details of the data model in this chapter involve the requirement for work efforts, creation of work efforts, scheduling of resources, and completion of work efforts (see Figure 6.13). Included are the complete breakdown of work efforts to other work efforts and the tracking of assignments of people, fixed assets, and inventory necessary for the completion of the tasks. Incorporated into the model as well are the entities needed to record the standards associated with type of work efforts as well as the actual results from work efforts.

With this data model, enterprises should be able to effectively maintain lists of ongoing efforts and the various resources that are available or already assigned to the completion of these efforts. The availability of this information could be critical to the continued success and development of the enterprise; it is therefore of importance and needs to be included in the overall corporate model.

Please refer to Appendix A for a listing of entities and attributes. SQL scripts to build tables and columns derived from the logical models in this book can be found on the full-blown CD-ROM, which is licensed separately.

CHAPTER 7

Invoicing

Ensuring that payment occurs is critical for organizations. Now that items have been ordered, shipped, or delivered in some fashion, it is critical for the enterprise to make sure that it requests payments; this is often done through invoices. It is important to send out correct invoices that correspond to the appropriate orders, shipments, or work efforts. The enterprise needs to set up systems that facilitate getting paid, and this could involve setting up appropriate billing accounts; matching invoices to orders, billing for shipments, invoicing for work efforts; sending out invoices; tracking payments against invoices; recording deposits, and issuing statements.

Questions that enterprises need to know about invoicing include the following:

- How does each invoice relate to orders, shipments, and/or work efforts?
- What are the products, features, and other charges for which payments are due?
- Who owes how much to whom?
- What is the status of each invoice?
- What is the payment history of each party?

Models discussed in this chapter are as follows:

- Invoice and invoice items (alternate model also provided)
- Invoice roles
- Invoice billing account
- Invoice specific roles
- Invoice status and terms
- Billing for shipment items
- Invoicing of work efforts and time entries
- Billing for order items
- Invoice payments (alternate model also provided)
- Financial accounts, withdrawals, and deposits

Invoices and Invoice Items

Invoices, like shipments and orders, may have many items showing the detailed information about the goods or services that are charged to parties. The items on an invoice may be for products, features, work efforts, time entries, or adjustments such as sales tax, shipping and handling charges, fees, and so on.

Figure 7.1a provides a data model with some of the key entities for invoicing. Each INVOICE is composed of INVOICE ITEMs that represent any items that are being charged. The INVOICE maintains header information about the transaction, and the INVOICE ITEM maintains the details of each item that is being charged. Each INVOICE ITEM may have a many-to-one relationship to either PRODUCT or PRODUCT FEATURE. The INVOICE ITEM may also be related to a SERIALIZED INVENTORY ITEM because maintaining the actual instance of the product that was bought with its serial number may be useful. For instance, computer manufacturers often record the serial number of the computer that was bought and invoiced.

Because INVOICE ITEMs do not relate only to products (i.e., they also relate to work efforts, time entries) other relationships to other entities will be covered later in this chapter. If the item represents a one-time charge item that is not catalogued, then the **item description** attribute within the INVOICE entity may be used to record what was charged. Each INVOICE ITEM may be categorized by an INVOICE ITEM TYPE, which could include values such as "invoice adjustment," "invoice item adjustment," "invoice product item," "invoice product feature item," "invoice work effort item," or "invoice time entry item." Each INVOICE ITEM has a recursive relationship as it may be adjusted by one or more other INVOICE ITEMs, which would be of INVOICE ITEM TYPE "invoice

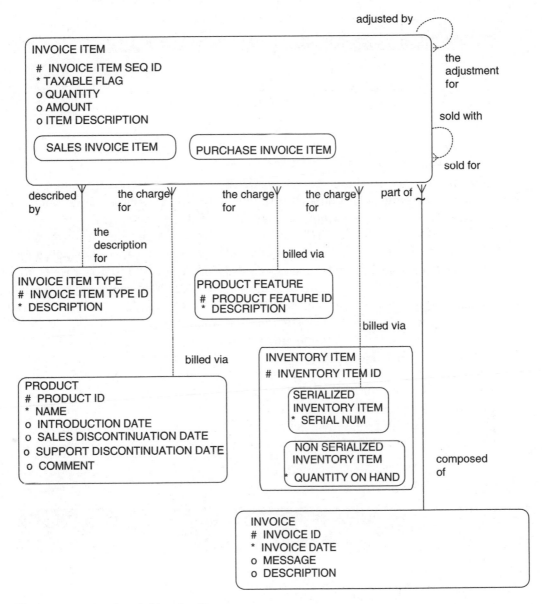

Figure 7.1a   Invoice and invoice items.

item adjustment." Each INVOICE ITEM may also be sold with other INVOICE ITEMs that would be of type "invoice product feature item."

As with shipments, many things are needed in order to send a correct bill to customers. The first thing to record about the invoice (besides a unique identifier) is the invoice creation date or **invoice date**. This will be an important

Table 7.1 Invoice Data

INVOICE ID	INVOICE DATE	MESSAGE	DESCRIPTION
30002	May 25, 2001		Fulfillment of office supply order
30005	June 5, 2001	Thanks for the business!	

piece of information used in tracking the progress of the invoice when a client calls to discuss his or her bill. Some systems may want to include a specific note or message to the customer on the invoice, so the model includes the attribute **message**. The **description** attribute describes the nature of the invoice. Table 7.1 shows sample data for the INVOICE entity.

Because each INVOICE ITEM may be for a product, product feature, work effort, or time entry or because it may be described via an **item description** for non-standard items, the relationships to PRODUCT and PRODUCT FEATURE are both optional. When features are shown in invoice items, the recursive relationship **sold with** should be recorded in order to indicate that the feature was invoiced for a specific invoice item that was for a product. The quantity is optional because there may only be an **amount** and not a **quantity** for items such as features where the quantity really isn't necessary and is not applicable.

Instead of tying an INVOICE ITEM recursively to another INVOICE ITEM to record the feature for a product, why not just record both the product and feature on an invoice item? This would not account for invoices that have the same product on two different invoice items. For instance, if an organization bought two different computer servers with different features on each, it would be

Table 7.2 Invoice Item Data

INVOICE ID	INVOICE ITEM SEQ ID	PRODUCT	PRODUCT FEATURE	SOLD WITH	QUANTITY	AMOUNT	TAXABLE FLAG?
30002	1	Johnson fine grade 8½ by 11 bond paper			10	$8.00	Y
	2		Product quality, Extra glossy finish	Invoice 30002, Seq ID 1		$2.00	Y
	3	Goldstein Elite pens			4	$12.00	Y
	4	HD 3½-inch diskettes			6	$7.00	Y

important to record which combination of features corresponded with which specific products. What if a feature was later added (and invoiced) on an existing product that the customer already has? The invoice item could be related to the initial invoice item that had the product charge.

Table 7.2 provides an example invoice with four items being charged, three for products and one for the feature of special glossy paper for the Johnson fine grade 8½ by 11 bond paper. The second item, which is for extra glossy finish for the Johnson fine grade 8½ by 11 bond paper, includes a recursive relationship to the invoice item for the product in order to show that the item is for a feature within the context of a product.

In addition to the invoice ID and product or feature, the details include the **quantity** of items being billed, the amount, and whether this is a taxable item through the **taxable flag** attribute. Note that product-specific information, such as unit of measure for the quantity, can be derived through the relationship from PRODUCT to UNIT OF MEASURE (see Chapter 3 for more on product definition). Also, notice that the extended price for the item is not an attribute because this is derivable information.

The **taxable flag** is stored on the invoice item to signify if the item is to be taxed. This cannot always be determined by the item being invoiced because the taxability of an item could vary depending on many circumstances, such as the source and destination of the shipment or the tax status of the purchasing organization. The information needed to calculate taxes is not included in this model because it is highly dependent on the rules and regulations of each geographic boundary.

Other information that enterprises may want to know about an invoice include adjustments to the invoice such as the total tax (after it is calculated), freight charges, and handling charges. Each adjustment is stored as an instance of INVOICE ITEM because these are also charged items. Why was ORDER ADJUSTMENT a separate entity in the order chapter, but invoices include adjustments as instances of an INVOICE ITEM? The reason is that when parties order something, they do not request adjustments such as sales tax, fees, handling charges, and so on. These adjustments are recorded as ORDER ADJUSTMENTs in order to maintain potential expected charges; however, they are still not "ordered items." INVOICE ITEMs represent charges that are incurred, and these adjustments are included in this definition.

The INVOICE ITEM TYPE could include different types of adjustments such as "miscellaneous charge," "sales tax," "discount adjustment," "shipping and handling charges," "surcharge adjustment," and "fee." If needed, a **percentage** attribute could be added to the INVOICE ITEM to store the percentage of the adjustment, such as .07 for sales tax.

Table 7.3 contains examples of adjustment data for an invoice.

Using this structure, an enterprise can include any number of adjustments to an invoice that could be of many different types. This is much more flexible

Table 7.3   Invoice Item Adjustment Data

INVOICE ID	INVOICE ITEM SEQ ID	INVOICE ITEM TYPE	AMOUNT	TAXABLE?
30002	5	Shipping and handling	$16.00	N
	6	Fee (order processing fee)	$5.00	N
	7	Tax	$25.65	N

than including attributes such as **tax amount** or **freight charge** on the IN-VOICE entity because new attributes would have to be added to the entity if the enterprise discovered that other adjustments needed to be tracked. With this model, the enterprise simply defines new invoice items that may have different INVOICE ITEM TYPEs and then relates additional instances to either the INVOICE or INVOICE ITEM (through a recursive relationship).

Invoice items may be adjusted by other invoice items in another way. For example, suppose there was a mistake in which the quantity of items invoiced was 10 instead of 8, the correct quantity. A future invoice item showing a credit of 2 items could be used to correct the invoice. This correction could be implemented using an INVOICE ITEM with a **quantity** of –2 that related back to the original INVOICE ITEM that had a **quantity** of 10. Many enterprises will show corrections using this approach as opposed to modifying the invoice, which could lead to control and audit issues. The recursive relationship around the INVOICE ITEM provides the information necessary for relating invoice items together.

Figure 7.1b provides an alternative model that more specifically illustrates the subtypes of INVOICE ITEM. The INVOICE ADJUSTMENT shows the various adjustment subtypes, and the INVOICE ACQUIRING ITEM represents the items that the party really got, whether they were a product, feature, work effort, or time. Instead of showing the recursive relationships around INVOICE ITEMs to handle features sold with products or adjustments to invoice items, this model has relationships from INVOICE PRODUCT ITEM to INVOICE PRODUCT FEATURE ITEM as well as from INVOICE ACQUIRING ITEM to INVOICE ADJUSTMENT, which enforce more specific business rules.

Invoice Roles

Of course, enterprises also need to know where to send the invoice and where it came from. Standard models often record only the customer address, and the supplier address is assumed to be the enterprise doing the billing (the "I" model). This model accommodates a more flexible structure for both sales and purchase invoices for a multilocation or multicompany organization.

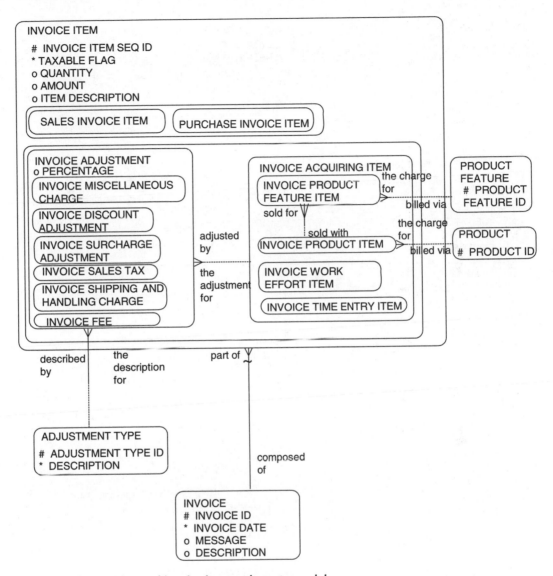

Figure 7.1b   Invoice and invoice items—alternate model.

Figure 7.2 provides a basic data model for the parties involved in the invoice. Each INVOICE may be **billed to** or **billed from** any PARTY, and therefore it may accommodate both incoming (PURCHASE INVOICE) and outgoing invoices (SALES INVOICES). The **billed to** and **billed from** are the two main roles and represent the party owing the money and the party that is requesting payment.

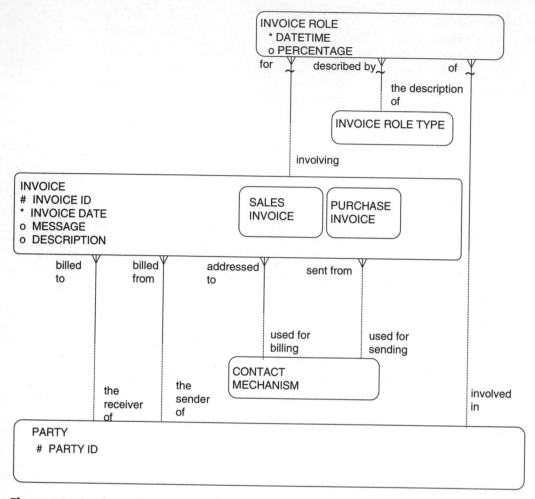

Figure 7.2 Invoice parties.

In addition to these two key roles, additional roles may be involved in the invoice. The additional roles are maintained by the INVOICE ROLE, which records each PARTY involved in each INVOICE ROLE TYPE for an INVOICE. For example, invoice role types may include "entered by," "approver," "sender," and "receiver." The **datetime** attribute indicates the date and time that the person or organization performed the role.

Flexible means of sending and receiving invoices are needed in order to record from where and to where the invoice was sent because there are many ways to send an invoice. Therefore, Figure 7.2 shows that each INVOICE also needs to maintain the CONTACT MECHANISMs to which the invoice is addressed and the CONTACT MECHANISM from which it was sent. This is related to the supertype, CONTACT MECHANISM, because the INVOICE may be sent or received via numerous subtypes of CONTACT MECHANISM including POSTAL ADDRESS, ELECTRONIC ADDRESS, or TELECOMMUNICATIONS NUMBER. In these days of e-commerce, sending an invoice via e-mail, which is a form of ELECTRONIC ADDRESS, is becoming more and more common. An invoice may be faxed, which is a type of TELECOMMUNICATIONS NUMBER. Finally, an invoice could be sent the old-fashioned way, by addressing it via a POSTAL ADDRESS.

Table 7.4 shows example data for the information maintained about the invoice parties.

Notice that invoice #30002 has standard **addressed to** and **sent from** locations, but #30005 is addressed to an Internet e-mail address. In this situation, the invoice is being sent via e-mail (however, the data shows only the physical address of the sender). For invoice #30010, the data indicates that the invoice is being sent from one electronic mail address to another e-mail.

As more and more enterprises and people get online, this type of transaction will become more prevalent; thus, the need for a more flexible data model will become apparent. Current invoicing systems that require a physical address to mail an invoice may become unusable in the future.

The PARTY CONTACT MECHANISM PURPOSE entity (see Chapter 2, Figure 2.10) could be used for additional validation if an enterprise wanted to implement additional business rules to see if the invoice contact mechanism recorded is valid for invoicing purposes. A possible example would be a rule that states that an invoice may be related only to a PARTY CONTACT MECHANISM with a role of "location for receiving invoices."

Billing Account

As shown in Figure 7.3a, there is another way to bill a customer in addition to sending a bill to a PARTY, namely through the use of a BILLING ACCOUNT. This

Table 7.4   Invoice Parties.

INVOICE ID	INVOICE DATE	BILLED TO PARTY	ADDRESSED TO CONTACT MECHANISM	SENDER OF PARTY	SENT FROM CONTACT MECHANISM
30002	May 25, 2001	ACME Corporation	123 Main Street	ABC Subsidiary	100 Bridge Street
30005	June 5, 2001	John Smith	jsmith@us.com	ABC Subsidiary	100 Bridge Street
30010	June 5, 2001	Tom Jones	1235,678@cis.com	ACME Corporation	acorp@ acme.com

method of billing is used only in certain circumstances for specific types of businesses. Therefore, the BILLING ACCOUNT, BILLING ACCOUNT ROLE, and PARTY entities and their associated relationships in Figure 7.3a are optional and are included only if the enterprise has a need to maintain billing accounts.

A BILLING ACCOUNT provides a mechanism for grouping different types of items on different invoices. A client might want one account for his or her office supplies and another account for furniture purchases. A billing account allows customers to receive separate invoices to track different types of items separately. Banks and credit card companies use this concept frequently to allow

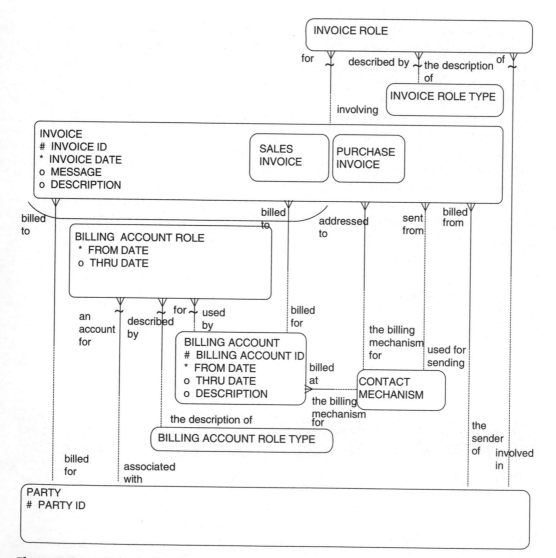

Figure 7.3a Billing account.

separation of various charges for their customers. A telecommunications company may set up separate billing accounts for different telecommunications lines. Perhaps one account is for standard telephone service, while another account is set up for the enterprise's dedicated lines.

Figure 7.3a adds to the previous model shown in Figure 7.2 by providing for invoices that may be sent to a BILLING ACCOUNT as an alternative to sending it directly to a PARTY. Some enterprises may have a need to track more than one party that is responsible for paying an invoice that is sent to a BILLING ACCOUNT. Therefore, the model in Figure 7.3a has an intersection entity called BILLING ACCOUNT ROLE between PARTY and BILLING ACCOUNT, allowing for maintenance of the various parties involved on the account. The BILLING ACCOUNT ROLE allows each PARTY to play a BILLING ACCOUNT ROLE TYPE in the account. Roles could include "primary payer," indicating the main party that is supposed to pay, or "secondary payer," indicating other parties that could pay in case of default. There may be other roles as well, such as "customer service representative," "manager," and "sales representative," that could be involved with the account as well. Other attributes needed on the BILLING ACCOUNT ROLE include the **from date**, which is when the party became active on the account, and the **thru date**, which indicates through when the role is involved.

Each invoice may then be billed to either a BILLING ACCOUNT or directly to a PARTY with this model. The BILLING ACCOUNT has a **from date** (when it became active), a **thru date,** and a **description** identifying the nature of the billing account. In order to determine where to send the invoice, the account in question must, in turn, be related to a CONTACT MECHANISM. Eventually, all invoices must end up at a location of some sort. Also, note that if the enterprise uses billing accounts, the order models in Chapter 4 (Figures 4.3 and 4.5) should include a **with a requested bill to** relationship to the BILLING ACCOUNT entity, with a mutually exclusive arc similar to the arc in the invoicing model.

Table 7.5 provides the example of ACME Corporation setting up an account for its office supplies and a separate account for using consulting services.

Table 7.5 Billing Account Data

BILLING ACCOUNT ID	FROM DATE	THRU DATE	PARTY	BILLING ACCOUNT ROLE	MECHANISM	CONTACT DESCRIPTION
1295	Apr 15, 2000		ACME Corporation	Primary payer	123 Main Street	All charges for office supplies
1296	Apr 15, 2000		ACME Corporation	Primary payer	123 Main Street	All charges for consulting services

Table 7.6 Billing Account with More Than One Party

BILLING ACCOUNT ID	BILLING ACCOUNT ROLE FROM DATE	BILLING ACCOUNT ROLE THRU DATE	PARTY	BILLING ACCOUNT ROLE TYPE
1459	Apr 15, 2000		Jane Smith	Primary payer
1459	Apr 15, 2000	June 15, 2001	John Smith	Secondary payer
1459	June 16, 2001		Joe Smith	Secondary payer

Table 7.6 shows sample data for an account with more than one party assigned to it. The sample data shows a typical situation that could occur for a credit card account, a bank account, a telecommunications account, or a utilities account, possibly with many individuals on it. Initially the account was opened with both Jane and Joe Smith assigned to the account on April 15, 2000. Jane had primary responsibility for paying for the account and if, for some reason, she did not pay, then John would be held accountable in his role as the secondary payer. Then, on June 16, 2001, Joe Smith was added to the account, replacing John Smith as the secondary payer on the account. Because the **thru date** is blank, it can be inferred that both Jane and Joe are still active on the account.

Cards can be issued against an account—for example, a banking card or credit card. If this is needed, then a CARD or MEDIA entity, maintaining banking card or credit card information, could be added and related to BILLING ACCOUNT as well as PARTY. Based on the business rules of the enterprise the relationship from the CARD entity could be a one-to-many or a many-to-many relationship to either the BILLING ACCOUNT or the PARTY.

Another common example of the usage of billing accounts is in the telecommunication industry. In some cases, all phone services for several phone numbers might appear on one billing account, while all charges for other phone numbers for the same location might appear on a different account. This could allow the charges for standard telephone service to be included on one account while other services, such as dedicated line and network services, might appear on another account. Again, telephone cards may be issued that give the customer the right numbers to charge calls to the account.

Invoice Specific Roles

An alternative to the data models in Figure 7.2 or Figure 7.3a is to relate the invoices to the specific entities that represent roles for invoicing. Figure 7.3b provides additional relationships to represent the key roles of BILL TO CUSTOMER, INTERNAL ORGANIZATION, and SUPPLIER, which are subtypes of PARTY ROLE and are still tied to PARTY.

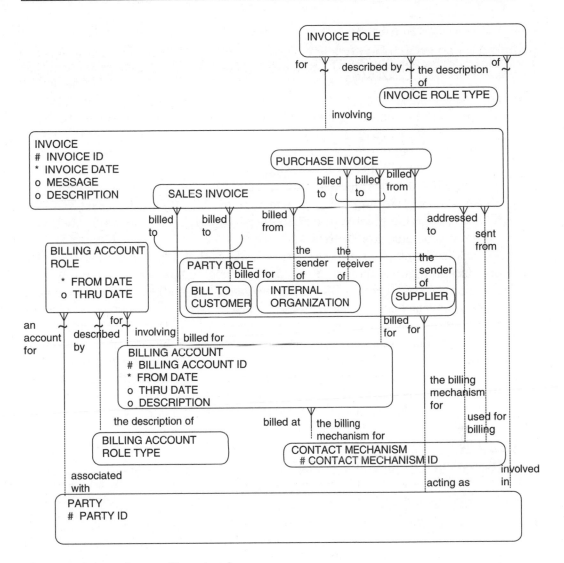

Figure 7.3b Invoice specific party roles.

This model defines more specific rules for the way that SALES INVOICES and PURCHASE INVOICES operate. A SALES INVOICE must be **billed to** a BILLING ACCOUNT or directly to a BILL TO CUSTOMER. If billing accounts are not used at the enterprise, then just remove the BILLING ACCOUNT entity relationships to this entity. The SALES INVOICE must be **billed from** an INTERNAL ORGANIZATION. A PURCHASE INVOICE must be **billed to** a BILLING ACCOUNT or an INTERNAL ORGANIZATION. The PURCHASE INVOICE must be **billed from** one and only one SUPPLIER.

Each of these roles, BILL TO CUSTOMER, INTERNAL ORGANIZATION, and SUPPLIER, are subtypes of PARTY ROLEs, which are each related to a PARTY. This allows the same PARTY to act in multiple PARTY ROLEs, each of which may be related to different invoices in different ways. Thus, this data structure still maintains the idea that a PARTY may have the same information that can still be stored once, independently of the information associated with the various roles that the party may play.

The advantage of this alternative data model over the more generic models in Figure 7.2 or Figure 7.3a is that it conveys more specific business rules showing the specific roles that parties are required to play in the sales and purchase invoicing. For instance, it shows that the INTERNAL ORGANIZATION is the party role that receives the PURCHASE INVOICE and the party role that is the sender of each SALES INVOICE.

The disadvantage of this alternative model is that it is less flexible than Figure 7.2 and Figure 7.3a because it conveys specific business rules that may or may not hold up over time. For instance, what if an AGENT of the enterprise is a party that may be the sender of the INVOICE? What if other roles change the nature of the way that INVOICEs are processed?

As a general guideline, one should use the more specific models such as the one in Figure 7.3b when the relationships between the entities are very stable and will probably not change over time. If one knows that there will always be one and only one SUPPLIER that is always going to be the sender of PURCHASE INVOICEs, then it is safe to model this relationship as such.

Invoice Terms and Status

Like orders, shipments, and many other transactions, invoices also have status and terms. Figure 7.4 shows that the INVOICE entity can have multiple INVOICE STATUSes and that either the INVOICE or INVOICE ITEM entity can have multiple INVOICE TERMs.

Invoice Status

Similar to orders, the state of an invoice changes over time. To track this, the entity INVOICE STATUS is used. It is an intersection entity between INVOICE and INVOICE STATUS TYPE (which is another subtype of STATUS TYPE). Examples of statuses include: "sent," "void," and "approved." "Paid" is not a valid status because it can be determined via payment transactions, which will be discussed later in this chapter. Additionally, the need to know when this status took effect is provided by the attribute **status date**. Table 7.7 shows how this data might look.

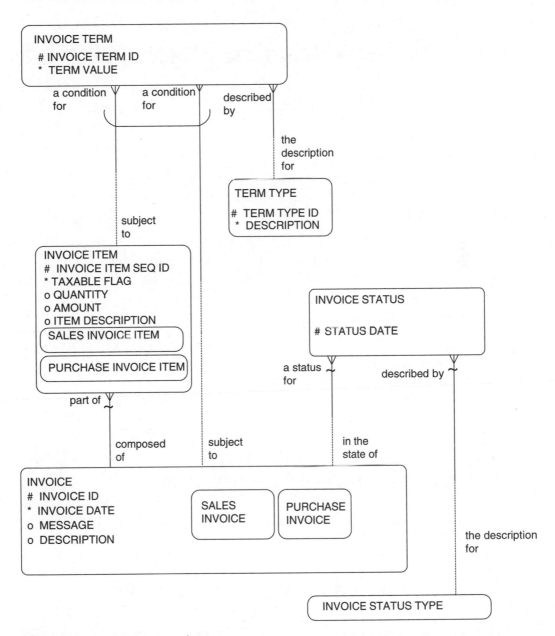

Figure 7.4   Invoice status and terms.

To find the current status, look for the most recent date. Note that if the number of statuses is somewhat limited, these items would be good candidates for denormalization in a physical model. If the model was denormalized, there may be **approved date**, **sent date**, and **void date** as attributes within the INVOICE entity instead of as records within the INVOICE STATUS entity.

Table 7.7 Invoice Status Data

INVOICE ID	STATUS TYPE	STATUS DATE
30002	Approved	May 25, 2001
	Sent	May 30, 2001
30005	Sent	June 5, 2001
	Void	June 6, 2001

Invoice Terms

Some systems or enterprises might need to record various terms and conditions on invoices, such as payment terms. Terms may sometimes apply at the item level. The model handles this with the INVOICE TERM entity, which must be related to either the INVOICE or INVOICE ITEM entities.

Table 7.8 shows three terms that were applied to an invoice and one term that is applied to only one of the items on that invoice. The first three rows describe terms for payment, late fees, and penalties that apply to the INVOICE. This data indicates that for invoice #30002, the payment is due in 30 days. If it is late, there is a 2 percent late fee added. If the invoice is sent to a collection agency, then there is an additional 5 percent added to the amount due. The last row provides an example of a term that is applied to the INVOICE ITEM, namely that the second item on invoice 30002 is nonrefundable.

Invoice and Associated Transactions

Invoices generally stem from associated transactions, which may include shipments, work efforts, and time entries, or directly from orders. An invoice represents a request for payment, and each invoice item identifies each part of the request as it relates to the items that are chargeable. Each invoice item may include moneys that are owed from shipment items, work efforts, time entries,

Table 7.8 Invoice Term Data

INVOICE ID	INVOICE ITEM SEQ ID	TERM TYPE DESCRIPTION	TERM VALUE
30002		Payment—net days	30
30002		Late fee—percent	2
30002		Penalty for collection agency—percent	5
30002	2	Non-returnable sales item	

or order items,. In each of these cases the invoice item may group together the items from which the charge came. There could be many shipment items, work efforts, time entries, or order items for an invoice item.

Also, there may be multiple invoice items for each order item, shipment item, or work effort due to two factors. The first factor is that the invoice item may only partially bill for the amount due and bill the rest at a later point in time. The second factor is that additional invoice items may be added in order to correct the initial shipment item, work effort, time entry, or order item.

The following three data models and corresponding sections describe how shipment items are related to shipment items, work efforts, and order items, respectively.

Billing for Shipment Items

A very common relationship is from the invoice item to the shipment item because these shipments often represent the delivery of goods that need to be paid after they have been received. How does one ensure that everything shipped actually gets billed?

The SHIPMENT ITEM BILLING entity allows enterprises to track this information (see Figure 7.5). This entity provides a means to store intersection information between INVOICE ITEM and SHIPMENT ITEM. Each of the invoice items should represent the bill for one or more shipment items. Conversely, one shipment item could be related to many invoice items in the case where adjustments to the original invoice item were needed. For example, if some of the goods for the original shipment were damaged, a credit for these items would be needed. The credit would take the form of an invoice item on a second invoice. Thus, the one shipment item would actually have a relationship to two different invoice items. It is unlikely that one shipment item would be related to two invoice items on the same invoice (though this would need to be enforced with a business rule).

Table 7.9 gives some examples of the data held by this entity. The table shows an example of a single shipment that resulted in two invoice items. Observe that the same shipment item (shipment ID #1235, item #1) is related to two invoice items. The first invoice item was a bill for the shipment of 1,000 items. On receipt, the customer found 10 items damaged; therefore, on a subsequent invoice another invoice item was to credit the customer for the 10 damaged items. This adjustment was then linked to the original shipment item to allow for proper tracking. Therefore, there were two invoice items for the same shipment item.

The example of shipment ID #1330 shows the opposite situation. In this case, three shipment items are mapped to only one invoice item. This can occur when the shipment items show component parts for an item, but the invoice shows only the price for the entire assembly. This situation could also occur

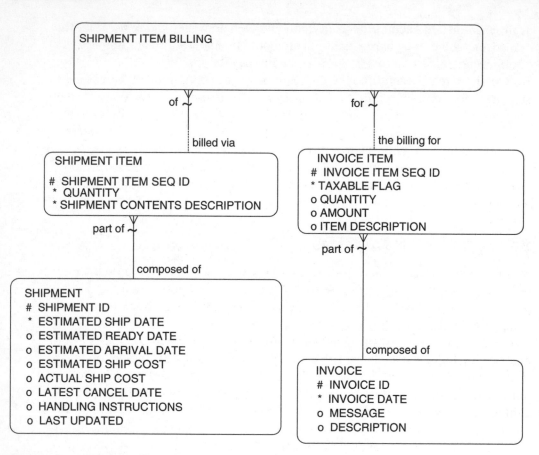

Figure 7.5   Billing for shipment items.

Table 7.9   Shipment Invoice Data

SHIPMENT ID	SHIPMENT ITEM SEQ ID	INVOICE ID	INVOICE ITEM SEQ ID	QUANTITY (FROM INVOICE ITEM)
1235	1	30002	1	1000
	2	30002	2	1000
	3	30002	3	100
1235	1	30045	1	−10
1330	1	30005	1	
	2	30005	1	
	3	30005	1	

when three shipments on different dates are grouped together into one invoice (perhaps due to a prearranged billing agreement).

Notice that there is not a **quantity** attribute on the SHIPMENT INVOICE and that the quantity shown in Table 7.9 comes from the INVOICE ITEM. The reason for this is that an enterprise will usually not partially invoice for items that have been shipped. If this case can exist and it is necessary to map quantities of invoice items to shipment items, then the **quantity** attribute could be added.

Keep in mind that there will not always be a SHIPMENT INVOICE record for every shipment. Some shipments, such as transfers, will not show up on an invoice unless the enterprise wants to keep track of internal transactions.

Billing for Work Efforts and Time Entries

The previous section identified how the delivery of goods is usually invoiced. How are services invoiced then? Services are generally invoiced one of two ways: The organization performing the services bills their client for either their time or for progress on specific work efforts.

Figure 7.6 provides a data model for billing of work efforts and/or time entries. For many of the same reasons that SHIPMENT ITEMS have a many-to-many relationship to INVOICE ITEMs, both WORK EFFORT and/or TIME ENTRY are also related in a many-to-many fashion to INVOICE ITEM. Each WORK EFFORT may be billed by many INVOICE ITEMs and vice versa. The associative entity WORK EFFORT BILLING accommodates this many-to-many relationship. Similarly, the associative entity TIME ENTRY BILLING resolves the many-to-many relationship from TIME ENTRY to INVOICE ITEM.

A WORK EFFORT may have many INVOICE ITEMs because it is common for companies to charge progress payments on the work effort. For instance, a professional services firm such as a consulting organization may charge a client 30 percent of a project (i.e., a type of work effort) on starting, 30 percent on initial delivery, and 40 percent 30 days after the project's completion. This would represent three INVOICE ITEMs for the same work effort. The **percentage** attribute allows recording of how much of the work effort was invoiced in that invoice item. Many WORK EFFORTS could be combined and invoiced in a single INVOICE ITEM. For example, a law firm may agree to perform three different efforts for a set fee, which is invoiced as a single INVOICE ITEM.

Each TIME ENTRY may have many INVOICE ITEMs associated with it. Suppose a TIME ENTRY was for five hours of consulting services. The client called and complained that he or she did not get what was expected in the five hours, and the consulting firm responded by agreeing to issue a credit of two hours regarding that time entry. Therefore, this led to two INVOICE ITEMs for the same TIME ENTRY. Usually partial invoicing of a time entry is not done; how-

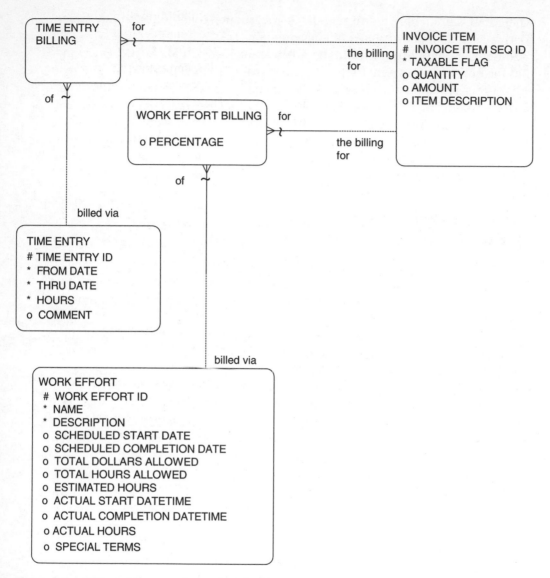

Figure 7.6 Billing of time entries and work efforts.

ever, if this is possible then an **hours** attribute could be added to the TIME ENTRY BILLING record to show how much of each time entry was billed.

Instead of assuming that each TIME ENTRY can be billed via more than one INVOICE ITEM to handle adjusting invoice item entries, can corrections to invoices be handled with a relationship from one INVOICE ITEM to the previous INVOICE ITEM? One of the problems with handling it via a recursive relationship on INVOICE ITEM is that the INVOICE ITEM may represent multiple time entries on different dates. In this case, it may be important to record to which of the three time entries the adjusting INVOICE ITEM applied. For this reason, this data model assumes that each should be related directly to the source transaction(s) that generated the invoice item.

Many TIME ENTRYs could also be combined on the same INVOICE ITEM, particularly if the time entries had similar information except for the date. An accountant may work two hours on Monday, three hours on Wednesday, and four hours on Friday, and the invoice may show an INVOICE ITEM for nine hours with an attached time sheet that could show the related time entries.

Billing for Order Items

What if the enterprise bills based on the order? Perhaps payment is due after ordering the goods and/or services. Or perhaps the enterprise does not track the shipment or work effort associated with the order and tracks only the order and its following invoice. For example, enterprises will not always track the work efforts associated with purchase orders for services rendered.

Figure 7.7 provides an additional data structure to show that ORDER ITEMs may also have a many-to-many relationship with INVOICE ITEMs. The associative entity ORDER ITEM BILLING lets order items be grouped together on an INVOICE ITEM or, conversely, more than one INVOICE ITEM for an ORDER ITEM. The **amount** and **quantity** attributes on the ORDER ITEM BILLING entity are provided to record the distribution of the amount or quantity from an order item to multiple invoices or vice versa.

Take, as an example, a purchase order item for a year's worth of accounting services at a cost of $120,000. The accounting firm invoices monthly. An invoice arrives with an invoice item for $10,000. This is then linked to the appropriate order item on the purchase order (using ORDER ITEM BILLING), and the amount of $10,000 is entered to show that $10,000 of the original $120,000 has been billed. This allows the enterprise to easily track over time how much of the original commitment has actually been billed to date (and also to notice if it has been billed beyond the amount of the purchase order). This example illustrated that a single ORDER ITEM may be related to many INVOICE ITEMs.

To show that a single INVOICE ITEM may be for multiple ORDER ITEMs, consider an enterprise in need of hardware support for its internal computer systems. Over the course of time, it executes three separate purchase orders to the same external company to provide this support. Each order has an order item for 40 hours of on-site support, for a total of 120 hours. Again, over time, the services are delivered, but due to the billing cycles at the vendor company, the first invoice has one order item for 100 hours. The final 20 hours are billed on the next invoice. Table 7.10 shows the details for these transactions.

Using this construct, it is possible to handle almost any combination of order and invoicing. Why go to such lengths to provide this flexibility in the data model? An enterprise has no real way of controlling service vendors and how

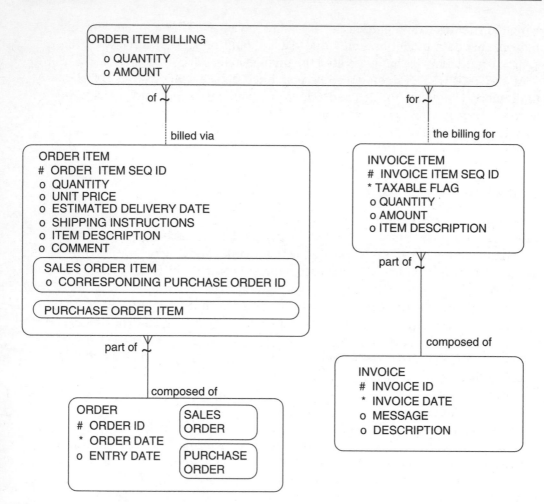

Figure 7.7 Billing for order items.

they invoice; with this model that does not matter. How the vendor chooses to do business regarding customer purchase orders will make no difference to the enterprise because this model is flexible enough to handle a variety of situations. Additionally, this model provides flexibility in recording the billing of both sales and purchase order items.

Payments

Invoices are issued to request payment. The tracking of payments issued and received is a very important universal data concept for most businesses because it represents the flow of money from and to the enterprise.

Table 7.10 Billing for Order Items

PURCHASE ORDER ID	ORDER ITEM SEQ ID	QUANTITY	UNIT PRICE	INVOICE ID	INVOICE ITEM SEQ ID	INVOICE QUANTITY	ORDER ITEM BILLING QUANTITY
10001	1	40 (hours)	$60	990023	1	100	40
10002	1	40 (hours)	$60				40
10003	1	40 (hours)	$60				20
10003	1	40 (hours)	$60	990026	1	20	20

Figure 7.8a provides a data model to track payments against invoices and billing accounts. Each PAYMENT may be applied toward many INVOICEs through the PAYMENT APPLICATION. Conversely, multiple payments may pay for a single INVOICE when partial payments are made.

Alternatively, the payment may be applied "on account," which means it is applied to a BILLING ACCOUNT without being applied to specific invoices.

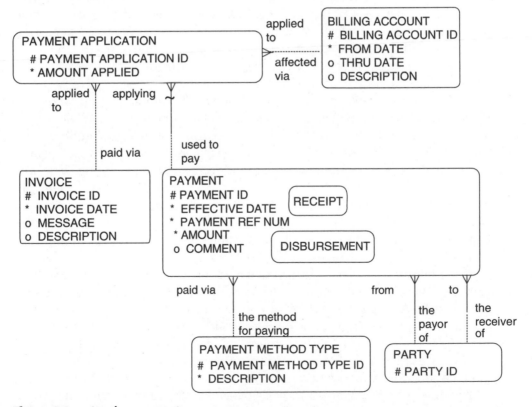

Figure 7.8a Invoice payments.

This allows for situations where a payment comes in and it is not clear for which invoice(s) it is paying. Also it allows moneys to be accepted in advance of charges. In either of these cases, the payments can be properly allocated later to the appropriate invoice items, once this is known.

The PAYMENT APPLICATION provides for the many-to-many relationships that can exist between the PAYMENT and INVOICE ITEM as well as between the PAYMENT and BILLING ACCOUNT.

The PAYMENT entity represents instances of moneys transferred from a PARTY and to a PARTY. A RECEIPT subtype represents incoming moneys to an internal organization of the enterprise, and a DISBURSEMENT represents outgoing payments of moneys sent by an internal organization of the enterprise. A payment made from one internal organization to another internal organization results in two PAYMENT instances; one internal organization will record a RECEIPT, and the other internal organization will record a DISBURSEMENT.

The PAYMENT entity is related to the PAYMENT METHOD TYPE entity whose description identifies the kind of payment such as "electronic" (for electronic transfers of moneys), "cash," "certified check," "personal check," or "credit card." The **payment ref num** references a payment identifier such as a check number or electronic transfer identifier. The **effective date** documents when the payment can be realized. For instance, an electronic transfer may be for a future time, or a check may be postdated and take effect at a later time. The **comment** provides an attribute to fully describe any circumstances involved in the transaction such as "payment was made with a message that complimented the service provided."

Table 7.11 shows example data for payments. The amount owed on invoice ID #30002 is $184.04, which can be calculated by extending each of the invoice items (multiplying the **quantity** times the **unit price**) and adding them together. The enterprise received a partial payment check for $182.20 against invoice #30002 because the paying organization had an outstanding issue with the Goldstein Elite pens and did not pay at first. After resolving the issue, they paid the other $12.84 (12.00 plus .84 for the sales tax for the pens) against the same invoice #30002, thus fully paying off the invoice. This example illustrates that when partial payments are issued against an invoice there can be more than one payment for an invoice.

The other two invoices, purchase invoices #990023 and #990026, have one payment that is for both of them. $6,000 of the $7,000 payment was applied to invoice #990023, and the enterprise decided to pay only $1,000 of the $1,200 due, leaving $200 additional due on the second invoice.

In some enterprises, invoices are very complex and are tracked at an invoice item level. For instance, a large consulting firm that outsources the information systems function of an organization may have a single bill for all the engaged consultants. The paying firm may pay against only the invoice items with which

Table 7.11 Invoice Payments

INVOICE ID	INVOICE ITEM SEQ ID	PRODUCT	PRODUCT FEATURE	ADJUSTMENT	QUANTITY	UNIT PRICE	PAYMENT APPLICATION AMOUNT	PAYMENT ID	PAYMENT AMOUNT
30002							$182.20	1298398	$182.20
							$12.84	1298412	$12.84
	1	Johnson fine grade 8½ by 11 bond paper			10	$8.00			
	2		Product quality, Extra glossy finish			$2.00			
	3	Goldstein Elite pens			4	$12.00			
	4	HD 3½-inch diskettes			6	$7.00			
	5			Sales tax		$12.04			
	6			Shipping and handling		$16.00			
	7			Fee (order processing fee)		$5.00			
990023	1	Accounting services				$6,000	$6,000	488893	$7,000
990026	1	Accounting services				$1,200	$1,000		

it is comfortable, and the receiving firm may want to track which invoice items have been paid.

The previous example in Table 7.11 for Invoice #30002 shows why the enterprise may also desire to track the payments against the invoice items to see which invoice items are outstanding. The company fully paid off three of the invoice items, and they may want to track which invoice items are outstanding as opposed to just recording that the invoice was partially paid off. The decision to track payments against invoice items would depend on the organization and how often individual invoice items are paid versus how often the full invoice is paid. The trade-off is that tracking by invoice item is more specific; however, it requires more work and more database records because there would be at least one PAYMENT APPLICATION record for every INVOICE ITEM.

Figure 7.8b provides an alternate data model to handle tracking payments at an invoice item level. In this model the PAYMENT APPLICATION relates to an INVOICE ITEM, thus tracking payment of each part of the invoice. This structure allows the enterprise to know for which invoice items they have received moneys and for which invoice items they have disbursed moneys. Of course, with this model, it assumes that the enterprise has the necessary information as well as the desire to record which items corresponded to which payments.

A common example of payments is to invoice item charges occurring in the banking industry. When loans are due, invoices may be issued. Then when a partial payment for a loan amount is received, business rules determine which invoice items should be paid off first. Therefore, tracking which invoice items are paid is important. For instance, the moneys could be first applied to fees, then applied to interest due, and then applied to the principal.

A third possible data model is to account for the PAYMENT APPLICATIONs being related to either INVOICEs or INVOICE ITEMs. This would allow the enterprise to record full payments of invoices easily and, when necessary, record payments against individual INVOICE ITEMS. This option has a large drawback because the option to apply payments against either invoices or invoice items may lead to more confusion (with procedures and invoice tracking) than it is worth.

Financial Accounts, Deposits, and Withdrawals

Once payments are received, it is important to deposit these receipts into a bank account, investment account, or some form of financial account where funds are kept. This section describes the handling of receipts and withdrawals that are recorded as transactions against financial accounts.

Figure 7.9 provides a data model to handle financial accounts, deposits, and withdrawals. A FINANCIAL ACCOUNT is a vehicle for maintaining funds, and

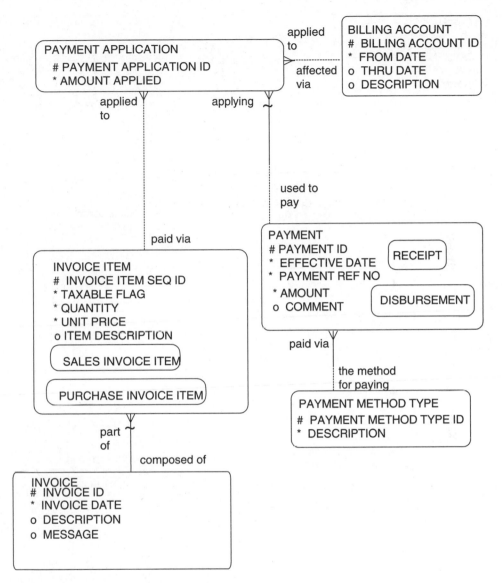

Figure 7.8b   Invoice item payments.

subtypes include a BANK ACCOUNT and an INVESTMENT ACCOUNT. There could be other types of FINANCIAL ACCOUNTs, such as a "checking account," "savings account," "IRA account," "mutual fund account," and so on, which could be described in the FINANCIAL ACCOUNT TYPE entity. Each PAYMENT may be either a RECEIPT or DISBURSEMENT, which is linked to different types of FINANCIAL ACCOUNT TRANSACTIONS, namely DEPOSIT and WITHDRAWAL. One or more RECEIPTs could be included in a DEPOSIT, which is a type of FINANCIAL ACCOUNT TRANSACTION that affects a FINANCIAL

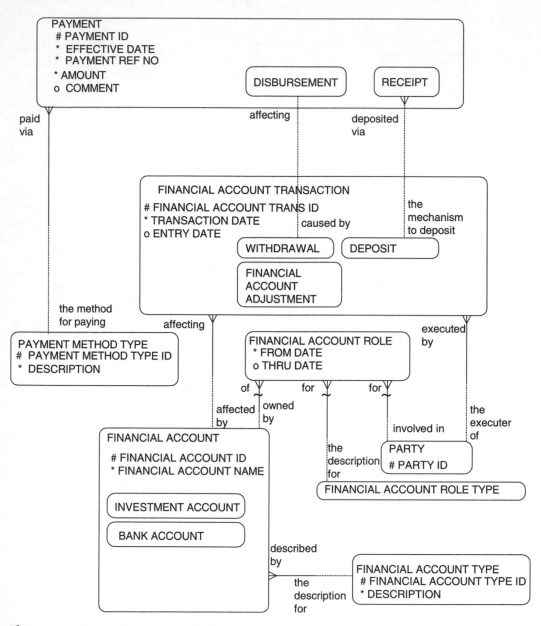

Figure 7.9   Financial accounts, withdrawals, and deposits.

ACCOUNT. Each DISBURSEMENT may be related to a WITHDRAWAL, which is a type of FINANCIAL ACCOUNT TRANSACTION that affects a FINANCIAL ACCOUNT.

For example, an enterprise may receive three incoming checks (i.e., RECEIPTs) and have a DEPOSIT transaction that records that these three checks

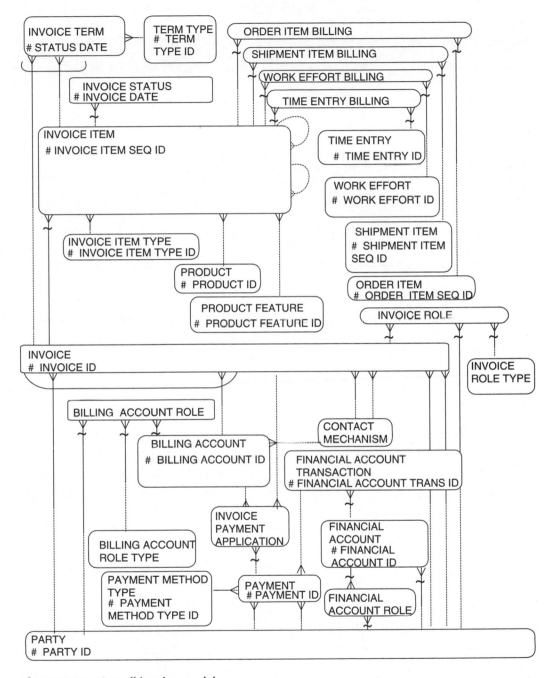

Figure 7.10   Overall invoice model.

Table 7.12 Deposits and Withdrawals.

PAYMENT ID	PAYMENT AMOUNT	DEPOSIT ID	DEPOSIT AMOUNT	WITHDRAWAL AMOUNT	FINANCIAL ACCOUNT ID (BANK ACCOUNT NUMBER OR INVESTMENT ACCOUNT ID)
1298398	$182.20	398749	$917.04		8389309984
1298412	$12.84				
394789	$343.00				
97873	$379.00				
88394	$480.00	398761		$480.00	8389309984
88756	$670.00	398762		$670.00	8389309984

have been deposited into a bank account (FINANCIAL ACCOUNT). This enterprise may issue a check (i.e., DISBURSEMENT) that ultimately results in a WITHDRAWAL of funds, which is a FINANCIAL ACCOUNT TRANSACTION, which also affects a FINANCIAL ACCOUNT, for example, a BANK ACCOUNT.

Table 7.12 provides an example of a typical case of a DEPOSIT, which consists of four RECEIPTs. There are also two withdrawals, which consist of two checks. The first two receipts are the receipts from the previous example in Table 7.11, and two additional receipts that have not previously been shown are included to illustrate the idea of recording each deposit and its corresponding receipts.

Summary

This chapter has provided models for invoice and invoice items for products, product features, adjustments, shipments, work efforts, and orders. Other models described in this chapter have been invoice roles, invoice billing accounts, invoice status and terms, invoice payments, and financial account deposits and withdrawals. The main entities and relationships are shown in Figure 7.10. It is the interrelationships with other parts of the model and the intersection entities that will allow for the development of a robust, integrated solution. These models should, once implemented, minimize the occurrence of redundant data and simplify the maintenance of the database.

Please refer to Appendix A for a listing of entities and attributes. SQL scripts to build tables and columns derived from the logical models in this book can be found on the full-blown CD-ROM, which is licensed separately.

Accounting and Budgeting

Many accounting functions are very similar across enterprises. Enterprises need to record transactions, post these transactions to each internal organization's chart of accounts, set up budgets, track variances to their budgets, and report on the results of their business operations.

An accounting and budgeting data model needs to maintain financial information to answer many important questions that affect an enterprise's existence:

- What is the financial position of the enterprise, and how did this change from previous periods?

- What types of transactions occurred in each period, and how much of each transaction occurred? For instance, what payments were made to which invoices, and what invoices are still outstanding?

- What expenses were incurred during various periods?

- What effect did transactions such as depreciation, capitalization, and amortization have on the enterprise?

- What budgets were set up, and how did the enterprise perform compared to these budgets?

This chapter illustrates data models with the following types of information:

- Chart of accounts
- Business transactions versus accounting transactions
- Accounting transactions
- Accounting transaction detail
- General ledger account associations and subsidiary ledger accounts
- Asset depreciation
- Budget definition
- Budget revision
- Budget review
- Budget scenario
- Use and sources of budgeted money
- Budget versus general ledger

Chart of Accounts for Internal Organizations

Generally, the first step in setting up an accounting system is determining a chart of accounts for each organization. A chart of accounts is simply a list of the buckets or categories of transactions that the enterprise will use to track its business activity for accounting purposes.

Figure 8.1 shows a data model that can establish and maintain a chart of accounts for each organization within the enterprise. The GENERAL LEDGER ACCOUNT represents a type of financial reporting *bucket* to which transactions are posted, for example a "cash" account or a "supplies expense" account. Each GENERAL LEDGER ACCOUNT may be categorized by one and only one GENERAL LEDGER ACCOUNT TYPE to specify the type of account (for instance, "asset" or "liability"). Each INTERNAL ORGANIZATION may be using many GENERAL LEDGER ACCOUNTs, and each GENERAL LEDGER ACCOUNT may be associated with more than one INTERNAL ORGANIZATION. The ORGANIZATION GL ACCOUNT resolves this many-to-many relationship. Each internal organization needs to establish the ACCOUNTING PERIOD for which it reports its business activities. Each ACCOUNTING PERIOD is of PERIOD TYPE such as "fiscal year," "calendar year," "fiscal quarter," and so on.

General Ledger Accounts and Types

General ledger accounts are mechanisms to categorize similar types of transactions together for the purpose of financial reporting. The field name shown

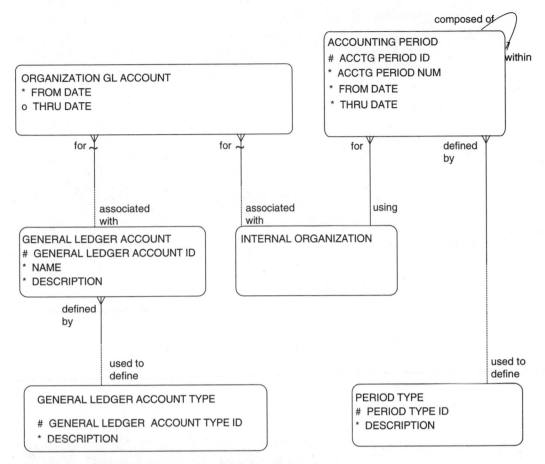

Figure 8.1 Chart of accounts for internal organizations.

in the GENERAL LEDGER entity identifies the **name** of the account that will be used for reporting purposes in financial statements. Examples of general ledger account names include "cash," "accounts receivable," "notes payable," or "advertising expense." The **description** attribute provides a definition behind the account to ensure that it is understood properly.

The key to a GENERAL LEDGER ACCOUNT entity in this model is the **general ledger account ID** and is filled with a *non-meaningful* unique number. Many other accounting systems assign a meaningful mnemonic to the general ledger account ID so that accounts are easily identified. The key may start with an organization component, then have a suborganization portion, then have the type of account, and then have a number representing the account. An example of this ID structure is ABC100-200-A-101, where "ABC100" represents the organization, "200" represents a specific division, "A" stands for asset, and "101" represents the account "cash." The problem with having a meaningful key is that if things change within the enterprise, such as a reorganization of the enterprise, then it creates a major problem for the system because key values and foreign key values need to be changed and there is a high chance of data inconsistencies. This is not what is desired, especially in an accounting system that needs to be precise.

The GENERAL LEDGER ACCOUNT TYPE entity identifies the classification of the GENERAL LEDGER ACCOUNT. Valid classifications include "asset," "liability," "owners equity," "revenue," and "expense." This information provides a mechanism to group information on financial statements. The "asset," "liability," and "owners equity" categories, along with the associated general ledger accounts, are generally used for the organization's balance sheet. The "revenue" and "expense" categories are generally used for the income statement.

Table 8.1 shows examples of general ledger accounts along with the type associated with each account.

Organization GL Account

Now that general ledger accounts have been established, they need to be related to the internal organizations that use them for reporting. Each INTERNAL ORGANIZATION may have many GENERAL LEDGER ACCOUNTs associated with it. Conversely, each GENERAL LEDGER ACCOUNT may be reused to sat-

Table 8.1   General Ledger Accounts

GL ACCOUNT ID	NAME	DESCRIPTION	GL ACCOUNT TYPE
110	Cash	Liquid amounts of money available	Asset
120	Accounts receivable	Total amount of moneys due from all sources	Asset
240	Notes Payable	Amounts due in the form of written contractual promissory notes	Liability
300	Retained Earnings	Identifies the difference between assets and liabilities that the owners have earned	Owners Equity
420	Interest Income	Amounts of revenues accumulated for a period due to interest earned	Revenue
520	Advertising expense	Costs due to all ads placed in newspapers, magazines, etc.	Expense
530	Office Supplies expense	Expenses for buying supplies needed for the office	Expense

isfy the needs of many INTERNAL ORGANIZATIONs. The ORGANIZATION GL ACCOUNT shows which internal organizations use which general ledger accounts. The **from date** and **thru date** attributes on the ORGANIZATION GL ACCOUNT entity indicate when general ledger accounts were added to an internal organization's chart of accounts and for what period of time they were valid.

The ORGANIZATION GL ACCOUNT represents the instance of a general ledger for a particular internal organization and is therefore a very significant entity. For instance, accounting transactions will be related to this entity, thus allowing maintenance of all the transactions for a particular balance sheet or income statement account.

Accounting Period

The ACCOUNTING PERIOD entity indicates the periods of time that the organization uses for its financial reporting. This may be to define a fiscal year, fiscal quarter, fiscal month, calendar year, calendar month, or any other time period that is available in the PERIOD TYPE. The **acctg period num(ber)** identifies the relative number of the accounting period. For instance, if there are 13 accounting periods in a year, the **acctg period num** would vary from "1" to "13" for this type of period. Quarters may vary from "1" to "4." The **from date** and **thru date** attributes define the time period for each instance.

An alternative structure is to use a **from day** and **thru day** to identify the starting *day* and ending *day* of a period, instead of the attributes **from date** and **thru date**. These would be character strings and not date domains because they specify only part of a date such as the month and day for the start and end of a period. The benefit of this design is to be able to define a period once. For example, the fiscal **from day** may be "Mar 1" and the fiscal **thru day** may be "Feb 28" to identify a PERIOD TYPE of "fiscal year," instead of having to reenter the accounting period for each year. One downside of this data structure is that it creates complications in handling leap years for periods ending at the end of Feb. Another downside of this data structure is that it is less practical to implement because date conversions will be needed to figure out which transactions should be posted to which periods, versus explicitly storing the dates, as shown in Figure 8.1.

Each ACCOUNTING PERIOD may be within one and only one ACCOUNTING PERIOD, as shown in the recursive relationship. This allows monthly periods to be rolled up to quarters, which can be rolled up to years.

Table 8.2 illustrates examples of the chart of accounts for ABC Corporation and ABC Subsidiary. Notice that while many general ledger accounts are used within both organizations, some accounts are different. For example, ABC Corporation has a "trade show expense" account whereas the subsidiary doesn't have this account because it is not involved in trade shows.

Table 8.2 Organization GL Account

INTERNAL ORGANIZATION	ACCTG PERIOD FROM DATE	ACCTG PERIOD THRU DATE	PERIOD TYPE	GENERAL LEDGER ACCOUNT TYPE	GENERAL LEDGER ACCOUNT	GL ACCOUNT FROM DATE	GL ACCOUNT THRU DATE
ABC Corporation	Jan 1, 2001	Dec 31, 2001	Fiscal Year	Asset	Cash	Jan 1, 1995	
					Accounts receivable	Jan 1, 1995	
				Liability	Notes payable	Jan 1, 1995	
				Owners Equity	Retained earnings	Jan 1, 1995	
				Revenue	Interest income	Jan 1, 1995	
				Expense	Marketing expense	Jan 1, 1995	Dec 31, 1996
					Advertising expense	Jan 1, 1997	
					Trade show expense	Jan 1, 1997	
					Office supplies	Jan 1, 1995	
ABC Subsidiary	Jan 1, 2001	Dec 31, 2001	Fiscal Year	Asset	Cash	Jun 1, 1997	
					Accounts receivable	Jun 1, 1997	
				Liability	Notes payable	Jun 1, 1997	
				Owners Equity	Retained earnings	Jun 1, 1997	
				Revenue	Interest income	Jun 1, 1997	
				Expense	Marketing expense	Jun 1, 1997	
					Office supplies	Jun 1, 1997	

Also, notice that each organization has its fiscal year accounting periods associated with it (ACCOUNTING PERIOD **from date** and **thru date**). The two organizations shown have the same fiscal year period; however, it is possible for internal organizations within the same enterprise to have different accounting periods. For example, an organization with a fiscal period from June 1 to May 31 may have been recently merged into an internal organization whose fiscal period is January 1 to December 31.

The ORGANIZATION GL ACCOUNT **from date** and **thru date** provide the ability to track which GL accounts existed for which INTERNAL ORGANIZATIONs at what periods of time. For example, Table 8.2 shows that on January 1, 1997, ABC Corporation divided its "marketing expense" account into two accounts: "advertising expense" and "trade show expense."

Accounting Transactions Definition

In various parts of this book, there are transactions that affect the accounting of the organization. For example, in Chapter 7, the creation of an INVOICE will result in a related accounting transaction, namely a SALES ACCTG TRANS. In Chapter 3, the identification of an ITEM VARIANCE to adjust INVENTORY ITEMs will lead to an ITEM VARIANCE ACCTG TRANS. Thus, there is a need in enterprises to maintain information about the accounting transactions.

Figure 8.2 provides the initial part of the accounting transaction data model. The ACCOUNTING TRANSACTION entity is a supertype that encompasses all the transactions that affect the financial statements of the enterprise. It includes INTERNAL ACCTG TRANS such as DEPRECIATION, CAPITALIZATION, AMORTIZATION, ITEM VARIANCE ACCTG TRANS, and OTHER INTERNAL ACCTG TRANS that document adjustments to the internal organization's financial position. Accounting transactions may also be EXTERNAL ACCTG TRANS that involve either OBLIGATION ACCTG TRANS or PAYMENT ACCTG TRANS made. Each PAYMENT ACCTG TRANS represents either a RECEIPT ACCTG TRANS for moneys coming in or a DISBURSEMENT ACCTG TRANS for moneys going out.

Each ACCOUNTING TRANSACTION may be related to its business transaction from which it originated. Thus the SALES ACCTG TRANS must be originated from each INVOICE instance, each PAYMENT ACCTG TRANS is originated from a PAYMENT instance, and each ITEM VARIANCE ACCTG TRANS must be originated from a INVENTORY ITEM VARIANCE instance that shows adjustments to inventory.

The relationship from ACCOUNTING TRANSACTION to ACCOUNTING TRANSACTION TYPE provides a specific low-level categorization of each transaction. Types may include further breakdowns of the subtypes such as "Payment Receipt for Asset Sale" or "Payment Disbursement for Purchase Order."

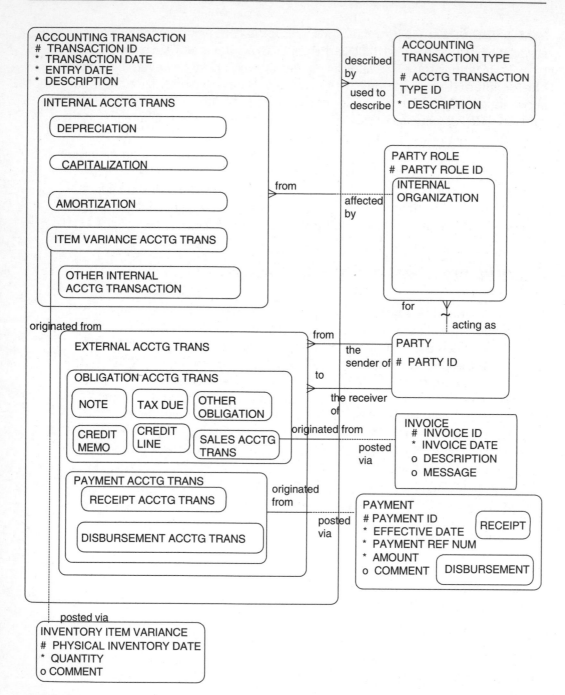

Figure 8.2   Accounting transactions.

Business Transactions versus Accounting Transactions?

Each ACCOUNTING TRANSACTION may be originated from a corresponding business transaction, which is any transaction through the enterprise's data model that will affect the financial status of the organization. The model shows a few of these corresponding business transaction relationships, and there may be many others depending on the nature of the organization. The model shows that INVENTORY ITEM VARIANCE instance may be posted via a corresponding ITEM VARIANCE ACCTG TRANS transaction. Similarly, each INVOICE may be posted via a SALES ACCTG TRANS, and each PAYMENT corresponds to a PAYMENT ACCTG TRANS.

Are each of these business transactions such as an INVOICE actually a separate entity tied to an accounting transaction, or are they really a subtype of an ACCOUNTING TRANSACTION? One may think that these business transactions and accounting transactions are the same thing because they have a one-to-one relationship and they represent the same thing: a transaction that affects the books of the enterprise. On the other hand, there may be a timing difference between the business transaction and the accounting transaction. For instance, an INVOICE may be maintained by the enterprise even though, at a particular point in time, there may not be a related accounting transaction because it has not yet been posted. Furthermore, the INVOICE may have a status of "pending approval from manager," thus maintaining it as an INVOICE but not as an ACCOUNTING TRANSACTION. Therefore, the data model shows that each of the business transactions is a separate entity from the corresponding accounting transactions.

Accounting Transaction

Each ACCOUNTING TRANSACTION instance represents a journal entry in accounting terms. The ACCOUNTING TRANSACTION entity has a **transaction ID** that uniquely identifies the particular transaction. The **transaction date** is the date on which the transaction occurred. The **entry date** is the date on which the entry was made into the system. The **description** attribute describes the details behind the transaction. Note that there is no **amount** attribute because the transaction amounts are maintained in the transaction detail, which will be covered in the next section.

Accounting deals with two main types of transactions. An ACCOUNTING TRANSACTION may be either an INTERNAL ACCTG TRANS or an EXTERNAL ACCTG TRANS. INTERNAL ACCTG TRANS are adjustment transactions that affect only the books of the internal organization being affected. EXTERNAL ACCT TRANS are transactions that involve transactions with a party that is external to the enterprise for whom the books are kept.

The subtypes reveal examples of INTERNAL ACCTG TRANS such as DEPRECIATION, CAPITALIZATION, AMORTIZATION, ITEM VARIANCE ACCTG TRANS, and OTHER INTERNAL ACCTG TRANS that adjust the financial position of the internal organization.

The OBLIGATION ACCTG TRANS subtype is broken down into various other subtypes that represent different forms of a party owing moneys to another party. One subtype of OBLIGATION is a NOTE. It may be a note payable, where the internal organization owes money, or a note receivable, where the organization is due money. Another subtype is CREDIT MEMO, which is a transaction where credit is given from one party to another party. TAX DUE is an obligation to pay taxes to government agencies. The SALES ACCTG TRANS entity represents the obligation to pay for products sold. CREDIT LINE represents money actually borrowed from a line of credit extended from a financial institute to another party. There may be other forms of obligations depending on the business; therefore, the OTHER OBLIGATION subtype is included.

The PAYMENT ACCTG TRANS subentity represents collections of moneys received by an internal organization (RECEIPT ACCTG TRANS) or payments of moneys sent by an internal organization (DISBURSEMENT ACCTG TRANS). A payment made from one internal organization to another internal organization results in two PAYMENT ACCTG TRANS instances; one internal organization will record a RECEIPT, and the other internal organization will record a DISBURSEMENT.

Accounting Transactions and Their Related Parties

The INTERNAL ACCTG TRANS identifies transactions that serve as adjustments to the books of an internal organization. Because there is only one organization involved in the transaction (namely, the internal organization whose books are being adjusted), there is a single relationship to an INTERNAL ORGANIZATION.

The EXTERNAL ACCTG TRANS subtype models accounting transactions that affect two parties. An EXTERNAL ACCTG TRANS may be either an OBLIGATION ACCTG TRANS or a PAYMENT ACCTG TRANS. An OBLIGATION ACCTG TRANS represents a transaction where one party has recognized that it owes moneys to another party. Therefore, the *from* and *to* relationships identify the parties involved on both sides of a transaction. A PAYMENT ACCTG TRANS represents a transaction where one party is paying another party; therefore it also relates to two parties.

Table 8.3 provides examples of various types of accounting transactions. The first row (transaction ID 32389) is an example of an internal transaction that records a depreciation expense for a piece of equipment. Only one party is

Table 8.3 Accounting Transaction

TRANSACTION ID	FROM PARTY	TO PARTY	TRANSACTION DATE	TRANSACTION AMOUNT	TRANSACTION TYPE	DESCRIPTION
32389	ABC Corporation		Jan 1, 2000	$200	Depreciation	Depreciation on pen engraver
38948	ABC Corporation	ACME Company	May 31, 2000	$900	Invoice	Invoiced amount due
39776	ACME Company	ABC Corporation	Jun 13, 2000	$700	Payment receipt for invoices	Payment against invoice
45783	ABC Corporation	ACME Company	Jul 2, 2000	$200	Credit memo	Credit to invoice #
45894	ACME Company	ABC Corporation	Aug 13, 2000	$300	Payment receipt for invoices	Payment made on account with invoice in mind
46325	ABC Corporation	ACME Company	Oct 10, 2000	–$300	Payment receipt for invoices	Returned payment for moneys held with no invoice
47874	Johnson Recycling	ABC Corporation	Oct 11, 2000	$1200	Payment receipt for asset sale	Payment received for sale of pen engraver

affected—the internal organization that owns that piece of equipment, ABC Corporation. The rest of the transactions are various types of external transactions that involve a "to" party and a "from" party. For instance, transaction 39776 describes a receipt (incoming payment) to pay off $700 owed by ACME Company to ABC Corporation.

Accounting Transaction Details

Figure 8.3a adds to the previous accounting transaction model by adding the transaction detail debit and credit entries to the accounting transaction as well as relating the transaction detail to the organizations' general ledger accounts. Each ACCOUNTING TRANSACTION is broken down into numerous TRANSACTION DETAILs that represent the debits and credit entries for the transaction. Each debit or credit entry will affect one of the internal organization's accounts and therefore is related to an ORGANIZATION GL ACCOUNT, which is the bucket for a GENERAL LEDGER ACCOUNT for an INTERNAL ORGANIZATION.

Transaction Detail

As shown in Figure 8.3a, each ACCOUNTING TRANSACTION must be composed of one or more TRANSACTION DETAILs, which show how each part of the transaction affects a specific ORGANIZATION GL ACCOUNT. A TRANSACTION DETAIL instance corresponds to a "journal entry line item" in accounting terms.

According to the principles of double-entry accounting, each transaction has at least two detail records, a debit and a credit. For instance, an ACCOUNTING TRANSACTION of type INVOICE may result in two TRANSACTION DETAIL instances: a debit to the general ledger account "accounts receivable" (showing that moneys are due) and a credit to the general ledger account "revenue" (showing that revenue is recognized). Table 8.4 illustrates the details of this transaction (transaction ID 38948 in the table).

Each transaction is related to the general ledger account within a specific internal organization, which is why the organization GL account column of Table 8.4 references the "ABC Corporation" in parentheses. Appropriate business rules need to be put in place to make sure that the organization associated with the ORGANIZATION GL ACCOUNT makes sense in relation to the PARTY associated with the ACCOUNTING TRANSACTION. For instance, if there is an INTERNAL TRANSACTION for ABC Corporation, then the TRANSACTION DETAIL records need to be related to ORGANIZATION GL ACCOUNTs of "ABC Corporation" and not of another internal organization.

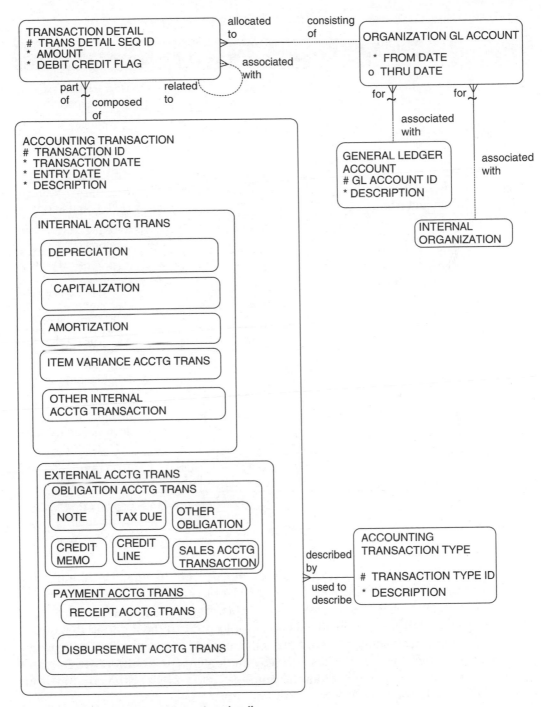

Figure 8.3a Accounting transaction details.

Table 8.4 Transaction Detail

TRANSACTION ID	TRANSACTION DESCRIPTION	TRANS DETAIL SEQ ID	AMOUNT	DEBIT/CREDIT FLAG	ORGANIZATION GL ACCOUNT
32389	Depreciation on equipment	1	$200	Debit	Depreciation expense (ABC Corporation)
		2	$200	Credit	Accumulated depreciation for equipment (ABC Corporation)
38948	Invoiced amount due	1	$900	Debit	Accounts receivable (ABC Corporation)
		2	$900	Credit	Revenue (ABC Corporation)
39776	Payment against invoice	1	$882	Debit	Cash (ABC Corporation)
		2	$18	Debit	Discount expense (ABC Corporation)
		3	$900	Credit	Accounts receivable
47874	Payment received for sale of pen engraver	1	$1000	Debit	Cash (ABC Corporation)
		2	$200	Debit	Accumulated depreciation (ABC Corporation)
		3	$800	Credit	Asset (ABC Corporation)
		4	$400	Credit	Capital gain (ABC Corporation)

The **transaction ID** and the **trans detail seq id** uniquely identify the TRANSACTION DETAIL because it is a detail record that breaks down the ACCOUNTING TRANSACTION. The **debit/credit flag** indicates whether the transaction detail is posted as a debit or credit to the appropriate general ledger account. The **amount** indicates the amount of that portion of the transaction. Many *physical* database designs implement the **debit/credit flag** as a positive or negative sign within the **amount** field so that arithmetic functions can be easily used to offset debits and credits.

It was stated that an ACCOUNTING TRANSACTION has at least two TRANSACTION DETAIL records. In many cases, an accounting transaction may have more than two detail entries. Consider the third transaction in Table 8.4, transaction ID 39776. This transaction was a payment against an invoice with a 2 percent discount taken for early payment. The transaction resulted in three detail records, a credit to clear the accounts receivable of $900, a cash increase of $882, and a discount expense of $18.

The fourth transaction in Table 8.4 (transaction ID 47874) provides an example of an accounting transaction with four detail records. The sale of a piece of equipment, in this case the pen engraving machine, resulted in a debit to cash of the $1,000 received, a debit of $200 that clears the accumulated depreciation of the machine, a credit of $800 that was the book value of the asset, and a credit to record the capital gain on the transaction of $400 ($1,000 received minus the net value of the equipment of $600).

Relationships between Accounting Transaction Details

Businesses need to answer questions regarding the relationships between certain transactions. For example, which invoices have been paid off through which payments, and which invoices are still outstanding? Which invoices have been reduced via credit memos issued to customers? Which payments were subsequently sent back to the originating party because they did not correspond to an invoice or amount due?

The recursive relationship around TRANSACTION DETAIL provides the capability to track which accounting transaction details are associated with other transaction details. Using this recursive relationship, the model can provide the information to answer the previous questions.

Is there a need for TRANSACTION DETAIL recursions showing which payment was for which obligation? Is this not derived information, as one can see that a payment for $500 paid off an obligation of $500? What if there were several obligations for $500? It is necessary to maintain which payment paid off which obligation. When partial payments occur, it is even more important to track which payments are paying off which obligations. Similarly, it is also important to track which obligations are related to which obligations (an invoice with a related credit, for example).

Table 8.5 illustrates how the model can be used to relate different accounting transactions to one another. A very common type of related transaction is what payments are made against which invoices. Transaction ID 38948 shows that $900 is due as an accounts receivable. The next transaction shown (39776) is a payment that is applied to this invoice. The last column, **Associated Transaction ID and TRANS Detail Seq ID**, represents the recursive relationship from one transaction detail to another transaction detail. In this case, it identifies that the credit to accounts receivable is specifically regarding transaction 38948, which was the original invoice that was paid off.

Table 8.5 Transaction Detail Relationships

TRANSACTION ID	TRANSACTION DESCRIPTION	TRANS DETAIL SEQ ID	AMOUNT	DEBIT/CREDIT	ORGANIZATION GL ACCOUNT	ASSOCIATED TRANSACTION ID AND TRANS DETAIL SEQ ID
38948	Invoiced amount due	1	$900	Debit	Accounts receivable (ABC Corporation)	
		2	$900	Credit	Revenue (ABC Corporation)	
39776	Payment against invoice	1	$882	Debit	Cash (ABC Corporation)	
		2	$18	Debit	Discount expense (ABC Corporation)	
		3	$900	Credit	Accounts receivable (ABC Corporation)	38948, 1
50984	Invoiced amount due	1	$1000	Debit	Accounts receivable (ABC Corporation)	
		2	$1000	Credit	Revenue (ABC Corporation)	
50999	Invoiced amount due	1	$2000	Debit	Accounts receivable (ABC Corporation)	
		2	$2000	Credit	Revenue (ABC Corporation)	
60985	Payment against invoice	1	$3000	Debit	Cash (ABC Corporation)	
		2	$1000	Credit	Accounts receivable (ABC Corporation)	50984, 1
		3	$2000	Credit	Accounts receivable (ABC Corporation)	50999, 1

Table 8.5 also shows that two invoices (transactions 50984 and 50999) were paid off via a single payment (transaction 60985). In this case, the transaction detail representing the "accounts receivable" entry was split into two detail records in order to identify the amounts allocated for each of the two invoices.

This model can accommodate any type of transaction relationship that occurs in accounting. For instance, it can provide the information to maintain credit memos that reduce invoice amounts (obligations related to other obligations), refunds of payments (payments related to other payments), partial payments applied to invoices (payments to obligations), and sales of depreciated equipment applied to the original purchase transaction (payments related to payments and to internal transactions; namely, depreciation).

Account Balances and Transactions

Should each TRANSACTION DETAIL be related to the ORGANIZATION GL ACCOUNT, as it is in the previous model, or should it be related to an entity that stores the balances for the account for each accounting period?

There is a strong argument for modeling the account balance as an entity. After all, the financial statements and other financial reporting will most likely be based on account balances, making this is a critical piece of information. Also, managers will frequently want to see the balance for a particular general ledger account for a period without necessarily looking up the related transactions. Furthermore, the related transactions may be archived for account balances for previous years.

The model in Figure 8.3a does not show the account balance as either an entity or attribute because the account balance amount is derived information from the transactions that affect the account. Whenever derived data is included in a data model, there is redundant information. When there is redundant information modeled in a system, data synchronization issues occur that can affect the accuracy of data. Regarding account balances, one can argue that the information doesn't change much after the period ends so it is not much of a data synchronization issue. Retroactive accounting adjustments for past periods could complicate matters and make the storing of account balances in a logical model unwise.

Certainly in the physical implementation of this logical model, it may be a good idea to include account balances for various time periods. Managers will no doubt need fast access to this information, and the physical design should not have to scan through the transactions associated with the general ledger account to determine the account balance.

Even though the modeling of account balance does not represent a "pure" data modeling practice, many data modelers would argue that it needs to be included for the model to be complete and practical. Therefore, Figure 8.3b shows an alternate model that includes account balance information. This data model would represent a very practical database design for implementation purposes.

Figure 8.3b shows that the ORGANZATION GL ACCOUNT BALANCE has been inserted between the TRANSACTION DETAIL and the ORGANIZATION GL ACCOUNT. This allows direct access to the critical attribute **amount** in the ORGANIZATION GL ACCOUNT BALANCE, which stores the current balance of the ORGANIZATION GL ACCOUNT for a certain ACCOUNTING PERIOD.

Subsidiary Accounts

In accounting, organizations often keep subsidiary ledgers to track the status of specific accounts. There may be an "accounts receivable" general ledger account to show how much is owed to the enterprise. This account may be composed of accounts receivable subsidiary ledger accounts showing the amounts owed and paid for each bill-to customer or other party that owes moneys. Similarly, the general ledger "accounts payable" account has subsidiary ledger accounts, each of which represents suppliers or other parties that owe money to the enterprise. General ledger accounts to represent various products or product categories may also be captured as separate general ledger accounts and rolled into an overall product revenue account.

Figure 8.4 provides a data model to capture the information requirements of subsidiary ledgers. The diagram has a recursive relationship showing that each ORGANIZATION GL ACCOUNT may comprise one or more other ORGANIZA-TION GL ACCOUNTs. The parent general ledger account represents an account such as accounts payable or accounts receivable. The recursive **comprised of** relationship relates to the associated subsidiary ledger accounts, which each maintain information about a specific customer, supplier, product, or product category. Each of those subsidiary accounts may be related to other entities in the data model such as BILL TO CUSTOMER (a subtype of PARTY ROLE), SUPPLIER (a subtype of PARTY ROLE), PRODUCT, or PRODUCT TYPE. General ledger accounts may be related to particular products in order to track the revenues produced by a specific product, or if there are a great deal of products, then the general ledger accounts may be related to product categories.

Subsidiary general ledger accounts are related to the roles of BILL TO CUSTOMER and SUPPLIER, which represent very specific roles of parties. It could be that other parties in other roles owe moneys to the enterprise and/or the enterprise owes moneys to them. Therefore, the model could show relationships to PARTY as an alternate, more generic structure, instead of tying them to the specific roles of BILL TO CUSTOMER and/or SUPPLIER.

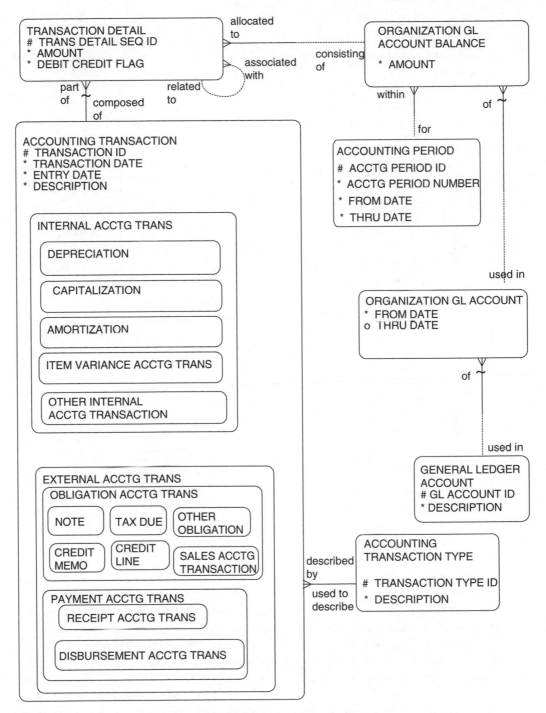

Figure 8.3b Accounting transactions detail with account balances.

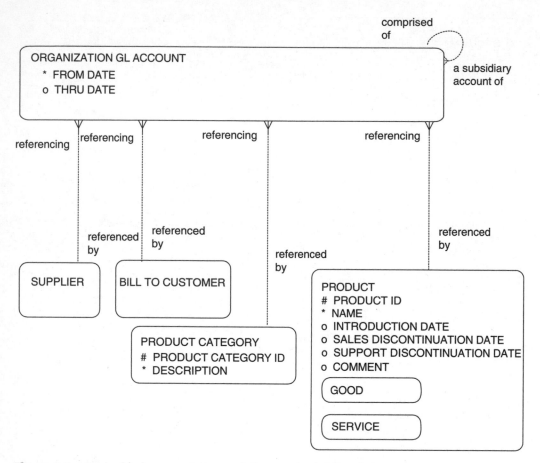

Figure 8.4 General ledger account associations and subsidiary ledger accounts.

Asset Depreciation

Additional entities are used to determine how certain accounting transactions are calculated. This section illustrates the means by which a common type of internal transaction, namely, depreciation, is calculated.

As shown in Figure 8.5, each DEPRECIATION transaction is specifically for one and only one FIXED ASSET (described in Chapter 6). A FIXED ASSET may be depreciated using DEPRECIATION METHODs. The same depreciation method may be used to depreciate more than one fixed asset, and a fixed asset may have more than one DEPRECIATION METHOD over time because a fixed asset's depreciation method may change (although this may be regulated by agencies such as the IRS). Therefore, the FIXED ASSET DEPRECIATION

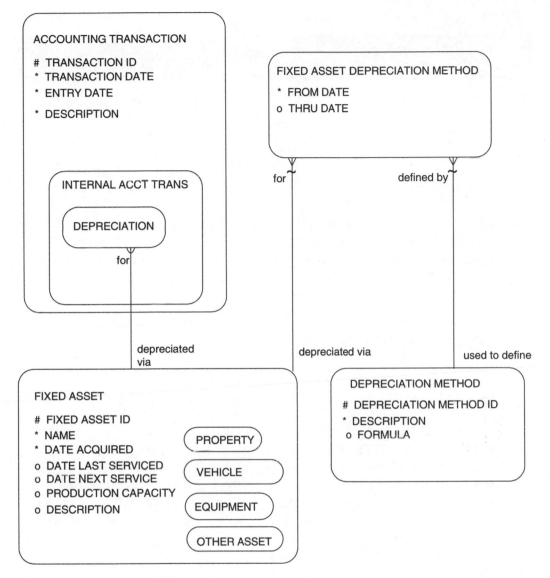

Figure 8.5   Asset depreciation.

METHOD entity documents which depreciation method was used on each fixed asset during various periods of time.

The DEPRECIATION METHOD entity has a **description** attribute that specifies the type of depreciation such as "straight line depreciation" or "double declining balance depreciation." It also describes the **formula** for calculating depreciation. Table 8.6 illustrates examples of the type of information maintained for depreciation calculation purposes. In this example, the pen engraver

Table 8.6 Fixed Asset Depreciation Method

FIXED ASSET NAME	DEPRECIATION METHOD DESCRIPTION	DEPRECIATION METHOD FORMULA	FROM DATE	THRU DATE
Pen Engraver	Double-declining balance depreciation	(Purchase cost – salvage cost)* (1/estimated life in years of the asset)*2	Jan 1, 1999	Dec 31, 1999
	Straight-line depreciation	(Purchase cost – salvage cost)/estimated life in years of the asset	Jan 1, 2000	

used "double-declining balance" as a method for the year 1999; starting in 2000, it began using the "straight-line depreciation" method of depreciation. Although it may be very interesting to describe the formulas behind these depreciation methods (for a very select breed), this information can be found in any accounting book and is beyond the scope of this book.

Budget Definition

Another aspect of financial control is budgeting. Figure 8.6 illustrates a data model that provides information on budgets that are set up to monitor the spending of moneys. Each BUDGET may be an OPERATING BUDGET for expense type items or a CAPITAL BUDGET for fixed assets and long-term items.

The BUDGET TYPE allows the flexibility to categorize other types of budgets according to the needs of the organization. The BUDGET entity describes the information about the amounts of moneys needed for a group of expense items over a certain period of time. STANDARD TIME PERIOD maintains possible time periods for which budgets could be allocated. Each BUDGET may have many parties involved in various BUDGET ROLEs and several BUDGET STATUSes over time. BUDGET ROLEs for PARTYs (which may be a person or an organization) include the initiator of the budget request, the party for whom the budget is requested, the reviewer(s) of a budget, and the approver of the budget. Each BUDGET must be composed of one or more BUDGET ITEMs, each of which is described by a BUDGET ITEM TYPE that describes the budgeted items. BUDGET ITEMs may be recursively related to other BUDGET ITEMs, allowing for a hierarchy of budget item rollups.

Budget

Budgets are mechanisms for planning the spending of moneys. Figure 8.6 has a BUDGET entity that describes the key information regarding budgets. A budget

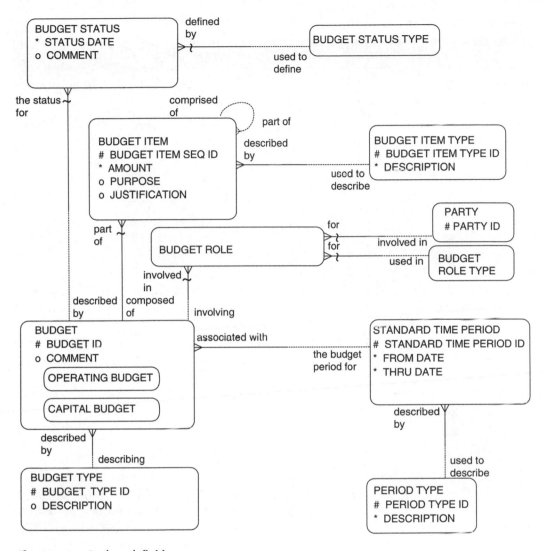

Figure 8.6 Budget definition.

is uniquely identified by a **budget ID**. The relationship to STANDARD TIME PERIOD identifies the time period for which the budget applies, including the **from date** and **thru date** for that period. This may represent different types of periods for different enterprises. The entity PERIOD TYPE identifies the particular type used by each defined period. Common period types are "month," "quarter," or "year." The **description** attribute describes the budget at a high level.

Table 8.7   Budget Data

BUDGET ID	BUDGET TYPE	PARTY FOR WHOM BUDGET IS REQUESTED	BUDGET PERIOD	PERIOD TYPE	BUDGET DESCRIPTION
29839	Operating budget	Marketing department	1/1/2001–12/31/2001	Year	Marketing budget
38576	Operating budget	Administration department	6/1/2002–6/30/2002	Month	Office expenses budget
39908	Capital budget	Manufacturing operations	1/1/2001–12/31/2001	Year	New manufacturing machines needed

Table 8.7 illustrates examples of the information in the BUDGET entity. Budget ID 29839 represents the 2001 annual budget submitted by the marketing department of ABC Corporation for its marketing expenses. Budget ID 38576 is a monthly budget, for June of 2002, from the administration department of ABC Corporation for its planned office expenses. Budget 39908 is a capital budget for the purchase of manufacturing machines in 2001.

Notice that budgets are defined for individual parties that may be departments, divisions, organizations, or whatever organizational structure the enterprise uses. The budget should be defined at the lowest level in the organizations, thus allowing the enterprise the ability to roll up budgeted amounts to various levels.

Budget Item

Each BUDGET must be composed of one or more BUDGET ITEMs, which store the details of exactly what is being budgeted. The **amount** attribute defines the total amount of funds required for the item within the time period. The **purpose** attribute identifies why the items are needed, and the **justification** attribute describes why the budgeted amount of money should be expended. Each BUDGET ITEM is described by a BUDGET ITEM TYPE so that common budget item descriptions can be reused. BUDGET ITEMs may be comprised of other BUDGET ITEMs via the recursive relationship around BUDGET ITEM. Table 8.8 provides two simple examples of budget items within the budgets described in the previous section.

Budget Status

Each BUDGET generally moves through various stages as the budget process unfolds. A budget is typically created on a certain date, reviewed, submitted for approval, then accepted, rejected, or sent back to the submitter for modifications.

Table 8.8   Budget Item

BUDGET ID	BUDGET DESCRIPTION	BUDGET ITEM SEQ	BUDGET ITEM DESCRIPTION	AMOUNT	PURPOSE	JUSTIFICATION
29839	Marketing budget	1	Trade shows	$20,000	Connect directly with various markets	Last year, this amount was spent and it resulted in three new clients
		2	Advertising	$30,000	Create public awareness of products	Competition demands product recognition
		3	Direct mail	$15,000	To generate sales leads	Experience predicts that one can expect 50 leads for every $5,000 expended
38576	Office expenses budget	1	Office supplies	$5,000	Supplies needed to perform office administration tasks	This is the amount expended last year and is required again
		2	Furniture	$10,000	For new facility on Benjamin Street	New facility needs some basic items of furniture

Figure 8.6 shows that each BUDGET has one or more BUDGET STATUSes over time, each of which is described by a BUDGET STATUS TYPE, which is another subtype of STATUS TYPE. This structure provides for the tracking of the history of a budget through its various stages.

Table 8.9 illustrates examples of budget statuses. Notice that on November 15 when the budget was sent back to the submitter for modifications, it created the need for a new revision of the budget, which will be discussed in the next section.

Budget Revision

Each budget will usually go through a process whereby several budget revisions are created for a BUDGET. Figure 8.7 provides two alternatives for how BUDGET REVISION information may be stored, depending on the needs of the enterprise. If the enterprise does not need to track each change to a budget and if it considers each revision to a budget a whole new budget, then the top model will work. If the enterprise wants to track changes to each budgeted item over time, then the bottom model is needed.

Table 8.9 Budget Status

BUDGET ID	STATUS DATE	BUDGET STATUS TYPE DESCRIPTION	COMMENT
29839	Oct 15, 2000	Created	
29839	Nov 1, 2000	Submitted	
29839	Nov 15, 2000	Sent back for modifications	Management agreed with the types of items budgeted; however, it asked that all amounts be lowered.
29839	Nov 20, 2000	Submitted	
29839	Nov 30, 2000	Approved	

The top model in Figure 8.7 simply shows that budget revisions may simply be handled by creating and maintaining a whole new budget each time a revision is needed. The old budget can then be related to the next budget via the recursive relationship around BUDGET. While this model is very simple, the disadvantage is that the whole budget needs to be rerecorded, even though many of the budgeted items may remain consistent from one revision to the next. Also, this model will not track the history of changes that were made from one budget revision to the next. This model is designed for organizations with relatively simply budgets and budgeting needs.

The bottom model in Figure 8.7 shows that each BUDGET may have one or more BUDGET REVISIONs over time, which can affect many parts of the BUDGET. Each BUDGET is composed of one or more BUDGET ITEMs, each of which may be affected by one or more BUDGET REVISION IMPACTs. Each BUDGET REVISION may affect more than one BUDGET ITEM and vice versa, thus resulting in the many-to-many relationship between BUDGET ITEMs and BUDGET REVISIONs, resolved by the BUDGET REVISION IMPACTs, which is an associative entity.

The **revised amount** attribute of BUDGET REVISION IMPACT maintains the reduction or increased amount of a budgeted item. The **add delete flag** shows which budget items have been added or deleted according to the budget revision. The **revision reason** attribute shows why each budgeted item needed to be changed.

Because budgets may go through many revisions or versions, the BUDGET REVISION entity is used to maintain each revision in its entirety. Each BUDGET REVISION is uniquely identified by the **budget ID** and the **revision seq** that specifies the version of the budget.

Table 8.10 illustrates examples of the information in the BUDGET REVISION entity. This example shows that budget 29839 had two revisions, 1.1 and 1.2.

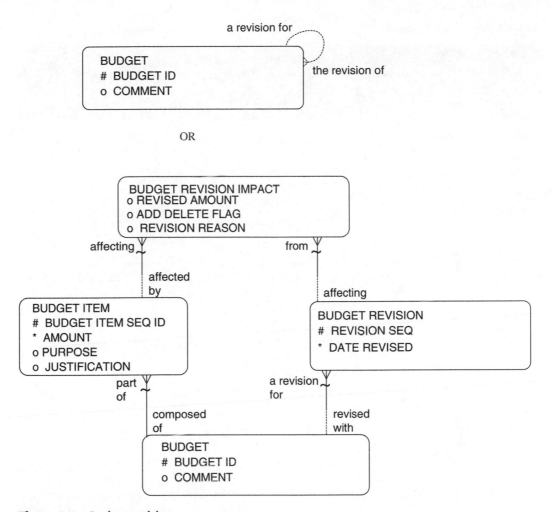

Figure 8.7 Budget revisions.

The initial budget was subsequently revised by revision 1.1. Revision 1.1 consisted of changes to items 2 and 3 and adding an item for Internet advertising. This shows that a BUDGET REVISION can affect more than one BUDGET ITEM. Revision 1.2 was needed to adjust the direct mail budget again, showing that the same BUDGET ITEM may be affected by more than one BUDGET REVISION. This example, which confirms the need for a many-to-many relationship, is accounted for using the BUDGET REVISION IMPACT entity, which stores the changes to the BUDGET ITEMs. With this structure, both the current and change history of the budget can be maintained and accessed.

Table 8.10 Budget Revision Impact

BUDGET ID	BUDGET DESCRIPTION	REVISION NUMBER	A REVISION OF	BUDGET REVISION IMPACT REASON	BUDGET REVISION IMPACT RELATIONSHIP TO BUDGET ITEM	BUDGET REVISION IMPACT AMOUNT	ADD DELETE FLAG
29839	Marketing budget						
29839	Marketing budget	1.1	29839	Needed to substantially cut advertising	29839, item 2	−$10,000	
				Needed to substantially cut direct mail	29839, item 3	−$7,000	
				Need to add budget for Iinternet advertising	29839, item 4	+$5,000	Added
29839	Marketing budget	1.2	29839	Direct mail budget still needs to be reduced	29839, items 3	−$2,000	

Budget Review

In the budgeting process several people may be involved in reviewing a budget for approval. Depending on the degree of formality in the budget process of the enterprise, there may be a need to track the results of each budget review. The BUDGET REVIEW, PARTY, and BUDGET REVIEW RESULT TYPE entities in Figure 8.8 provide for the tracking of the parties involved in budget reviews as well as the results of the budget review process.

The BUDGET REVIEW entity provides the information about which parties were involved in the review process via the relationship from BUDGET REVIEW to PARTY. The **review date** identifies when they were involved in the review. The **comment** attribute allows any personal opinions about the review to be documented. Each person's decision regarding the budget review is indicated via the relationship to BUDGET REVIEW RESULT TYPE.

Is the budget review process related to the BUDGET entity or the BUDGET REVISION? While each revision may be reviewed, each BUDGET REVISION is really a part of the BUDGET and is thus covered in the review process. There-

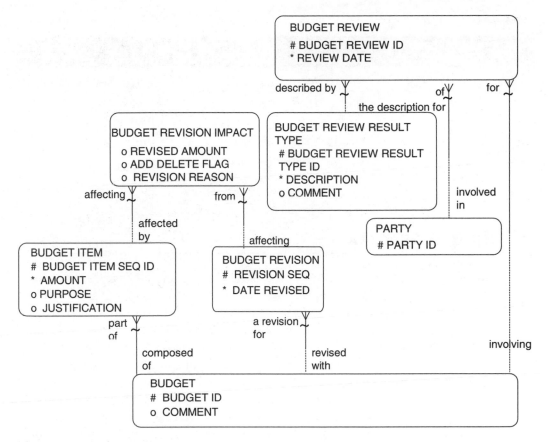

Figure 8.8   Budget review.

fore, the BUDGET REVIEW is related to the BUDGET, which may include one or more BUDGET REVISIONs.

Table 8.11 illustrates the information that may be contained in the BUDGET REVIEW process. The example provides information on the people involved in the budget review process and their comments and conclusions. This information serves as supporting information regarding budget reviews and could ultimately affect the BUDGET STATUS, which was defined in Figure 8.6.

One may think that the BUDGET REVIEW entity is related to the BUDGET STATUS because the result of the reviews may affect the budget revision status. In reality, there is not really a direct data relationship between these entities because reviews and statuses each exist independently for a budget. The enterprise, however, may maintain business rules to determine what review results would constitute moving from one status to the next.

Table 8.11 Budget Review

BUDGET ID	BUDGET REVISION PARTY ID	REVIEW DATE	BUDGET REVIEW RESULT DESCRIPTION	COMMENT
29839	Susan Jones	Nov 10, 2000	Accepted	Budget seems reasonable
	John Smith	Nov 15, 2000	Rejected	Budgeted amount is too high
29839	Susan Jones	Nov 22, 2000	Accepted	Budget is OK
	John Smith	Nov 30, 2000	Accepted	Budget is OK

Budget Scenarios

Budgeted items frequently have different figures associated with them based on various scenarios. For example, there may be different moneys allocated to a budgeted item depending on whether the market conditions are excellent, fair, or poor. The data model then needs a way to show what the budgeted amount is for the items under different conditions or scenarios.

Figure 8.9 provides a model that allows variations on the amounts budgeted based on different BUDGET SCENARIOS. Each BUDGET SCENARIO has a **description** that stores the type of scenario such as "excellent market condition," "poor market conditions," "worst case," "best case," "major deal signed," "no major deal signed." This allows maintaining multiple budgeted figures based on these conditions. Each BUDGET or BUDGET ITEM may have several BUDGET SCENARIO APPLICATIONs, which store either an **amount change** or a **percentage change** for each BUDGET SCENARIO. This means that these amounts or percentages may be applied uniformly across the whole budget (if it is related to the BUDGET) or may vary for each budgeted item (if it is related to the BUDGET ITEM). The **amount change** or **percentage change** maintains either the dollar amount of the change or the percentage of the change that is applied to each BUDGET ITEM amount, which will vary based on the particular BUDGET SCENARIO. For instance, there may be $10,000 more in the budget item for "marketing" if the BUDGET SCENARIO description is "excellent market conditions," but there will be –$5,000 for the same BUDGET ITEM with a BUDGET SCENARIO of "poor market conditions."

The BUDGET SCENARIO RULE stores the standard **percentage change** or **amount change** with which to raise or lower the amounts or percentages for standard BUDGET ITEM TYPEs. These rules may be the default amounts or percentages tied to the BUDGET ITEM SCENARIO; however, they may be different than the values for specific budgeted items because more might be known at budgeting time.

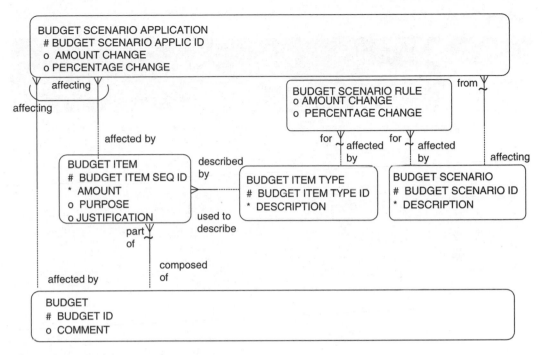

Figure 8.9 Budget scenario.

Table 8.12 provides an example of the values that may be in budget scenarios. The table shows that the budgeted item amounts may vary based on different scenarios. The "trade show" budget is $20,000; however the data structures provide for a 20 percent higher budget if there are excellent marketing conditions and 20 percent lower if poor marketing conditions. This implies that the budget is still $20,000 and is not changed in average marketing conditions. THE BUDGET SCENARIO *RULE* PERCENTAGE CHANGE column represents the suggested increase or decrease for the budget item *type*. The BUDGET SCENARIO APPLICATION PERCENTAGE CHANGE represents the actual percentage change that was used for the specific budget. The example that follows shows that the rule was used to define changes on scenarios for all budget items except for trade shows under "poor marketing conditions," where the budget specified –20 percent instead of the suggested –15 percent.

Usage and Sources of Budgeted Amounts

Now that budgets have been set up, how does the organization monitor whether financial commitments have the proper budgeting appropriated for them and monitor what commitments and expenses have been made to each budget

Table 8.12 Budget Scenarios

BUDGET ID	BUDGET DESCRIPTION	BUDGET ITEM SEQ	BUDGET ITEM TYPE DESCRIPTION	AMOUNT	BUDGET ITEM SCENARIO	BUDGET SCENARIO RULE PERCENTAGE CHANGE	BUDGET SCENARIO PERCENTAGE CHANGE
29839	Marketing budget	1	Trade shows	$20,000	Excellent marketing conditions	+20%	+20%
					Poor marketing conditions	−15%	−20%
		2	Advertising	$30,000	Excellent marketing conditions	+25%	+25%
					Poor marketing conditions	−15%	−15%
		3	Direct mail	$15,000	Over 2% return responses	+30%	+30%
					Less than 1% return responses	−40%	−40%

item? Certain transactions, such as requirements, orders, and payments, may need to be related to budgeted items in order to monitor ongoing use of budgets. The following models may be used to track budgets for expenditures (usages of budgeted amounts) or to track budget revenues (sources of budgeted amounts).

Figure 8.10 provides a data model to answer these questions. Each ORDER ITEM may be authorized via and allocated to a specific BUDGET ITEM. This relationship establishes what commitments (and dollar amounts) have been made to various budget items. A REQUIREMENT may be funded via many BUDGET ITEMS (and vice versa) through the entity REQUIRMENT BUDGET ALLOCATION. This relationship provides information about the outstanding needs for the use of budgets.

The many-to-many relationship between PAYMENT and BUDGET ITEM is resolved by using a PAYMENT BUDGET ALLOCATION entity. The PAYMENT BUDGET ALLOCATION records both disbursements and receipts against budget items, but only for disbursements that *do not have* a corresponding order associated with them. For disbursements that have a purchase order, the rela-

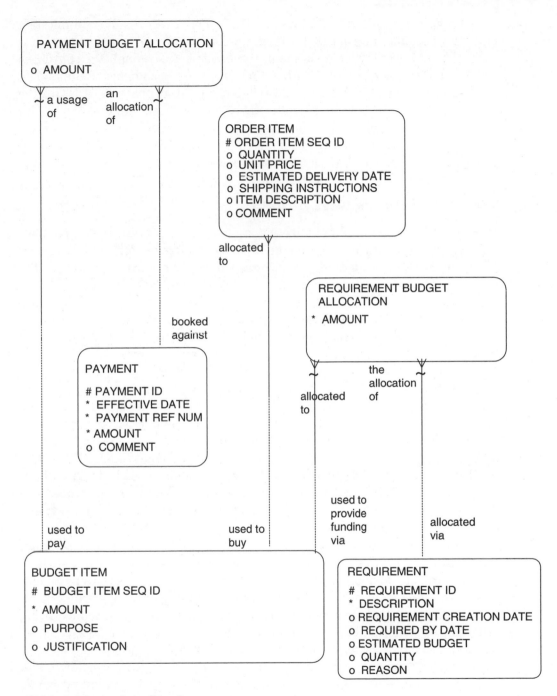

Figure 8.10 Budget allocations.

tionship between ORDER ITEM and BUDGET ITEM records the commitment of moneys against the budget. To determine the payment of moneys (which is the next step beyond the commitment) for disbursements that have a purchase order, the PAYMENT BUDGET ALLOCATION is not used because the budget item allocation can be derived from relationships from the PAYMENT to the corresponding PURCHASE ORDER ITEM of the purchase order.

The next two sections describe the model in Figure 8.10, which illustrates how to track commitments against budgeted amount, such as placing an order, as well as payments against budgets, such as the disbursement of funds.

Commitments against Budgets

Most enterprises involved in budgeting are interested in two types of comparisons against the budget: what commitments exist against a budget item, and what has been expended against a budget item. This section addresses the information needed to track commitments against a budget.

After a budget is approved, enterprises are interested in tracking commitments against a budget. An item on a purchase order may establish a commitment against a budget item. Therefore, in Figure 8.10, the data model illustrates that each ORDER ITEM may be allocated to one and only one BUDGET ITEM. The order item will generally be from a purchase order; however, for revenue budgets the same model can also be used for sales orders. For example, a purchase order item for 20 "Johnson Elite Pens" may be recorded against an administration department's budget item for "office supplies."

One may conclude that each purchase order item is for a specific product and that each product corresponds to a particular budget item. This would result in a PRODUCT to BUDGET ITEM relationship instead of the ORDER ITEM to BUDGET ITEM. Although this may work in some circumstances, the allocation of a commitment is very dependent on the particular situation and usually cannot be generalized.

Consider the purchase of a personal computer (PC). On one purchase order, the PC is used for a systems development project and is tied to the budget item for that project. On another purchase order for a PC, the PC is for a particular employee and may be allocated to a computer equipment budget item. Therefore, rather than perform budget allocations based on the product being ordered, the ORDER ITEM determines the allocation to a BUDGET ITEM so that individual circumstances can be accommodated.

Budget items may also be used to provide funding for REQUIREMENTs to determine if those requirements can actually be implemented. In other words, before committing to a requirement, there may be a need to allocate it to a budget item in order to determine if there is enough money in the budget for this item. The cost of the requirement may need allocation to one or more BUDGET ITEMs. Figure 8.10 shows that each REQUIREMENT may be allocated to many

BUDGET ITEMs and that one BUDGET ITEM may be used to fund more than one REQUIREMENT. Hence, this many-to-many relationship is resolved with the entity REQUIREMENT BUDGET ALLOCATION. The **amount** attribute is used to store the dollar allocation information so that total requirements for any given item are easily calculated.

For example, an internal repair order (i.e., a work requirement) to repair a personal computer may have an estimated cost of $50 per hour for the employee who is fixing it. This may represent a possible commitment toward a specific budget item such as "PC Repairs" (if the requirement is acted on). Over time, there could be many such orders against the same budgeted item.

On the other hand, a WORK REQUIREMENT for a project may require $100,000 total from several different budget items. In order to pay the project staff, the work order may need $80,000 from the BUDGET ITEM for "salary" that is included in a budget for research projects. In addition, the project may also need $20,000 for office supplies, which comes from a budget item for "office supplies" in the overhead budget for the enterprise.

Payments against Budgets

In addition to knowing what commitments have been made against budget items, organizations also want to know what payments have been made against each budget item. The commitment, such as a purchase order item, represents an obligation to pay, whereas the payment, such as a disbursement, represents actual payments made against the budget item.

The data model shown in Figure 8.10 provides the ability to capture payments against budgets under two different scenarios: when there is an order prior to the disbursement and when there is an payment without an order preceding it.

When there is an order prior to the payment, the payment may be traced back to the corresponding order item. This is necessary to determine how much of the purchase order item is now expended versus what was committed against the budget item. In other words, the data model tracks disbursements against the corresponding order that is tied to the budget item. For instance, a $50,000 purchase order for an "office supplies" budget item may have a $25,000 disbursement against it. The $50,000 represents the budget item commitment. The $25,000 represents disbursements against that commitment.

The PAYMENT is related back to the ORDER ITEM through a series of data model transversals. The PAYMENT is related to the INVOICE ITEM entity through the INVOICE PAYMENT ITEM APPLICATION. Then each INVOICE ITEM is related to either SHIPMENT ITEMs (for goods) or directly to the ORDER ITEM (for services purchased). The SHIPMENT ITEM is then related back to an ORDER ITEM of a purchase order.

Needless to say, the relationships from a disbursement back to the originating order item are very complex and require numerous business rules. For instance, payments may pay off partial orders or many orders for various shipments. The enterprise will need business rules regarding how to allocate the disbursements to the appropriate purchase orders.

While it may be complex to trace back a payment to an order, it is also necessary if the budget is to accurately reflect committed and expended amounts against a budget item. Whether the information is stored in the database or a person manually figures out the budget allocation, the same process needs to occur: The disbursement needs to be mapped to the corresponding invoice, mapped to the shipment, then mapped to the order details, in order to figure out the proper budget allocation.

In some circumstances, an order may not be in place before the payment is made. For example, an employee may go out to a store and pay for items with a check, without a purchase order. Yet, this disbursement may still need to be allocated against a budget item. The data model shown in Figure 8.10 accommodates this circumstance by using the PAYMENT BUDGET ALLOCATION entity. This is an intersection entity between the BUDGET ITEM and the PAYMENT. The **amount** attribute records how much of each payment is allocated to each budget item.

Table 8.13 gives an example of a disbursement budget allocation. In this case, an employee went out to an office supplies store and wrote out a check for $2,000 for the purchase of a chair and some office supplies. This payment needs to be allocated between two budget items: office supplies and furniture. The first two columns of the table describe the budget and the item budgeted. The next three columns describe information about the disbursement. The last column shows that $500 of the transaction was allocated to the "office supplies" budget item and $1,500 was allocated to the "furniture" budget item.

Table 8.13 Disbursement Budget Allocation

BUDGET ID	BUDGET ITEM TYPE DESCRIPTION	PAYMENT (DISBURSEMENT) ID	PAYMENT TRANSACTION DESCRIPTION	PAYMENT TRANSACTION AMOUNT	PAYMENT BUDGET ALLOCATION AMOUNT
38576	Office supplies	2903	Payment by check for a chair and office supplies	$2,000	$500
38576	Furniture	2903	Payment by check for a chair and office supplies	$2,000	$1,500

This budget data model is intended to accommodate not only the purchase order commitment and disbursement side of budgeting but also the projected revenue and receipts of moneys. The model in Figure 8.10 can be used to accommodate the usage *and source* of moneys, meaning tracking sales order commitments and receipts against budgeted projections.

The PAYMENT BUDGET ALLOCATION may be for a RECEIPT or DISBURSEMENT, thereby including receipts of moneys as they relate to projected sales invoices. Also, the relationship from BUDGET ITEM to ORDER ITEM should allow tracking of items on sales orders as well as purchase orders. This model allows the enterprise to set up budgets for incoming and outgoing moneys.

Budget Relationship to General Ledger

Budgets are used for different purposes than general ledger accounts. Budgets are used to monitor disbursements; general ledger accounts are used to report the financial performance of an enterprise. Department managers may define budget items in any fashion that helps them control costs. Accountants categorize their chart of accounts to meet tax needs and various financial reporting needs.

Therefore, budget items may not correspond directly with general ledger accounts. It is very helpful (and sometimes required) to be able to tie budget items to general ledger accounts. An enterprise may want to see how much was budgeted and expended for a specific general ledger account such as "marketing expense."

Figure 8.11 shows a data model that relates budget item types to general ledger accounts. Each BUDGET ITEM TYPE may be related to many GENERAL LEDGER ACCOUNTs and vice versa. Therefore, the GL BUDGET XREF entity resolves the many-to-many relationship.

Table 8.14 illustrates examples of relationships between budget items and general ledger accounts. The first example illustrates a situation that accountants love! When a departmental manager uses the general ledger account name for budgeting purposes, then the budget item ("office supplies") has a one-to-one mapping to the general ledger account ("office supplies expense").

The second example, illustrated by the second and third rows in Table 8.14, shows that many budget item types may correspond to a single general ledger account (this is still easy for accountants to track and audit). Budget items were set up for a sales director position and for a sales representative. These are both mapped to a general ledger account called "salaries expense."

The third example is the most complex and will require more work on the part of the enterprise to maintain correctly. The fourth and fifth rows of Table

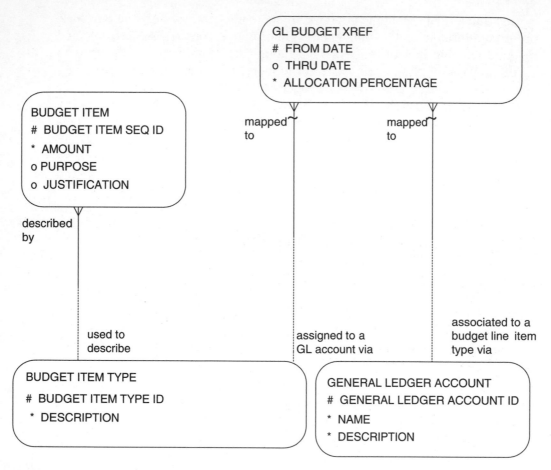

Figure 8.11   Budget relationship to general ledger.

Table 8.14   General Ledger Budget Xref

GENERAL LEDGER ACCOUNT NAME	BUDGET ITEM TYPE DESCRIPTION	GL BUDGET XREF ALLOCATION PERCENTAGE	GL BUDGET XREF FROM DATE	GL BUDGET XREF THRU DATE
Office Supplies Expense	Office supplies	100	Jan 1, 2001	
Salaries Expense	Sales director	100	Jan 1, 2001	
Salaries Expense	Sales representative	100	Jan 1, 2001	
Trade Show Expense	Marketing	50	Jan 1, 2001	
Advertising Expense	Marketing	50	Jan 1, 2001	

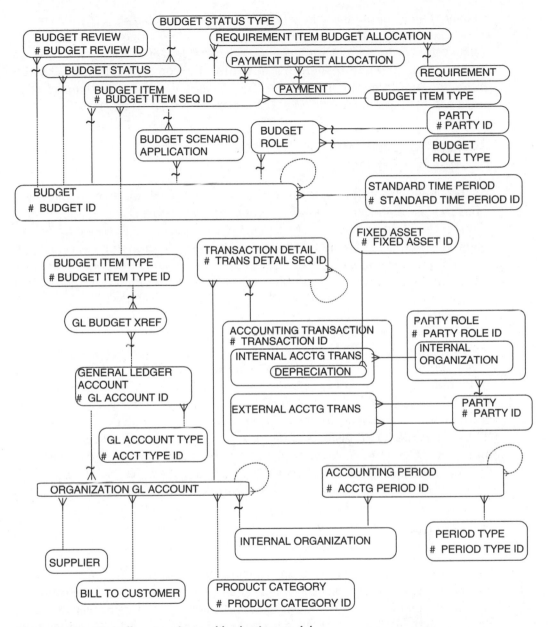

Figure 8.12 Overall accounting and budgeting model.

8.14 show that "marketing" budget items should be mapped 50 percent to "trade show" and 50 percent to "advertising expense" general ledger accounts.

The rules for how budget items map to general ledger accounts may change over time. The **from date** and **thru date** attributes on the GL BUDGET XREF entity allow different mappings over time. This model assumes that the mappings will be the same for different organizations within an enterprise.

Budgeted Items versus General Ledger Accounts

The previous model showed that there are standard mappings from budget item types to general ledger accounts. Another common information requirement is to show the budgeted figures as they compare to general ledger accounts. For example, there may be budgets for certain classifications of expenses, for depreciation, for projected revenues, or for any other general ledger account.

The model in Figure 8.11 can be used to find out the budgeted amount for each general ledger account. Each BUDGET ITEM is of a BUDGET ITEM TYPE that relates to one or more GENERAL LEDGER ACCOUNTs (thru GL BUDGET XREF), which then relates to the ORGANIZATION GL ACCOUNT, hence tying the budget item amount back to the specific general account for an organization. This relationship transversal is complex because of the fact that there may be many-to-many relationships between general ledger accounts and budgets. If there is always a one-to-one correspondence, the model could be changed to put in a one-to-one relationship between the GENERAL LEDGER ACCOUNT and BUDGET ITEM TYPE instead of the associative GL BUDGET XREF. Furthermore, with a one-to-one relationship, one could show **budgeted amount** as a field in the ORGANIZATION GL ACCOUNT in lieu of the BUDGET and BUDGET ITEM structures, if there was no need to store other budget information.

Summary

There are many similar accounting and budgeting information requirements among various enterprises. This chapter has included data models to establish charts of accounts for internal organizations, track accounting transactions, set up budgets, record budget revisions, maintain budget scenarios, maintain budget review process information, record commitments and allocations against budgets, and cross-reference budgets to general ledger accounts.

Figure 8.12 shows an overall view of the accounting and budgeting models included in this chapter.

Please refer to Appendix A for a listing of entities and attributes. SQL scripts to build tables and columns derived from the logical models in this book can be found on the full-blown CD-ROM, which is sold separately.

CHAPTER

9

Human Resources

So far, this book has discussed models for handling much of the information an enterprise needs to conduct business: parties, products, orders, shipments, invoices, work efforts, and accounting. One critical section of the business remains for discussion: human resources, or HR. Without human resources, an enterprise cannot employ and use the key resources it needs to stay in business.

Information that an enterprise may want to keep includes the following:

- Who is employed, and what is the history of employments?
- What positions exist in the company?
- Are they filled? If so, who has what position, and what are his or her responsibilities?
- Who reports to whom?
- What is the rate of pay for these positions?
- Who received raises and when?
- What benefits does the enterprise provide and to whom?
- What is the cost of these benefits?
- What is the status of employment applications?
- What are the skills of employees?

- What is the performance of employees?

- What are the preferences, deductions, and payroll information needed to process payroll?

- What applicants have there been, and how many of them have turned into employees?

- What has been the rate of turnover and the causes of turnover?

Why is it necessary to model human resource data given that enterprises usually buy a standard human resources package with its own data structure? One reason is that it is important to know what the information requirements are for the enterprise in order to drive a proper package selection. Another reason is that many enterprises implement a separate HR system, very often through a package that may not integrate well with other in-house systems.

This chapter illustrates a model that allows an enterprise to track basic human resources information and have it tied to other models presented in this book. The models presented in this chapter include the following:

- Standard human resources model (EMP DEPT model)

- Employment

- Position definition

- Position type definition

- Position fulfillment

- Position reporting

- Position fulfillment and tracking

- Salary determination and pay history

- Benefits tracking

- Payroll information

- Employee application

- Employee skills and qualifications

- Employee performance (alternate model also provided)

- Employee termination

Standard Human Resources Model

A very basic model for employees, shown in many textbooks, is called the EMP DEPT model. Figure 9.1 shows this model. Each EMP (employee) has information such as his or her employee id (**emp id**), **emp name**, **position**, and **date hired**. Each EMP reports to another EMP, who is the manager, as shown in the

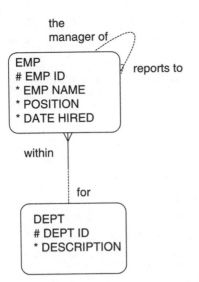

Figure 9.1 Standard emp dept model.

recursive relationship from EMP to EMP. Each EMP is within a DEPT, which also has an ID and description.

Figure 9.1 is useful to demonstrate data model principles by using this simplified model of human resources. The models shown in this book will illustrate a much more effective human resources data model to maintain real-life human resource information requirements.

There are several simplifying structures in this standard model:

- Employee, manager, and departments are roles that should be ideally maintained as a subtype of PARTY ROLE so that a person or organization is not redundantly stated for each role played.

- The employment of an individual to an internal organization is an important PARTY RELATIONSHIP that is not shown.

- Positions are shown as an attribute in the standard model. POSITION is an important entity, which has its own information as well as a many-to-many relationship with the employee (this will be explained later).

- The reporting structure showing one employee reporting to one and only one other employee is overly simplistic. For one thing, an employee may report to more than one manager through a dotted line or matrix structure. Another issue is whether the reporting structure really is from one employee to another. If John Jones gets promoted, do all the people that John had reporting to him also get promoted at that time? Is the reporting structure based on the person, or do positions really report to other positions?

■ There is no history reflected in these data models. When did each employee have each position? When was he or she in each department? When was he employed with the organization?

The following universal data models for human resources will handle these questions and provide for a much more robust human resources data structure.

Employment

What data structure could one use to model the employee-employer relationship? There is a **from date** and a **thru date** for the relationship, there is a status of the relationship, there may be associated agreements within the context of the relationship and communication events within the relationship. These all represent information requirements for any relationship between two parties, or in other words, a PARTY RELATIONSHIP.

Figure 9.2 provides a data model to maintain employment information. EMPLOYMENT is a subtype of PARTY RELATIONSHIP and represents a rela-

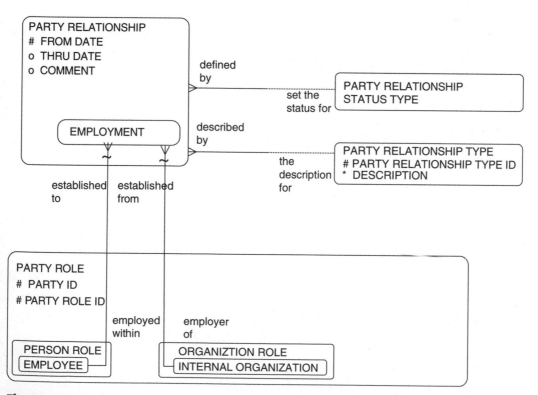

Figure 9.2 Employment.

tionship between the PARTY ROLES of EMPLOYEE and INTERNAL ORGANI-ZATION. This assumes that the enterprise is interested only in tracking its own employees. If the model needs to accommodate employees of external organizations as well, then the EMPLOYMENT entity should be between the EMPLOYEE and EMPLOYER instead.

The EMPLOYMENT inherits the properties of PARTY RELATIONSHIP because it is a type of relationship between two parties. It inherits the fact that it has a **from date**, which would represent the start of the relationship or the hire date, as well as the **thru date**, which would be the last date of the employment. It inherits the relationship to PARTY RELATIONSHIP STATUS TYPE because each employment will have a status such as "active," "inactive," "pending," "terminated," and so on.

The EMPLOYMENT entity allows important pieces of information to be placed where they belong. For example, many data models will show the status of the employee when the data really represents the status of the *employment*. The status of "resigned" is not really the status of that employee. That employee may have resigned from one subsidiary and then been hired by another subsidiary within the enterprise. The status of resigned is really the status of the EMPLOYMENT because it represents a piece of information about two parties, namely that the employee resigned from an internal organization.

This provides yet another example of the importance of distinguishing between attributes of the party versus those of the relationship (two parties). When these two entities get mixed up, (and they will get mixed up if there are not two different entities in the data model from which to reference a party versus a relationship), data inconsistencies and errors occur, leading to inaccurate data.

Position Definition

What does a position represent? A POSITION represents a job slot in an enterprise that can be occupied by more than one person over time. In some enterprises, this may also be referred to as an FTE or full-time equivalent. For example, if the HR department of an organization was told that there were two positions (two FTEs) open for a junior programmer, that would indicate that they could hire two people. Each of these people may perform the same type of duties, but they would be filling two separate job slots. Over time, one of these people may resign and be replaced by a third person. This third person would fill the existing position that had been vacated. This would not constitute a new position. (This will be explained further in the section on position fulfillment.)

In Figure 9.3 the entities used to define a position are modeled. The POSITION entity contains the basic information to track about any given job slot. The POSITION TYPE entity provides information for further defining and cate-

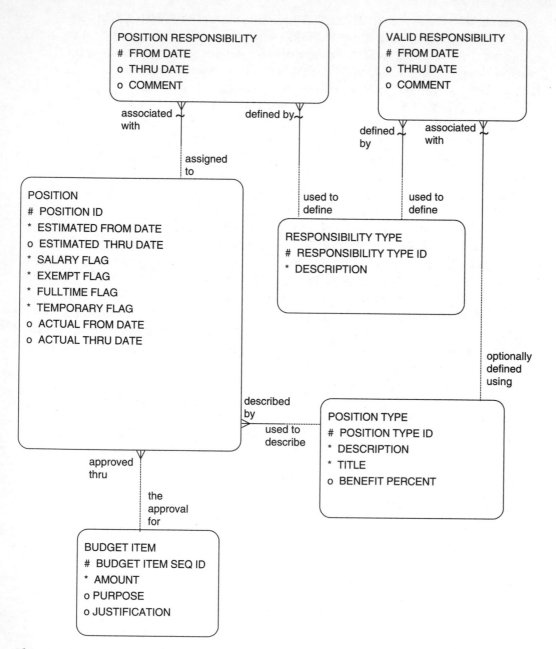

Figure 9.3   Position definition.

gorizing a job, while the BUDGET ITEM provides a possible means of authorizing a slot. The entities RESPONSIBILITY TYPE, VALID RESPONSIBILITY, and POSITION RESPONSIBILITY provide a mechanism for assigning and tracking what are the possible and actual responsibilities for any position.

Position

Some of the data an enterprise may wish to track about a POSITION is shown in Figure 9.3. The **estimated from date** and **estimated thru date** can be used for planning. This data is the first indication of when the enterprise expects to need a person to fill this role in the organization. If the position is for an indefinite period, the **estimated thru date** would remain blank.

The various flags included in the entity help to define the particular circumstances under which a person hired for a position will be employed. Will the person be salaried or hourly? Is the position exempt or nonexempt under the Fair Labor Standards Act (FLSA)? Will this be a full-time or part-time position? Is it temporary or permanent? The answers to these questions will be very important for benefits administrators and payroll personnel. Additionally, the model includes an **actual from date** and **actual thru date** to allow tracking of this data once it is known. Sample data for some of these attributes is shown in Table 9.1.

Position Authorization

First, for a job to even exist in an enterprise, it must usually be approved and funded in some manner. In this model, positions can be approved through a BUDGET ITEM. One BUDGET ITEM may approve or fund one or more positions. For example, there may be a budget item for programmers. The amount of this budget item is then used to fund the multiple programmer positions that the enterprise has. If a position is tied to a budget, then the position is considered "authorized" when the BUDGET STATUS for the BUDGET that affects BUDGET ITEM has been approved (see Chapter 8 for more on the BUDGET model).

Table 9.1 Position Data

POSITION ID	ESTIMATED FROM DATE	ESTIMATED THRU DATE	SALARY?	EXEMPT?	FULL-TIME?	TEMP?
101	Jan 1, 2001		Yes	No	Yes	No
204	Jun 1, 2001	Aug 31, 2001	Yes	Yes	Yes	Yes

Position Type

Even though each job opening represents a single occurrence of POSITION, several of these openings could have some characteristics in common, such as a title or description of the type of job. Those common characteristics are represented by a common POSITION TYPE. The entity POSITION TYPE maintains information associated with all the slots that exist for a kind of job. Table 9.2 contains examples of this data.

As shown in the data, each POSITION TYPE will have a **position type ID** for identification, a brief **description**, and a standard job **title**. Other data that could be stored is the **benefit percent**, which records the percentage of benefits that an enterprise will pay for a particular type of position. For example, the data in Table 9.2 indicates that the enterprise has made a decision to pay 100 percent of the benefits for all "business analyst" positions.

Position Responsibilities

Also shown in Figure 9.1 are the entities RESPONSIBILITY TYPE, VALID RESPONSIBILITY, and POSITION RESPONSIBILITY. These will allow for the definition of various job responsibilities, identification of which responsibilities are appropriate for the different position types, and identification of responsibilities that are actually assigned to a given position. Notice that both VALID RESPONSIBILITY and POSITION RESPONSIBILITY have a **from date** and a **thru date.** These allow the enterprise to assign and track historically changing responsibilities for jobs and positions. In this way very specific and detailed job descriptions can be developed, while at the same time allowing for ongoing change.

To maintain a tightly integrated system, the enterprise may wish to establish business rules to control some of this data. Data checks could be developed to ensure that, if a certain RESPONSIBILITY TYPE is assigned as a POSITION RESPONSIBILITY, it is first identified as a VALID RESPONSIBILITY for the POSITION TYPE with which the POSITION is associated. For example, a new

Table 9.2 Position Type Data

POSITION TYPE ID	DESCRIPTION	TITLE	BENEFIT PERCENT
1100	Recommend proper policies, procedures, and mechanisms for conducting effective business.	Business Analyst	100
2200	Enter bookkeeping figures, file appropriate accounting papers, and perform administrative accounting tasks.	Accounting Clerk	50

position for an "account representative" is created. One of the responsibilities is to "create monthly sales report." Before that could be assigned, "create monthly sales report" would have to already exist as a VALID RESPONSIBILITY associated with the POSITION TYPE of "account representative." In addition, the **from date** and **thru date** in both entities could be compared to be sure that the assigned responsibility is actually valid for the assigned time period.

Position Type Definition

Some enterprises may need to further classify the types of positions they have. To help with this, the model shown in Figure 9.4 was developed. In it an optional entity POSITION TYPE CLASS is shown as an intersection between POSITION TYPE and POSITION CLASSIFICATION TYPE. Using these entities, additional groupings of types of positions can be done. Because it is possible that a POSITION TYPE could be reclassified over time, the POSITION TYPE CLASS entity with its attributes of **from date** and **thru date** are included to support the many-to-many relationship between POSITION TYPE and POSITION CLASSIFICATION TYPE. An example of possible data is shown in Table 9.3

The data shown in Table 9.3 indicates that for the enterprise in question, the position types "programmer," "system administrator," and "business analyst" were at one time all classified as "computer" positions. Then in 2000, the "business analyst" was reclassified to "MIS." In addition to the "computer" classification, "programmer" is also classified as "technical" while the "system administrator" is considered "admin support." In any of the cases where the **thru date** is not included, it is assumed that the classification is still valid. Using this model, the enterprise can develop a very detailed and flexible classification system to meet its needs.

Some enterprises may wish to use the POSITION CLASSIFICATION TYPE entity to categorize how the position will offer pay. POSITION CLASSIFICATION TYPEs could include data such as "hourly," "salary," "exempt," "nonexempt," "part-time," "full-time," "regular," or "temporary." Then, the entity POSITION TYPE CLASS would act as an historical list of these base classifications for a POSITION. Note that the POSITION entity currently shows binary attributes for pairs of these classifications. If this use is implemented with the listed data, then these attributes could be removed from POSITION. (In a physical model the enterprise may also want to implement this data as flags associated with a position slot for easier reporting of current data.)

Organization

Certain enterprises may need to track whether certain types of positions are unionized. This is handled through the relationship to UNION, which is a sub-

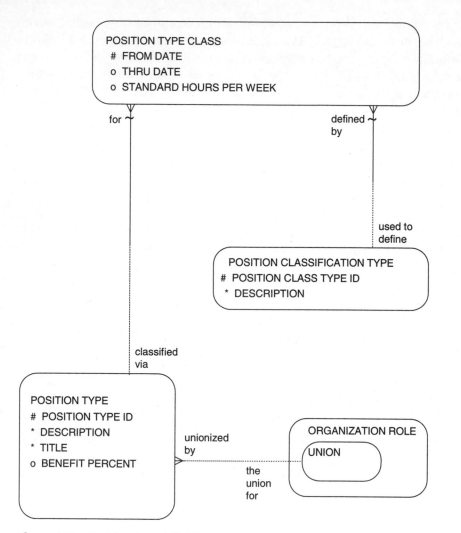

Figure 9.4 Position type definition.

Table 9.3 Position Type Classification Data

POSITION TYPE	CLASSIFICATION TYPE	FROM DATE	THRU DATE
Programmer	Computer	Jan 1, 1995	
	Technical	Jan 1, 1995	
System Administrator	Computer	Jan 1, 1995	
	Admin Support	Apr 1, 1997	
Business Analyst	Computer	Jan 1, 1995	Dec 31, 1999
	MIS	Jan 1, 2000	

type of ORGANIZATION ROLE because a union is one type of organization. This information could be of vital importance during salary and benefits negotiations or in the case of a pending strike. If a position is protected through a union relationship, then the enterprise may have certain guidelines regarding these types of positions.

Position Fulfillment and Tracking

Figure 9.5 shows a model that will allow the enterprise to track each person's position history within the organization. It includes entities for tracking POSITION FULFILLMENT and POSITION STATUS TYPE. The model needs the entities POSITION and PERSON for context. ORGANIZATION is also included to provide information on the hiring company.

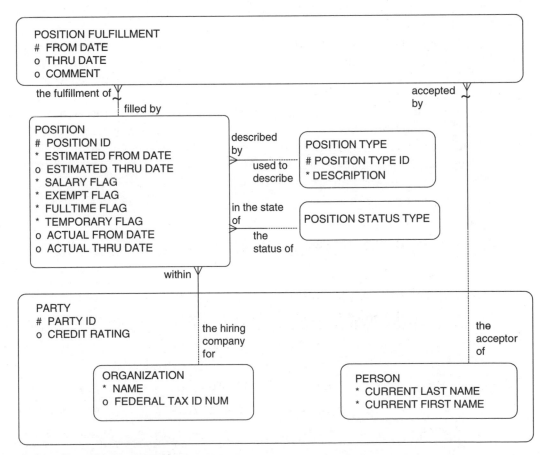

Figure 9.5 Position fulfillment.

Position Fulfillment

A person can, of course, occupy more than one position either over time or at the same time. Conversely, a position may be filled by more than one person over time (and even at the same time through job sharing). The POSITION FULFILLMENT entity provides a very flexible way to retain the history of this activity. The attributes **from date** and **thru date** will allow the enterprise to keep historically accurate information about this data. It is a convenient and effective way to resolve the many-to-many relationship that really exists between PERSON and POSITION. Some possible data is shown in Table 9.5.

The data given shows the career path of Mike Johnson as he moved progressively up the corporate ladder from the position of "mail clerk" to "CEO." Because the **thru date** for the "CEO" entry is blank, it is assumed that he currently holds that position. Also shown is the career of Sue Jones. She started in the position of "programmer" in 1995 then in 1997 took on the additional role of "business analyst." She was then promoted to "MIS manager" in 1999. Finally, she earned her current position as "CIO" (Chief Information Officer) on November 2, 2000.

A popular trend in many enterprises is the concept of job sharing. In this situation, two people fill one position. Both work part-time and share the responsibilities of the position. This is where the concept of an FTE (full-time equivalent) is most useful. With a job-share situation, the enterprise has authorized only one full-time position (one FTE), which constitutes one "head count." One half-time person plus another half-time person equals one FTE. The number of FTEs is the information needed for resource allocation, budgeting, reporting relationships, and such. Again, the information is related to or dependent on the position, not the person.

Table 9.5   Position Fulfillment Data

PERSON	POSITION	FROM DATE	THRU DATE
Mike Johnson	Mail Clerk	May 31, 1980	Jun 1, 1980
	Mail Supervisor	Jun 1, 1980	Dec 31, 1983
	Office Manager	Jan 1, 1984	May 31, 1990
	Regional Manager	Jun 1, 1990	May 31, 1996
	CEO	Jun 1, 1996	
Sue Jones	Programmer	Mar 1, 1995	Feb 27, 1997
	Business Analyst	Feb 28, 1997	Mar 14, 1999
	MIS Manager	Mar 15, 1999	Nov 1, 2000
	CIO	Nov 2, 2000	

Another feature of the POSITION FULFILLMENT entity is that it can be used to record employee assignments in a job-sharing situation without confusing the FTE or head count. This is due to the fact that the primary key of this entity is the combination of an inherited key from POSITION (**position ID**), an inherited key from PERSON (**party ID**), and the attribute **from date**. With this three-part key, it is possible to record more than one person as having accepted the same position during the same time period. Of course, whether this is allowable could be controlled by implementing some business rules. If an enterprise never does job sharing, then the model could be changed to enforce this by removing the relationship to PERSON and hence removing the **party ID** from the compound key. If that were done, then the model would allow one and only one person to occupy a position during the same time period (even in this case, some business rules will be needed).

Note that it is also possible that a person from outside of the organization could fill a position that was authorized, such as a contractor. Because this model shows that POSITION FULFILLMENT must be accepted by a PERSON and not an EMPLOYEE, it is much more flexible than standard models and can handle this situation. To determine if the person is an employee or a person external to the enterprise the PARTY RELATIONSHIP entity may be used (refer to Chapter 2). Because it contains this information, PARTY RELATIONSHIP could also be used to enforce business rules such as whether positions may be filled by non-employees.

Position Status Type

The POSITION STATUS TYPE identifies the current state of a position. When a position is first identified, it is in a state of "planned for." When the enterprise decides to pursue fulfillment of the position, it may then change to a state of "active" or "open." If the enterprise then decides that it no longer needs that position, the status may be "inactive" or "closed." A "fulfilled" status would not be a value because this information can be derived from the POSITION FULFILLMENT entity.

Hiring Organization

What is the hiring company for the position? This is easily tracked via a relationship between POSITION and ORGANIZATION. Without the enterprise doing the hiring, there would be no need for a position.

Other Considerations

Some other information not obvious in this model concerns how a person actually gets offered an open position. In fact, the interview process can be tracked through the PARTY COMMUNICATION EVENT model (see Figure 2.12). An interview is a COMMUNICATION EVENT PURPOSE TYPE with interview notes stored in the entity COMMUNICATION EVENT. See Chapter 2 for more details on this model.

By using the POSITION FULFILLMENT model, combined with the model for position reporting, an enterprise can retain and access a complete picture of its organization and structure at any point in time.

Position Reporting Relationships

Most data models show people reporting to and managed by other people. As discussed in Chapter 2, common models for people and organizations are generally oversimplified. Many models show an EMPLOYEE entity with a recursive relationship for the manager. In a large and dynamic organization, this structure could result in a lot of updating and possible data inconsistencies.

The problem is that in reality the reporting structure is a function of the organizational structure of the enterprise, not of the people in the positions. If it really was a function of the person, then when a person gets promoted, everyone who was previously reporting to that person would still be reporting to that person after the promotion. This is usually not the case. In most instances, when a supervisor is promoted, the vacated supervisory position is filled by another person. The people who originally reported to the supervisor now report to a new person, but they still report to the same position. Instead of changing everyone's reporting relationships, the position reporting model handles this situation by changing one person's position assignment (further demonstrated later in the chapter).

Additionally, an enterprise may identify its position hierarchy before assigning people to the various positions. Certainly this is the case when an organization is first created. This situation also occurs when enterprises reorganize.

What happens when the simplified model is implemented is that usually only a picture of the organization structure at the current time is maintained. All history of reorganizations and promotions is lost. This can be a serious problem when, for example, an EEOC suit is filed against the enterprise and it becomes necessary to determine who occupied a position at a particular point in time and who was the supervisor. The model presented in Figure 9.6 solves this and other challenges.

Position Reporting Structure

The model in Figure 9.6 shows the entity POSITION REPORTING STRUCTURE, which links POSITION back to itself. The attributes **from date** and **thru date** are provided to allow for tracking organizational changes through time, as previously discussed. The **primary flag** attribute is included to help model flexible, matrix-type structures. In these cases, certain positions may report to more than one position at the same time. This indicator allows the enterprise to indicate which reporting relationship is the overriding one.

In the examples shown in Table 9.4, business analysts, system administrators, and programmer/analysts report to the director of IS. Suppose that the enterprise grows and subsequently creates an IS development manager position and a maintenance manager position that report to the director of IS. Instead of changing the reporting relationship of each of the people, the old reporting relationships of the positions would be expired (using the **thru date**) and new records could be added to show the revised structure. In this way, the enterprise can more easily implement the new reporting structure and at the same time retain an accurate history of previous structures.

Notice that in the sample data, the current reporting relationships are identified where the **thru date** is blank. Alternatively, a **thru date** in the future could

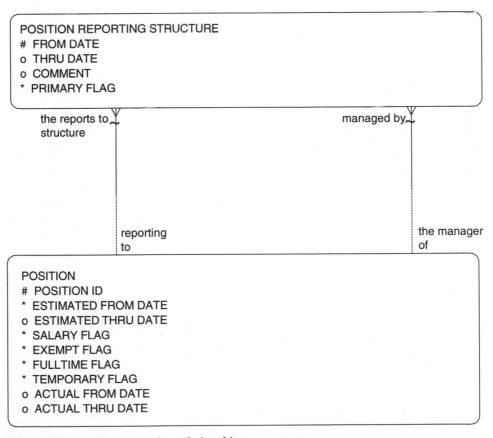

Figure 9.6 Position reporting relationships.

Table 9.4 Position Reporting Relationship Data

REPORTING TO POSITION	THE MANAGER OF POSITION	FROM DATE	THRU DATE	PRIMARY FLAG
Director of Business Information Systems	Business Analyst	Jan 1, 2000	Dec 30, 2000	Yes
	Systems Administrator	Jan 1, 2000	Dec 31, 2000	Yes
	Programmer/Analyst	Jan 1, 2000	Dec 31, 2000	Yes
IS Development Manager	Business Analyst	Jan 1, 2001		Yes
	Systems Administrator	Jan 1, 2001		No
	Programmer/Analyst	Jan 1, 2001		Yes
Maintenance Manager	Systems Administrator	Jan 1, 2001		Yes
	Programmer/Analyst	Jan 1, 2001		No

also indicate a current relationship with a preplanned end date. Note also that with the new structure, the "programmer/analyst" and "systems administrator" positions now report to both the "IS development manager" and the "maintenance manager" (these positions represent actual slots within the enterprise and not position types). They have split duties. In the case of the "systems administrator," the **primary flag** is set to "yes" for the relationship to the "maintenance manager"; it is the opposite for the "programmer/analyst" position. In this way it is possible to identify to which position each of these ultimately reports.

In larger enterprises, these changes to organization structure may affect hundreds or thousands of people. By designing a system that merely changes the reporting relationship of the position instead of the actual parties involved, fewer updates will be required and presumably data will be much cleaner in the long run.

The point is that positions and people are separate entities. The next section will discuss how people and positions are actually related.

Salary Determination and Pay History

The model presented in this section is an extended compensation model that handles both highly structured organizations such as the government or less structured organizations such as small private businesses (see Figure 9.7). This is done using the entities POSITION TYPE RATE, RANGE TYPE, PERIOD TYPE, PAY GRADE, and SALARY STEP. In addition, this model also includes

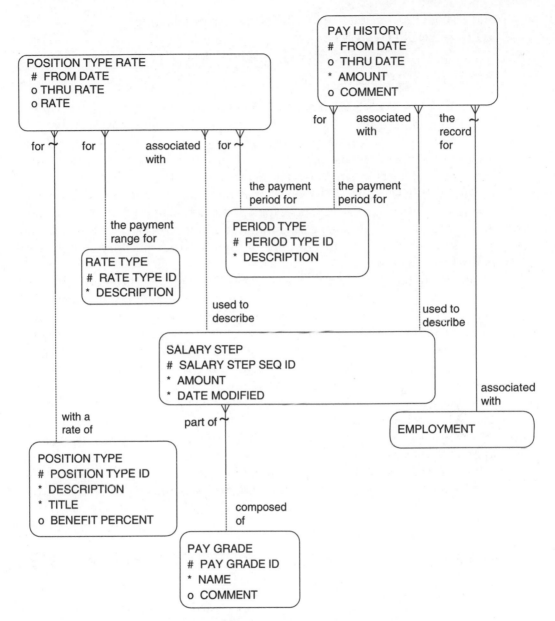

Figure 9.7   Salary determination and history.

entities and relationships to allow the tracking of salary history (i.e., PAY HISTORY and EMPLOYMENT).

Position Type Rate

The POSITION TYPE RATE and RATE TYPE entities were defined in Chapter 6 (see Figure 6.7) to provide the costs and standard rates for various types of positions in order to capture appropriate cost estimates for work efforts. This section will expand the use of this entity to incorporate other types of position rates for tracking standard pay rates and ranges.

The POSITION RATE TYPE entity may be used to record the allowable or acceptable salary and salary ranges for a particular position type. This information could be used by managers during the hiring process when negotiating salary. A **from date** and **thru date** are included so that a history of these standards can also be kept.

The relationship to RATE TYPE provides the ability to record reference information such as "highest pay rate," "lowest pay rate," "average pay rate," and "standard pay rate," which represent different types of pay rates that can be captured for each type of position. This would indicate such things as the upper limit, average amount paid, lower limit, and the default, standard amount of pay for a type of position. The relationship to PERIOD TYPE will allow an enterprise to define various pay period types for which rates can be recorded. Examples of PERIOD TYPE include "per year," "per week," "per month," and so on. This relationship is part of the primary key to allow an enterprise to record information for multiple period types (i.e., average per hour and average per month). Table 9.6 contains sample pay rate data.

The sample data indicates that the enterprise in question has updated rate information for the position type "programmer" only once in 10 years. The rate

Table 9.6   Rate of Pay Data

POSITION TYPE	RATE TYPE	AMOUNT	PERIOD TYPE	FROM DATE	THRU DATE
Programmer	Average pay rate	$45,000	per year	Jan 1, 1990	Dec 31, 1999
	Highest pay rate	$70,000	per year	Jan 1, 1990	Dec 31, 1999
	Lowest pay rate	$25,000	per year	Jan 1, 1990	Dec 31, 1999
	Standard pay rate	$30.00	per hour	Jan 1, 1990	Dec 31, 1999
	Average pay rate	$55,000	per year	Jan 1, 2000	
	Highest pay rate	$90,000	per year	Jan 1, 2000	
	Lowest pay rate	$30,000	per year	Jan 1, 2000	
	Standard pay rate	$55.00	per hour	Jan 1, 2000	

of pay stayed the same from 1990 through 1999, then was increased in 2000. This organization kept information on the average, high, and low annual salary that it was willing to pay to programmers. It also kept track of a standard rate that was used to establish hourly pay.

Pay Grade and Salary Step

Additional information stored in this entity could also include a PAY GRADE and SALARY STEP for use in enterprises that have a predefined, highly structured pay system (such as the federal government). This is done by reference to a structured pay schedule. These types of schedules normally have two levels: a grade and a step. The SALARY STEP entity includes an **amount** attribute and is generally described in the context of a PAY GRADE. Table 9.7 includes part of a sample grade schedule.

Notice that there is an overlap in the pay scale between "GG-1" and "GG-2." Step #1 for GG-2 falls between step #3 and step #4 of GG-1. This is not uncommon in these types of pay systems. It allows HR administrators some flexibility in negotiating pay for new employees. Because the grades are basically "set in stone" and tied to specific position types, the administrators are restricted as to what grades can be offered for any given position. To compensate for these restrictions, the range of pay covered by the steps of a grade are often very wide. Table 9.8 gives sample data for POSITION TYPE RATE where a grade system is used.

There are several things to notice in the data shown in Table 9.8. First, there are no values in the POSITION TYPE RATE **rate** column because, when using a pay grade system, the amount is taken directly from SALARY STEP. Business

Table 9.7 Pay Grade System Sample

GRADE ID	PAY GRADE NAME	SALARY STEP SEQ ID	SALARY STEP AMOUNT
1	GG-1	1	$10,000
		2	$10,200
		3	$10,400
		4	$10,500
		5	$10,800
2	GG-2	1	$10,450
		2	$10,780
		3	$11,200
		4	$11,650

Table 9.8 Rate of Pay Sample #2

POSITION TYPE	RATE TYPE	POSITION TYPE RATE	GRADE	SALARY STEP SEQ ID	PERIOD TYPE	FROM DATE	THRU DATE
Programmer	Average pay rate		GG-6	6	per year	Jan 1, 1990	
	Highest pay rate		GG-8	10	per year	Jan 1, 1990	
	Lowest pay rate		GG-5	1	per year	Jan 1, 1990	

processes would, of course, need to be implemented to ensure that **rate** was not filled in; otherwise, there could be conflicting information. In implementing this model for use with a pay schedule, this attribute could be dropped. Conversely, when implementing the model for an enterprise that *will not* use a schedule, the POSITION TYPE RATE **rate** attribute should be mandatory.

Second, note that the **thru date** is also blank. This illustrates the concept that, over time, the dollar amount for a selected pay grade and step may increase, but the step assignment related to the POSITION TYPE RATE does not need to change. In this case, nothing needs to be changed in the pay rate records to indicate the increase in pay. In other words, there is no need to enter a **thru date**, then create a new record to show the pay increase because the pay increase is reflected via an update to the SALARY STEP information.

Pay History and Actual Salary

Actual salary or pay, represented by PAY HISTORY, is related to a person, *not* POSITION or POSITION TYPE. In fact, it is really related to the EMPLOYMENT (which is a subtype of PARTY RELATIONSHIP) that exists between the employer and employee.

Salary is *not* related to POSITION because the position the person occupies can change over time, but that doesn't mean the salary will automatically change as well. Sometimes, a person is given more responsibility and placed in a higher-level position but is not given the salary raise until he or she demonstrates the capability of performing the duties appropriately. Also, consider again the job-sharing scenario. If the pay were tied to the position, both people would have to be paid the same. This would limit the flexibility of the enterprise to pay one party more than the other based on differing levels of skill or experience.

Depending on the nature of the enterprise, salary is represented by actual dollar amounts and optionally by the relationship to SALARY STEP. Unlike the POSITION TYPE RATE attribute of **rate**, **amount** is always recorded in PAY HISTORY to ensure that there is no confusion on what the person was paid during a given time period. Also, note that because this is a record of the actual rate of pay for a person, not a list of possible rates, there can be only one record for

Table 9.9 Pay History Data

EMPLOYER	EMPLOYEE	FROM DATE	THRU DATE	AMOUNT	PERIOD TYPE
ABC Corporation	John Smith	Jan 1, 1995	Dec 31, 1997	$45,000	per year
		Jan 1, 1998	Dec 31, 2000	$55,000	per year
		Jan 1, 2001		$62,500	per year

the person for any selected time period. The PERIOD TYPE associated with this record is determined by how the enterprise wants to see this data. See Table 9.9 for examples of this data.

The data shown gives the record of pay for John Smith, who works for ABC Corporation. It shows his salary and increases over the past six years. Where the **thru date** is missing, assume that this indicates his current annual salary. With this kind of data, an enterprise can accurately track the salary history of its employees. If it is necessary to track the pay of outside parties, such as contractors, then the data model should relate PAY HISTORY to the supertype of PARTY RELATIONSHIP instead of the subtype EMPLOYMENT.

Benefits Definition and Tracking

In addition to salary or pay, most enterprises provide compensation through a benefits package. This could include vacation, health or life insurance, sick leave, or a retirement plan. The cost of these benefits may be partly or completely absorbed by the enterprise. Figure 9.8 demonstrates a simplified model for benefits tracking. It includes the information on the PARTY BENEFITs for each BENEFIT TYPE within an EMPLOYMENT for each PERIOD TYPE.

Employment

Similar to PAY HISTORY, PARTY BENEFIT is also related to the EMPLOYMENT subtype of PARTY RELATIONSHIP, not the PARTY or PERSON, because the benefits are associated with a particular employer and employee relationship. In a large multicompany enterprise people may move from one company to another, so sometimes their benefits may come from different organizations at different times in their career. If the enterprise wants to track benefits costs at the lower levels of the organization, then associating the costs simply with the employee will not be sufficient. Why not associate the benefit with the employee and the organization directly? By using EMPLOYMENT, the enterprise can enforce business rules that would prevent such things as contractors accidentally being given benefits.

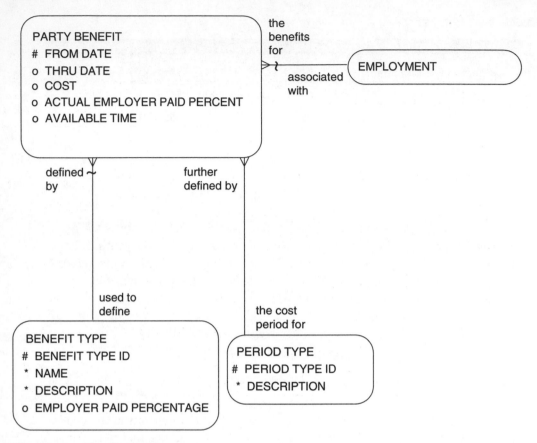

Figure 9.8   Benefits tracking.

For insurance purposes, there may be a need to determine the benefits for a person for more than one organization (through the EMPLOYMENT instances for that person). Some of its employees may have two part-time jobs; it may be important to know the benefits offered by each job to avoid duplication of benefits (a coordination of benefits issue). This is also useful for determining which insurance policy should pay for an illness. The information could be critical in helping the insurance company control its costs.

Party Benefit

In PARTY BENEFIT there can be several pieces of information that the enterprise may wish to track. First is the **from date** and **thru date**. These allow the tracking of benefits through time. Additionally, the enterprise may want to track the actual **cost** of the benefit and the **actual employer paid percentage**. With that information it would be possible to calculate the cost not only to

Table 9.10 Party Benefit Data

EMPLOYER	EMPLOYEE	BENEFIT TYPE	FROM DATE	THRU DATE	COST	PERIOD TYPE	ACTUAL EMPLOYER PAID %	AVAILABLE TIME
ABC Corporation	John Smith	Health	Jan 1, 1998	Dec 31, 2000	$1200	per year	50	
			Jan 1, 2001		$1500	per year	60	
		Vacation				days	100	15
		Sick leave				days	100	10
		401k	Jan 1, 2001		$50.00	per year	100	

the employee but to the enterprise as well. Another attribute, **available time**, is also included for tracking allowable time off such as vacation and sick leave. Example benefit data is shown in Table 9.10.

The examples given deal with John Smith, who works for ABC Corporation. Over the years, the cost of his health insurance has risen from $1,200 to $1,500 per year. During that time ABC Corporation initially paid 50 percent of the cost for him, but it now pays 60 percent. The data also shows that he has 15 vacation days and 10 sick days as a current balance and that the company absorbs the full cost of that time off. Mr. Smith also has a 401k plan that he started when he was eligible in 2001. The information indicates that the plan cost is $50 per year (for administration), with the company picking up 100 percent of the cost.

Period Type

Notice that Table 9.10 includes **Period Type.** This is the result of the resolution of the relationship to the entity PERIOD TYPE (see Figure 9.8). This information is used primarily to modify the **cost** attribute. Without it, there would be no context for the dollars reported and thus no way to determine the enterprise's costs accurately. Additionally, it could also be used as the context for types like "vacation" and "sick leave," as shown in the table.

Benefit Type

The various types of benefits provided by the enterprise are listed in the entity BENEFIT TYPE. Samples of that data are included in Table 9.10. In addition to the identification of the benefit, this entity may also store a standard **employer paid percentage** that can be used to calculate costs related to all employees with a particular benefit.

Percentages for employer contribution are included not only in BENEFIT TYPE but also in PARTY BENEFIT and POSITION TYPE to allow recording this information at various levels of detail. Because of this, certain business rules need to be put in place. A likely set of rules would be as follows:

- If **actual employer paid percent** exists in PARTY BENEFIT, that number takes precedence.

- If that is blank, then **benefit percent** on the POSITION TYPE associated with the person's current position (as indicated in POSITION FULFILL-MENT) is used.

- If both of these values are blank, then the **employer paid percentage** in BENEFIT TYPE would be the override.

Note that this section has provided a general data structure for handling benefits; if a more comprehensive model is needed for enterprises in the insurance industry, there is a more complete model in Chapter 5 of Volume 2— "Insurance."

Payroll Information

Another item to consider for a standard human resources model is payroll (see Figure 9.9). Without payroll, there won't be many human resources working for the enterprise for long! This model considers what to many people will be the most critical portion of payroll: getting paid correctly. Information about payroll is included in the entities EMPLOYEE, INTERNAL ORGANIZATION, PAYMENT METHOD TYPE, PAYROLL PREFERENCE, PAYCHECK, DEDUCTION, and DEDUCTION TYPE.

PAYCHECK is a subtype of the DISBURSEMENT entity and is modeled separately because of some of the unique aspects of a paycheck as opposed to other disbursements. The payment model in Chapter 7 describes a generic data model for making any type of payments, and this section elaborates on that model by adding the specifics of payroll payments.

Employee

As with benefits and salary, all payroll information is related to the EMPLOYEE and INTERNAL ORGANIZATION. These relationships represent more specific modeling of the relationships of PAYMENT from and to PARTY. The relationships are mandatory because if there were no employer (internal organization) and employee or similar relationship, there would be no need for a paycheck. By using the relationships as a base, business rules can be used to ensure that not just any party within the system can be issued a paycheck.

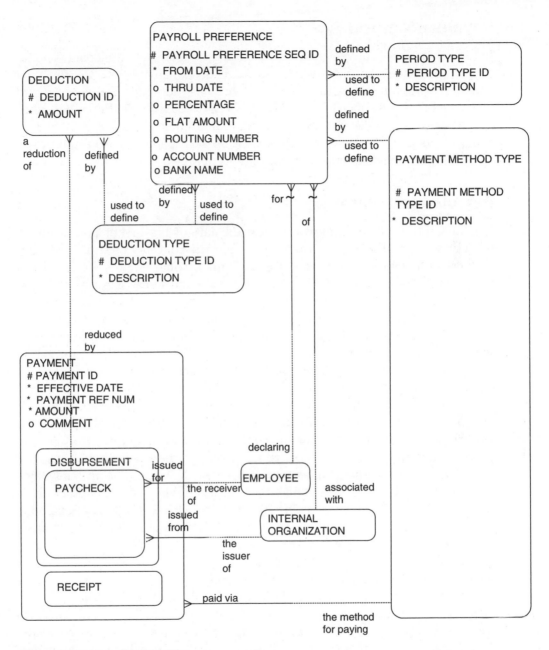

Figure 9.9   Payroll information.

Payment Method Type

In today's world of convenience and electronic commerce, getting paid is not as simple as it once was. Now employers can choose many options to offer their employees when it comes to methods of receiving their pay. The basic form of these options is described by the entity PAYMENT METHOD TYPE, as described in the payment models section of Chapter 7. In it could be stored data such as "cash," "check," and "electronic." Depending on the capabilities of an enterprise's payroll department, any or all of these options may be offered to employees.

Payroll Preference

It is possible that an employee may want part of his or her pay in check form and the rest in cash. Others may want their money split up and electronically deposited to several different banks. Some employees may want standard deductions to be accounted for each and every paycheck, unless overridden.

In order to handle this type of information, the model includes the entity PAYROLL PREFERENCE. Because an employee may change preferences over time, the attributes **from date** and **thru date** are included. Other information that is needed includes the **percentage** of total pay or a **flat amount** that the employee wants designated to a particular PAYMENT METHOD TYPE or designated for certain recurring deductions that are maintained through the relationship from PAYROLL PREFERENCE to DEDUCTION TYPE. If the type of pay selected is "electronic," then the **routing number**, **account number,** and **bank name** may be used to successfully complete the transaction. These are stored as attributes instead of as entities because the enterprise probably does not have the will and means to maintain these as their own entity. Each PAYROLL PREFERENCE may be defined for certain PERIOD TYPEs. For example, a particular standard deduction that is desired may be specified for pay period types of "per year," "per month," or "weekly."

Sample data is included in Table 9.11.

As in previous examples, assume that the employer is still ABC Corporation and the employee is John Smith. The sample data contains what is a very common scenario that payroll departments encounter today. When Mr. Smith starts with the company, he chooses to have his paycheck deposited electronically. As indicated in the data, he wants it split between a checking and a savings account. Then in 1999, he decides to close one checking account and open a new one at a different bank. The payroll department is informed, and the first preference is then expired, and a new one is entered to take effect on November 2. The fourth row shows that there is a standard deduction for insurance each month.

Table 9.11 Payroll Preference Data

PAYROLL PREFERENCE SEQ ID	PAYMENT METHOD TYPE	FROM DATE	THRU DATE	PERCENTAGE	FLAT AMOUNT	ROUTING NO AND ACCOUNT NUMBER	DEDUCTION TYPE	PERIOD TYPE
1	Electronic	Jan 1, 1995	Nov 1, 1999	50		99986-99, 30984098		
2	Electronic	Jan 1, 1995		50		99986-98, 93485999		
3	Electronic	Nov 2, 1999		50		11111-22, 67567676		
4		Nov 2, 1999			$125		Insurance	Per month

Note that the primary key for PAYROLL PREFERENCE is a simple sequence number compounded with the primary keys from EMPLOYEE and INTERNAL ORGANIZATION (the hiring firm). This is needed because, depending on the type of payroll preference, different information will be recorded in the PAYROLL PREFERENCE entity.

Paycheck

Now that method of payment has been established, it is time to consider the actual payment itself. The PAYCHECK entity contains basic information an enterprise needs to record about the checks it writes to its employees. As seen in Figure 9.9, this entity inherits the attributes it needs from PAYMENT, namely a **payment ID**, **payment ref num** (could be a check number or electronic transfer number), **effective date** (date of check or electronic transfer), **amount**, and optionally a **comment**.

Financial account information for a check may be determined after depositing a check, using the payment financial account data model in Figure 7.9 in Chapter 7. This information, along with the **payment ref num,** will contain the information to uniquely identify a particular paycheck and to know where it has been deposited. Even electronically deposited checks need a source account and a check number, which show up on the paper confirmation. The **effective date** is the actual date the payroll disbursement was issued. In the case of electronic deposit, this may or may not correspond to the bank posting date. The **amount** is recorded as part of the PAYMENT entity and inherited by the subtype PAYCHECK as the gross amount of pay. The net amount of the paycheck can be *calculated* by subtracting from the PAYCHECK **amount**, the amounts recorded in the associated instances of the DEDUCTION entity.

Deduction and Deduction Type

The DEDUCTION entity stores information about the various deductions that occur on a particular check. The DEDUCTION TYPE entity contains a list of the valid types of deductions that are allowed by the enterprise or are required by law. Some of these include: "federal tax," "FICA," "state tax," "401k," "retirement," "insurance," or "cafeteria plan."

DEDUCTION TYPEs may be applied to the actual payroll disbursements when they are related to DEDUCTIONs. These DEDUCTIONs represent instances of moneys deducted from actual payroll checks (or electronic transfers). DEDUCTION TYPEs may also be used to provide standard deductions that employees want on an ongoing basis.

Table 9.12 contains examples of deductions as they have been applied to a particular paycheck.

Again, assume that the sample data is related to John Smith and ABC Corporation. The data shows an example that would be typical in most organizations. The check number 10001 is cut on January 1, 2001, with a gross amount of $2,000. The deductions include the standard ones that everybody sees, plus an additional deduction for insurance. The total deductions add up to $459.50, making the net amount for the check $1,540.50

So where did the $1,540.50 go? It should be deposited or distributed based on what was recorded in the PAYROLL PREFERENCE occurrence that is associated with the same EMPLOYEE that the PAYCHECK is associated with (i.e., if a paycheck is issued for John Smith at ABC Corporation, then the preferences for John Smith at ABC Corporation should be used). If there were no preference records, then what happens? Is a paper check cut by default, or is the check processing held up until preferences are declared? Again, more business rules need to be in place to make these decisions and ensure that the entire transaction is completed correctly.

Table 9.12   Payroll Data

CHECK NO	EFFECTIVE DATE	AMOUNT	DEDUCTION ID	DEDUCTION TYPE	AMOUNT
1001	Jan 1, 2001	$2,000	1	Federal tax	$200.00
			2	FICA	$54.50
			3	State tax	$80.00
			4	Insurance	$125.00

Employment Application

Each employment may have started with an employment application. Applications may be maintained in order to ensure that they are properly reviewed and processed. Also this information can provide valuable analysis of the recruiting process, yielding information such as how many applications are received, from where are they received (the source of the application), and the ratio of applications that turn into employees.

Figure 9.10 provides a data model that shows information about employment applications. Each EMPLOYMENT APPLICATION may be for a POSITION. This relationship is optional because applications may be for employment without knowing if a specific position slot is available. Each EMPLOYMENT APPLICA-

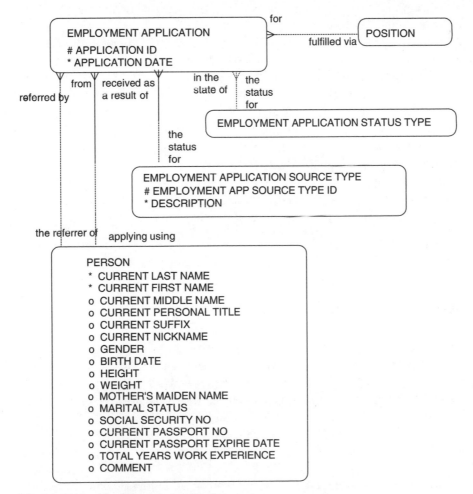

Figure 9.10 Employment application.

TION may have an EMPLOYMENT APPLICATION STATUS TYPE associated with it such as "received," "reviewed," "filed," "rejected," "notified candidate of non-interest," and so on. Each EMPLOYMENT APPLICATION may also be from an EMPLOYMENT APPLICATION SOURCE TYPE such as "newspaper," "personal referral," "Internet," and so on. Each application may be from one and only one PERSON who represents the candidate. The application may also be referred from a PERSON that is the referrer of the candidate.

Employee Skills and Qualifications

An important aspect of human resources is keeping track of the skills, qualifications, and training levels for people and organizations. This information is needed to facilitate parties being placed in the most suitable positions based on their skills and qualifications.

Figure 9.11 provides a model that helps to maintain the skills, qualifications, and training of not only employees, but of all people and organizations for whom this is useful. Each PARTY may have one or more PARTY QUALIFICA-TIONs or PARTY SKILLs because it may be useful to track these for both a person and/or an organization in assessing to whom to assign responsibilities. In order to maintain the level of training that people have, each PERSON may have one or more PERSON TRAINING instances, indicating which training programs he or she has attended. The RESUME entity records one or more textual descriptions regarding the background and qualifications of each PARTY.

One may think that qualifications, skills, and resumes should be related to PERSON and not PARTY. Organizations may also have qualifications about which they are judged, skills that they specialize in, and resumes that describe their talents.

Employee Performance

Part of the human resource function is tracking the effectiveness of employees over time. Employees are generally evaluated periodically, and an audit trail of comments or notes may be recorded about employees.

Figure 9.12a provides a data model that maintains information regarding performance reviews and notes that can be used to provide an audit trail for employees. Each EMPLOYEE may be the receiver of one or more PERFOR-MANCE REVIEWs. The receiver is the person for whom the performance review is written. Each EMPLOYEE PERFORMANCE REVIEW is from one and only one MANAGER responsible for the review. If the enterprise has a need to

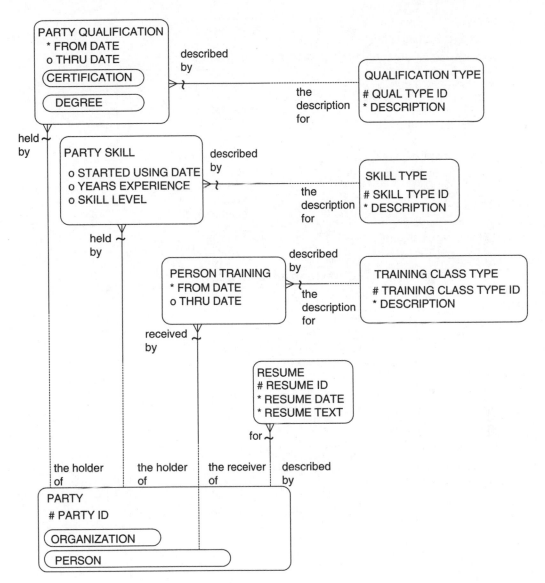

Figure 9.11 Employee skills and qualifications.

track more than one manager who may give a specific review, then this relationship may need to be many-to-many. Each EMPLOYEE PERFORMANCE REVIEW may be composed of PERFORMANCE REVIEW ITEMs that represent the various questions that may be asked on a performance review. An example of this is "Rate employee's promptness" or "Describe employee's teamwork

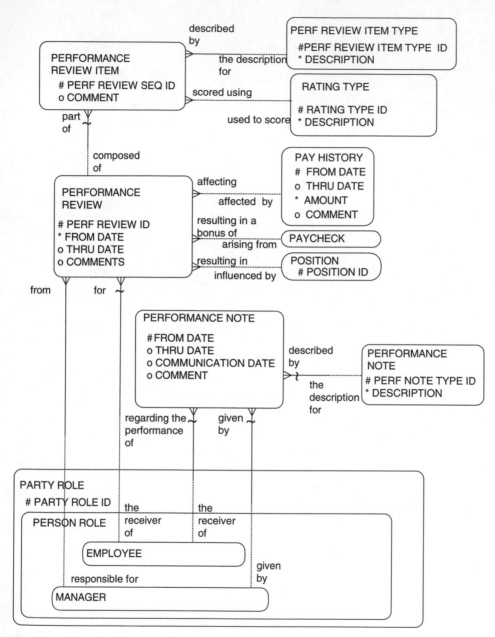

Figure 9.12a Employee performance.

style." Each PERFORMANCE REVIEW ITEM represents the specific item as it relates to that review, along with a possible RATING, as illustrated by relationship to the RATING TYPE, for that item and a **comment** (some items may not have a rating and only a comment if the item asks only for a description).

Each EMPLOYEE may be the receiver of one or more PERFORMANCE NOTEs, which is another mechanism for documenting an employee's performance. An example is that there may be NOTE on particular communication dates on January 20, 2001, with a comment of "Hal Smith was insubordinate and refused to listen to the direction of his manager."

The information maintained in Figure 9.12a is mandatory for employees in most organizations. The model may also be expanded to include this information for other people such as contractors for whom performance reviews may also be given, if this is a need of the enterprise. Some enterprises may even want to track performance reviews for organizations that provide goods and/or services to them. In order for the model to be expanded, the relationships for PERFORMANCE NOTE and PERFORMANCE REVIEW would be to either PERSON or PARTY, depending on whether organizations also were going to receive performance reviews and performance notes.

Raises, bonuses, promotions, and demotions are important pieces of information that may arise from a PERFORMANCE REVIEW. Therefore, the PAY HISTORY, PAYCHECK, and POSITION entities are related to the review. Raises or cuts in salary are maintained within instances of PAY HISTORY and may be **affected by** a PERFORMANCE REVIEW. Bonuses would be maintained as a PAYCHECK and may be **arising from** a PERFORMANCE REVIEW. A POSITION may be influenced by a PERFORMANCE REVIEW, as the review may lead to a promotion or demotion if it is related to a certain POSITION.

Another alternative to the model in Figure 9.12a is shown in Figure 9.12b. This model maintains the PERFORMANCE NOTE as well as the PERFORMANCE REVIEW information as a subtype of COMMUNICATION EVENT PURPOSE with a corresponding COMMUNICATION EVENT describing the purpose for a PARTY RELATIONSHIP of EMPLOYMENT. This model also provides for the fact that a PERFORMANCE NOTE or PERFORMANCE REVIEW may be for any PARTY that is involved in the COMMUNICATION EVENT. For example, performance notes or reviews could be kept for contractors who would have a "contractor being reviewed" COMMUNICATION EVENT ROLE.

Should performance notes and reviews be considered types of communication events? The answer could be "yes," as many of the same attributes and relationships are applicable. However the first model (Figure 9.12a) treats performance notes and performance reviews as separate entities, as they are very sensitive in nature and would most likely be maintained separately. The modeler needs to decide which model is most appropriate for the enterprise being modeled.

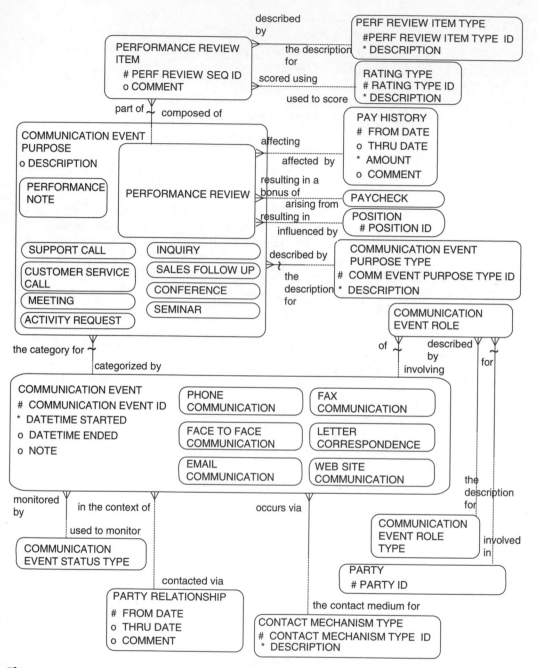

Figure 9.12b Employee performance—alternate model.

Employee Termination

Unfortunately, or fortunately, depending on how you look at it, there is a need to track information about the termination of employees. The dates of termination, reason for termination, and type of termination, as well as possible after-effects such as unemployment claims, are important pieces of information to capture.

Figure 9.13 captures information about employee terminations. As stated previously, the EMPLOYMENT entity is a subtype of PARTY RELATIONSHIP that establishes a relationship between an EMPLOYEE and an INTERNAL ORGANIZATION. When the EMPLOYMENT ends, the **thru date** of the PARTY RELATIONSHIP stores the date of termination. On termination, the PARTY RELATIONSHIP STATUS TYPE instance of "terminated" is now used to signify that the employment has ended. The TERMINATION TYPE stores what kind of termination happened, such as "resignation," "firing," or "retirement." The TERMINATION REASON maintains the description explaining the circumstances and cause of the termination. Examples include "insubordination," "took new job," "non-performance," "moved," and so on.

The UNEMPLOYMENT CLAIM maintains information about unemployment claims that may be related to terminations of employees. The **claim date** shows what date the unemployment claim was filed. The **description** provides information on the background of the claim, and the relationship to UNEMPLOYMENT CLAIM STATUS TYPE stores whether the claim was "filed," "pending," "accepted," "rejected," or any other important status. If a history of statuses is needed, then the model needs to include a many-to-many relationship between UNEMPLOYMENT CLAIM and UNEMPLOYMEN CLAIM STATUS TYPE. Other information may be associated with the UNEMPLOYMENT CLAIM, such as the various parties involved, notes about the claim, dollar figures involved in the claim, and so on, depending on the needs of the enterprise.

It is important to note that the employee has not really been terminated (unless the person passes away), even though that is the common means of expressing this fact. The employment is the thing that has really terminated. This is why the PARTY RELATIONSHIP STATUS TYPE is used to record the termination status as opposed to the PARTY STATUS, which is used to record information about the party irrespective of any relationship (this would be used to record if someone were "deceased").

Summary

This chapter has discussed one of the more complex aspects of operating a business: the tracking and management of human resources information (see

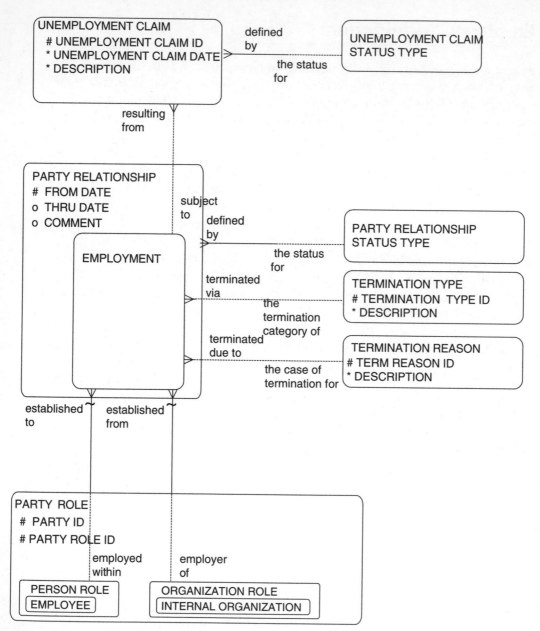

Figure 9.13 Employee termination.

Figure 9.14). The models presented allow an enterprise to more efficiently track positions and assignments associated with its employees and contractors. In addition, the models contain elements for position classifications, reporting structures, determining pay rates, tracking the salary history of those people associated with the enterprise, benefits tracking, payroll infor-

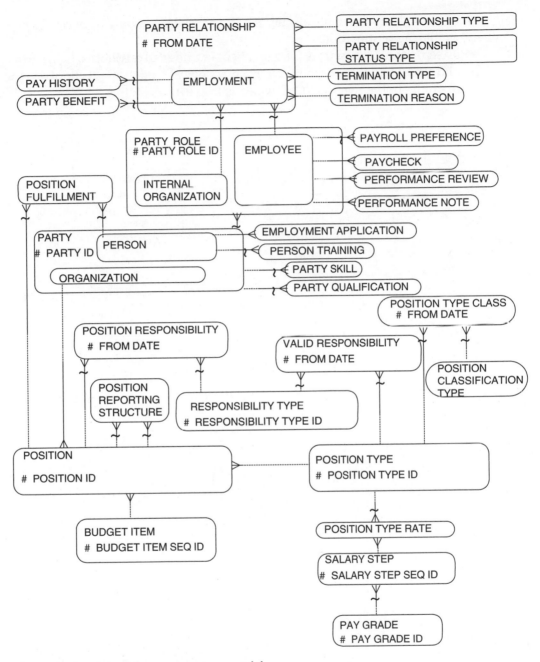

Figure 9.14 Overall human resources model.

mation, employment applications, employee skills, employee performance, and employee termination.

Please refer to Appendix A for a listing of entities and attributes. SQL scripts to build tables and columns derived from the logical models in this book can be found on the full-blown CD-ROM, which is licensed separately.

CHAPTER

10

Creating the Data Warehouse Data Model from the Enterprise Data Model

Each of the previous chapters focused on the data model for a specific subject data area, namely parties, products, orders, shipments, work efforts, accounting, and human resources. These data models are essential for building not only a data warehouse but also *any* type of system because it is critical to understand the nature of the data and their relationships.

What is the process for using these data models to build a data warehouse? This chapter not only describes the transformation process, but also provides examples of each type of transformation by using the logical data models from the previous chapters as a basis.

The Data Warehouse Architecture

Before discussing how to convert the logical data models into a data warehouse, it is important to understand the three types of models involved in the transformation process from the operational environment to a decision support system:

- The enterprise data model
- The data warehouse design
- The departmental data warehouse design or data mart

The Enterprise Data Model

The enterprise data model is an enterprise-wide view of the data and its relationships. It normally includes a high-level model that is an overview of each subject data area and the relationships between them, as well as logical data models for each subject data area. These models are the basis for developing both the enterprise's online transaction processing (OLTP) systems and its data warehouses. The models presented in the previous chapters could serve as a starting point for an enterprise's enterprise data model.

The Data Warehouse Design

The data warehouse design is sometimes referred to as a data warehouse data model. It represents an integrated, subject-oriented, and very granular base of strategic information that serves as a single source for the decision support environment. This allows an architecture where information is extracted from the operational environment, cleansed, and transformed into a central, integrated enterprise-wide data warehouse environment. The data warehouse data model maintains this integrated, detailed level of information so that all the departments and other internal organizations of the enterprise can benefit from a consistent, integrated source of decision support information.

The Departmental Data Warehouse Design or Data Mart

The departmental data warehouse design is used to maintain departmental information that is extracted from the enterprise data warehouse. This is sometimes referred to as lightly and highly summarized data or as data marts. An example of a departmental data warehouse is the maintaining of a particular department's sales analysis information such as its product sales by customer, by date, and by sales representative. This department can create a departmental data warehouse and pull the information into its own data warehouse (or data mart) from the enterprise data warehouse.

Another department of the corporation, for example, the marketing department, may be interested in higher-level sales information across the enterprise such as sales by month, by product, and by geographic area. This department can create a departmental data warehouse design for its own purposes. Rather than building its own extraction, transformation, and cleansing routines against the operational systems to gather this information, it can rely on the enterprise data warehouse.

An Architected Data Warehouse Environment

By using this architected approach, as illustrated in Figure 10.1, the enterprise will avoid the pitfall of having each department extracting different views of the enterprise's information. These inconsistent extractions lead to more unintegrated and inconsistent data. After all, the primary goal of decision support is to provide strategic, meaningful management information. The most ideal method of doing this is by focusing on developing integrated data; then, once this is done, passing it on to different departments that have various information needs.

It is important to note that as the enterprise moves from the enterprise data model to the data warehouse data model to the departmental data warehouse, the models become more dependent on the particular enterprise. For instance, many parts of the logical data models in the prior chapters can be used by many different enterprises. The data warehouse data model is more specific to an enterprise because it is based on numerous assumptions concerning the type of decision support information that is considered useful to the enterprise. The departmental data warehouse is even more dependent on the specific needs of a department. Therefore, the data warehouse models presented later in this chapter and in subsequent chapters serve only as examples because each enterprise's data warehouse designs will be highly dependent on its own specific business needs.

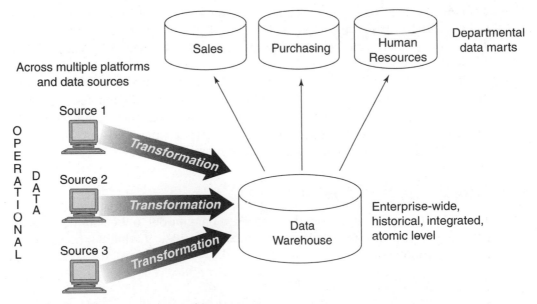

Figure 10.1   Data warehouse architecture.

This chapter will focus specifically on the transformation of the enterprise data model to the data warehouse data models. Chapter 11 provides an example of a data warehouse data model containing several subject areas. Chapters 12, 13, and 14 provide examples of *departmental* data models and illustrate various designs for structuring the departmental warehouse using the **star schema** representation for multidimensional analysis.

The Enterprise Data Model

The point of departure for the design and construction of the data warehouse is the enterprise data model. Without a data model it is very difficult to organize the structure and content of data in the data warehouse.

The enterprise data model may cover a very wide scope; when it does, it is often called an enterprise data model (corporate data model is a synonym). On the other hand, a data model within an enterprise may cover a restricted scope; for instance, it may cover the information within a particular department or division. In either case—that of the enterprise data model or the data model for a part of the enterprise—the data model is the starting point for creating the data warehouse data model.

Many organizations have recognized the importance of the data model over the years and have invested the time and effort to build such a model. One of the problems with classical data modeling techniques is that there is no distinction between modeling for the operational and decision support environments. Classical data modeling techniques gather and synthesize the informational needs of the entire enterprise without consideration for the context of the information. The result of such a model is the enterprise data model, which tends to be very normalized.

The enterprise data model is a very good place to start the process of building a data warehouse. It provides a foundation for integration and unification at an intellectual level. Because the enterprise data model is not built specifically for the data warehouse, some amount of transformation is necessary to adapt it to the design to build the data warehouse data model.

Transformation Requirements

To do the transformation from the enterprise data model to the data warehouse data model, the enterprise data model must have identified and structured, at least, the following:

- Major subjects of the enterprise
- Relationships between the subjects
- Definitions of the subject areas

- Logical data models for each subject data area (sometimes referred to as entity relationship diagrams)

Also, for each major logical data model, the following must be identified and structured:

- Entities
- Key(s) of the entity
- Attributes of the entity
- Subtypes of the entity
- Relationships between entities

Figure 10.2 identifies the minimum components of the enterprise data model.

The logical models in the previous chapters can be used as a starting point toward the development of an enterprise data model. The models presented represent many of the major subject data areas within enterprises. Each of the previous chapters of this book, Chapters 2–9, correspond roughly to a possible subject data area for an enterprise. For instance, there is often a PARTY subject data area, PRODUCT subject data area, and so on. Each enterprise needs to select the appropriate subject data areas for its specific business and add any other subject data areas needed.

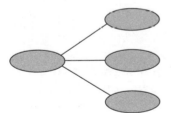

High-level data model:
Major subject areas
Relationships between subjects/areas

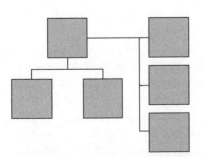

Logical data model:
Entities
Keys
Attributes
Sub-types
Relationships

Figure 10.2   The components of a data model.

Process Models

Many more design and modeling components may be used in conjunction with an enterprise data model. For example, the enterprise may model the design and synthesis of processes as well. Process analysis typically consists of the following:

- Functional decomposition
- Data and process matrices
- Data flow diagrams
- State transition diagrams
- HIPO charts
- Pseudocode

These are generally included in an enterprise *process* model, as opposed to being part of the enterprise data model. This book addresses "universal data models," but there is also a great need for "universal process models"—or templates to help develop these enterprise process models.

While these corporate process models are interesting to some, the process model usually is not of much interest to the data warehouse designer because the process analysis applies directly to the operational environment, not the data warehouse or the decision support system (DSS) environment. It is the enterprise data model that forms the backbone of design for the data warehouse, not the process models.

High-Level and Logical Data Models

As stated previously, the enterprise data model is usually divided into multiple levels—a high-level model and logical data models for each subject area. The high level of the enterprise data model contains the major subject areas and the relationship between the subject areas. Figure 10.3 shows a simple example of a high-level enterprise data model.

In Figure 10.3 there are five subject areas: party, order, product, shipment, and work effort. A direct relationship exists between party and order, order and work effort, order and shipment, and order and product. Of course, many indirect relationships are inferred from the high-level data model, but only the direct relationships are shown. Note that the high-level enterprise data model does not contain any amount of detail at all; at this level, detail only clutters up the model unnecessarily.

The next level of modeling found in the enterprise data model is logical data modeling. Here is where much of the detail of the model is found. These models contain entities, keys, attributes, subtypes, and relationships, and they are

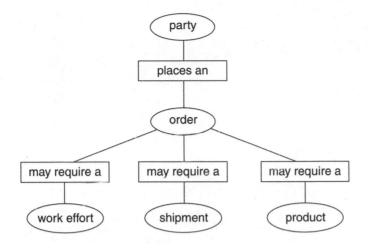

Figure 10.3   A simple example of a high-level model.

fully normalized. Each of the previous chapters generally corresponds to a subject data area and includes a normalized logical data model for that area. There is a relationship between each subject area identified in the high-level model and the logical data models. For each subject area identified, there is a single logical data model, as shown in Figure 10.4.

Note that in many organizations the logical data model is not fleshed out to the same level of detail. Some logical data models are completely designed and fully attributed, while other models are only sketched out, with little or no detail.

The degree of completion of the larger enterprise data model is of little concern to the data warehouse developer because the data warehouse will be developed iteratively, one stage at a time. In other words, it is very unusual to develop the data warehouse on a massive frontal assault, where all logical data models are developed at once. Therefore, the fact that the enterprise data model is in a state of differing degrees of readiness is not a concern to the data warehouse developer. Figure 10.5 shows that the data warehouse will be built one step at a time. First, one part of the data model (perhaps a particular subject data area such as "product") is transformed and readied for data warehouse design, then another part of the data model is transformed, and so forth.

Making the Transformation

Once the enterprise has an enterprise data model, the transformation process into the data warehouse data model can begin. Following are a set of procedures

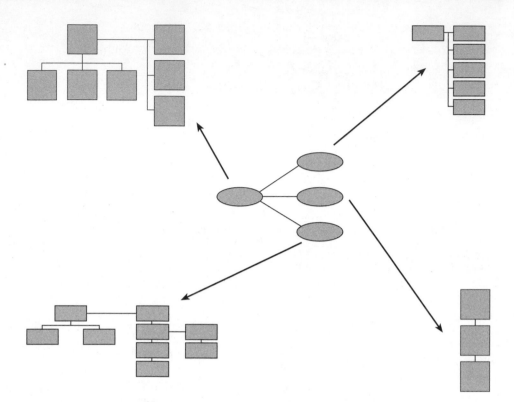

Figure 10.4 Each major subject area has its own mid-level model.

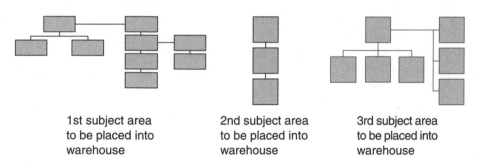

1st subject area
to be placed into
warehouse

2nd subject area
to be placed into
warehouse

3rd subject area
to be placed into
warehouse

Figure 10.5 Each major subject area will be integrated one step at a time.

for how to transform the enterprise data model to a data warehouse data model:

- Removal of purely operational data
- Addition of an element of time to the key structure of the data warehouse if one is not already present
- Addition of appropriate derived data

- Transformation of data relationships into data artifacts
- Accommodation for the different levels of granularity found in the data warehouse
- Merging of like data from different tables together
- Creation of arrays of data
- Separation of data attributes according to their stability characteristics

These activities serve as guidelines in creating the data warehouse data model. Transformation decisions should be based largely on the enterprise's specific decision support requirements. The following sections will discuss each of these aspects in detail.

Removing Operational Data

The first task is to examine the enterprise data model and remove all data that is purely operational, as illustrated in Figure 10.6. The figure shows that some data found in the enterprise data model finds its way into the data model for the data warehouse. Some data, such as **message, description, terms** and **status**, usually apply to the operational environment. These should be removed as a first step in building the data warehouse data model. They are *not* removed from the logical data models; they are simply not useful in the data warehouse. Note that the box represents information about the INVOICE within the corporate data model and may be either an attribute such as **message** or **description**, or related information such as INVOICE TERM or INVOICE STATUS.

The removal of operational data is seldom a straightforward decision. It always centers around the question, "What is the chance the data will be used for DSS?" Unfortunately, circumstances can be contrived such that almost *any* data can be used for DSS. A more rational approach is to ask, "What is the *reasonable* chance that the data will be used for DSS?"

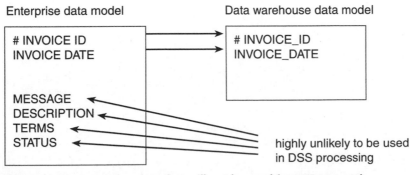

Figure 10.6 Removing data that will not be used for DSS processing.

The argument that can always be raised is that one never knows what is to be used for DSS because it always involves the unknown. On that basis, *any* and *all* data should be kept. The cost of managing volumes of data in the data warehouse environment, however, is such that it is patently a mistake not to weed out data that will be used for DSS only in farfetched or contrived circumstances.

Adding an Element of Time to the Warehouse Key

The second necessary modification to the enterprise data model is the addition of an element of time to the data warehouse key if one does not already exist, as shown in Figure 10.7.

In the figure, **snapshot_date** has been added as a key to the customer record. The enterprise data model has specified party information with only a party ID as the key. But in the warehouse, snapshots of customer-related party data are made because customer demographics may change over time. The effective date of those snapshots is added to the key structure. Note that there are many different ways to take these snapshots and a few common ways to add an element of time to the data warehouse key. The technique shown in the example is a common one.

Another common technique is the addition of a from and thru date to the key structure. This technique has the advantage of representing continuous data rather than snapshots at a specified point in time. An example of this technique is illustrated in the sample data warehouse data model in Figure 11.2.

If data identified in the logical data model already has an element of time, such as a **from datetime** or **thru datetime** attribute, then there is no need to add another element of time to the data warehouse key structure.

Adding Derived Data

The next transformation to the logical data models is the addition of derived data to the data warehouse data model where it is appropriate, as shown in Fig-

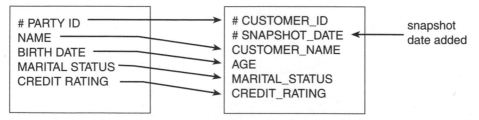

Figure 10.7 Adding an element of time to the data warehouse data model.

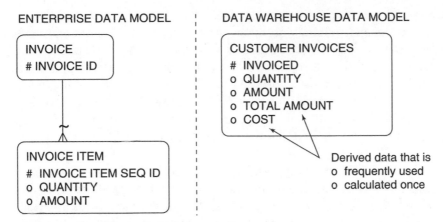

Figure 10.8   Adding appropriate derived data.

ure 10.8. The **total_amount** field is derived by multiplying the **quantity** times the **amount** field of the INVOICE.

As a rule, data modelers do not include derived data as part of the data modeling process. Logical models show only the data *requirements* of an enterprise. The reason for the omission of derived data in logical data models is that when derived data is included, certain processes are inferred regarding the derivation or calculation of that data. Derived data is added only to the *physical* database design for performance or ease of access reasons.

It is appropriate to add derived data to the data warehouse data model where the derived data is popularly accessed and calculated once. The addition of derived data makes sense because it reduces the amount of processing required on accessing the data in the warehouse. In addition, once properly calculated, there is little fear in the integrity of the calculation. Said another way, once the derived data is properly calculated, there is no chance that someone will come along and use an incorrect algorithm to calculate the data, thus enhancing the credibility of the data in the data warehouse.

Of course, any time that data is added to the data warehouse, the following question must be asked: "Is the addition of the data worth it?" The issue of volume of data in a data warehouse is such that every byte of data needs to be questioned. Otherwise, the data warehouse will quickly grow to unmanageable proportions.

Creating Relationship Artifacts

The data relationships found in classical data modeling assume that there is one and only one business value underlying the relationship (i.e., there is only one primary supplier for a product). For the assumption that data is accurate as of the moment of access (i.e., operational data), the classical representation of a relationship is correct. A data warehouse usually has *many* relationship values between tables of data because data in a warehouse represents data over a long spectrum of time; therefore, there will naturally be many relationship values over time (i.e., there are many product suppliers for a product over time). Thus, the classical representation of relationships between tables as found in classical data modeling is inadequate for the data warehouse. Relationships between tables in the data warehouse are achieved by means of the creation of *artifacts*.

One means of describing a *relationship artifact* is that it is the existence of a relationship that existed at one point in time and no longer exists. If one is married and gets a divorce, an alimony payment is an indication of a relationship artifact. It is the reminder of a relationship that used to exist and that no longer exists. For sales analysis purposes within businesses, old customer relationships are important to record in the data warehouse even though they may no longer exist in the operational system.

An artifact of a relationship that is maintained in the warehouse is merely that part of a relationship that is obvious and tangible at the moment the snapshot of data is made for the data warehouse. In other words, when the snapshot is made the data associated with the relationship that is useful and obvious will be pulled into the warehouse table.

The artifact may include foreign keys and other relevant data, such as columns from the associated table, or the snapshot may include only relevant data and no foreign keys. This is one of the most complex subjects facing the data warehouse designer. Consider the simple data relationship shown in Figure 10.9.

Figure 10.9 shows that there is a relationship between a PRODUCT and a SUPPLIER. This information is shown in Chapter 3, Figure 3.5, in the entities PRODUCT, SUPPLIER PRODUCT, and PREFERENCE TYPE. In the example, each PRODUCT has a primary SUPPLIER (a PREFERENCE TYPE of *primary*). Integrity constraints dictate that if a SUPPLIER (or organization) is deleted, a SUPPLIER PRODUCT record may not exist that has that SUPPLIER

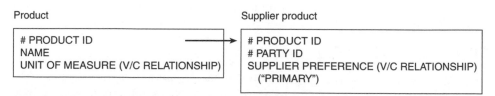

Figure 10.9 An operational relationship between product and supplier.

DATA WAREHOUSE DATA MODEL

PRODUCT SNAPSHOT TABLE

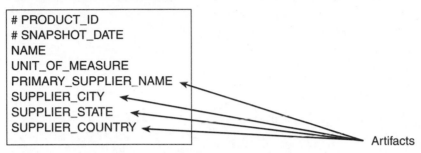

Figure 10.10 Artifacts of the operational data relationship.

as the primary source. In other words, the information about who was the primary supplier is lost because the supplier record was deleted. The relationship represents an ongoing relationship of data that is active and accurate as of the moment of access.

Now consider how snapshots of data might be made and how the relationship information might be captured. Figure 10.10 shows a snapshot of PRODUCT and SUPPLIER data that might appear in the data warehouse.

The PRODUCT snapshot table is one that is created periodically—at the end of the week, the end of the month, and so on. Much detailed information about a PRODUCT is captured at this time. One of the pieces of information that is captured is **primary supplier name** as of the moment of snapshot. Another artifact is the supplier location that is extracted from the supplier information found in the operational system at that point in time. Even if the enterprise stops doing business with a supplier and the supplier record is deleted, the data warehouse still maintains a history of the primary suppliers for the product. This, then, is an example of an artifact of a relationship being captured. Note that the relationship is accurate as of the moment of capture. No other implications are intended or implied.

The snapshot previously discussed has one major drawback: It is incomplete. It shows only the relationship as it exists as of some moment in time. Major events may have occurred that the snapshots never capture. For example, suppose the PRODUCT SNAPSHOT is made every week. A product may have had three primary suppliers during the week, yet the snapshot would never reflect this fact.

Snapshots are easy to make and are an essential part of the data warehouse, but they do have their drawbacks. To capture a complete record of data, an historical record rather than a snapshot is required for data in the data warehouse. Figure 10.11 shows an example of historical data in a data warehouse.

DATA WAREHOUSE DATA MODEL

PRODUCT HISTORY TABLE

```
# PRODUCT_ID
# SHIPMENT_ID
DATE_RECEIVED
SUPPLIER_ID
SUPPLIER_NAME
UNIT_OF_MEASURE
CONDITION
RECEIVED_BY
STORAGE_CONTAINER
```

Figure 10.11   Another form of warehouse data is discrete historical data in which all activities are captured.

In the PRODUCT HISTORY table, a shipment has been received at the loading dock and relevant information is recorded. Among other things, the SUPPLIER of the PRODUCT is recorded. This is another form of artifact relationship information being recorded inside a data warehouse. Assuming that *all* deliveries have an historical record created for them, the record of the relationship between the two tables, over time, is complete.

Changing Granularity of Data

One of the features of a data warehouse is the different levels of granularity. In some cases, the level of granularity does not change as data passes from the operational environment to the data warehouse environment. In other cases, the level of granularity does change as data is passed into the data warehouse. When there is a change in the level of granularity, the data warehouse data model needs to reflect those changes, as shown in Figure 10.12.

In the figure, the enterprise data model shows shipment activity data that is gathered each time a shipment is made. Due to the requirements specified by end users, data granularity is changed as the data passes into the data warehouse. Two summarizations of shipment data are made—the monthly summarization of total shipments and the summarization of shipments made by the **shipped from** location.

The issues in the changing of granularity (insofar as the data warehouse data modeler is concerned) revolve around the following questions:

- What period of time should be used to summarize the data (i.e., summarized by day, by week, by month, etc.)?
- What elements of data should be in the summarized table?

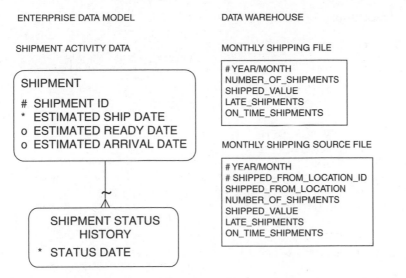

ENTERPRISE DATA MODEL   DATA WAREHOUSE

SHIPMENT ACTIVITY DATA   MONTHLY SHIPPING FILE

SHIPMENT

\# SHIPMENT ID
* ESTIMATED SHIP DATE
o ESTIMATED READY DATE
o ESTIMATED ARRIVAL DATE

\# YEAR/MONTH
NUMBER_OF_SHIPMENTS
SHIPPED_VALUE
LATE_SHIPMENTS
ON_TIME_SHIPMENTS

MONTHLY SHIPPING SOURCE FILE

\# YEAR/MONTH
\# SHIPPED_FROM_LOCATION_ID
SHIPPED_FROM_LOCATION
NUMBER_OF_SHIPMENTS
SHIPPED_VALUE
LATE_SHIPMENTS
ON_TIME_SHIPMENTS

SHIPMENT STATUS
HISTORY
* STATUS DATE

Figure 10.12 Accommodating the different changes in granularity in going from the operations environment to the data warehouse environment.

- Will the operational environment support the summarized data elements (i.e., has the data warehouse designer specified data in the warehouse that cannot be calculated from the operational data source)?

- What is the trade-off between keeping lower levels of granularity for detailed analysis versus the cost of storing those details? The costs include disk space, performance, and database management overhead, especially for very large databases (VLDB).

Merging Tables

The next transformation consideration involves merging corporate tables into one data warehouse table, as illustrated in Figure 10.13.

The figure shows two tables, INVOICEs and INVOICE_ ITEMs (the top two boxes), from an operational environment (see Chapter 7). The tables are normalized. As they are placed in the data warehouse environment, they are merged together. The merge can greatly improve query performance and can simplify the data structure by eliminating a commonly required join.

The conditions under which a merge makes sense are when the following situations occur:

- The tables share a common key (or partial key).

- The data from the different tables is used together frequently.

- The pattern of insertion is roughly the same.

TWO NORMALIZED TABLES FROM THE ENTERPRISE DATA MODEL

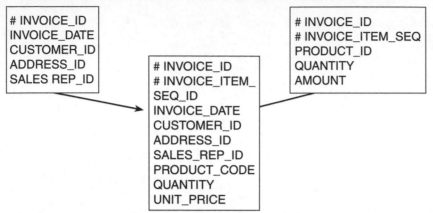

Figure 10.13   Merging corporate data tables into a warehouse data model.

If any one of these conditions is not met, it may *not* make sense to merge the tables together.

In the example given, the common portion of the key is **invoice_id.** In many situations the information in the two tables is used together and the pattern of insertion is exactly the same (i.e., there would be no need for an invoice without invoice items).

Creation of Arrays of Data

The next transformation activity is the consideration of the creation of arrays of data in the data warehouse data model. Data in the enterprise data model is usually normalized. This means that repeating groups are not shown as part of the data model. But, under the proper conditions, the data warehouse can and should contain repeating groups. Figure 10.14 shows an example creating a data warehouse data model containing arrays of data.

The enterprise data model has shown that the budget record (from BUDGET and BUDGET_ ITEMs in Chapter 8) is created on a month-by-month basis. However, as data goes into the data warehouse, it is organized into an array so that each month of the year is an occurrence of the array.

There are several benefits to this structuring of data. One is that by not having individual records of data for each month, a certain amount of space is saved. In the data warehouse case, the values **budget_id** and **year** appear in only one row for each year, while in the case of the enterprise data model, the values appear in 12 rows for each year (assuming that the budget period is

ENTERPRISE DATA MODEL   DATA WAREHOUSE
                         DATA MODEL

```
#BUDGET ID
BUDGET
YEAR/MONTH
BUDGET AMOUNT
```

```
#BUDGET_ID
#YEAR
JANUARY_AMOUNT
FEBRUARY_AMOUNT
MARCH_AMOUNT
...
...
DECEMBER_AMOUNT
```

Figure 10.14   Under the right conditions, creating an array of data in the data warehouse data model is the correct design choice.

monthly). The savings of this space may not be trivial at all. In some cases, it amounts to as much as 25 percent of the total space required for the table. In addition, the data warehouse structuring of data requires one twelfth the index entries as the enterprise data model structuring of data.

The other advantage is the possibility of organizing all yearly occurrences of data in a single physical location, creating the possibility of performance enhancement. This is due to a reduction in the number of physical inputs/outputs (I/Os) needed to retrieve the same data because many logical records are stored in one physical record. Whether this turns out to be a significant factor depends on many considerations, such as the use of data, which database management system (DBMS) is being used, the physical organization of the records within the DBMS, and so forth.

The creation of arrays of data is not a general-purpose option. Only under the correct circumstances does it pay off to create arrays of data in the data warehouse data model. Those conditions are as follows:

- When the number of occurrences of data are predictable
- When the occurrence of data is relatively small (in terms of physical size)
- When the occurrences of data are frequently used together
- When the pattern of insertion and deletion is stable

One of the interesting aspects of the data warehouse is that because the key structure of the data in the warehouse often contains an element of time and because the units of time occur predictably, then the techniques of arrays of data in a data warehouse table are peculiarly appropriate. In other words, there is a strong affinity between the technique of creating arrays of data in a single table and the data warehouse.

Organizing Data According to Its Stability

The final transformation technique is organizing data in the data warehouse according to its propensity for change. The enterprise data model makes little or no distinction in the rate of change of the variables contained inside a table. But a data warehouse is very sensitive to the rate of change of data within the warehouse. The optimal organization of data inside a data warehouse is where data in one table changes slowly and data in another changes rapidly. The reason for this is that if all the data for an entity is stored in only table with a snapshot, then a change to any of the values will necessitate making a copy of all the values. Rapidly changing values should be stored in a separate table to avoid many instances of the stable data.

An illustration of how this transformation works is shown in Figure 10.15. The figure shows that the enterprise data model has gathered some data for customers. That data is then divided into three categories—data that rarely changes, data that sometimes changes, and data that often changes. The data warehouse data structure finally ends up with structures that are compatible, in terms of volatility. This provides a mechanism to minimize the data within the warehouse, so that stable information such as **date-of-birth** doesn't have to be rerecorded each time a more rapidly changing attribute such as **customer_ status** changes.

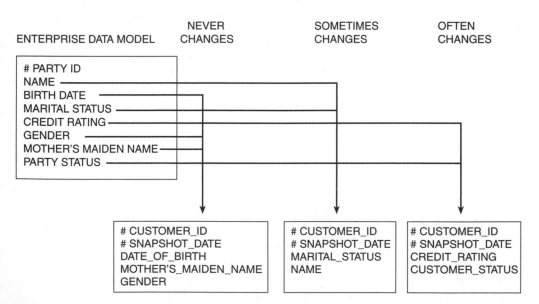

Figure 10.15 Data in the enterprise data model may be further divided according to its propensity for change.

THE ORDER OF APPLYING THE TRANSFORMATION CRITERIA

The order in which the transformation criteria are applied is as previously presented, with the removal of purely operational data first and the grouping of data according to stability last. Of course, as with every design process, a certain amount of iteration occurs. The order in which the transformation criteria is applied is not set in concrete. As a general guideline, though, the criteria should be applied as presented.

Summary

The enterprise data model is the basis for building the data warehouse. However the enterprise data model needs a fair amount of design activity as it is turned into a design for the data warehouse. The data warehouse data model is created from the enterprise data model by going through the following design activities, as they relate to user requirements:

- Removing all purely operational data
- Adding an element of time to the warehouse key if one isn't already there
- Adding appropriate derived data
- Creating relationship artifacts
- Accommodating the granularity changes in warehouse data
- Merging tables where appropriate
- Specifying arrays of data where appropriate
- Organizing data according to its stability

The next chapter will illustrate the design of a sample data warehouse data model using these principles.

CHAPTER

11

A Sample Data Warehouse
Data Model

Each enterprise has its own unique requirements regarding the types of information that are valuable for decision support. In general, though, the decision support environment provides information to illustrate trends, depict performance, and provide key business indicators in order to make informed strategic decisions.

There are a variety of decision support questions that many different departments across an enterprise may need to have answered, such as the following:

- How did sales representatives perform over different periods of time?

- What products are most popular to whom and when?

- What types of customers are buying what types of products?

- How much are the various internal organizations spending on what products?

- What were the variances between the amounts budgeted and the amounts spent?

- What positions are being filled by people with what types of backgrounds?

- What is the average pay for people within different age brackets or Equal Employment Opportunity Commission (EEOC) categories?

This chapter provides a sample data warehouse data model that answers these types of questions. The model was developed using the logical data models from Chapters 2 through 9 as a basis, then utilizing the principles outlined in Chapter 10 to perform the appropriate transformations. The model in this chapter will serve as the source for the data in the departmental models in Chapters 12, 13, and 14.

This data warehouse data model serves as the enterprise-wide source of decision support information. It is an integral piece for an architecture, as described in Chapter 10, that allows a central process for the extraction, cleansing, and transformation of data from the operational environment into the data warehouse environment. Using this approach, various departments with differing needs can use an integrated, consistent source of information to build departmental data warehouses or data marts.

Transformation to Customer Invoice

Two key factors are needed in describing the transformation of data from the operational environment to the data warehouse environment: the selection (or non-selection) of data and the transformation rules describing how the data is moved into the data warehouse.

This section gives an example of the transformation process used to develop the CUSTOMER_INVOICES subject data area of an enterprise-wide data warehouse data model in order to move toward the data warehouse design in Figure 11.1, which is a portion of the data warehouse design. Selection criteria and algorithms for extracting the data are provided solely for the purpose of illustrating the process. Remember, these selection criteria and algorithms may vary across enterprises based on business requirements.

The information in the CUSTOMER_INVOICES table is the result of transforming INVOICE and INVOICE_ ITEM (see Chapter 7, Figure 7.1), according to the principles described in Chapter 10. Details of this process are outlined in the following sections.

Removing Operational Data

First, any operational information, such as messages, descriptions, status, and invoice terms, was removed from INVOICE. This left **invoice_id** and **invoice_date** as part of the CUSTOMER_INVOICES data warehouse table. The column **invoice_id** was left to allow the user to do analysis on a specific transaction. Looking at the invoice items, **taxable_flag** was removed in this model because it was deemed not important for strategic sales management decisions (although some organizations may deem this as valid decision support infor-

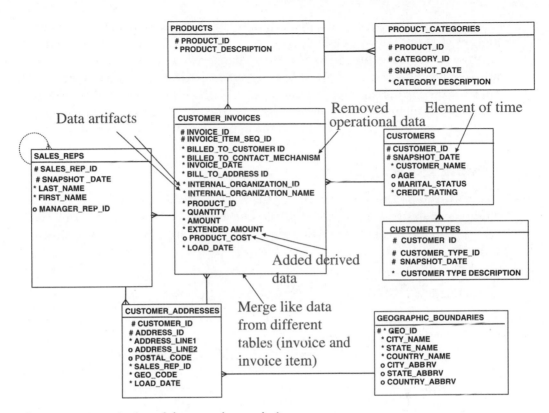

Figure 11.1   Beginning of data warehouse design.

mation—again, these decisions are dependent on the enterprise involved). Therefore, **product_id**, **quantity**, and **amount** were left.

Adding an Element of Time

In order to make sure that the element of time is present, the **invoice_date** was left from the INVOICE entity. Because the table CUSTOMER_INVOICES represents particular invoice item transactions, it is not necessary to include the **invoice_date** as part of the key. The transaction itself is identified uniquely by the **invoice_id** and the **invoice_item_seq_id** and is not time-variant; in other words, the transaction information will not change over time. (This model assumes that the enterprise has a business rule that prevents invoice items from being updated once they are sent out. Any adjustments must be made as separate invoice items that may adjust the original invoice.)

The CUSTOMERS table includes demographics about a customer that *can* change over time. This table includes a **snapshot_date** as part of the key to provide for the storage of historical data and is discussed later in this chapter.

Figure 11.2 is a more complete data warehouse design and is discussed later in this chapter. The POSITIONS table in Figure 11.2 illustrates the use of another common technique to represent changes to data over time. It includes an effective date range as part of the key by using the columns **from_date** and **thru_date**. This is an appropriate technique when the data changes less frequently and changes over time need to be recorded. (The snapshot method gives information only at specific points in time, not for time intervals.)

Adding Derived Data

The **extended amount** column in the CUSTOMER_INVOICES table is included as a derived value. It was added because it can be calculated once and will be commonly accessed. The formula for calculating this field is **amount* quantity**.

Creating Relationship Artifacts

Where did the **billed to_customer_id** and **billed_to_contact_mechanism** in CUSTOMER_INVOICES come from? They were derived through the resolution of the **billed to** relationships described in the logical model (see Figure 7.2, 7.3a and 7.3b). Those relationships ultimately point a **party ID** either directly to a PARTY or through a BILLING ACCOUNT that has a BILLING ACCOUNT ROLE of role type "bill to customer" that is related to a PARTY (Figure 7.3a). In any case, for the purposes of *this* decision support model, the information required is the *who* and *where* portion of these relationships. In order to make the design more understandable for the DSS analyst or other end users, the column is called **billed to_customer_id** rather than **party_id**. The **billed_to_customer_id** is a foreign key to the **customer_id** columns in CUSTOMERS as well as CUSTOMER_ADDRESSES.

The **billed_to_customer_id** and **billed_to_contact_mechanism** identify the customer who was responsible for the bill and the contact mechanism of where the invoice was sent. For this model it was decided that billed to customer information was important to capture within the data warehouse. Other fields could be added if deemed valuable for decision support, such as using the party to whom the order was shipped as the customer or the party placing the order. This model could have included additional artifact information about the customer and their contact mechanisms in this entity; however, another design decision was made to store additional customer information in the CUSTOMER ADDRESSES and CUSTOMERS tables because this would reduce the overall storage space required (by reducing the amount of redundantly stored data). The customer address being stored is the primary work address for the customer.

Another question the DSS analyst may need to answer is this: Who were the sales representatives involved in the transaction? To answer this, there is a relationship to the SALES_REPS table from the CUSTOMER_INVOICES table. The salespersons can again be derived from the Invoice Role model of Figure 7.2, which shows that each INVOICE has INVOICE ROLE, of which one may be an INVOICE ROLE TYPE of "sales representative". In this case, a relationship similar to customer/sales rep between an external organization (i.e., customer) and internal persons (i.e., sales reps or employees) needs to be traced.

The **sales_rep_last_name** and **sales_rep_first_name** columns *could* be included in CUSTOMER_INVOICES as data artifacts to allow for the occasions when the sales rep perhaps has left the enterprise. This model, however, includes the sales rep names in the SALES REPs table with snapshot dates to store what the name was and who the manager was at various points in time. This allows maintaining multiple sales reps for each invoice with a snapshot date that will probably correspond to the **invoice date**.

Additionally, if user requirements indicated that the names of the sales reps would be used frequently, then it would make the analysis simpler and more efficient by including these columns with the details and eliminating the need for a join to SALES_REPS to find the rep's name. In this way, the DSS analyst could more easily access the sales information by the sales rep's name. It would require more disk space for storage, however, and also require a design decision to maintain a preestablished number of names.

Who was the manager of the sales rep at the time of the transaction? The column **manager_rep_id** in the SALES REPS table provides this data through a recursive relationship. This column indicates the **party id** for the sales rep's manager at the current time. Because this relationship can change over time, the snapshot date on the SALES REPS table allows capturing who the manager was at various points in time. To make analysis easier, a **manager_last_name** and **manager_first_name** *could* have also been stored as artifacts in the CUSTOMER_INVOICE, if user requirements so indicated. These fields were stored in the SALES REPS table to reduce storage requirements (instead of storing them redundantly for every CUSTOMER INVOICE record) and to allow for the possibility of multiple sales reps and managers.

Assuming the models from this book have been implemented, the manager ID can be obtained from the operational data by examining the POSITION REPORTING STRUCTURE (see Figure 9.6). This data can be derived by determining the **party ID** of the person holding the position that is "reported to" by the position that the sales rep is currently filling. The recursive foreign key shown on the SALES_REP table is meant to indicate that the **manager_rep_id** will exist as a **sales_rep_id** in the SALES_REP table. This model assumes then that all sales rep managers are also sales reps themselves. In addition, this recursive relationship could be used for a higher-level grouping by which sales data could be summarized (i.e., a salesperson may report to a local manager who may report to a regional manager). Because the only information stored by this model is **first_name** and **last_name**, this relationship also saves the overhead of having an additional table for the manager information (this may or may not be a benefit, depending on the DBMS being used).

The **internal_organization_id** and **internal_organization_name** columns in CUSTOMER_INVOICES provide a mechanism for tracking which internal organization is responsible for the sale. The party is derived from tracing the **billed from** relationship from INVOICE to INTERNAL ORGANIZATION in Figure 7.3b. If internal organizational information changes quickly, the designer may also consider storing artifacts of additional internal organization information in the CUSTOMER_INVOICES table.

The **product_cost** is a derived field based on relationship artifacts. It represents what the actual product cost was at the time of the sale. Some of the information for item costs can be selected by traversing the relationships from INVOICE ITEM to the associated costs of the item that is being invoiced. This can be a complex field to derive because the costs may be stored in various parts of the model, such as the PURCHASE ORDER ITEM **amount** (see Chapter 4), the **actual ship cost** in the SHIPMENT (see Chapter 5), or the cost maintained as a rate in that are applied through TIME ENTRYs in WORK EFFORTs (see Chapter 6). This is further complicated by the applications of various costing methods [i.e., First In First Out (FIFO), Last In First Out (LIFO), or average cost] to determine the product cost. The INVOICE ITEM entity stores the **quantity** and **amount** as well as any INVOICE ADJUSTMENTS (see Figure 7.1b) that provide some of the information necessary to determine the costs of purchased items. While this example provides some of the selection criteria involved, the algorithms involved in determining product costs can be quite complex and are highly dependent on the business rules of the enterprise in terms of how they calculate costs.

Accommodating Levels of Granularity

By storing sales information at an invoice item level in the CUSTOMER_ INVOICES table, the enterprise has chosen to maintain the lowest level of granularity in its enterprise data warehouse. In other words, the data is stored at the transaction level and cannot be further subdivided. This allows departmental data warehouses the ability to summarize the sales information at whatever level of detail is required because the most detailed level of data (sometimes referred to as *atomic level*) is present in the data warehouse data model.

In some cases, it may be prudent to store multiple levels of granularity in an enterprise warehouse. This should be done only if there are good business reasons and requirements available to define the additional levels. If real requirements are not known, then the space required to store these extra levels, and the resources to build them, may be wasted. When it is known that the warehouse will be used to feed departmental warehouses, it is best to defer the definition of higher levels of granularity to the designers of these data marts. Then the specific requirements of the department can be used in producing meaningful summaries.

Merging Tables

As implied from the previous sections, the basis for CUSTOMER_INVOICES was the merging of the INVOICE and INVOICE ITEM entities. This was done on the basis that the two tables shared a common key (i.e., **invoice_id**), the data from the different tables is used together frequently, and the pattern for insertion is the same for both tables.

Separation Based on Stability

In the CUSTOMERS table, the **snapshot_date** column, which is part of the primary key, provides the ability to maintain a history of some of the more volatile demographics associated with each customer. If some of this data was more volatile, such as age and credit rating, it could have been separated into a CUSTOMER_DEMOGRAPHICS table to save space. This would have illustrated the concept of separation of data attributes according to its stability.

The customer information can be directly extracted from the operational systems of the enterprise. In terms of the models presented in this book, this data comes from the PARTY entity as described in Chapter 2. The data could be extracted by gathering all the parties that had a PARTY ROLE TYPE of "bill to customer". In the case of a customer that is an organization or company, the column **customer_name** is derived from ORGANIZATION **name** of the PARTY and, more specifically, the ORGANIZATION that was billed for the **INVOICE**. If the customer is a person, then the **current first name** and **current last name** from the PERSON entity would be combined into the **name** column (in which order will need to be determined by detailed *enterprise-specific* transformation rules).

Other Considerations

The **load_date** in CUSTOMER_INVOICES identifies the date that data was loaded into the data warehouse. This provides the ability to replace some records in the data warehouse with more up-to-date information if there are changes in the operational environment that affect history.

As may be obvious by the discussion so far, even though the design of the tables for the warehouse may be simple, getting the data into the proposed format could be quite an ominous task. Considering that the data may be coming from many separate source systems, there could be a need to scrub (or clean) the data and integrate it, as well as transform it into the warehouse model. For example, customer data may exist in two operational systems running on different platforms. Getting this information into one warehouse table will require careful examination of the data to see where the two systems match and where they do not. Then processes must be developed to convert that data into a common format that fits in the warehouse.

This point is precisely why a properly designed data warehouse can be of such incredible benefit to executives and analysts in an enterprise. It can allow them to view data and trends in ways that were not possible before without a substantial amount of time and effort on the part of the IS staff. With the data prearranged as described, the amount of time and system resources needed to process the various reports is also reduced.

The Sample Data Warehouse Data Model

Figure 11.2 illustrates an example of a data warehouse data model to support the information needs across an enterprise. This model illustrates the idea that while a data warehouse data model may start with a single subject data area, other subject areas may be integrated as time moves forward.

This sample data warehouse model builds on the previous section's customer invoicing model and integrates other subject data areas into the model. In particular, human resources, budget, and purchasing information has been added to the model.

Notice that while this model may contain a large part of the information that an enterprise may find useful for decision support, it is not all-inclusive. For instance, it doesn't cover all financial information, work efforts, or ordering and shipment information. This model illustrates the principle that the data warehouse is developed iteratively and other subject areas may be integrated, one at a time, into this model over time. Three subject data areas are integrated and included in this model:

- *Sales analysis.* This decision support information is primarily provided via the PRODUCTS, CUSTOMER_INVOICES, SALES_REPS, CUSTOMER_ ADDRESSES, CUSTOMERS, and GEOGRAPHIC_BOUNDARIES tables.

- *Budgeting and purchasing.* This decision support information is provided via the PRODUCTS, PRODUCT_SNAPSHOTS, PURCHASE_ INVOICES, SUPPLIER_ADDRESSES, BUDGET_DETAILS, INTERNAL_ ORG_ADDRESSES, and GEOGRAPHIC_BOUNDARIES tables.

- *Human resources.* This decision support information is provided through the INTERNAL_ORG_ADDRESSES, POSITIONS, and EMPLOYEES tables.

Common Reference Tables

Notice in Figure 11.2 that certain tables span subject data areas and are useful for several departmental views of data. The GEOGRAPHIC_BOUNDARIES table is useful to identify the types of boundaries included in different types of analysis. Notice that **geo_id** is present in several tables such as the CUSTOMER_ADDRESSES, SUPPLIER_ADDRESSES, and INTERNAL_ORG_ADDRESSES. The GEOGRAPHIC_BOUNDARIES table provides the look-up information linked to **geo_id**. This table can be used for extracting data based on city, state, or country (this will be discussed in future chapters). Because this information is maintained in a central prescrubbed decision support environment, it can be easily extracted into various departmental data marts (thus ensuring consistency across the data marts).

The PRODUCTS table is another example of standard information that may be used in purchasing, sales, and budgeting departmental data marts. The products sold are very often the products purchased, especially in retail and distribution organizations. For instance, a distributor may purchase a certain type of pencil in order to resell it. The fact that this information is being transformed only once from the operational environment to the data warehouse can save a great deal of development time in the long run and can lead to better quality decision support information.

Summary

This chapter has discussed details of the design of a sample data warehouse built to support the enterprise's needs. The methods discussed in Chapter 10 for transforming a corporate data model to a data warehouse model were applied specifically to the logical data models related to invoicing as presented in this book. The resulting data warehouse design contains some denormalization and various levels of granularity to assist in answering questions posed by the enterprise. The data warehouse data model as presented could be used as a starting point for developing departmental models for use in DSS, online analytical processing (OLAP), and multidimensional analysis. Some examples of these models are presented in the next three chapters.

It should be noted that what has been presented is one of many possible warehouse designs that could result from transforming the logical data models. The structure of a data warehouse will be influenced greatly by the questions it is designed to answer. If the corporate end users are asked enough questions during analysis, then the resulting design should provide the enterprise with the information it needs. If this does not occur, then more questions must be asked and another design developed. This is why it has been said that building a data warehouse is an *iterative* process.

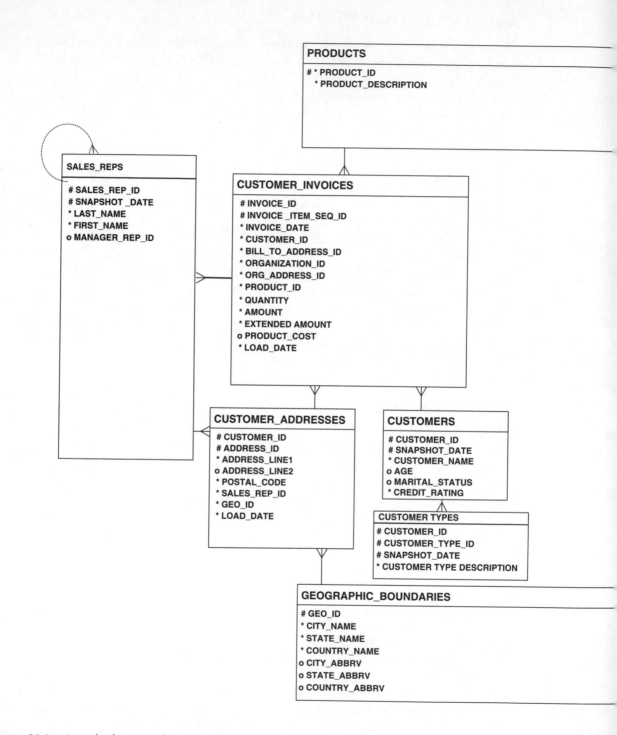

Figure 11.2 Sample data warehouse design.

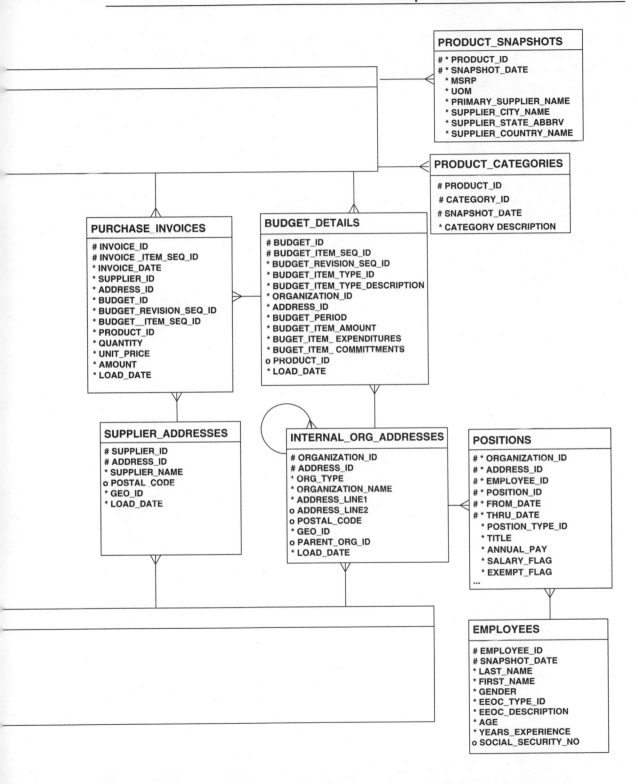

PRODUCT_SNAPSHOTS

\# * PRODUCT_ID
\# * SNAPSHOT_DATE
  * MSRP
  * UOM
  * PRIMARY_SUPPLIER_NAME
  * SUPPLIER_CITY_NAME
  * SUPPLIER_STATE_ABBRV
  * SUPPLIER_COUNTRY_NAME

PRODUCT_CATEGORIES

\# PRODUCT_ID
\# CATEGORY_ID
\# SNAPSHOT_DATE
  * CATEGORY DESCRIPTION

PURCHASE_INVOICES

\# INVOICE_ID
\# INVOICE _ITEM_SEQ_ID
  * INVOICE_DATE
  * SUPPLIER_ID
  * ADDRESS_ID
  * BUDGET_ID
  * BUDGET_REVISION_SEQ_ID
  * BUDGET__ITEM_SEQ_ID
  * PRODUCT_ID
  * QUANTITY
  * UNIT_PRICE
  * AMOUNT
  * LOAD_DATE

BUDGET_DETAILS

\# BUDGET_ID
\# BUDGET_ITEM_SEQ_ID
  * BUDGET_REVISION_SEQ_ID
  * BUDGET_ITEM_TYPE_ID
  * BUDGET_ITEM_TYPE_DESCRIPTION
  * ORGANIZATION_ID
  * ADDRESS_ID
  * BUDGET_PERIOD
  * BUDGET_ITEM_AMOUNT
  * BUGET_ITEM_ EXPENDITURES
  * BUGET_ITEM_ COMMITTMENTS
o PRODUCT_ID
  * LOAD_DATE

SUPPLIER_ADDRESSES

\# SUPPLIER_ID
\# ADDRESS_ID
  * SUPPLIER_NAME
o POSTAL_CODE
  * GEO_ID
  * LOAD_DATE

INTERNAL_ORG_ADDRESSES

\# ORGANIZATION_ID
\# ADDRESS_ID
  * ORG_TYPE
  * ORGANIZATION_NAME
  * ADDRESS_LINE1
o ADDRESS_LINE2
o POSTAL_CODE
  * GEO_ID
o PARENT_ORG_ID
  * LOAD_DATE

POSITIONS

\# * ORGANIZATION_ID
\# * ADDRESS_ID
\# * EMPLOYEE_ID
\# * POSITION_ID
\# * FROM_DATE
\# * THRU_DATE
  * POSTION_TYPE_ID
  * TITLE
  * ANNUAL_PAY
  * SALARY_FLAG
  * EXEMPT_FLAG
...

EMPLOYEES

\# EMPLOYEE_ID
\# SNAPSHOT_DATE
  * LAST_NAME
  * FIRST_NAME
  * GENDER
  * EEOC_TYPE_ID
  * EEOC_DESCRIPTION
  * AGE
  * YEARS_EXPERIENCE
o SOCIAL_SECURITY_NO

Please refer to Appendix B for a listing of tables and columns for this data warehouse design. SQL scripts to build tables and columns derived from this data warehouse design can be found on the full-blown CD-ROM, which is licensed separately.

Star Schema Designs for Sales Analysis

Suppose that ABC Corporation has built the data warehouse depicted in Chapter 11. Excited about the opportunity to get meaningful sales analysis information, the eastern regional sales manager has approached the IS department to see how and when the data would be available. The IS department, knowing that nothing is as simple as it seems, gathered some specific requirements. After a review of the real requirements, it was obvious that the sales manager did not need access to the entire warehouse. In fact, that would be too much information and ultimately result in confusion and dissatisfaction. IS decided the best solution was to develop a departmental data warehouse (or *data mart*).

The data warehouse stores all the atomic data necessary to capture all-important historic details. The data mart provides a mechanism to take a slice of this data for easy analysis by the end user. Each data mart usually takes a portion of the data warehouse and is designed to handle the needs of a specific department or part of the enterprise.

As pointed out in the previous chapters, a data warehouse is generally developed one subject area at a time. This chapter will briefly discuss possible star schema structures for a departmental warehouse containing the subject area of sales analysis to be transformed.

The purpose of the designs in this chapter is to provide an example of a department-specific data warehouse (or data mart) that could be developed from the data warehouse. Each enterprise may choose to modify this sales analysis departmental warehouse to meet its own specific needs. The models are presented in a standard *star schema* format to allow for multidimensional analysis. A star schema is a database design that contains a central table, called a *fact* table, with relationships to several look-up tables called *dimensions*. When the schema is diagrammed, it often forms a pattern resembling a star, thus the name *star* schema.

The models in this chapter will allow the DSS analyst to answer questions such as the following:

- What was the sales volume for a product during a specific time period?
- What was the sales volume for a category of products for a specific time period?
- How much of each product did various customers buy?
- How much of each product category did a selected customer buy?
- How much are the sales reps selling? To whom are they selling?
- Which products or product categories are they selling?
- When were sales the best? When were sales the worst?
- During those times who was buying and who was making the sale?
- Which products and/or customers are most profitable?

The specific schemas presented in the following pages include the following:

- Sales analysis data mart design
- Transaction-oriented sales data mart
- Sales performance data mart
- Product analysis data mart design

Sales Analysis Data Mart

Continuing with the example, the requirements analysis determined that the eastern region sales manager needs to see sales information by product, customer, sales representative, and geographic area. All this information must be available for analysis over daily, weekly, monthly, quarterly, and yearly time periods. In addition, the sales manager needs the ability to view information at a transaction level on an occasional basis when supporting detail is required.

Figure 12.1 shows a star schema that allows sales to be analyzed many different ways. The diagram shows a simple database star schema containing a central fact table and several dimension tables. The fact table is CUSTOMER_ SALES, which contains all the keys to the various dimensions and columns to hold the data to be reported (sometimes called *measures*). This table provides summarized extracts from the data warehouse to show sales via each of the desired dimensions. The dimensions by which the facts can be queried are CUSTOMERS, CUSTOMER_DEMOGRAPHICS, INTERNAL ORGANIZATIONs, SALES_REPS, ADDRESSES, PRODUCTS, and TIME_BY_DAY. This schema will likely be summarized and loaded on a daily basis so that current data is available every 24 hours. This means the level of granularity is fairly precise because the data is captured daily.

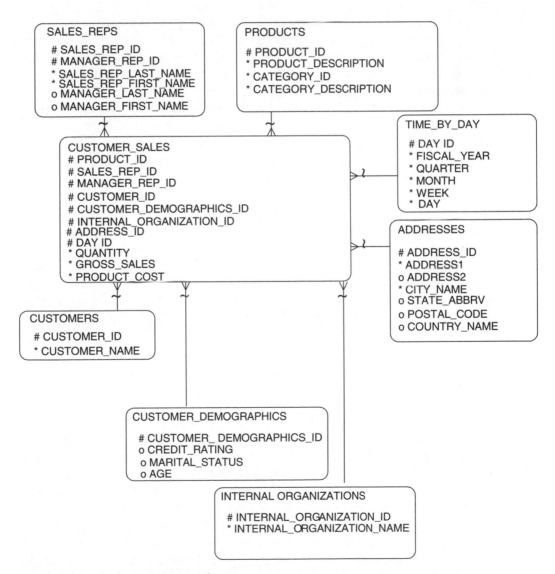

Figure 12.1 Sales analysis star schema.

Customer Sales Facts

The information in the CUSTOMER_INVOICES table is the result of transforming the data warehouse table CUSTOMER_INVOICES and its related tables (see Figure 11.1) into an effective data mart design. In order to allow the sales manager (or any DSS analyst) to use a multidimensional analysis approach, the data in the data warehouse is transformed into a (star) schema that is simple to query and performs well.

The key to the fact table is the combination of the various dimension keys: **product_id**, **sales_rep_id**, **customer_id**, **customer_demographics_id**, **internal_organization_id**, **address_id** and **day_id**. The information from the data warehouse summarizes each invoice and stores the resulting invoice summarizations in the fact table, partitioned by the combination of these dimensions. In other words, there would be a record in the CUSTOMER SALES fact table for every combination of the dimensions that has historically occurred.

If analysts wanted to see the resulting detailed transactions for a particular query, they could drill through to the main data warehouse by using the selected dimensions of the query as the parameters to the query to the data warehouse. Many data warehouse tools provide the facility of automatically passing the parameters of a query on a data mart to the data warehouse, in order to query the transactions that made up the summarized data.

The columns **quantity**, **gross sales**, and **product_cost** are the *measures* on which summaries and trend analysis will be done. The **quantity** column represents the actual product quantity that was invoiced, and it is from the INVOICE ITEM **quantity** attribute in the invoices data models from Chapter 7. The **gross sales** is the summary of the extended amounts (the INVOICE ITEM **quantity * amount**) for all the invoice items plus or minus any adjustments related to that invoice item, and it is also sourced from the INVOICE ITEM entity. The **product cost** is the product cost and may be calculated by using information from the PRODUCT COST COMPONENT models in Chapter 2 (V1:3.8). If actual costs are desired, the formulas can be much more complicated, and cost data may be gathered from the order models (to capture the cost of the invoice items), the shipment models (to capture the costs of shipments), and the work effort models (to capture the cost of producing products).

Data transformations that occur from the data warehouse to the data mart include summarizing the data (there could be several sales in the same day for the same dimensions), adding derived data, such as the gross invoice amount, and determining product costs. There could also be restrictions on the data selected. For example, as previously indicated, the process to extract the warehouse data may include customer invoice data only for particular internal organizations, such as certain departments or divisions. This would be done by limiting the selection process to specific organizations. Other possible restrictions could be on sales representatives or customers, or on a date-range basis.

The particular algorithm used must be based on the specific business analysis requirements of the enterprise using the data.

Customer Dimension

During the user interviews, the IS department learned that sales for each bill-to customer were desired. The sales manager, however, was *not* interested in historical changes to customer names, so the **customer_name** field is stored in the CUSTOMERS dimension table along with **customer_id**. The data selected from the warehouse into this table should be the most current data available on each customer.

The star schema shows a relationship to CUSTOMER, which is a subtype of PARTY ROLE. CUSTOMERs may also be further subtyped to define more specific roles such as BILL TO CUSTOMER, SHIP TO CUSTOMER, or END USER CUSTOMER. Because this data mart design is for INVOICE ITEMs, the customer that is represented is the bill-to customer. Additional, separate dimensions may be needed to show the ship-to customer or the end user customer if this information is needed. Ship-to information would be extracted using the relationships from the invoice item to the shipment item.

The data mart design could show ship-to and bill-to customers within a single dimension (as levels within the dimension); however, because there is a many-to-many relationship between bill-to customers and ship-to customers, the designer may want to have separate dimensions of a ship-to customer and a bill-to customer.

Customer Demographics Dimensions

To allow the analyst to get more detail on the demographics behind customers, the CUSTOMER_DEMOGRAPHICS table is included. The data for this dimension table can be directly extracted from the CUSTOMER DEMOGRAPHICS data table found in the enterprise data warehouse.

This table stores a record for each combination of the values for each of the fields in the table. For example, the table could store a **credit_rating** of "AAA," **marital_status** of "married," and an **age** of "20–25." Notice that age uses a range of ages in order to limit the possibilities to a reasonable size instead of allowing a number for each age year.* This would represent a unique row in the CUSTOMER_DEMOGRAPHIC dimension table that could be related to the CUSTOMER_INVOICES fact table.

If the analyst is interested in seeing sales data for all customers within an age of "20–25" that could be done with this data using a restrictive query against

---

The Data Warehouse Toolkit. Ralph Kimball. John Wiley & Sons. 2000.

CUSTOMER_DEMOGRAPHICS (e.g., select all customer IDs where the age is "20–25"). The same approach could be used to gather data based on **marital_status** or **credit_rating** as well.

In order to get meaningful information, the sales manager did indicate a need for demographic data *as it was* when the sale was made. It does not matter what age the customer is this month. The important information is what age was the customer last year when the sale was closed. In order to provide this level of detail, the CUSTOMER_DEMOGRAPHICS table was built using the columns **age**, **marital_status**, and **credit_rating**. Note that **age** and **marital_status** are optional columns because not all customers are people (they could be organizations). The column **credit_rating** may apply to both people and organizations; however it is also optional as it may not be known.

In the enterprise warehouse, the key to the CUSTOMER_DEMOGRAPHICS table is **customer_id** and **snapshot_date**. The data warehouse stores all the changes to customers' demographics. This data mart is interested in demographics only as it applies to invoices. Therefore, the table is loaded by extracting the appropriate snapshots of the demographics as they apply to each invoice. The table could be loaded by extracting the demographics of each customer as applied at the time of each invoice and creating a relationship to the existing CUSTOMER_DEMOGRAPHICS dimension instance or inserting records in the CUSTOMER_DEMOGRAPHICS dimension whenever there is a new combination.

Sales Reps Dimension

Another question the DSS analyst may need answered is this: What was the sales volume attributed to each sales representative during a certain time period? Also, who was the sales manager who managed the salesperson and was responsible for the sale? To answer these needs, the **sales_rep_id** and **manager_rep_id** columns are included as part of the key to CUSTOMER_INVOICES and are the key to the dimension SALES_REPS. The unique combination of the sales rep and manager allows querying on either of these attributes in order to analyze performance.

In the data warehouse, each SALES_REP has a recursive relationship to manager using the recursive relationship and linking the **manager_rep_id** to see who the sales reps are for that manager or, conversely, seeing who the manager of the sales rep is. The SALES_REPs is stored as a relationship to CUSTOMER_INVOICES. This information is extracted into the data mart and added to the SALES_REPS dimension. The details about a particular rep, including his or her name, are included in the dimension table SALES_REPS. This table corresponds to the SALES_REPS table in the warehouse. The only possible restriction to consider when populating this table would be to select only those reps that are involved in the required sales data. If the warehouse table is small, copying the entire table may be simpler and pose no performance impact. (Note that the definition of "small" varies from one enterprise to another.)

According to the data model, there may be more than one sales representative for an invoice. In these cases, the invoice amounts, quantities, and costs would need to be appropriately split (according to the **percentage** credit that each salesperson received, as shown in Figure 7.2) to accommodate for correct credit to each sales representative and manager.

Internal Organizations Dimension

Analysts may also want to analyze sales by different internal organizations to assess performance of various subsidiaries, departments, divisions, and so on. The INTERNAL ORGANIZATION dimension allows such analysis.

This data would come from the **internal_organization_id** and **internal_ organization_name** fields stored in the INTERNAL ORGANIZATIONS dimension table of the data warehouse.

Addresses Dimension

Another component, or dimension, commonly required in DSS and multidimensional analysis is geographic area, region, or location. For example, the eastern region sales manager needs to know sales volume not only by the various geographic areas, but also by the various customer locations or sites. In some cases, it may be critical to know the actual address where sales were made. This will provide the region with information to assess how well different products are selling at various customer locations.

The **address_id** columns and the ADDRESSES dimension will provide that information for this model. This data is extracted from the warehouse tables CUSTOMER_ADDRESSES and GEOGRAPHIC_BOUNDARIES. The values for **city_name**, **state_abbrv**, and **country_name** will be extracted from the warehouse table GEOGRAPHIC_BOUNDARIES using the column **geo_id**. As with customer and sales rep data, the only restriction to consider would be to pull only addresses referenced by the selected sales data.

Also dropped from the ADDRESSES table was the **customer_id** column as a way to identify that the address is for a particular customer (a CONTACT MECHANISM such as a POSTAL ADDRESS may be used by many PARTYs). Because the identifiers for an address are unique and the characteristics of an address rarely change, it was determined (through user interviews) that this dimension needed unique address records only. In other words, the extraction process from the enterprise warehouse needs to pull information for a particular **address_id** only once, regardless of how many customers are associated with it. This serves to save some space in the departmental warehouse because redundant data is eliminated. Because there is a many-to-many relationship between customers and their addresses, having separate dimensions provides the best flexibility to handle either customer analysis or location analysis.

Notice that the ADDRESSES table includes not only city, state, country, and postal codes but also **address_line1** and **address_line2**. This allows the regional sales manager to compare sales for a single customer that may have several locations within the same city. While some DSS analysts may be interested in performance at specific customer locations, others may be more interested in grouping sales by the large geographic areas like city, state, and country; both levels of detail are included.

Product Dimension

The PRODUCTS table provides description and category information about the various products that have been sold. Using this dimension, the DSS analyst can determine product sales by product or product category for higher-level analysis. The data in this table is a direct extract or copy of the PRODUCTS table found in the enterprise warehouse model.

The data model in Chapter 3, Figure 3.2, shows that a product may be categorized into more than one category. The current warehouse and this data mart determined that it would select only the primary categorization for the product (as indicated by the **primary_flag** attribute in the PRODUCT CLASSIFICATION CATEGORY entity in Figure 3.2). If it was necessary to store products in many categories, then the **product_id** and **product_category_id** would both need to be the keys to the CUSTOMER_SALES fact table.

Time Dimension

An accepted standard in the industry is that most star schema designs will have a time dimension. To accommodate this, the dimension table TIME_BY_DAY is used to store various time periods. It includes **fiscal_year**, **quarter**, **month**, and **week** and **day**. In this way, the data in the warehouse can be accessed and summarized to accommodate any of these time periods, not just a single period such as year. Table 12.1 contains examples of the data that could fill the TIME_BY_DAY table.

Table 12.1   Time Period Data

DAY	FISCAL YEAR	QUARTER	MONTH	WEEK
03-JAN-2000	2000	1	1	1
04-JAN-2000	2000	1	1	1
27-JAN-2000	2000	1	1	4
02-MAY-2000	1996	2	5	1

As indicated by the data, the table key, **day_id**, references the day of the invoice in the fact table. These dates are then associated with the appropriate year, month, quarter, and week. What dates are loaded into this table are again dependent on the time periods over which the enterprise wishes to conduct analysis.

At this point, it should be noted that this time data could mean several things depending on the rules of the enterprise. The table can be used to store organizationally defined time periods. Because many businesses operate on a fiscal year basis, the column for year is called just that: **fiscal_year**. This allows analysts to work within the bounds of their companies' standard time frames without too much confusion. If the year stored was only a calendar year, confusion could occur when interpreting the data and trends as there would be a mismatch between the time IDs in the dimension table and the time periods expected on company reports. A column for calendar year could be added if both year values are needed for analysis. Other extensions could be made to the model to categorize days into other classifications such as work days, weekends, or holidays.

Using this construct, it is possible to summarize the detailed data in CUSTOMER_SALES by the time element **day**. It could be summarized by fiscal year so that annual trends could be observed or by month so that the trends within a year could be observed or seasonal trends could be analyzed (e.g., compare gross sales for June, July, and August, for 1995 through 2000). Likewise, summary data by quarter or week could also be constructed. This would be done by selecting data associated with time ID values that have a particular year, month, or week (the actual mechanics of this will vary according to the DSS tool being used). This model is very flexible because one time dimension table could be used to produce many different summaries.

Note that this may or may not provide fast query retrieval, depending on many factors such as the DBMS and amount of data. If performance becomes an issue, then separate tables could be constructed to hold data summarized by the various time periods. For example, a *highly* summarized table containing this sales data by year could be built simply by substituting a TIME_BY_DAY dimension with a TIME_BY_YEAR dimension. Then a different time dimension table would be required that simply contained the list of years available. (If this was done, then the **quantity**, **gross_sales**, and **product_cost** fields would represent the sum of those values over a year's worth of invoices.) Depending on the needs of the enterprise, a weekly, monthly, or yearly data mart may be used in lieu of the daily data mart, in order to improve performance and save space.

Transaction-Oriented Sales Data Mart

Is a data mart with a granularity level of individual transactions an acceptable data mart design? The data warehouse stores the individual transaction data, so is it necessary to bring these transactions into a data mart because it can be viewed from the data warehouse? With the drill-through capabilities that exist to map back to the original transactions in the warehouse, is it necessary to store these transactions at the data mart level also? Perhaps a particular department just wants to have access to its own invoice transactions and be able to slice and dice these transactions easily by various dimensions.

Suppose we modified the previous data mart design to maintain the data at a lower level of granularity, namely at a transaction level. Figure 12.2 provides an example of this model. The model from Figure 12.1 has been modified by changing the key to **invoice_id** and **invoice_item_id**; the foreign keys to the dimension tables in this design are not part of the key to the fact table. (This will be the only fact table in Volume 1 and Volume 2 that does not have all of the foreign keys as part of the key to the fact table.)

On the surface it looks as if it is just a finer granularity for sales analysis. There is the added advantage of being able to view invoices at a summary level and then drill down until one gets to the individual transaction. Complications can occur when showing a star schema at a transaction level. Because the transaction needs to be kept intact and some of the relationships for the transaction may involve complex relationships, some information may not be able to be stored correctly.

For example, as shown in the invoices data model, there may be more than one salesperson for the invoice and each received a different percentage for the invoice. This is recorded in the data warehouse design of Figure 11.2, allowing many SALES_REPS for the CUSTOMER INVOICES table. This structure is not supported by a star schema because a star schema is defined by one-to-many relationships from the dimension to the fact table. The truth is that there can be many SALES_REPS for each CUSTOMER_INVOICES instance. Figure 12.2 has simplified the constraint of many salespeople by showing a single salesperson; however, it is not completely accurate.

The previous model, Figure 12.1, took care of this by allocating each salesperson's percentage to each salesperson and transforming the amount in the fact table's measures appropriately. This could be done because the fact instances represent summarized amounts. On a transaction basis, though, this is harder to do. Each transaction could be split into multiple transactions to accommodate the various salespersons. This could double or triple the number of transactions, a number that already may be quite large. If this is done it also may be confusing because the same transaction is stored multiple times. For instance, when counts of transactions are queried, the results may be misleading.

This example shows a key consideration when designing the data warehouse and data marts. The data warehouse is designed to capture the atomic transactions and their history. This may mean capturing data in non-star schema data

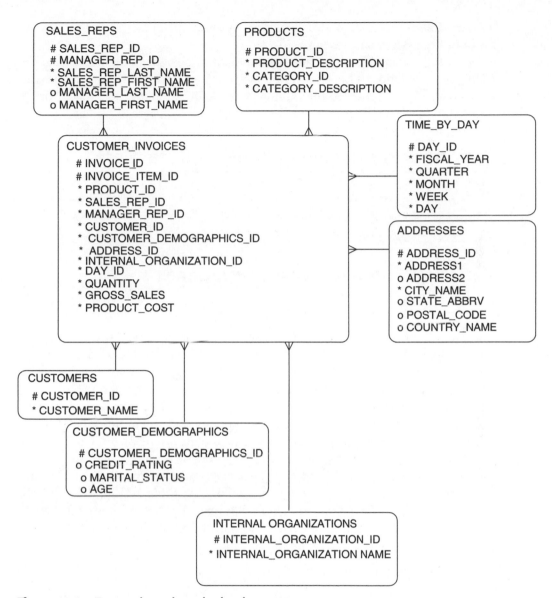

Figure 12.2   Transaction-oriented sales data mart.

structures because more complex relationships may be required, such as many-to-many relationships or recursive relationships.

The data mart is designed to capture data in a very easy-to-query and performance-oriented fashion. The star schema format is an example of a data structure that best meets these needs because it is very easy to slice and dice the information in this simple structure; due to its simple data structure, it can be more easily performance optimized.

Thus, the remainder of the universal data mart designs presented in the rest of this book will not be based on granularity of transactions. They will be based on measures that relate to the combination of the dimensions shown for the fact table.

Variations on the Sales Analysis Data Mart

There may be several variations on the star schema design represented in Figure 12.1. Depending on the business questions that need to be answered, the star schema design may vary.

Variation 1: Sales Rep Performance Data Mart

An example of a sales analysis data mart that may have very specific goals is one to measure salesperson performance. Take, for example, the need to analyze the performance of sales reps on a monthly basis. This may be done by the previously mentioned regional sales manager or, in other enterprises, by a human resources manager. These managers may need to evaluate the performance of the sales reps that report to them or develop and monitor sales incentive plans. They generally do not care what products are being sold, nor do they care about customer demographics. Their concern is sales performance and perhaps how much is sold to various customers to determine how diverse the sales rep's market is. To answer these needs, the table SALES_REP_SALES (see Figure 12.3) was designed. This table provides presummarized data by sales rep, customer, and address, by month. For example, suppose the questions that are needed are the following:

- What was the sales volume for a specific sales rep over the last 12 months?
- Which customer bought the highest volume through a particular sales rep for a specific month?
- What was the distribution of sales across a sales rep's customers?
- How much does each sales rep sell across each of his or her assigned states?
- Within each state, which city had the greatest volume for a sales rep?

To answer these questions, the model in Figure 12.3 may be the best sales analysis star schema for this application. This star schema may be in lieu of the star schema in Figure 12.1, or it may be in addition to the star schema in Figure 12.1. It may be in addition to the previous star schema because a more summarized version of the star schema may be needed for quicker access. Another reason is that different departments may have different needs regarding access to the data, so there may be several different data mart designs to meet each department's needs. They all, however, should extract data from the same company-wide data warehouse, so that one consistent, integrated source of decision support data can feed many data mart designs.

Customer Rep Sales Fact

Notice that there is no longer a PRODUCT dimension table because the table CUSTOMER_REP_SALES is a summarization of data about the performance of the sales reps, regardless of the individual products. Customer demographics

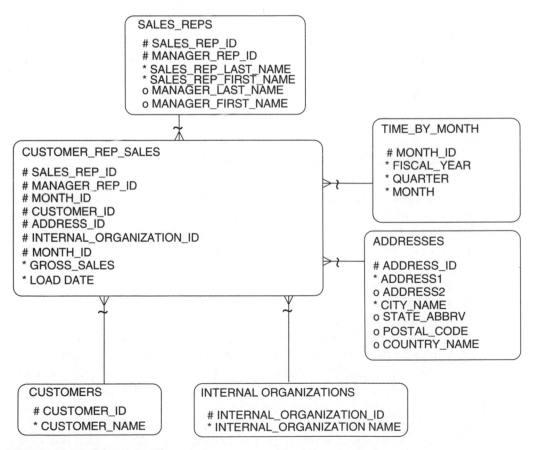

Figure 12.3 Sales rep performance.

are also deemed unimportant, and the CUSTOMER_DEMOGRAPHICS dimension has also been dropped. This table then represents a slightly higher level of summarization than the previous ones because two of the dimensions have been eliminated. The measures **quantity** and **product cost** have also been dropped because their values are dependent on product and cannot be summarized correctly in this context.

Time Dimension

In this star schema, there is a slight variation in the time dimension table. It is now summarized by month. When the sales manager was interviewed by the IS department, it became clear that daily information was not required to answer the questions posed; however, a monthly view of the data would be most useful. Therefore, the fact table has a column (**month_id**) that contains the ID to uniquely identify a specific month within the enterprise's fiscal year. This is matched in the time dimension table.

Because the data is to be summarized only by month, the time dimension needs only the columns **month**, **quarter**, and **fiscal_year**. The column **week** is no longer needed as it makes no sense in a monthly summary view of the data. Another point to note is that summarizing data to the monthly level also represents another higher level of summarization.

Thus, this table can provide the DSS analyst or department manager with another very flexible means of viewing the data.

Variation 2: Product Analysis Data Mart

Suppose a product analyst for ABC Corporation needs information to assess product performance. The information will be used to make strategic decisions on product offerings for various geographic areas. Interviews with the analyst determine that specific customer, customer address, or customer demographic information is unimportant for this type of analysis. It is also determined that monthly summaries will provide an appropriate level of granularity.

Figure 12.4 shows a schema containing PRODUCT_SALES as the central fact table. This is considered more highly summarized because it contains fewer dimensions than the previously discussed tables and because records are summarized by month. Thus, this table can be used to hold presummarized data for product sales by geographic area by month. While previous tables also included customer and sales rep information, this one does not (as the analysis indicated it was not required). Thus, the columns **sales_rep_id**, **customer_id**, and **address_id** are not included in this table. The only dimensions tables needed in this schema are GEOGRAPHIC_BOUNDARIES, PRODUCTS, and TIME_BY_MONTH.

Product Sales Facts

The measures in this table are again **quantity**, **gross_sales**, and **product_ cost**. Data in this table could be created by summing all the information in CUS-TOMER_INVOICES by **product_id**, **city_name** (from the ADDRESSES dimension), month, and year. The cities selected would be referenced by a new column, **geo_id**. As in the previous examples, this data could also be taken directly from the main warehouse by selecting and summing data from the data warehouse CUSTOMER_INVOICES table for the products of interest. An additional restriction on the data extracted would need to be made through a join to CUSTOMER_ADDRESSES with a summarization based on the **city name** via the column **geo_id**.

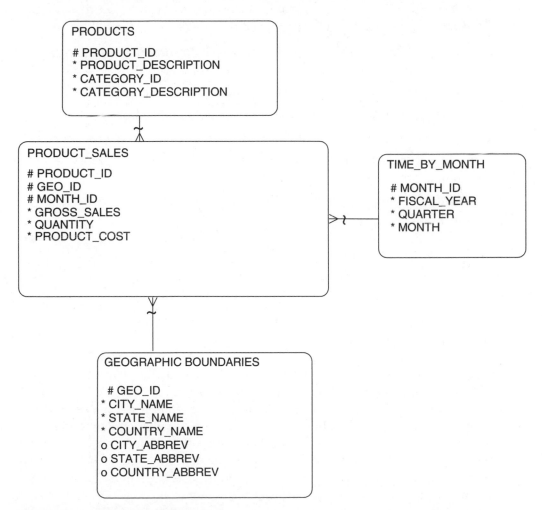

Figure 12.4   Product analysis star schema.

Geographic Boundaries Dimension

What is this **geo_id**? In the case of this warehouse, these IDs are tied to city names, so the data can be summed to the level of city-related data. The table GEOGRAPHIC_BOUNDARIES contains a hierarchy of geographic areas—namely, cities, states, and countries. By using this dimension, an analyst could gather data for all the cities within a selected state or country. Additionally, data could be selected for multiple states or countries.

Thus, for each product for a city, all the sales dollars and quantities for that product would be added up to give a grand total by product and city. Once compiled, this data could be very useful for product analysts and other executives who need a quick, high-level view of how their products are performing with respect to the various geographic areas. Even getting a view of total sales by product would be quick using this table because there are far fewer rows to sum.

Questions that could be answered from this data include the following:

- What was the sales revenue from a specific product over the last 12 months?
- What was the highest volume of a product for a specific month?
- Which product had the greatest revenue across all sales?
- Within that product, which geographic region had the greatest revenue?
- What was the profitability for each product or product category in a certain country for a specific year?
- Which country has generated the greatest average annual revenue by product?

Summary

This chapter presented details of the design of sample star schemas built to support sales analysis. The movement of data from the enterprise data warehouse to a data mart was discussed. The resulting design contained various levels of granularity to assist in answering the questions posed. The models presented could be effectively used to support DSS, OLAP, and multidimensional analysis.

It should again be noted that what has been presented is one of many possible designs that could result from building departmental warehouses based on the enterprise warehouse. The structure of a schema will be influenced greatly by the questions it is designed to answer. With a thorough end-user interview process, the resulting design should provide the departmental analyst with useful information. When this is not the case, more questions must be asked and another design developed. Again, this is why building a data warehouse or data mart *must* be an iterative process.

As may be obvious by the discussion so far, even though getting the data into the enterprise data warehouse may have been difficult, once in place, the warehouse provides an excellent basis for developing departmental data marts (star schemas). All the major transformation and integration work has already been done *and documented*. To state again, this is why a properly designed data warehouse can be of such incredible benefit to executives and analysts in an enterprise. It allows them to get data extracts more easily for viewing trends in ways that were not possible before without a substantial amount of time and effort on the part of the IS staff. With the data prearranged as described, the amount of time and system resources needed to produce various data marts can be reduced. The accuracy of data is also increased because there is an integrated source (from the data warehouse data model) allowing for consistent decision support information that may be useful in many departmental data warehouses.

Please refer to Appendix C for a listing of tables and columns for these star schema designs. SQL scripts to build tables and columns derived from these data mart designs can be found on the full-blown CD-ROM, which is licensed separately.

CHAPTER 13

Star Schema Designs for Human Resources

As in the previous chapter, the design of another proposed departmental data warehouse will be discussed. The EEOC (Equal Employment Opportunity Commission) Compliance Division of the Human Resources Department of ABC Corporation has been hearing how happy the eastern regional sales manager is with the data mart produced for that group. The division has heard that the data mart has drastically reduced the time and energy required to get reports on strategically important data and that with some appropriate DSS tools, it is fairly easy to analyze trends effectively.

Not wanting to be behind the times and having a real need, the EEOC division manager asks the IS department for assistance in producing a small data warehouse for the division. Elated that the data mart concept is catching on, the IS manager is more than willing to assign some people to the task. After a series of interviews, the IS team determines what questions the EEOC team is most interested in answering and develops a couple of star schemas for the data marts to specifically address those questions. This chapter will examine the structure for these data marts.

As stated before, the purpose of the models in this chapter is to provide examples that demonstrate the concepts of building a departmental data warehouse. This model may be tailored to fit a specific enterprise's needs; however, it should be understood that the design of this departmental data warehouse is highly dependent on the enterprise implementing it.

This model will, however, allow the DSS analyst in the EEOC division to answer questions such as the following:

- How many programmer/analysts are African-American or Hispanic?
- What is their annual salary in comparison to that of those who are white?
- What is the average salary for female versus male workers?
- Is there any group that has a higher or lower rate of salary increase compared to others?
- How do annual salaries compare with respect to years of experience or years employed by the company?
- How many minority workers are there in total? What percentage does this group represent?
- How many employees of different statuses are there and what are their characteristics? For, instance how many part-time employees are there, and what is their average annual pay?
- How many employees for what types of positions have been employed during what lengths of service? How many employees have been employed more than 10 years? More than 20 years?

The specific schemas presented in the following pages include the following:

- Human resources star schema
- Human resources star schema at a higher level of granularization

Human Resources Star Schema

Given the results of the interviews with the EEOC staff, the IS department determined that initially it would be very useful to be able to look at human resource measures such as number of employees, the average age, the average years of experience, the average years employed, and the average annual pay for all employees, across all departments, and to group them by position, EEOC category (white, Hispanic, African-American, Asian, Native American, etc.), status, pay grade, length of service, and gender. Discussions with the staff indicated that daily information would not be needed but that a picture of the organization at month end would allow for observation of some meaningful trends.

The star schema depicted in Figure 13.1 was developed—based on the data in the enterprise data warehouse—to address these needs. The central fact table, HUMAN_RESOURCES_FACT, contains not only the keys to the various dimensions, but also the important measures to be analyzed. The dimen-

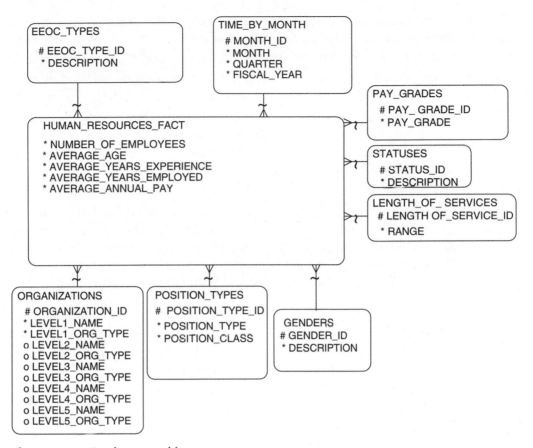

Figure 13.1 Employee pay history.

sions for this star schema include ORGANIZATIONS, POSITION_TYPES, GENDERS, LENGTH_OF_SERVICES, STATUSES, PAY GRADES, EEOC_ TYPES, and TIME_BY_MONTH. As indicated, the data for this schema will likely be loaded at the end of each month.

Human Resource Fact Table

The measures for this fact table are as follows:

Number_of_employees. The count of employees meeting the specified dimension values.

Average_age. The mean age for employees meeting the specified dimension values.

Average_years_experience. This indicates the total number of years of work experience both in and outside ABC Corporation. In other words, the mean number of years experience that the employee has working in the field.

Average_years_employed. The average number of years that the employee has been employed for the enterprise.

Average_annual_pay. This represents the annualized salary for a given employee as of the end of the month in question. In other words, at the point in time when the snapshot was taken, this is the amount of money that an employee would make over the period of one year if the current pay rate remained the same.

The **average_years_employed** is a calculated measure based on the **from_ date** and **thru_date** of all the positions an employee has held for the company as indicated in the enterprise warehouse. Even though these columns have changing values for employees, the fact that month is part of the key provides a history of what these values were at various points in time (in this case, at each month end).

As measures, the analysts can find out such things as the average age of employees in the company or the total years of experience within a position type in a department (this is calculated by dividing the **average_years_experience** by the **number_of_employees** for the selected dimensions). Questions such as these can be asked:

- What is the average salary for those between the ages of 55 and 60 compared to those between 25 and 30?

- What is the salary for those with over 15 years of experience (or employment) within each position type or each department?

The notation in chapter 12 for star schemas explicitly showed the primary key to each fact table. Since the key to the remaining fact tables in this book will always be a combination of the primary keys from each dimension, the key to each of the remaining fact tables will not be explicitly stated. The reader should know that the primary key to each fact table will be the combination of the primary keys of each dimension.

Organizations Dimension

Information about the internal organizations is taken from the warehouse table INTERNAL_ORG_ADDRESSES. Because no geographic information was required for this data mart, only the unique organization identifiers and names were selected to be moved from the enterprise warehouse. In addition, there are numerous **org_type** columns (i.e. **level1_org_type**, **level2_org_type**, and so on) that were also extracted to allow analysts to select the organizations to be analyzed based on a type such as department, division, or branch.

The structure of this table is somewhat different from that of the other tables seen so far. It has been denormalized to store the organizational hierarchy that is represented in the main warehouse by the **org_type** columns. The **level1_org_type** information represents the data associated directly with the lowest level HUMAN RESOURCE FACT measures records that were extracted. **Level2_org_type** is the name and type of the parent organization to the "level 1" organization, for example the division to which a department is within. **Level3_org_type** is the parent of "level 2," and so on. The columns with **name** such as **level1_name** and **level2_name** function in a similar manner as was just explained.

The "level 2" and higher levels do not include an ID as that information is not needed. Each dimension record is defined by its **organization_id**, which is a "level 1" or lowest level unit. For instance, a dimension record may show that the "accounting department" is a "level 1" that is within a "level 2" finance division that is within a "level 3" eastern region that is within a "level 4" ABC Subsidiary that is part of "level 5" ABC Corporation. The inclusion of only five levels of structure was a decision based on the levels of organization found in ABC Corporation. This model could easily be adapted to other organizations by adding or subtracting levels as required.

Table 13.1 gives examples of the data that may be found in the organization dimension. It is shown only to "level 3" for illustration purposes. The key point is that each organization dimension represents the lowest level in an enterprise structure, allowing analysis to be summarized to any level desired. The flat structure of this table serves to enhance performance and simplify queries, rather than imposing a recursive structure on end users.

Position Types Dimension

This information is extracted directly from the POSITIONS table in the enterprise warehouse which corresponds to the POSITION and POSITION TYPE entities in the logical data models. This dimension represents a *unique* list of all types of positions (**position_type**) represented along with the **position_class**

Table 13.1 Organization Dimension

ORGANIZATION ID	LEVEL 1 NAME	LEVEL 1 ORG TYPE	LEVEL 2 NAME	LEVEL 2 ORG TYPE	LEVEL 3 NAME	LEVEL 3 ORG TYPE
10929	Accounting	Department	Finance	Division	Eastern	Region
23948	Investments	Department	Finance	Division	Eastern	Region
29039	Sales	Department	Marketing	Division	Western	Region

associated with that position. It was assumed that for any given position there was one and only one position type associated with it throughout time. Using this dimension, an analyst can select from HUMAN_RESOURCE_FACT by **position_type** or **position_class** (from the POSITION TYPE CLASSIFICATION entity), which is a higher-level position classification. This is similar in construct to the PRODUCTS dimension (discussed in the previous chapter), which includes both **product_description** and **category_description** columns (see Figure 12.1).

Genders Dimension

The enterprise may want to do analysis to see how many positions are occupied by males or females, how much they are getting paid on the average, and how much experience they have. Many human resource enterprises are required to maintain five categories of GENDERS **description**s: "male," "female," "male to female," "female to male," and "not provided."

Length of Services Dimension

This dimension allows the analysis of various ranges regarding lengths of employment with the enterprise. For instance, how many employees have worked for the **range** 10–15 years. and what is their average annual pay? This LENGTH_OF_SERVICEs dimension may be used in conjunction with the **average_years_employed** measure. The analyst could determine the **average_years_employed** measure for employees in the length of service of 5–9 years, thus further refining their knowledge of employment history.

Statuses Dimension

The status provides information on number of employees, average salaries, or other metrics for each status in the organization. Possible statuses may be "part time," "full_time," "exempt," "temporary," and so on. This allows the enterprise to conduct analysis about different types of employees.

Pay Grades Dimension

This dimension allows for querying human resource measures by various pay grades and this dimension corresponds to the PAY GRADE entity from chapter 9, Figure 9.7. If more specific information is needed such as SALARY STEP, this could also be included as a level of this dimension.

This dimension can help analyze how much different types of human resource positions are paid. For instance, how many employees are in pay grade 5, and what is their average annual pay?

EEOC Types Dimension

This dimension is built by gathering the unique **eeoc_type_id** and associated **description** values from the EMPLOYEES table in the enterprise warehouse. Based on the analysis requirements, it was critical that this information be included as a dimension because the project is sponsored by the EEOC (Equal Employment Opportunity Commission) Compliance Division of the Human Resources Department.

Time_By_Month Dimension

The TIME_BY_MONTH table used for this schema is the same table used in the sales analysis data mart discussed in Chapter 12. To review, it contains a **month_id** that uniquely represents a fiscal year and month combination. The data loaded in this table should represent all time periods covered by the data in the fact table. It provides the EEOC analysts with the ability to gather data not only by month, but by quarter and year as well. In this way they should be able to comply with their reporting requirements easily.

The **month_id** column acts as the link to the time dimension. This information then represents the human resource facts for each month the enterprise does business.

Human Resources Star Schema at a Higher Level of Granularization

As previously stated, another principle in data warehousing is that of accommodating different levels of granularity. As in the sales analysis model, interviews with EEOC compliance staff members did indeed indicate that they needed some common averages for reporting to the federal government. They needed to evaluate average annual salaries based on the position type, EEOC category, and gender, across the organization. To accommodate this need, the IS department developed the higher-level schema based around the HUMAN_RESOURCES_SUMMARY_FACT table (see Figure 13.2).

How is this table loaded? It could be loaded from the enterprise warehouse or from the HUMAN_RESOURCE_FACT table. Because these two schemas will be used by the same division, it may be most efficient to load the summary data from the HUMAN_RESOURCE_FACT table after completing the monthly load process (this saves having to scan the entire warehouse—data in the details table is essentially preselected). If this is the case, then the table would be loaded by selecting the detail data for a month, then selecting each of the measures from the previous star schema. Next, those sums are summed and allocated across a broader range using the same **organization_id**, **position_**

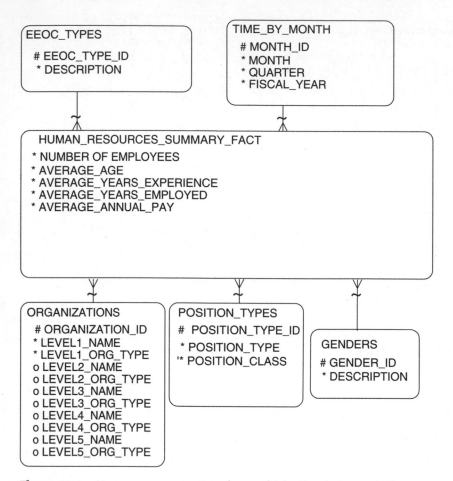

Figure 13.2 Human resources star schema—higher level of granularity.

type_id, **eeoc_type_id**, and **gender_id**. The calculations are then loaded into the columns **number_of_employees**, **average_age**, **average_years_experience**, **average_years_employed**, and **average_annual_pay**. (Note that in most relational DBMSs, there will likely be a SQL function that calculates averages easily.)

With this data in hand, the EEOC division at ABC Corporation can easily answer such questions as these:

- What is the average salary for Hispanic females in data modeling positions compared to that of white males?

- How do average age and average salary compare between female supervisors and male supervisors?

- Is there any obvious trend comparing years of experience, salary, and EEOC category within a particular division?

WHY CREATE ANOTHER SUMMARIZED VIEW OF THIS HUMAN RESOURCE INFORMATION?

Any of the questions that can be answered by the schema in Figure 13.2 can also be answered in the schema of Figure 13.1. With this in mind, why would there be a need to create a less granular schema such as the one presented in Figure 13.2? The schema in Figure 13.2 is optimized for performance and will result in much quicker queries than the last schema. There may be many other variations of higher-level summarizations, which may be used by specific departments that need only certain data. The other reason for a more summarized star schema, such as this one, is that some personnel may be allowed to view only certain human resources information, and one method for providing data security to different parts of the enterprise is by providing different views of overlapping data while restricting sensitive data to certain groups of individuals.

Summary

This chapter contained details of the design of two sample star schemas built to support analysis of human resources data. The resulting design demonstrated some additional denormalization and several levels of summarization to assist in answering the questions revealed during end-user interviews.

As previously noted, what has been presented are several of the many possible schemas that could be derived from an enterprise data warehouse. The structure of a departmental model is in a large part determined by the questions it is designed to answer. It cannot be over-emphasized that end users of the data must be interviewed to determine their *real* business and information needs if a data warehouse strategy is going to be successful.

As illustrated, it is not uncommon for one department to wait to see how successful another department's venture is before it is willing to commit time and money to the effort. Once the methodology and technology have been proven, by producing not only data marts but *happy and satisfied* users, then others will soon want to join in that success.

Please refer to Appendix C for a listing of tables and columns for these mart designs. SQL scripts to build tables and columns derived from these data star schema designs can be found on the full-blown CD-ROM, which is licensed separately.

Additional Star Schema Designs

This chapter provides some additional star schema designs for common functions of the organization, such as inventory management analysis, purchase order analysis, logistics/shipment analysis, work effort analysis, and financial analysis.

Each of the Universal Data Model chapters (Chapters 3 through 9) have corresponding data analysis or star schema designs that can help analyze data. Chapter 2, which covers parties, provides constructs that are used in many of the star schemas such as CUSTOMER, SUPPLIER, INTERNAL ORGANIZATION, FACILITY, and so on. The following illustrates the corresponding data model chapter for the star schemas defined in this chapter.

Chapter 3, which includes inventory management models, corresponds to the inventory management star schema of this chapter.

Chapter 4, which includes purchase order and purchase order item models, corresponds to the purchase order star schema of this chapter.

Chapter 5, which includes shipment models, corresponds to the shipment star schema of this chapter.

Chapter 6, which includes work effort models, corresponds to the work effort star schema of this chapter.

Chapter 7, which includes invoicing models, corresponds to the customer invoices star schemas in chapter 12, Figures 12.1–12.4.

Chapter 8, which includes accounting and budgeting models, corresponds to the financial analysis star schema of this chapter.

Chapter 9, which includes human resources models, corresponds to the human resources star schemas in Chapter 13, Figures, 13.1, and 13.2.

For each star schema, common questions are provided that are useful starting points for discussions of data warehouse requirements. Template measures and dimensions are provided in each diagram, and the questions may be used as sample data warehouse questions to facilitate discussions about what data warehouse users may need.

Inventory Management Analysis

Figure 14.1 provides a template star schema design to analyze inventory items. The design assumes that the enterprise manages inventory by part and that a part may be a raw material, subassembly, or finished good, as shown in Chapter 3 (V1:3.10b). If parts are not tracked and the enterprise only manages their goods, then substitute GOOD for PART. The information for this star schema can be extracted from a combination of entities in Chapter 3 and Chapter 5.

The geo level and org levels in the dimensions provide for flexible hierarchies of geographies and organization rollup structures. For instance, the geo level may indicate city, state, or country, or it may be changed at a later date to state, country, continent. The **level_org_type** columns were explained in Figure 13.2 only they are now applied to the INTERNAL ORGANIZATIONS instead of the ORGANIZATIONS. The org levels may be department, division, and parent company, and they could also change as time goes by. This convention is used for subsequent star schema designs in this chapter.

Figure 14.1 is designed to handle the following types of questions:

- How much inventory does the enterprise have of different types of parts (or goods if the enterprise just tracks goods)?

- How much has been committed for use?

- How can the enterprise optimize inventory levels and store what is needed and where it is needed? How can the enterprise forecast what we need?

- What is the status of inventory in various locations? How much inventory has been shipped, received, and issued over time for various locations and for various types of goods?

- How much inventory of what types of parts has been scrapped in various facilities over time?

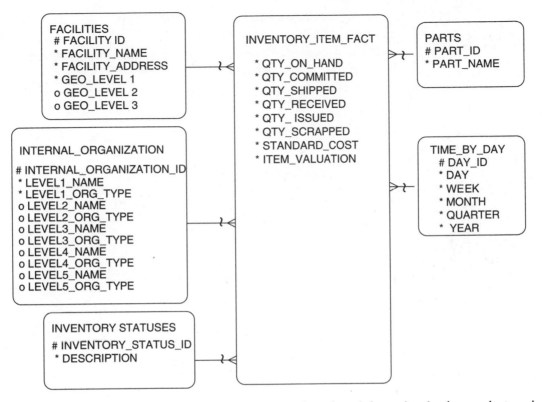

Figure 14.1   Inventory management star schema—based on information in the product and shipments data models.

- What is the count and item valuation of inventory items?
- What are the trends over time for inventory balances and needs for inventory by various facilities and internal organizations?
- What are the inventory costs by facility and by internal organization?

Purchase Order Analysis

Figure 14.2 provides a template star schema design to analyze purchase orders. The information from this design is sourced from implementations of the PURCHASE ORDER and PURCHASE ORDER ITEM entities described in Chapter 4.

The purchase order star schema is designed to handle the following types of questions:

- What types of products are being ordered by various internal organizations?

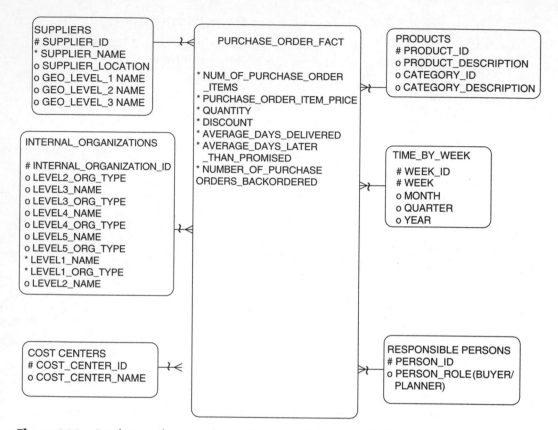

Figure 14.2 Purchase order star schema—based on information in the order chapter.

- How many purchase orders of what types of products and for how many items occur over time?

- What are the average prices for different types of products from different suppliers?

- What types of discounts have been offered by various suppliers for different types of products?

- What suppliers have offered the best prices for different products over time?

- How prompt are various suppliers, as measured by the average number of days later than they have promised for their purchase orders?

- What are the expected lead times for various products, as measured by the history of the average number of days that it took for various products to be delivered?

- What buyers are more effective at negotiating better prices and discounts for various products?

- How many purchase orders are back-ordered for various types of products by different suppliers?

- Which cost centers have had the greatest purchase order amounts allocated to them?

- What is the breakdown by product of the amounts spent within each cost center?

Shipment Analysis

Figure 14.3 provides a star schema to analyze shipments and help organizations analyze their logistics operations. The data that is analyzed is sourced mainly from the SHIPMENT ITEM entity and its related information. A key benefit to

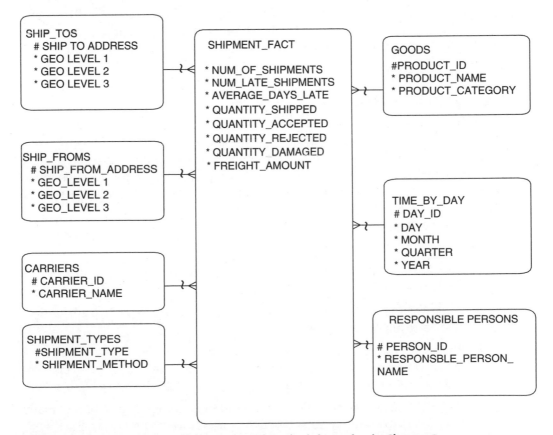

Figure 14.3 Shipments star schema—based on the information in Chapter 5.

this shipment analysis star schema design is that it provides the ability to analyze all types of movements of goods including customer shipments, purchase shipments, transfers, drop shipments, and any other SHIPMENT TYPE. The star schema allows the enterprise to assess the following questions:

- How well are shipment delivery expectations being met?
- How many damaged or rejected shipments are being received or delivered (via the **quantity_damaged** and **quantity_rejected** measures)?
- How many shipments are late by which carriers? (A late shipment occurs when the **shipment received date** is greater than the **promised order shipment date.**)
- How many shipments are rejected for which types of goods for which carriers?
- How many shipments are damaged for which types of goods for which carriers?
- What have been the freight charges (**freight_amount** measure) for various types of shipments for various carriers to and from various locations?
- Which people responsible for the shipments have been most effective at keeping the freight costs lower and minimizing rejected shipments?

Work Effort Analysis

Figure 14.4 provides a work effort analysis star schema to analyze how effective various work efforts are, such as production runs, repair efforts, consulting engagements, internal projects, or any other type of work efforts as described in Chapter 6. The work effort star schema is sourced from the WORK EFFORT entity and its related information.

The types of questions that are meant to be answered by this data analysis design are the following:

- How successful were our work efforts based on on-time, on-budget performance?
- What was the performance for various types of parties such as for project managers and/or workers?
- What was the average amount of time spent on various work efforts? (Keep in mind that work efforts were defined at multiple levels. For instance, they may be plans, projects, phases, activities, tasks, and so on.)
- Which facilities have had the best record of keeping their labor and materials costs down for various types of work efforts?

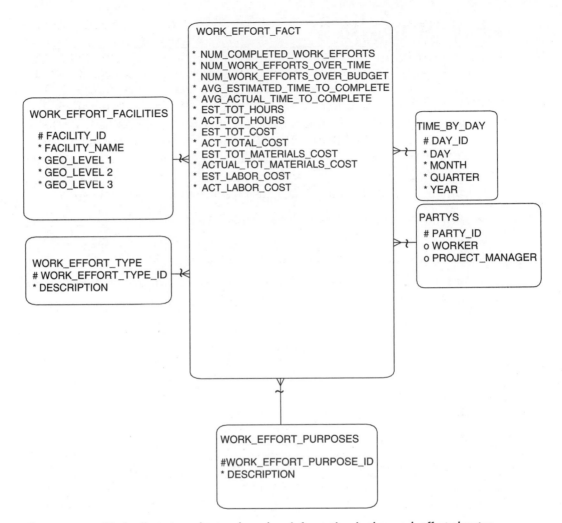

Figure 14.4 Work effort star schema—based on information in the work effort chapter.

- How have actual labor, material, and total costs compared to the estimated costs for these items?
- How have costs for various types of work efforts changed over time?
- How long do various types of work efforts take to complete by facility and by the project manager?
- How many work efforts for what purposes have been completed at which facilities?

Financial Analysis

Figure 14.5 provides a template star schema design to analyze accounting transactions from Chapter 8 and is based on the summarized ACCOUNTING TRANSACTION instances. The ACCOUNT_BALANCES star schema allows balance sheet and income statement account analysis by GENERAL_LEDGER ACCOUNTS, by the INTERNAL ORGANIZATIONS that are being analyzed, by the LOCATIONS (for various country and continent analysis), and over TIME_BY_MONTH.

This financial analysis star schema answers questions such as these:

- How do actual revenues compare to planned revenues?

- How can one graphically depict the financial performance of various business units (an example type of org level) over time?

- How well are various departments (an example org level) controlling their costs against their allocated budgets?

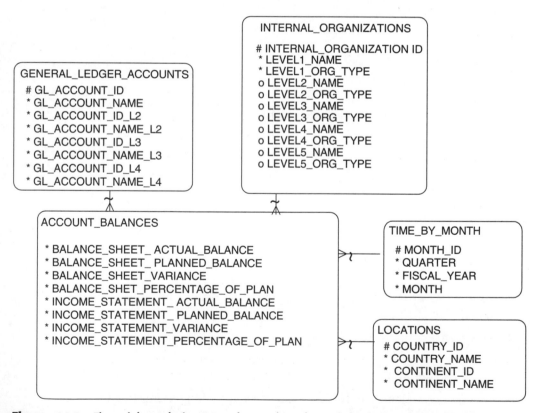

Figure 14.5 Financial analysis star schema—based on information from Chapter 8, and specifically accounting transactions.

- What significant variances occurred for income and expense accounts (GENERAL LEDGER ACCOUNTS) from period to period that may flag possible business concerns?

- What trends are apparent in the area of accounts receivable (a type of general ledger account)? What indications do these trends have for increasing or decreasing the expense of sales (another type of general ledger account)?

- How can cash flow trends be used to predict how much capital is available for business expansion?

- What trends exist over time in key financial ratios such as debt to equity, current assets, and liquidity ratio? (These can be calculated via formulas applied to various general ledger accounts and could also be included as additional measures even though the information is derivable with the current star schema.)

Summary

This chapter has provided some examples of Universal Data Models for jump-starting the design of data marts for inventory management analysis, purchase order analysis, logistics analysis, work effort analysis, and financial analysis.

Many other star schema designs may apply to enterprises, and this chapter has provided a sampling of some of the more common designs as well as common questions that may be used to facilitate data warehouse and data mart requirements sessions.

Appendix C provides a listing of tables and columns for star schemas, including the ones in this chapter. The full-blown CD-ROM contains SQL scripts to implement these star schemas.

CHAPTER

15

Implementing the Universal Data Models

In this book, numerous models have been provided that can help jump-start data modeling efforts. But what are the purposes for these models, and how can the enterprise use them to build higher-quality operational and data warehouse databases? The models in this book, as well as those in Volume 2, can facilitate the building of more integrated systems, help the enterprise better manage its information, and can lead to higher-quality database designs in shorter periods of time. This chapter will cover the life cycle of the model from the development of an enterprise data model, to the development of the logical data model for a project, to the development of a physical database design which is the basis for implementing a database. Using these models for data warehouse implementations will also be discussed.

Effective methods for incorporating the Universal Data Models can be summarized as follows:

- Develop the enterprise data model by customizing and adding to the Universal Data Models using the business terms that are commonly known in the enterprise and adding appropriate information requirements.

- Build the appropriate logical data models for each project according to the business requirements for that specific application.

- Create the necessary physical database designs based on the logical data model and the technical requirements.

- Customize the database design to the appropriate target DBMS (database management system).

Questions to be answered in approaching this area are the following:

- What are valid purposes and applications for using Universal Data Models?

- What are the appropriate models to create, and how can the Universal Data Models support them?

- What customizations are needed for the Universal Data Models to adequately reflect the business of a particular enterprise?

- How do the business functions and process impact the data models?

- What options are available in creating the logical data models for a specific project?

- How flexible are the Universal Data Models? Is there only one right way to implement them?

- What considerations are needed in creating the physical database designs?

- How does DBMS platform choice affect the design?

The chapter will address each of these subjects in the areas of business analysis, system design, and database design. The Universal Data Models will be used to demonstrate principles and to assist in understanding. The focus for each section will highlight the outlined areas and answer the appropriate questions.

The Enterprise Data Model—An Integrated Business View of the Enterprise's Information

One of the key information issues today is how to develop integrated systems that facilitate consistent information for use by the enterprise. When projects develop their database designs independent of an overall model, the same information items are often implemented in separate tables and sometimes with different meanings, leading to redundant, inconsistent data and non-integrated systems.

The Universal Data Models in this book can be used to jump-start an enterprise data model effort, providing the enterprise with a "road map" of their information and showing how information relates to other information. If proj-

PURPOSES OF THE UNIVERSAL DATA MODELS

The Universal Data Models in this book can be used to do the following:

- Help build an enterprise data model that illustrates the interrelationships between information in various applications. This is a key aspect of helping enterprises integrate their information.

- Provide a starting point in developing a logical data model.

- Add a new section of a data model to an enterprise's existing data model.

- Validate an enterprise's existing logical data models and provide ideas for additions or modifications.

- Help systems developers to understand the nature of various pieces of data and offer possible options and solutions to providing better information to the enterprise.

- Help understand the information requirements of the enterprise and be used as the basis for helping to select and implement application packages. Requirements for application packages generally consist of functional requirements, data requirements, and technical requirements. The data model can serve as the data requirements. Why let the package dictate the information requirements of the enterprise? The enterprise needs to know its own requirements in order to properly select and implement application packages.

- Help to serve as an information road map to identify and synchronize data from multiple systems. Even if an enterprise has decided to use mostly application packages instead of custom building systems, it may use the enterprise data model to identify the information requirements and where application packages store redundant information.

ects had such road maps, then they could use this model to facilitate each project using the same format for their data structures and the same definitions behind data items, or possibly even sharing the same physical data structures. This approach can lead to much more data consistency, data quality, and ultimately to better information to be used to improve the operations of the enterprise. The enterprise data model documents the information requirements of the enterprise and helps the enterprise integrate their information.

In addition to an enterprise data model, an enterprise process model can help the enterprise identify the business functions across the enterprise and facilitate building systems that do not redundantly or inconsistently develop the same processes. For instance, a "quoting" process would be represented and defined once in the enterprise process model, and this function should be implemented the same way for the quoting system, order entry system, and invoicing system that is developed. Template or Universal Process Models, can help jump-start and validate an enterprise's process model. There is a great need in the industry to develop re-usable process models to assist in systems development projects.

Very large enterprises may want to consider developing an integrated view of a portion of their business. For instance, a large international firm may decide it needs to get a handle on the information and/or processes involved in its customer service and support division, which handles customer service, sales support, technical support, and training worldwide. Although having an enterprise model across the entire enterprise may also be valuable, perhaps developing a model for this portion of the business may be a more manageable effort.

In order to be successful in adapting and using the Universal Data Models (and/or universal process models) as a basis for creating this enterprise data model, it must begin with the business community. Any understanding of information begins with the business. It is important to keep the information at a level that business people can understand. In preparing the enterprise data model, the business concepts need to be complete. In order to represent the broadest viewpoint, the models need to be flexible and able to solve multiple business problems.

Customizing the Universal Data Models

The logical data models in this book were designed to give an enterprise a head start in designing a system or in developing a corporate data model. As noted in many sections of this book, enterprises will invariably have specific business needs that are not addressed by these models or changes in terminology that necessitate model changes The following sections address the various degrees of change that may be required as well as how to handle changes in terminology to suit the enterprise.

Degrees of Customization

Varying degrees of changes may be made to these data models. The changes range from very easy modifications to more difficult data model changes. An example of an easy change is adding additional attributes to one or more entities in the model. This is considered a very easy change because the structure of the data model is kept intact and because it is not necessary to evaluate the impact that this change has on other parts of the model. Care should be taken, though, not to introduce attributes that represent the denormalization of existing structures.

A slightly harder modification is adding a new entity or relationship to the data model. In this case, it is necessary to determine if the new entity or relationship already exists in some other portion of the model. For instance, if there is a proposal to add an entity named PRODUCT PACKAGE, does that information already exist within the MARKETING PACKAGE entity (see Figure 3.9b)? This depends on how the enterprise defines PRODUCT PACKAGING and therefore requires careful analysis.

Data modelers need to be a little more cautious when modifying or deleting entities and relationships in the data models. Because the data models are highly integrated, many entities and relationships in these data models are reused in many different diagrams and for many different purposes. There should be some consideration and analysis of how the change may affect other portions of the model. For example, if the enterprise decides to model ORGANIZATION and PERSON as two separate entities instead of as subtypes of PARTY, how this change affects other portions of the model must be considered. Some changes may be dramatic while other changes to entities and relationships may have lesser impacts on the whole model. If the enterprise is using only a small, specific portion of these data models, the impact of proposed changes may not be as significant.

While care should be taken when modifying these models, one purpose of these models is to provide a starting point for data modelers. If the models are used for this purpose, modifications to the models *should be expected* and encouraged in order to meet the information requirements of each enterprise.

Because these data models are integrated and many changes may require impact analysis, the systems development team should consider the use of appropriate change control and data administration procedures. These procedures include, but are not limited to, defining the following: Who is responsible for maintaining the models; how change requests are documented, prioritized, evaluated, and approved; how data model versions are maintained; and what mechanisms are provided to support the change control process (i.e., regular review meetings, systems, forms, etc.).

Customizing the Models for Unique Business Terminology

In using the Universal Data Models within this book , it is important to adapt the models to fit the terminology of a specific enterprise. Each enterprise is unique, and what works for some does not work for others. In working with the business, it is important to capture the business language. Important concepts are presented within the Universal Data Models, but they may not directly relate to the organization's business community. This is the first task in modifying the Universal Data Models for an enterprise.

There are various methods of understanding these terms. Documentation reviews, interviews, and facilitated sessions are some common methods used to discover this important aspect of the enterprise. In discussing this, it will most likely be discovered that different segments of the enterprise have different terms for similar things or the opposite—similar terms for different things. This inconsistency in language needs to be dealt with during the customization of the Universal Data Models. Depending on the scope and nature of the work, this may be very involved. Typically, this will require some consensus within the business community. While some items must have a common understanding, such as CUSTOMER, PARTY, and so on, others may not require it. Time must be spent with the business community to prioritize the items and gain the full support of all required business representatives.

The best path is to identify with the generic terms from the models all the business aliases for that term. This will allow for the business view to be included, but it will move the effort toward a unified standard. If consensus (or a majority of participants agreeing) is achieved, the terms can be modified to support the enterprise viewpoint. Documenting all aliases during this process in order to gain a complete understanding of any concept is usually recommended.

The key is to reuse as many of the constructs provided as possible in order to save time in reanalyzing generic constructs so that the modeler can focus on the specific needs of the enterprise. If the data structures apply however the terms used are different, then to gain buy-in, keep the data structure idea and change the names of the entity.

To demonstrate the concept of using the business terminology of an enterprise, this next section will review the party contact mechanism model from Chapter 2 (Figure 2.10).

Again, the model in Figure 15.1 shows the CONTACT MECHANISM used by each PARTY as the PARTY CONTACT MECHANISM. This consists of several subtypes: POSTAL ADDRESS, TELECOMMUNICATIONS NUMBER, and ELECTRONIC ADDRESS. Included is the PARTY CONTACT MECHANISM PURPOSE. This structure as described earlier represents all the potential methods of contact for any PARTY.

Example of Changing the Terms for the Specific Enterprise

In our example, John Doe, a data analyst working to customize the party contact mechanism for XYZ Company, reviews the business requests given to him regarding the PARTY CONTACT MECHANISM. He discovers that there are many aliases for different entities within the model.

These aliases are the candidate entity names in the customized Universal Data Model. As you can see from Figure 15.2, the customized names are applied in the appropriate entities.

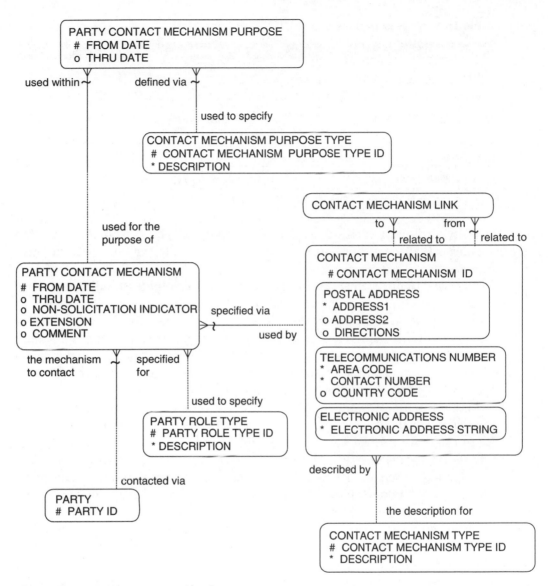

Figure 15.1 Party contact mechanism.

The updates made to the Universal Data Model are the application of the XYZ Company business names: PARTY is replaced with BUSINESS ENTITY, CONTACT MECHANISM with CONTACT METHOD, and TELECOMMUNICATIONS NUMBER with PHONE NUMBER. Notice that ELECTRONIC ADDRESS was kept, but because the business used two prominent names, EMAIL ADDRESS and WEB ADDRESS, they were added as subtypes to the enterprise data model. Often adding alias entities as subtypes gains two benefits: One is that the

Table 15.1 Aliases for the PARTY CONTACT MECHANISM

UNIVERSAL DATA NAME	XYZ CO. ALIAS NAMES
PARTY	BUSINESS ENTITY
CONTACT MECHANISM	CONTACT METHOD, CONTACT TYPE
TELECOMMUNICATIONS NUMBER	PHONE NUMBER (includes fax, cell, beeper, pager, and so on)
ELECTRONIC ADDRESS	EMAIL ADDRESS, WEB ADDRESS
CONTACT MECHANISM LINK	CONTACT METHOD RELATIONSHIP

specific attribution for each type may be captured as it is discovered, and the second is that the old business names can be linked to the new, generic business names.

It is good to mention at this point that an important understanding is the use of language. If a particular term has traditionally meant one thing, it may be best to choose a new, previously unused word or term for the concept. For example, if ORGANIZATION within XYZ Company always means a subsidiary of XYZ Company, it may be unwise to use it to represent any outside company. The analysts should seek an alternate term for that concept rather than forcing the word to mean something that it never has meant before.

Another important concept is to choose words that reflect a great majority of the business thought. In the previous example, two terms are very common in XYZ Company for ELECTRONIC ADDRESS. Because ELECTRONIC ADDRESS has not been used before, it was decided to add this to the enterprise's vocabulary, but to add the two known terms as types of the higher concept. This helps business users understand the new term and achieves a common feel by having the two known concepts included.

The other question to answer is how to choose which alias, if any, should be used within the business models. Usually the majority of business users will be able to substantiate the most common business terms. The best term to use is the one used the most. The benefit of this approach is that the majority of the business groups will understand the term. The downside is that all known terms have embedded subtleties that may not be apparent. These must be understood and documented in order to properly evaluate the usefulness of a term.

In our example, John Doe has learned that the commonly used term for PARTY is BUSINESS ENTITY. In his research, he discovers that many parts of the enterprise refer to the people and organization as "business entities." In light of his findings and discussions with many business groups, BUSINESS ENTITY instead of PARTY is used for the model. The term PARTY is avoided, as this is not a sufficiently understood term; however, the same data constructs from the party model may be used.

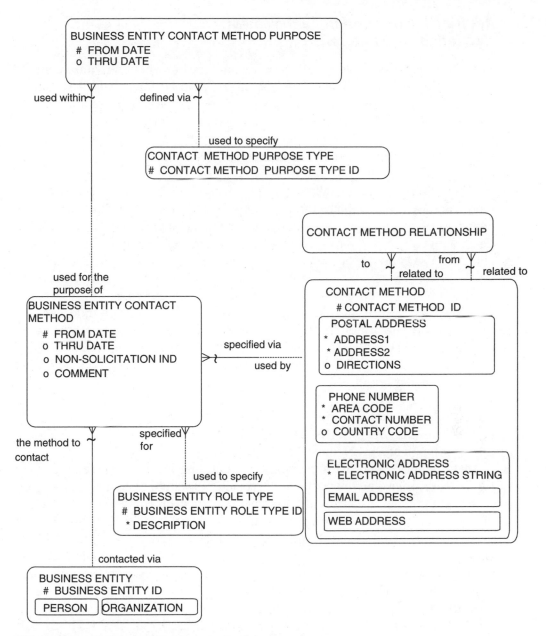

Figure 15.2 Customized party contact mechanism.

Additional Information Requirements Needed for the Enterprise

The enterprise data model needs to encompass the information requirements of the specific enterprise. While many common constructs may be used as a jump-start to the model, the information requirements of the enterprise still need to be captured and added to the model. The modelers developing the enterprise model need to capture this information, typically through interviews, group sessions, and modeling sessions, to gain a more complete understanding of the information requirements.

The Universal Data Models can serve as the basis for the enterprise data model and then may require modifications to support the specific enterprise's needs. As an example, suppose that John Doe finds that the majority of the entities, relationships, and data objects within the Universal Data Model are applicable for XYZ Company; however, he finds that there are additional needs as well.

For instance, suppose that John Doe learned that XYZ Company needs to capture the preferred times to contact each person or organization and that they need to capture these preferred times for each contact method because the times may vary for different contact methods. A person or organization may specify that it is OK to contact them anytime using an e-mail address; however, they may specify that they should be contacted only at a certain phone during normal business hours.

Additionally, XYZ enterprise needs to add more subtypes to the Universal Data Models in their enterprise data model. They have a need to specifically identify the subtypes of WEB ADDRESS, EMAIL ADRESS, and IP ADDRESS as different types of ELECTRONIC ADDRESSes.

These requirements would represent additional information requirements for the enterprise, and thus data model structures should be added to the enterprise's data model to represent these and any other information needs that are discovered. Figure 15.3 shows the additional entities of PREFERRED CONTACT TIME as well as the IP ADDRESS subtype as additions to the Universal Data Models. (These could also be considered Universal Data Model constructs; however, for illustration purposes, these are shown as additional requirements for a specific enterprise.)

Figure 15.3 shows that each PARTY CONTACT MECHANISM may be preferred to be contacted at one or more PREFERRED CONTACT TIME. This entity indicates the **from datetime** and/or the **thru datetime**. Each contact mechanism may have different time preferences. For instance, the preferred contact time for Marc Martinez as a customer of ACME may be from Monday through Friday from 9 AM to 5 PM. Another customer may specify to contact him or her only from Thursday to Friday from 3 to 5 PM. That customer may also specify that it is OK to call him or her at the home number from 10 AM to 4 PM on Saturday or Sunday.

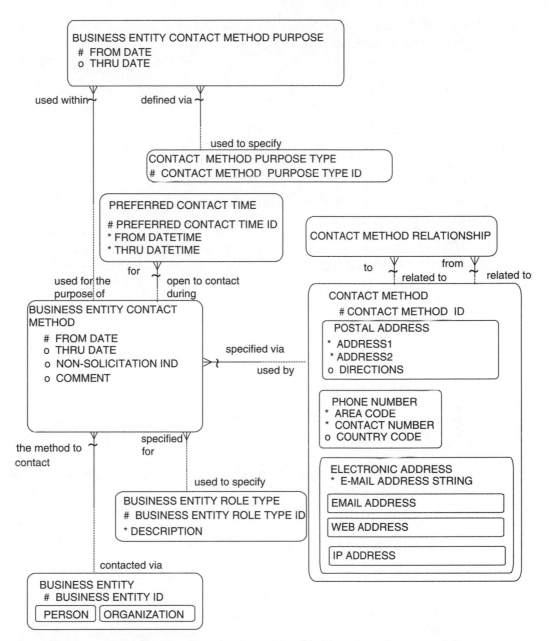

Figure 15.3 Additional information requirements added to Universal Data Models.

Once all the information is gathered for the Universal Data Models, they should be linked together into a single model to form a consistent enterprise view. The full-blown CD contains all the models that may be uploaded to a modeling tool. This allows for the models to be created and modified within the targeted tool set. Once created, the model should be segmented by business concept (or subject data area), such as Party, Product, Order, Shipment, Work Effort, Invoicing, Accounting, and Human Resources, in order to more easily maintain the model going forward.

How the Universal Data Models and Enterprise Data Model Solve Business Problems

Once completed, the enterprise data model will reflect the business understanding of critical information. This is an ongoing process that requires support, time, and resources. One may question the need for such a facility, as it is costly and requires time. The benefits far outweigh the challenges in many ways. One important benefit of this model is in facilitating the ability to solve business problems.

In order to properly solve any problem, the business needs to have a clear view of all information. A past understanding that is assumed to be common knowledge often clouds this view. These assumptions need to be brought out and understood. The information in the model allows for the clear understanding of what should be and what is currently requiring improvement. Once challenged, the information can be redesigned in order to support the true business need.

A clear, concise picture of the information can validate understanding. In a model, clear business rules, concepts, and ideas are captured in a graphical form. The model can support the walk-through of any business group to assist in understanding that information. Once a full understanding is gained, the group is able to discuss potential changes and modifications. Further assumptions can be challenged and modified as required.

This clear picture of the information can support out-of-the-box thinking. When the business is able to see its information, this leads to a clear understanding of potential alternatives, supporting various viewpoints. The enterprise data model is then enhanced to support the multiple viewpoints discovered.

There are many complex concepts in doing business. Often, the downfall of the business community is not enough foresight. The modeled information is able to assist in identifying potential traps that can cause serious efficiency, performance or support problems. One of the biggest benefits in supporting an enterprise data model of information is understanding all the potential solutions. This is accomplished through a detailed, thorough picture of the information in order to see all the possibilities.

In the example, John Doe outlines the key business information involved in contacting a business entity. By modeling this information, the business leaders of XYZ Company begin to understand that electronic mail, postal mail, and telephone calls are essentially alternate means of accomplishing the same thing (contacting a business entity) and are hence similar types of information. Hence, if the resulting systems are able to display this information together in order to show all the methods for getting in touch with various parties, then it may facilitate easier contacting of parties. Contacts with the business entities are understood according to their purpose in order to know when a contact is valid. It also shows that communication events are within the context of relationships (this information is available in Figure 2.12) and that it is important to maintain how well communication events were followed up (this information is available in Figure 2.13).

The enterprise data model can help identify data redundancies and systems that do not serve as well as they could. For instance, it may point out that the customer service personnel and sales personnel are both using the same type of communication events and that the data is not currently integrated. This could lead to scenarios of a sales account manager calling on a customer, without even realizing that the customer has just communicated a complaint in the customer service department.

The model could point out the importance of maintaining information on the complete profile of a person or organization so that, when dealing with people or organizations, a complete picture can be viewed. What would be the consequences of selecting a supplier in a Request for Proposal process, not even realizing that one of the suppliers that was not selected also happened to be your best customer?

In a decision support environment, it may be important to analyze what types of contact methods generally lead to the greatest amount and dollar volume of sales for customers in order to maximize revenues. For instance, perhaps e-mail contacts (as opposed to telephone contacts or mailings) are shown to produce more leads that result in sales.

With the insight into the required information of an enterprise and associated relationships as presented in a data model, the enterprise can validate, update, improve, and remove redundancies in systems.

Using a Data Model for a Particular Application

While the enterprise data model enables an overall view of the enterprise's information, it is important to be able to build individual applications based on a high-quality data design. The enterprise data model can be used to provide a jump-start to the development of a solid database design for an individual application while providing a good context so that the individual application is integrated into the whole system of the enterprise.

The enterprise data model and the individual application data design (sometimes referred to as the logical data model for the application) can support and contribute to each other. The enterprise data model can provide a starting point for the individual application, and then the application data design can feed its insight and learning back into the enterprise data model so that other applications can benefit from this knowledge of the business.

The main objective of a good system design for a specific application is to solve the business problem and produce a system that the targeted community can use. This requires much communication and leverage in order to complete a good design. The Universal Data Models within the chapter facilitate a quicker and higher-quality data design by already addressing the most common needs and providing a better business understanding of the data. Once that is established, the next steps of design and implementation become easier.

Understanding Business Processes

One of the biggest challenges in working with business people to gain a clear understanding of information is that they just do not think in terms of data. Most business people think in terms of a known business process. It is important to approach them from their vantage point to drive a data understanding. In order to accomplish this, a solid understanding of the business processes behind the data is required.

In any interview or facilitated session, an effective approach is to outline the business processes that can help to validate and further refine the data model. This can be as formal as a process modeling methodology or as simple as a procedural flow of the business process to aid in discussion. In the natural course of conversation, "how" something is done will inevitably require "what" is involved. "How" something is done may be modeled with process models. "What" information is needed may be modeled using data models. The data modeler may ask questions about the goals, process, data, systems used, reports needed, issues, and possible solutions, thereby driving out the details of the data.

As pointed out previously, template process models can help jump start the analysis of the processes. Template models can help save time by allowing the analyst to reuse process models for common functions that most organizations conduct, such as sales, marketing or product development, or customer service functions. Template process models can also help to provide a checkpoint to make sure that no required processes are missing.

In our example, John Doe meets with XYZ Company executives to discuss their business issues to be solved with regard to better managing their contact

Table 15.2   Sample Required Business Processes

BUSINESS PROCESS	RELATED INFORMATION
Retrieve current contact methods	CUSTOMER, CUSTOMER CONTACT METHOD, POSTAL ADDRESS, PHONE NUMBER, ELECTRONIC MAIL ADDRESS, WEB ADDRESS
Determine most effective method for making contact for the desired purpose	CUSTOMER CONTACT METHOD AND CUSTOMER CONTACT METHOD PURPOSE
Establish that permission was granted for contacting customer(s)	CUSTOMER, CUSTOMER CONTACT METHOD, **non-solicitation ind, use permission ind**, CONTACT METHOD,
Establish best time(s) to make contact	CUSTOMER CONTACT METHOD, PREFERRED CONTACT TIME
Make customer contact	CUSTOMER, CUSTOMER CONTACT METHOD, CONTACT METHOD
Update Customer Contacts and Contact Method Relationships	CUSTOMER, CUSTOMER CONTACT MECHANISM, CONTACT METHOD, CONTACT METHOD RELATIONSHIP

management systems. Apparently, XYZ is planning to expand its Internet capacity and have decided to increase its presence on the Web. Traditional contact methods of telephone and mail arc not to be abandoned, but enhanced with the use of e-mail, Web sites, and direct access to many customers. XYZ will contact each customer and determine the best method of contact. The overall process is discussed with the business team, and they design how they will gather the information and make decisions. John then captures both the process and data requirements of XYZ Company.

Table 15.2 illustrates the processes needed for better managing contacts. Each process is documented during the design of the application to gain an understanding of how the system should work. The associated data is also defined and modeled (the next section will show this), maintaining the business requirements and rules.

The completed processes are helpful in determining the information needs for the needed application. With the supporting business process, the business people can review the developed processes and then identify what information is needed to support that process. In this way, the data requirements may be further driven from the understanding of process. The process model can also serve to validate that the data model is correct or if changes need to be made.

Building the Logical Data Model

Once a clear understanding of the business processes is established, the logical data model for the application can be completed. The logical data model needs to address the specific information requirements and business issues outlined in the process. It is critical to have the business view; otherwise, there is a risk that the resulting system will not solve the particular business issues.

Enterprise data models are important to capture the overall needs of the enterprise and show how the information is integrated across the enterprise. In building a logical data model for an application, it is important to flesh out the model in more detail so that the business processes and data requirements of the specific application are completely met. The enterprise data model will help the designer keep the various views of the enterprise in perspective, so that the resulting data model fits into the enterprise's integrated structure. It is important to know when to use the constructs from the enterprise data model and when to provide specific customizations needed for that specific application.

Suppose the enterprise data model structures are used to jump-start an application for the sales force, which is interested in tracking their customer's phone numbers, fax numbers, e-mail addresses, and any other contact methods. While other parts of the enterprise have a need to track information about their people and organizations, the sales force may have specific needs that they want to ensure are met.

In developing the needs for this application it is important to understand the specific needs of the sales force, while recognizing the benefits of being able to track contact methods and communication events for the entire enterprise. The same customer information that the sales force tracks may also be tracked by the customer service department, the accounting department, and the quality assurance department.

In the detailed system model, John Doe finds that some additional needs are important to the sales force. They may be important to other parts of the enterprise as well and thus be integrated back into the enterprise data model. Because it is not known if the other parts of the enterprise are willing to maintain this information, these information requirements may be included only in the specific application's model.

As an example, suppose that John Doe finds that the majority of the entities, relationships, and attributes listed within the enterprise data model are applicable for the sales force. He finds, though, that there are additional needs as well, shown in Figure 15.4. For instance, John Doe finds that there is an additional attribute, **use permission ind**, to the CUSTOMER CONTACT METHOD PURPOSE entity for purposes of gaining permission from customers to make "sales solicitation" calls to them. This was a process requirement that was outlined in the detailed process breakdown, and it is to show that the customer has granted permission to contact them for a particular purpose. For example, a

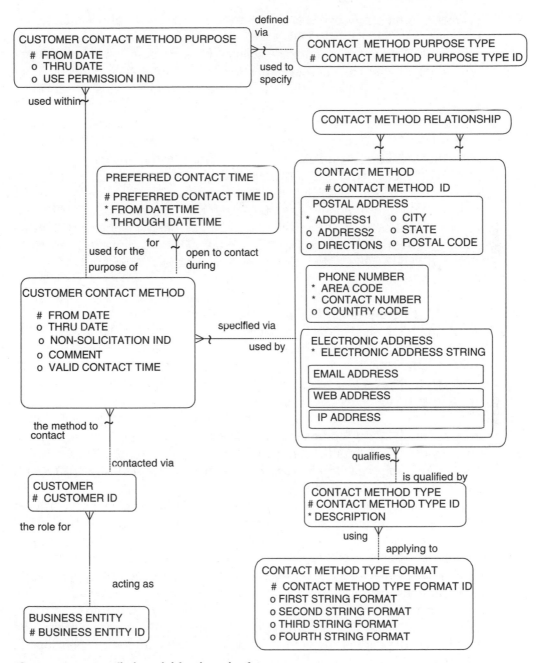

Figure 15.4 Detailed model for the sales force.

customer may have approved being contacted at a particular phone number for a CONTACT METHOD PURPOSE TYPE of "sales solicitation." XYZ needs this requirement for customer contacts because the enterprise holds it important that customers who have not given permission are not solicited by phone. In many other parts of the enterprise, this may not be required; thus, the attribute may not be included in the enterprise data model.

Another difference between the enterprise data model and the specific application model is that the enterprise tracks the CONTACT METHODs for all BUSINESS ENTITYs regardless of the role. The specific application is interested only in these CONTACT METHODs for their customers (in this case, they consider prospects to be a subtype of customers). The application-specific model may therefore model the CONTACT METHODs for CUSTOMERs and relate CUSTOMERs back to a BUSINESS ENTITY, thereby staying within the data structures of the enterprise data model. (This relationship from CUSTOMER to BUSINESS ENTITY can be implemented by using a foreign key to a business entity ID.)

Typically the logical data model will cover the generic structures of the enterprise data in greater detail and in a more explicit way. John found that there was an additional need in this application to create a CONTACT MECHANISM TYPE FORMAT entity to provide additional validation for different types of contact mechanism. For example a CONTACT MECHANISM TYPE FORMAT for "electronic mail address" may have an "@" as the **second string format** to identify that this is a necessary part of the second part of the string. A CONTACT METHOD TYPE of "phone number within country" may have a **first string format** of "###" to indicate that this type of contact mechanism must start with three numbers (i.e., the area code) in order to be valid. This additional information requirement was to eliminate errors and to supply XYZ with extremely accurate information.

It is also important to keep the detail explicit enough to support a robust solution. The depth of detail required is set by the requirements of the system. This is an important area, as this will determine the usability of the system. Once the details are captured, the information needs are also detailed. In the example, the details for a CONTACT METHOD were enhanced to support additional requirements. In this discussion, it is important to underline that there is no one way to approach a given problem, but it is based on the needs identified. The Universal Data Models support a guideline approach and will give the group using them a starting point as well as additional ideas to consider in developing the application.

Once all the requirements are understood and modeled, the business and design teams can review them to ensure that everything that is required is covered. It is at this time that any adjustments need to be made to cover all information. The design team should now accept the design as complete to move to the development of a physical database design that can be implemented in a database to support an applications.

Physical Database Design

The Universal Data Models can be used as the basis for an effective physical database design. The flexibility built into them allows for applications to be more stable and more easily maintained. It is important to provide flexible databases because the business rules of an enterprise may change over time, and the database design should be capable of handling many of these changes without restructuring the database design (which is an extremely costly process). Following the basic database principles itemized here, a successful design can be accomplished for any database. These are given as an overview to assist in creating a solid design.

Basic Database Design Principles

Any database design needs to be based on a solid logical datamodel. This is a critical step to ensure that the system developed meets the expectations of the business community using it. The Universal Data Models can be used to facilitate creation of the needed logical data models. Those models can then be implemented in a physical database design. The physical database design implements the information requirements of the logical data model while considering database performance for the selected database management system. A logical data model may be physically implemented many different ways depending on how the data will be maintained and accessed. The processes behind the data are critical to understanding how the data will be used and what the physical requirements of the data are: currency, update frequency, volume of transactions, and retention. It is also important to understand if the data will be used for analytical capabilities, such as a data warehouse or mart. These are some of the main considerations that need to be discussed.

Another key consideration is the type of database engine that will be used for the database. Important information is needed in order to support a design, as each has its special considerations. The requirements of the enterprise's systems should drive the choice of database platforms. Each company should have architectural guidelines to assist in the database choice. Once determined, a skilled database administrator (DBA) should work with the data modeler to create the required physical database design.

Using the logical data model that is based on the Universal Data Models, the physical design can be derived using standard principles. The goal of the following section is to show how the logical data models, built using Universal

Data Models as a starting point, can be used to create a physical database design that encompasses performance and implementation considerations. The following section will focus on several examples of how the Universal Data Models can be physically implemented as well as some standard practices used for converting a logical data model into a physical database design.

The database design should follow from the logical data model. The reasons are clear as the important efforts to maintain the business view and requirements are reflected in the logical model. Because the logical data model is linked to the process, the database administrator will be able to understand the usage, currency, security, and other factors required in the design. When using a modeled approach, the assumptions are easily tested prior to physical database creation and loading.

The logical data model should be normalized to third-normal form (3NF) to eliminate any redundancy. This means that each attribute is stored only once and is directly associated with the key, the whole key and nothing but the primary key. The models in this book are in third-normal form since each attribute is associated with an entity with a key that determines that attribute. For instance, the **non-solicitation_ind** is an attribute of the CUSTOMER CONTACT METHOD since it can be determined from the primary key of that entity, namely, the **customer id**, **contact method id** and **from date**. Stated differently, if one knows the primary key, then one can determine the attribute.

Once physical design is begun, the process of denormalizing begins. The physical database design may not be normalized and may include redundant attributes for speed in maintaining or accessing data. For instance, keeping the contact method fields, such as **address1**, in the CUSTOMER CONTACT METHOD entity will result in redundant data, but performance may be improved. It is best to denormalize based on performance issues: number of table joins, indexes, number of queries, updates, inserts, etc. At this point, the needs to support the process are considered and factored into the performance requirements. As in the previous step, the data is modeled and the assumptions tested prior to the actual creation and loading of data.

An important task in creating the database from the physical database design is the mapping of existing data to the new or enhanced structure. Transformation of data will need to be accounted for as well as when the data will be loaded in the process.

Many tools exist today to create the needed code to generate the database from a modeled solution. Once created, the required data objects are loaded into the DBMS, and the database is ready for data loading. Application testing can begin once all data is loaded to the DBMS. Modifications should be made at this point, beginning with the enterprise and logical data models, as new information requirements are discovered. Once the system is tested for the suitability of the application, the database is ready for production.

Creating a Physical Database Design

The logical data models in this book do not represent physical database designs; they illustrate the information needs of an enterprise. The physical database design converts the information requirements represented by the logical data model into a design for the database that can be implemented.

The main difference between the logical data models and the physical database design is that the latter may be optimized for performance. The physical database designer uses the logical database design as a starting point for the database design and denormalizes the structures where appropriate for performance and ease-of-access reasons. For instance, derived data may be included, tables may be merged, and arrays of data may replace one-to-many relationships in certain circumstances.

Several different ways exist to convert the same logical data model into various physical database designs. Many of the design decisions depend on transaction frequencies, use of the data, data volume statistics, and the chosen relational database management system (RDBMS).

Additionally, supertypes and subtypes from the logical data model may be implemented in many different ways in a physical database design:

1. The entire supertype with its subtypes may be implemented as a single table with a relationship to a look-up table to indicate the subtype. For example, the PARTY, PERSON, and ORGANIZATION entities could be implemented as a PARTY table with a look-up to a PARTY TYPE to indicate if it is a "person" or an "organization."

2. Each subtype may be established as a separate table with the supertype attributes included in each table. For example, the PARTY entity with its subtypes of PERSON and ORGANIZATION could be implemented as a PERSON table and an ORGANIZATION table. Any relationships to PARTY would now point to the PERSON table, ORGANIZATION table, or both, and any attributes of PARTY would be columns in both tables.

3. The supertype and one subtype may be merged into one table, and the other subtypes may be implemented as their own tables. For example, the PARTY, PERSON, and ORGANIZATION entities could be implemented as a PARTY table that includes all the attributes of PARTY and all the attributes of PERSON. In this scenario ORGANIZATION would be a separate table and related to the PARTY table. This design assumes that the PERSON table is accessed much more often than the ORGANIZATION table. And that is why the ORGANIZATION table is split out.

4. The supertype may be implemented as one table, and each subtype may be implemented in separate tables. In this physical database design, the PARTY, PERSON, and ORGANIZATION entities would each be

implemented as their own tables leading to a PARTY table, PERSON table, and ORGANIZATION tables with relationships from PERSON to PARTY and ORGANIZATION to PARTY.

The physical database designer needs to make these and other decisions to arrive at a physical database design.

Physical Database Design Examples

Based on the previous examples, the different design options available will be explained. We will use the party model from Chapter 2 (V1:2.5) as the target for discussion of physical design. Although physical design options are discussed for this model, all the Universal Data Models may be physically implemented using a similar physical database design approach.

Review of the Party Role and Relationship Model

The next section will briefly review the party role and relationship model from Chapter 2 (V1:2.5); the following sections will provide examples of possible physical database designs for this model.

As explained in Chapter 2, each PARTY may participate in many different ROLE TYPEs that describe various roles of the PARTY. These ROLE TYPEs are influenced by the type of PARTY, which may be subtyped into PERSON or ORGANIZATION. Some ROLE TYPEs may be for either a PERSON or an ORGANIZATION, specifically SHAREHOLDER, CUSTOMER, and PROSPECT, while others are specific PERSON ROLEs or ORGANIZATION ROLEs. (See Figure 15.5.)

As also explained in Chapter 2, PARTY RELATIONSHIP stores the information about the relationship between two parties such as the relationship status, priority, or communication events within the relationship. The CUSTOMER RELATIONSHIP is an example of a party relationship and at XYZ Company, one of the most critical information requirements is tracking and maintaining this relationship. There are other potential PARTY RELATIONSHIP subtypes, such as EMPLOYMENT, ORGANIZATION ROLLUP, and many other party relationships and corresponding PARTY ROLEs; however, the following discussion will focus on the physical implementation of the PARTY, PERSON, ORGANIZATION, CUSTOMER, EMPLOYEE, INTERNAL ORGANIZATION, CUSTOMER RELATIONSHIP EMPLOYMET and ORGANIZATION ROLLUP entities.

The enterprise data model and logical data model development efforts are normally followed for this model as described by the previous discussions on the contact mechanism model. The upcoming sections will discuss physical database design options for implementing the model, assuming that the enterprise and/or logical data modeling efforts have already occurred.

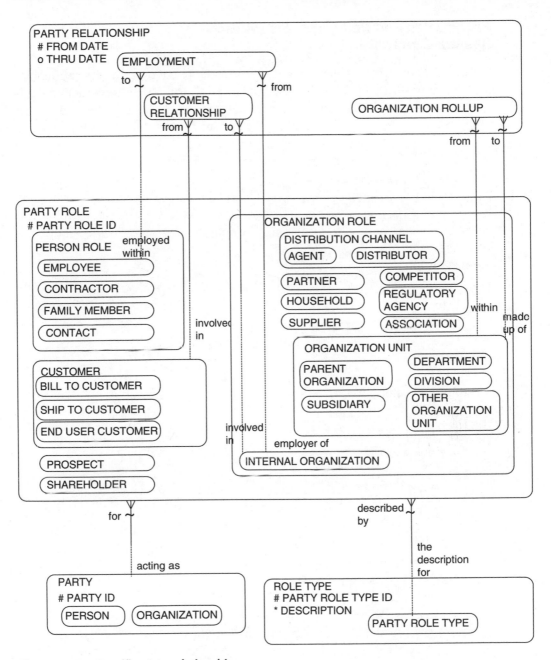

Figure 15.5 Specific party relationships.

Party Roles and Relationships Physical Design, Option 1

Figure 15.6 illustrates a database design for the party roles and relationships model just described and mostly uses the second strategy of implementing subtyping discussed earlier. Namely, each subtype may be established as a separate table with the supertype attributes included in each table.

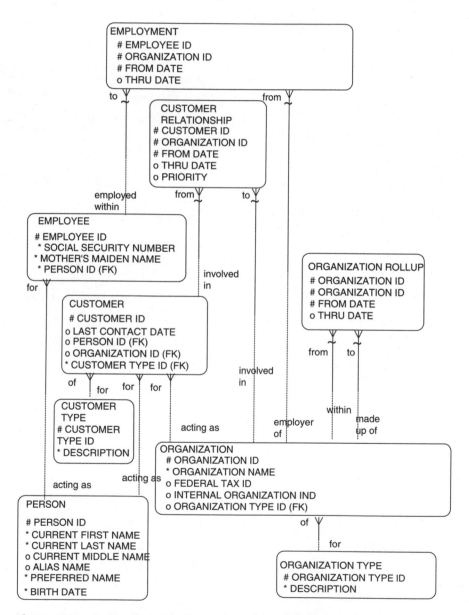

Figure 15.6   Party roles and relationships physical design, Option 1.

Separate tables are set up for the PERSON and ORGANIZATION subtypes instead of implementing a PARTY table. This helps performance because the number of rows in each table is far less than one big PARTY table. The disadvantage is that when either a person or an organization is related to another entity, such as the relationship to CUSTOMER or relationships from both people and organization to ORDERs, then the design is more complex, and the resulting system tends to be complex. For example, the application would have to reference either a PERSON or ORGANIZATION that is related to the ORDER and applications would need additional logic instead of simply showing the PARTY that was related to the order.

Separate tables are also set up for some of the PARTY ROLEs such as EMPLOYEE and CUSTOMER. This is a very practical implementation because most of the PARTY ROLEs are viewed as needing their own tables by most application development efforts. Even though there is a separate CUSTOMER and EMPLOYEE table, the holistic, integrated perspective is preserved because each of these tables is linked to the PERSON and/or ORGANIZATION that plays the role. Therefore, a PERSON could still play multiple roles without storing that person's information redundantly. In this example, the PERSON could act as a CUSTOMER or could act as an EMPLOYEE, which would be valuable to know. Perhaps EMPLOYEEs that are CUSTOMERs are entitled to special considerations such as discounts, or perhaps they are, at least, given special courtesies.

Each CUSTOMER has its own **customer id** and certain information that is unique to the CUSTOMER role such as **last contact date**, which is the last date that the customer was contacted by anyone in the enterprise. The BILL TO CUSTOMER and SHIP TO CUSTOMER subtypes were converted to a **customer type id** foreign key to the CUSTOMER TYPE table, indicating if the CUSTOMER TYPE **description** is "bill-to customer" or "ship-to customer." This is an example of using the first subtype implementation option because there is one table for the supertype and the subtypes. (The entire supertype with its subtypes may be implemented as a single table.)

Each EMPLOYEE has its own employee id as well as information that is appropriate to maintain for that specific role. For instance, the enterprise has deemed that the **social security number** and **mother's maiden name** will be maintained only for employees.

Attributes about people that are needed in more than one role are maintained in the PERSON table. This preserves the holistic principle that information about people should be stored once and not redundantly duplicated for each role they play. For instance, the **current first name**, **current last name**, **current middle name**, **alias name**, **preferred name**, and **birthdate** of a person may be needed for many different roles and in many different applications. Rather than repeat this information, for instance, by storing the employee name and the customer name in the CUSTOMER and EMPLOYEE tables (and repeating the name in any other role tables that are set up for people), the design recognizes that this is information about the PERSON so each EMPLOYEE and/or CUSTOMER is related to the PERSON, allowing access to this information.

A possible objection to this design for a specific database is that it is not performance oriented because a join needs to take place from CUSTOMER to PERSON to access the customer name, and a similar join from EMPLOYEE to PERSON needs to occur to access the employee name. The CUSTOMER table could include customer name attributes, and the EMPLOYEE table could include employee name attributes. There is, however, a drawback. What if the person is both an employee and a customer? This would mean storing the name twice and possibly storing it inconsistently in the case of a name change.

The database design could provide for a view of each role to its PERSON or ORGANIZATION table so that the required join from the role table to the person or organization table does not complicate the database query. Of course, there is still a performance issue involved, and the designer will need to weigh this trade-off against the redundant data possibility, which could have significant business impacts.

Even if the customer name attributes were put into the CUSTOMER table and EMPLOYEE name attributes were put into the EMPLOYEE table, at least the common **person id** foreign key would allow the enterprise to identify the presence of the same party that may play more than one role.

Some of the PARTY ROLE subtypes are designed with slight modifications to the logical data model to improve performance and simplify the physical table designs. INTERNAL ORGANIZATION and ORGANIZATION UNIT were PARTY ROLE subtypes in the logical model and provided information on whether the organization was an internal organization of the enterprise as well as whether the organization acted as a department, division, subsidiary, parent company, or other type of role. The physical database design handles the INTERNAL ORGANIZATION information requirements by maintaining an **internal organization ind**(icator) attribute that specifies if the organization is part of the enterprise (a "yes" value) or not (a "no" value).

The physical database design handles the ORGANIZATION UNIT requirement by relating each ORGANIZATION to an ORGANIZATION TYPE **description** of "department," "division," "subsidiary," and "parent organization." The relationships between departments, divisions, subsidiaries, parent organizations, and other organization units is handled through the ORGANIZATION ROLLUP entity, which was a subtype of PARTY RELATIONSHIP.

Each of the PARTY RELATIONSHIP entities is implemented as a separate table, and they inherit the attributes and any relationships of the supertype. (This is the second subtype implementation strategy—each subtype may be established as a separate table with the supertype attributes included in each table.) This is a practical implementation showing the EMPLOYMENT, CUS-

TOMER RELATIONSHIP and ORGANIZATION ROLLUPs as separate tables. Although they are implemented as separate tables, the enterprise model points out that they share common information, such as **from date** and **thru date,** as well as attributes not shown in the figure, such as status, priority, and communication events. The model therefore helps point out common information that should be considered for any PARTY RELATIONSHIP subtype table.

Example Data for Physical Database Design, Option 1

The following tables provide examples of the data that may be stored in the PERSON, ORGANIZATION, CUSTOMER, EMPLOYEE, CUSTOMER RELATIONSHIP, EMPLOYMENT, and ORGANIZATION ROLLUP.

Table 15.3 shows the contents of the PERSON table. In this, the common information regarding the PERSON is defined, such as the PERSON ID, a generated unique identifier, used as the key to the table. Each instance has the appropriate **current first name** and **current last name**, "John Doe," "Mary Smith," "Joe Jones," "John Jones," "Jane Doe," and "K Smith." These columns in the table are required. The **current middle name** and **alias name** are optional and are filled in only when necessary. In the majority of cases, the **current middle name** contains the first initial for rows "1234," "1345," and "7890." Rows "9900" and "7823" have left this blank, as this information was not applicable. For entry "6723," the value in this case is "Frank," as the PERSON's name is "K Frank Smith," and the person uses his middle name instead of his first name. Only two rows contain an **alias** name: Row "9900" has a value of "Jack," and row "6723" has a value of "Bud."

Table 15.4 provides a few examples of organizations with which the enterprise is concerned. The organization ID of each organization is stored as well as the name and federal tax ID; thus, information about each organization may be stored just once and not for each role the organization may play.

Table 15.3   Person Table

PERSON ID	CURRENT FIRST NAME	CURRENT LAST NAME	CURRENT MIDDLE NAME	ALIAS NAME
1234	John	Doe	P	
1345	Mary	Smith	E	
7890	Joe	Jones	W	
9900	John	Jones		Jack
7823	Jane	Doe		
6723	K	Smith	Frank	Bud

Table 15.4 Organization Table

ORGANIZATION ID	ORGANIZATION NAME	FEDERAL TAX ID
8457	Goodcusto, Inc	84-1111-222
8890	ABC Inc.	84-3333-444
8789	Twin Systems	84-6666-777
8821	Consultants Inc.	84-2222-444
8845	DEF Supplies	84-5455-333
9923	XYZ Co	84-7777-444
9924	XYZ Subsidiary	84-7777-456

Table 15.5 provides information about people or organizations that are customers and hence are in the CUSTOMER table. Because either people or organizations may be customers, the customer ID is set up for each customer (perhaps by the sales force) and linked back to either the PERSON **person id** or the ORGANIZATION **organization id,** thus providing for the individual needs of the applications using CUSTOMER as well as the enterprise view allowing anyone to see the complete profile for the ORGANIZATION or PERSON, including information about any role they may play.

The **last contact date** is a field that may apply only to people or organizations that are customers; therefore, it is a field of the CUSTOMER table. If it is deemed that other applications also need this information, then it should be a field in the PERSON or ORGANIZATION tables, or both. Notice that this is a derived field because it could be figured out from the last COMMUNICATION EVENT (V1:2.12); however, the physical designer has decided to include this as a field for performance reasons. Application code would need to synchronize this date with the last COMMUNICATION EVENT date so that this information is consistent.

Table 15.5 Customer Table

PERSON ID	ORGANIZATION ID	CUSTOMER ID	CUSTOMER FIRST AND LAST NAME (FROM THE PERSON TABLE)	ORGANIZATION NAME	LAST CONTACT DATE
1345		87487	Mary Smith		3/13/00
7890		49795	Joe Jones		4/15/00
7823		49859	Jane Doe		5/16/00
6723		98785	K. Smith		2/12/00
	8457	84989		Goodcusto, Inc	4/20/00

Table 15.6   Employee Table

PERSON ID	EMPLOYEE ID	CURRENT FIRST NAME AND CURRENT LAST NAME	SOCIAL SECURITY NUMBER	MOTHER'S MAIDEN NAME
1234	387847	John Doe	234-29-8015	Barr
7890	934789	Joe Jones	178-90-2137	Stevens
7823	466765	Jane Doe	186-09-2918	Kylie

Table 15.6 provides information that may be in the EMPLOYEE table. An employee ID may be provided for a particular application, such as a human resources application. Again, the application can store its own data, such as the **social security number** and **mother's maiden name** if these are deemed fields that are solely for use within human resources. The fact that each **employee id** relates to a **person id** allows the enterprise to link to any other information about that person and thus provide a complete view of each person.

Notice that Joe Jones (person ID 7890) is an employee of XYZ Company, and he was also identified as a customer in Table 15.5. This type of information can be used to provide better service to Joe, and it can also be beneficial for XYZ company to know how many of their employees are actually customers.

Table 15.7 provides information that may be in the CUSTOMER RELATION-SHIP table. This table links PERSONs or ORGANIZATIONs with the ORGANI-ZATION for which they are a customer. This allows each customer to have several CUSTOMER RELATIONSHIPs with each of the organizations of the enterprise. For instance, the table shows that Mary Smith has a CUSTOMER RELATIONSHIP with XYZ Company, which has a priority of 1, which is the highest priority. She also has a CUSTOMER RELATIONSHIP with the XYZ

Table 15.7   Customer Relationship Table

CUSTOMER ID	FIRST AND LAST NAME (FROM THE PERSON TABLE)	ORGANIZATION NAME (FROM THE ORGANIZATION TABLE)	ORGANIZATION ID	ORGANIZATION NAME	PRIORITY
87487	Mary Smith		9923	XYZ Co	1
87487	Mary Smith		9924	XYZ Subsidiary	5
49795	Joe Jones		9923	XYZ Co	5
49859	Jane Doe		9923	XYZ subsidiary	3
98785	K. Smith		9923	XYZ Co	5/15/2000
84989		Goodcusto, Inc	9923	XYZ Co	5/30/2000

Table 15.8 Employment Table

EMPLOYEE ID	PERSON ID	FIRST AND LAST NAME (FROM THE PERSON TABLE)	ORGANIZATION ID	ORGANIZATION NAME	EMPLOYMENT FROM DATE	EMPLOYMENT THRU DATE
387847	1234	John Doe	9923	XYZ Co	3/14/1999	
934789	7890	Joe Jones	9923	XYZ Co	2/13/1999	
466765	7823	Jane Doe	9923	XYZ Co	5/12/1999	1/14/00

Subsidiary organization, where her priority is 5 (perhaps she hasn't done much business with that organization). There may be other information, such as the relationship status, about each relationship that may vary by the relationship even though the customer is the same party.

Table 15.8 records information about which employee is employed by which organization. The table shows three employees of XYZ Company. The table could be expanded to include who was an employee of what external organizations; however, the enterprise would need to establish that it had the will and means to maintain this information. A person may be employed many times by a single organization; however, the information in the EMPLOYEE table or in the PERSON table may not change as a result of being employed numerous times.

Finally, Table 15.9 provides a couple of examples of ORGANIZATION ROLLUPs. The table shows that XYZ Subsidiary (an ORGANIZATION TYPE of "subsidiary") may be rolled up into XYZ Company (an ORGANIZATION TYPE of "parent organization"). The structures of the enterprises' departments, divisions, subsidiaries, or parent companies may be rolled up in order to show the organization structure of the enterprise at any point in time (the **from date** and **thru date** on ORGANIZATION ROLLUP provide for capturing changes). Alternatively, the enterprise can capture the organization structures for external organizations to help find out about these companies. For example, the second

Table 15.9 Organization Roll-up Table

ORGANIZATION ID	ORGANIZATION NAME	ORGANIZATION TYPE	ORGANIZATION ID	ORGANIZATION NAME	ORGANIZATION TYPE
9924	XYZ Subsidiary	Subsidiary	9923	XYZ Co	Parent organization
8789	Twin Systems	Division	8890	Goodcusto	Parent organization

row shows that Twin Systems (an external supplier) is a division of Goodcusto (an external customer).

One advantage of this physical database design implementation is that it provides a very practical strategy for different parts of the enterprise to more easily "own" and steward their own information (because it is in separate tables) while providing the infrastructure to enable integrating the various roles to capture a complete profile on either a PERSON or an ORGANIZATION. For instance, the sales force can more easily steward the CUSTOMER specific information while the human resource department can steward the EMPLOYEE information. Both departments may be able to see a more complete profile on a person that is both an employee and a customer.

A disadvantage of this design is that as new roles and relationships become known, it may require new tables. Also each role and relationship may need redundant attributes and relationships instead of being able to relate tables like STATUS TYPE or PRIORITY TYPE to the PARTY ROLEs and PARTY RELATIONSHIPs. Although there are advantages in separating the PERSON and ORGANIZATION subtypes, some redundant structures and relationships may be required in lieu of being able to relate entities to a PARTY entity.

To summarize, each of the PARTY ROLEs and each of the PARTY RELATIONSHIPs can be implemented as separate tables and linked together with common **person ids** and **organization ids** to provide an integrated view of people and organizations, while also meeting the needs of specific applications.

Party Roles and Relationships Physical Design, Option 2

Figure 15.7 provides a slightly different version of the previous design for implementing the party roles and relationships model. This design is similar in that most PARTY ROLEs and PARTY RELATIONSHIPs are set up as separate tables. This design shows that instead of separating PERSON and ORGANIZATION into separate tables, a PARTY table stores information on both people and organizations. The data examples would be similar to the first design option except that the **party id** would link each of the roles to a common profile of people and organizations, instead of linking them with a **person id** and an **organization id**.

This provides the benefit of sharing the same data structures between people and organizations. For instance, the same PARTY CONTACT MECHANISM structures can be used for PARTYs instead of having to relate them to both PERSONs and ORGANIZATIONs. Agreements and/or orders can be related to PARTYs instead of both PERSONs and ORGANIZATION. Responsibilities can be assigned to PARTYs, which could be either people or organizations. Many other circumstances exist for which this design is beneficial.

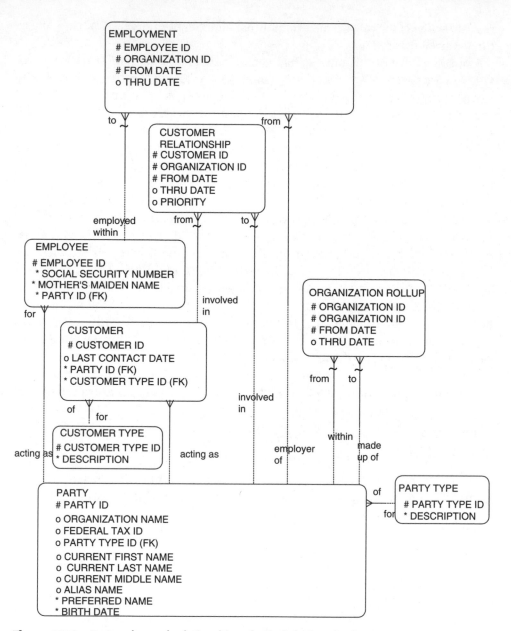

Figure 15.7 Party roles and relationships physical design, Option 2.

The trade-off is that this PARTY table could be quite large if it stores all the people and organizations in the enterprise. Various physical access strategies could be incorporated to handle this issue. For instance, the table could be heavily indexed, or more powerful processors could be used to access this information.

Another option is just to store the party ID as a foreign key in each of the role tables and redundantly store the common party attributes in each of the role tables. At least the enterprise will be able to identify the existence of the same party playing many roles. In this scenario, it is easier to reconcile data inconsistencies because the key to the party is known.

Nevertheless, the designer needs to weigh the clean, normalized, data-consistent design against performance considerations.

Party Roles and Relationships Generic Design, Option 3

The next example will review how to set up a generic overall set of tables to handle all roles and relationships within one model. This will show the flexibility of the Universal Data Models to provide a very flexible database design that will remain stable even when information requirements change.

Figure 15.8 provides a design that incorporates the first strategy for implementing subtypes (the entire supertype with its subtypes may be implemented as a single table with a relationship to a look-up table to indicate the subtype) throughout the design. In this design, it varies from option 1 and is similar to option 2 because it incorporates the PERSON and ORGANIZATION information back into the overall PARTY concept. A major change is that the specific roles played by each party are kept in one table, PARTY ROLE. In this case, the generic table of ROLE TYPE and the various types of roles that parties may play are maintained in the PARTY ROLE TYPE table. Another difference in this design from the previous two designs is that relationships are also placed together into the PARTY RELATIONSHIP table, without separating them into different tables.

This design option could be used for an application such as a staging data warehouse or operational data store. It could also be used in cases where the number of rows is relatively small or where very powerful processors are available to handle this flexible design. The benefit of this design is that it is very flexible and allows any information to be pulled together for overall viewing. Another potential application is where the maintenance and support of the information are centralized and managed by one group. In either case, this design would be appropriate.

As an example, XYZ Company maintains a decision support environment where the information from the various groups is pulled together on a daily basis into an operational data store and then is transferred to the data

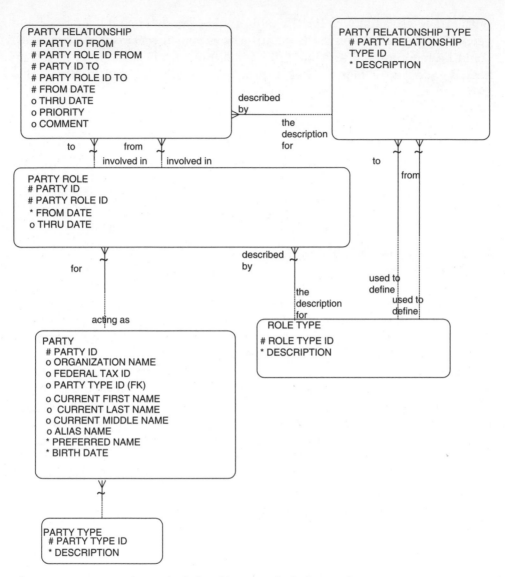

Figure 15.8 Party roles and relationships generic design, Option 3.

warehouse at the end of the month. This design is needed to capture all of the data given in the previous examples.

As seen before, all the information that XYZ Company has gathered either in the PERSON or ORGANIZATION tables has been moved into the PARTY table. The associated PARTY TYPE has been assigned based on the source of the original data. Included is the **current first name**, **current last name**, **current middle name**, taken from the PERSON table and the **organization name** from the ORGANIZATION table. Note that the first name and last name for each person have been concatenated to form PARTY NAME.

Table 15.10   Party Table

PARTY ID	PARTY NAME	PARTY TYPE
1234	John Doe	Person
1345	Mary Smith	Person
1567	John Smith	Person
1876	Jerry Wright	Person
7890	Joe Jones	Person
9900	John Jones	Person
7823	Jane Doe	Person
6723	Bud Smith	Person
1567	Ken Harris	Person
1990	Uma Key	Person
5134	Bill Jake	Person
6712	Betty King	Person
7876	Jeff Dane	Person
7890	Linda Kinney	Person
7721	Bob Mason	Person
7723	Larry Ink	Person
8457	Goodcusto, Inc	Organization
8890	ABC Inc.	Organization
8789	Twin Systems	Organization
8821	Consultants Inc.	Organization
8845	DEF Supplies	Organization
9923	XYZ Company	Organization
9924	XYZ Subsidiary	Organization
9925	Accounting department (of XYZ)	Organization

By adding the ROLE TYPE to the PARTY ROLE, as shown in Table 15.12, the information from the PARTY table is now linked to the role each party participates in with XYZ Company. Notice that there is the capability of tracking the many roles for each person; for example, "John Doe" is both a "Prospect" and an "Employee." "Joe Jones" is a "Customer" and an "Employee," as is "Jane Doe." In this case, the ROLE TYPE clarifies the different potential roles that each PARTY has. In addition, the ORGANIZATION type of PARTY plays the role of a SUPPLIER, as it provides the required people or supplies to XYZ Company.

Table 15.11 Party Role with Role Type

PARTY ID	PARTY NAME (EITHER PERSON CURRENT FIRST NAME AND CURRENT LAST NAME OR ORGANIZATION NAME)	PARTY TYPE	PARTY ROLE TYPE
1234	John Doe	Person	Prospect
1234	John Doe	Person	Employee
1345	Mary Smith	Person	Customer
1567	John Smith	Person	Employee
1876	Jerry Wright	Person	Employee
7890	Joe Jones	Person	Customer
7890	Joe Jones	Person	Employee
9900	John Jones	Person	Prospect
7823	Jane Doe	Person	Customer
7823	Jane Doe	Person	Employee
6723	Bud Smith	Person	Customer
1567	Ken Harris	Person	Contractor
1990	Uma Key	Person	Contractor
5134	Bill Jake	Person	Contractor
6712	Betty King	Person	Contractor
7876	Jeff Dane	Person	Contact
7890	Linda Kinney	Person	Contact
7721	Bob Mason	Person	Contact
7723	Larry Ink	Person	Contact
8457	Goodcusto, Inc	Organization	Customer
8890	ABC Inc.	Organization	Supplier
8789	Twin Systems	Organization	Supplier
8821	Consultants Inc.	Organization	Supplier
8845	DEF Supplies	Organization	Supplier
9923	XYZ Company	Organization	Internal organization, parent company
9924	XYZ, Subsidiary	Organization	Internal organization, subsidiary
9924	Accounting department (of XYZ)	Organization	Internal organization, department

Table 15.12 Party Relationship Table

FROM PARTY ID	FROM PARTY NAME	FROM PARTY ROLE	TO PARTY ID	TO PARTY NAME	TO PARTY ROLE	PARTY RELATIONSHIP
1345	Mary Smith	Customer	9923	XYZ Co	Internal organization	Customer relationship
9900	John Jones	Customer	9923	XYZ Co	Internal organization	Customer relationship
7823	Jane Doe	Customer	9923	XYZ Co	Internal organization	Customer relationship
8457	Goodcusto, Inc	Organization	9923	XYZ Co	Internal organization	Customer relationship
1567	Ken Harris	Contractor	9923	XYZ Co	Internal organization	Contractor relationship
1990	Uma Key	Contractor	9923	XYZ Co	Internal organization	Contractor relationship
5134	Bill Jake	Contractor	9923	XYZ Co	Internal organization	Contractor relationship
6712	Betty King	Contractor	9923	XYZ Co	Internal organization	Contractor relationship
1567	John Smith	Employee	9923	XYZ Co	Internal organization	Employee relationship
1876	Jerry Wright	Employee	9923	XYZ Co	Internal organization	Employee relationship
1567	Ken Harris	Employee	8789	Twin Systems	Employer	Employee relationship
1990	Uma Key	Employee	8789	Twin Systems	Employer	Employee relationship
5134	Bill Jake	Employee	8821	Consultants Inc.	Employer	Employee relationship
6712	Betty King	Employee	8821	Consultants Inc.	Employer	Employee relationship
7876	Jeff Dane	Contact	8890	ABC Inc.	Organization	Contact relationship
7890	Linda Kinney	Contact	8890	ABC Inc.	Organization	Contact relationship
7721	Bob Mason	Contact	8845	DEF Supplies	Organization	Contact relationship
7723	Larry Ink	Contact	8845	DEF Supplies	Organization	Contact relationship
8890	ABC Inc.	Supplier	9923	XYZ Co	Internal organization	Supplier relationship
8789	Twin Systems	Supplier	9923	XYZ Co	Internal organization	Supplier relationship
8821	Consultants Inc.	Supplier	9923	XYZ Co	Internal organization	Supplier relationship
8845	DEF Supplies	Supplier	9923	XYZ Co	Internal organization	Supplier relationship

Figure 15.12 provides an example of various relationships that could be stored in the PARTY RELATIONSHIP table.

Table 15.12 illustrates the flexibility offered with this physical implementation of the party roles and relationships model. As new roles or relationships are discovered, perhaps through new business rules, this database design can support these new roles without any database changes, unlike the previous two implementations, which would require additional tables. Again, the designer needs to evaluate performance considerations versus flexibility and maintainability.

Using the Data Warehouse Models

The data warehouse models presented in this book serve to illustrate examples of how to move from the corporate or logical data models to an enterprise-wide data warehouse data model, then to departmental data models. The most important point of these chapters is to show the transformation process so that enterprises can understand the importance of setting up an appropriate data warehouse architecture.

Chapter 10 presented the transformation steps for converting a corporate data model into a data warehouse data model. Chapter 11 then provided a sample data warehouse data model that was developed using these transformation concepts. These transformation steps should be used selectively; it is not necessary to use all of these steps when developing the data warehouse data model. They serve merely as guidelines.

For instance, denormalizations such as including derived data, merging tables, and creating arrays of data may not always be required, or they may be postponed until later. They should be included only when it is obvious that there are enterprise-wide requirements for the information provided by these transformations.

There has been much debate in the data warehouse community regarding the architecture involved in moving data to a data warehouse environment. Specifically, there seems to be many schools of thought. Some say that it is necessary to first extract data into an enterprise-wide data warehouse, then move it to departmental data warehouses. Others contend that they can simply move the information directly from the operational systems to departmental data warehouses. There are debates about the structure of an enterprise-wide data warehouse and whether it should be a series of interconnected star schemas, or a denormalized version of the enterprise data model.

Should there be an enterprise-wide data warehouse or just extractions into departmental data warehouses (i.e., data marts)? Certainly, it is initially easier to move the data directly into the departmental data warehouses. Only one transformation is needed instead of moving the data to an intermediate stage first, then to the departmental data warehouse. Business managers want information quickly and easily. There is an urgent need to provide the user community with the information it needs. This is exactly why the data warehouse concept has caught on. Why not take the direct route and provide the information directly to the departmental warehouse?

There is a major drawback in moving the information directly into the departmental warehouse. The drawback is *not* on the first implementation of the departmental data warehouse but on subsequent departmental implementations. If each department moves the data from the operational systems directly into its own departmental data warehouse, there is a great exposure in creating more inconsistent data sources than already exist in the operational systems.

Most enterprises that are creating data warehouses are faced with complex transformation routines that need to cleanse and consolidate data from several operational systems. The largest challenge in creating data warehouses is in deciphering the source of the most reliable data of the enterprise. This is complicated by the fact that the same data is often stored redundantly and inconsistently in most organizations (see Chapter 1 for a discussion on separate and redundant data in enterprises). Therefore, in the transformation process, the data inconsistencies need to be dealt with.

To illustrate the problems of inconsistent data, a project engagement comes to mind where data was being transformed into a new database. When the database design was reviewed, it was noticed that there were two fields for **blood type** in the person table. The obvious question created some concern: How can there be two blood types for a single person—a person, of course, has only one blood type! When the problem was tracked down, there actually *were* two blood types for each person; one from system A and the other from system B! It was extremely difficult to find out which system held the more accurate information for each person, so the enterprise decided to keep both values in the system. This is only one example showing the challenge of trying to consolidate information from several sources.

If each department uses its own transformation routines, think of the potential for inconsistent management information. Many of the departments may use the same information regarding people, organizations, products, sales, purchases, projects, and so forth in their decision support environment. The transformation routines are bound to be different for each department, if they are done separately, leading to inconsistent and confusing results. For instance, it is conceivable that a marketing organization may produce executive decision information that may be inconsistent with the data produced by the order processing department if it used different sources or transformations to gather its sales information. This can have devastating effects on an enterprise. The consequences of having inconsistent information between several systems, is that the enterprise may either start to question the credibility of the information, or worse, they act on incorrect information.

The entire enterprise can capitalize on sharing the results behind this difficult process of transforming data. The only way this can happen is by having *one central* transformation process for decision support. By building an enterprise-wide data warehouse data model, common transformation routines can be built that serve the needs of the entire enterprise. In addition, the enterprise can identify data inconsistencies that are discovered in the transformation process and make *a consistent* decision on how these discrepancies will be handled. This knowledge can help the enterprise move toward more integrated operational systems by pinpointing existing problems. Finally, the enterprise can save time and money in the long run by doing the transformation process once for the enterprise instead of transforming similar types of data for each departmental data warehouse.

The enterprise needs to be willing to make an investment in its data and information architecture in order to be successful with data warehousing in the long run. An analogy is that it often seems easier to jump in and develop a program without taking the time to formally analyze the requirements or design. Experience has shown, though, that the lack of up-front investment will usually lead to increased programming and maintenance costs over the life of the program.

If an enterprise wants to get a quick head start into the data warehouse arena, another strategy would be to use template data warehouse designs, either from this book or from another source, to create a prototype departmental data warehouse, then load it with a limited amount of data. This allows the enterprise to evaluate the benefits of a decision support environment and make strategic decisions regarding its data warehouse environment. After an initial prototype is built, the enterprise may want to consider building an enterprise-wide data warehouse to support future departmental information needs.

Summary

This chapter discussed how to implement the Universal Data Models to support various types of systems development efforts: models to provide an integrated view of the enterprise, models required to design a specific application, and physical database design models used to generate a database. The chapter also looked at strategies for implementing a data warehouse. The design points to emphasize are the following:

- Establish an enterprise data model in order to facilitate integration of information across the enterprise and also to gain understanding of the information requirements of the enterprise.

- Maintain contact with the business experts to adequately capture the business needs.

- Review the models with the business to ensure that the business understanding is adequately captured.

- Using the enterprise data model as the basis for building a logical data model for a specific application. This can facilitate better integration of that application into the overall system of the enterprise, thus enabling more effective sharing and communication of information. It can also provide a jump-start to the modeling effort for that application by allowing reuse of data structures that have already been modeled.

- Use process models as another source of input into developing a logical data model. Automate the business processes based on a clear understanding of them.

- Create the required physical database design models based upon the logical data models and with performance considerations in mind for the intended database management system (DBMS).

- Convert subtypes from the logical data models to a physical database design, choosing from among the four approaches shown in this chapter.

- Use the enterprise and logical data models as the basis for building an integrated decision support (data warehouse) environment.

As seen in the examples, there are a number of ways to implement each Universal Data Model. By following clearly defined design principles, the Universal Data Models can be used and adapted to build the physical design. After applying the needed database-specific requirements, the design can be used to generate a physical database schema that is ready for loading and testing. The Universal Data Models can then also serve as the basis for a data warehouse design and implementation.

The intent of this last chapter has been to illustrate how Universal Data Models can be used to build quality, integrated database implementations.

We hope that this is just the beginning of more widespread efforts toward building Universal Data Models and that the information systems industry will continue to develop more reusable models. The results of these efforts will allow developers to shorten systems development cycles and produce higher-quality, better integrated information systems at reduced cost for the user community at large.

For More Information

We encourage and would appreciate any suggestions, questions, or comments to help the further development of Universal Data Models, data integration, or holistic systems.

To find out more information, ask questions, contribute, or if we can be of further assistance to you, please feel free to e-mail us at info@univdata. com, visit the book's companion Web site at silverston.wiley.com, or visit www. universaldatamodels.com.

Logical Data Model Entities and Attributes

This appendix lists the entities and attributes from the models found in Chapters 2 through 9. This listing includes the entity names, attribute names, primary key indicators, foreign key indicators, and the domain for each attribute.

The domain indicates a standard set of characteristics that can be applied to attributes, including its datatype and length. Table A.1 defines the nature of each domain. When applying the domains to the attributes listed in these appendices, refer to Table A.1 for recommendations for what datatype and length to use when implementing these models. Of course, the datatype and length of each attribute should be adjusted as appropriate to meet the specific needs of the enterprise.

The domain definitions as they are applied to the attributes in the appendices are used for the SQL code that is contained on the full-blown CD-ROM (sold separately).

Table A.1 Appendices Domain Definitions

DOMAIN NAME	DATATYPE	SUGGESTED LENGTH	USED FOR
Blob	Blob		Images, graphics, binary information, and any attributes storing electronic object information
Comment	Varchar (variable length character string)	255	Used to store comment attributes that provide for free-form text describing the entity
Currency Amount	Number or money with two decimal places for the cents	9 digits with 2 decimals	Any currency amounts that may store monetary figures
Datetime	Date		Used to maintain any date or datetime attribute
Description	Varchar	255	Used for attributes that maintain descriptive information about the entity
Floating point	Float	9 with 4 more decimal points	Used to record information about percentages, calculated fields, variances, statistical attributes, or any attribute needing multiple decimal points
ID	Number	10	A sequential number to establish uniqueness of the entity, to be used for foreign key relationships
Indicator	Character	1	Any flag, indicator, or single character attribute used to indicate the value of an attribute. For example: Yes/No, Male/Female
Long Varchar	Varchar	255	Used to record attributes that generally need a longer string value
Name	Varchar	40	Used to record name information
Numeric	Number		Numbered values without decimal points
Short Varchar	Varchar	40	Used for attributes that generally need a longer string value
Very Long	Varchar	2000	Used for attributes that need a very long string value
Very Short	Varchar	10	Used for attributes that need a very short string value

Logical Data Model Entities and Attributes Listing

ENTITY NAME	ATTRIBUTE NAME	PK?	FK?	DOMAIN
ACCOUNTING PERIOD	ACCOUNTING PERIOD ID	Yes	No	ID
	ROLE TYPE ID	No	Yes	ID
	PERIOD TYPE ID	No	Yes	ID
	ACCTG PERIOD NUM	No	No	Numeric
	FROM DATE	No	No	Datetime
	THRU DATE	No	No	Datetime
	PARTY ID	No	Yes	ID
	INTERNAL ORGANIZATION ID	No	Yes	ID
ACCOUNTING TRANSACTION	TRANSACTION ID	Yes	No	ID
	ACCTG TRANSACTION TYPE ID	No	Yes	ID
	DESCRIPTION	No	No	Description
	TRANSACTION DATE	No	No	Datetime
	ENTRY DATE	No	No	Datetime
ACCOUNTING TRANSACTION TYPE	ACCTG TRANSACTION TYPE ID	Yes	No	ID
	DESCRIPTION	No	No	Description
ACTIVITY	WORK EFFORT ID	Yes	Yes	ID
ACTIVITY REQUEST	COMMUNICATION EVENT PRP TYP ID	Yes	Yes	ID
	COMMUNICATION EVENT ID	Yes	Yes	ID
ADDENDUM	ADDENDUM ID	Yes	No	ID
	AGREEMENT ID	No	Yes	ID
	AGREEMENT ITEM SEQ ID	No	Yes	ID
	ADDENDUM CREATION DATE	No	No	Datetime
	ADDENDUM EFFECTIVE DATE	No	No	Datetime
	ADDENDUM TEXT	No	No	Long varchar
AGENT	PARTY ID	Yes	Yes	ID
	ROLE TYPE ID	Yes	Yes	ID
AGREEMENT	AGREEMENT ID	Yes	No	ID
	PRODUCT ID	No	Yes	ID

ENTITY NAME	ATTRIBUTE NAME	PK?	FK?	DOMAIN
	PARTY ID FROM	No	Yes	ID
	PARTY ID TO	No	Yes	ID
	ROLE TYPE ID TO	No	Yes	ID
	ROLE TYPE ID FROM	No	Yes	ID
	AGREEMENT TYPE ID	No	Yes	ID
	AGREEMENT DATE	No	No	Datetime
	FROM DATE	No	Yes	Datetime
	THRU DATE	No	No	Datetime
	DESCRIPTION	No	No	Description
	TEXT	No	No	Long varchar
AGREEMENT EXHIBIT	AGREEMENT ITEM SEQ ID	Yes	Yes	ID
	AGREEMENT ID	Yes	Yes	ID
AGREEMENT GEOGRAPHICAL APPLICABILITY	GEO ID	Yes	Yes	ID
	AGREEMENT ID	Yes	Yes	ID
	AGREEMENT ITEM SEQ ID	Yes	Yes	ID
AGREEMENT ITEM	AGREEMENT ID	Yes	Yes	ID
	AGREEMENT ITEM SEQ ID	Yes	No	ID
	AGREEMENT TEXT	No	No	Long varchar
	AGREEMENT IMAGE	No	No	Blob
AGREEMENT ORGANIZATION APPLICABILITY	PARTY ID	Yes	Yes	ID
	AGREEMENT ID	Yes	Yes	ID
	AGREEMENT ITEM SEQ ID	Yes	Yes	ID
AGREEMENT PRICING PROGRAM	AGREEMENT ITEM SEQ ID	Yes	Yes	ID
	AGREEMENT ID	Yes	Yes	ID
AGREEMENT PRODUCT APPLICABILITY	PRODUCT ID	Yes	Yes	ID
	AGREEMENT ID	Yes	Yes	ID
	AGREEMENT ITEM SEQ ID	Yes	Yes	ID
AGREEMENT ROLE	PARTY ID	Yes	Yes	ID

ENTITY NAME	ATTRIBUTE NAME	PK?	FK?	DOMAIN
	AGREEMENT ID	Yes	Yes	ID
	ROLE TYPE ID	Yes	Yes	ID
AGREEMENT ROLE TYPE	ROLE TYPE ID	Yes	Yes	ID
AGREEMENT SECTION	AGREEMENT ITEM SEQ ID	Yes	Yes	ID
	AGREEMENT ID	Yes	Yes	ID
AGREEMENT TERM	AGREEMENT TERM ID	Yes	No	ID
	TERM TYPE ID	No	Yes	ID
	AGREEMENT ID	No	Yes	ID
	AGREEMENT ITEM SEQ ID	No	Yes	ID
	FROM DATE	No	No	Datetime
	THRU DATE	No	No	Datetime
	TERM VALUE	No	No	Numeric
AGREEMENT TYPE	AGREEMENT TYPE ID	Yes	No	ID
	DESCRIPTION	No	No	Description
AMORTIZATION	TRANSACTION ID	Yes	Yes	ID
ASSOCIATION	PARTY ID	Yes	Yes	ID
	ROLE TYPE ID	Yes	Yes	ID
BANK ACCOUNT	FINANCIAL ACCOUNT ID	Yes	Yes	ID
BASE PRICE	PRICE COMPONENT ID	Yes	Yes	ID
BENEFIT TYPE	BENEFIT TYPE ID	Yes	No	ID
	NAME	No	No	Name
	DESCRIPTION	No	No	Description
	EMPLOYER PAID PERCENTAGE	No	No	Floating point
BILL OF LADING	DOCUMENT ID	Yes	Yes	ID
BILL TO CUSTOMER	CUSTOMER ID	Yes	Yes	ID
	PARTY ID	Yes	Yes	ID
	ROLE TYPE ID	Yes	Yes	ID
BILLING ACCOUNT	BILLING ACCOUNT ID	Yes	No	ID
	CONTACT MECHANISM ID	No	Yes	ID
	FROM DATE	No	No	Datetime
	THRU DATE	No	No	Datetime
	DESCRIPTION	No	No	Description

ENTITY NAME	ATTRIBUTE NAME	PK?	FK?	DOMAIN
BILLING ACCOUNT ROLE	PARTY ID	Yes	Yes	ID
	BILLING ACCOUNT ID	Yes	Yes	ID
	ROLE TYPE ID	Yes	Yes	ID
	FROM DATE	No	No	Datetime
	THRU DATE	No	No	Datetime
BILLING ACCOUNT ROLE TYPE	ROLE TYPE ID	Yes	Yes	ID
BILLING FEATURE	PRODUCT FEATURE ID	Yes	Yes	ID
BRAND	PRODUCT FEATURE ID	Yes	Yes	ID
BUDGET	BUDGET TYPE ID	Yes	Yes	ID
	BUDGET ID	Yes	No	ID
	STANDARD TIME PERIOD ID	No	Yes	ID
	COMMENT	No	No	Comment
BUDGET ITEM	BUDGET ID	Yes	Yes	ID
	BUDGET TYPE ID	No	Yes	ID
	BUDGET ITEM SEQ ID	Yes	No	ID
	BUDGET ITEM TYPE ID	No	Yes	ID
	AMOUNT	No	No	Currency amount
	PURPOSE	No	No	Long varchar
	JUSTIFICATION	No	No	Long varchar
BUDGET ITEM TYPE	BUDGET ITEM TYPE ID	Yes	No	ID
	DESCRIPTION	No	No	Description
BUDGET REVIEW	BUDGET TYPE ID	Yes	Yes	ID
	BUDGET REVIEW ID	Yes	No	ID
	BUDGET ID	Yes	Yes	ID
	PARTY ID	Yes	Yes	ID
	BUDGET REVIEW RESULT TYPE ID	Yes	Yes	ID
	REVIEW DATE	No	No	Datetime
BUDGET REVIEW RESULTS TYPE	BUDGET REVIEW RESULT TYPE ID	Yes	No	ID
	DESCRIPTION	No	No	Description
	COMMENT	No	No	Comment

ENTITY NAME	ATTRIBUTE NAME	PK?	FK?	DOMAIN
BUDGET REVISION	REVISION SEQ ID	Yes	No	ID
	BUDGET TYPE ID	Yes	Yes	ID
	BUDGET ID	Yes	Yes	ID
	DATE REVISED	No	No	Datetime
BUDGET REVISION IMPACT	BUDGET ID	Yes	Yes	ID
	BUDGET ITEM SEQ ID	Yes	Yes	ID
	REVISION SEQ ID	Yes	Yes	ID
	REVISED AMOUNT	No	No	Currency amount
	ADD DELETE FLAG	No	No	Indicator
	REVISION REASON	No	No	Long varchar
BUDGET ROLE	BUDGET TYPE ID	Yes	Yes	ID
	BUDGET ID	Yes	Yes	ID
	PARTY ID	Yes	Yes	ID
	ROLE TYPE ID	Yes	Yes	ID
BUDGET ROLE TYPE	ROLE TYPE ID	Yes	Yes	ID
BUDGET SCENARIO	BUDGET SCENARIO ID	Yes	No	ID
	DESCRIPTION	No	No	Description
BUDGET SCENARIO APPLICATION	BUDGET SCENARIO APPLIC ID	Yes	No	ID
	BUDGET SCENARIO ID	Yes	Yes	ID
	BUDGET ID	No	Yes	ID
	BUDGET ITEM SEQ ID	No	Yes	ID
	AMOUNT CHANGE	No	No	Currency amount
	PERCENTAGE CHANGE	No	No	Floating point
BUDGET SCENARIO RULE	BUDGET SCENARIO ID	Yes	Yes	ID
	BUDGET ITEM TYPE ID	Yes	Yes	ID
	AMOUNT CHANGE	No	No	Currency amount
	PERCENTAGE CHANGE	No	No	Floating point
BUDGET STATUS	BUDGET ID	Yes	Yes	ID
	STATUS TYPE ID	Yes	Yes	ID

ENTITY NAME	ATTRIBUTE NAME	PK?	FK?	DOMAIN
	STATUS DATE	No	No	Datetime
	COMMENT	No	No	Comment
BUDGET STATUS TYPE	STATUS TYPE ID	Yes	Yes	ID
BUDGET TYPE	BUDGET TYPE ID	Yes	No	ID
	DESCRIPTION	No	No	Description
BUILDING	FACILITY ID	Yes	Yes	ID
CAPITAL BUDGET	BUDGET ID	Yes	Yes	ID
	BUDGET TYPE ID	Yes	Yes	ID
CAPITALIZATION	TRANSACTION ID	Yes	Yes	ID
CARRIER	PARTY ID	Yes	Yes	ID
	ROLE TYPE ID	Yes	Yes	ID
CARRIER SHIPMENT METHOD	SHIPMENT METHOD TYPE ID	Yes	Yes	ID
	PARTY ID	Yes	Yes	ID
	ROLE TYPE ID	Yes	Yes	ID
CASE	CASE ID	Yes	No	ID
	STATUS TYPE ID	No	Yes	ID
	DESCRIPTION	No	No	Description
	START DATETIME	No	No	Datetime
CASE ROLE	CASE ID	Yes	Yes	ID
	PARTY ID	Yes	Yes	ID
	ROLE TYPE ID	Yes	Yes	ID
CASE ROLE TYPE	ROLE TYPE ID	Yes	Yes	ID
CASE STATUS TYPE	STATUS TYPE ID	Yes	Yes	ID
CERTIFICATION	QUAL TYPE ID	Yes	Yes	ID
	PARTY ID	Yes	Yes	ID
CITY	GEO ID	Yes	Yes	ID
COLOR	PRODUCT FEATURE ID	Yes	Yes	ID
COMMUNICATION EVENT	COMMUNICATION EVENT ID	Yes	No	ID
	STATUS TYPE ID	No	Yes	ID

ENTITY NAME	ATTRIBUTE NAME	PK?	FK?	DOMAIN
	CASE ID	No	Yes	ID
	CONTACT MECHANISM TYPE ID	No	Yes	ID
	ROLE TYPE ID FROM	No	Yes	ID
	ROLE TYPE ID TO	No	Yes	ID
	PARTY ID TO	No	Yes	ID
	PARTY ID FROM	No	Yes	ID
	FROM DATE	No	Yes	Datetime
	DATETIME STARTED	No	No	Datetime
	NOTE	No	No	Comment
	DATETIME ENDED	No	No	Datetime
COMMUNICATION EVENT PURPOSE	COMMUNICATION EVENT PRP TYP ID	Yes	Yes	ID
	COMMUNICATION EVENT ID	Yes	Yes	ID
	DESCRIPTION	No	No	Description
COMMUNICATION EVENT PURPOSE TYPE	COMMUNICATION EVENT PRP TYP ID	Yes	No	ID
	DESCRIPTION	No	No	Description
COMMUNICATION EVENT ROLE	COMMUNICATION EVENT ID	Yes	Yes	ID
	PARTY ID	Yes	Yes	ID
	ROLE TYPE ID	Yes	Yes	ID
COMMUNICATION EVENT ROLE TYPE	ROLE TYPE ID	Yes	Yes	ID
COMMUNICATION EVENT STATUS TYPE	STATUS TYPE ID	Yes	Yes	ID
COMMUNICATION EVENT WORK EFFORT	WORK EFFORT ID	Yes	Yes	ID
	COMMUNICATION EVENT ID	Yes	Yes	ID
	DESCRIPTION	No	No	Description
COMPETITOR	PARTY ID	Yes	Yes	ID
	ROLE TYPE ID	Yes	Yes	ID
CONFERENCE	COMMUNICATION EVENT PRP TYP ID	Yes	Yes	ID

ENTITY NAME	ATTRIBUTE NAME	PK?	FK?	DOMAIN
	COMMUNICATION EVENT ID	Yes	Yes	ID
CONTACT	PARTY ID	Yes	Yes	ID
	ROLE TYPE ID	Yes	Yes	ID
CONTACT MECHANISM	CONTACT MECHANISM ID	Yes	No	ID
	CONTACT MECHANISM TYPE ID	No	Yes	ID
CONTACT MECHANISM LINK	CONTACT MECHANISM ID TO	Yes	Yes	ID
	CONTACT MECHANISM ID FROM	Yes	Yes	ID
CONTACT MECHANISM PURPOSE TYPE	CONTACT MECHANISM PURPOSE TYPE ID	Yes	No	ID
	DESCRIPTION	No	No	Description
CONTACT MECHANISM TYPE	CONTACT MECHANISM TYPE ID	Yes	No	ID
	DESCRIPTION	No	No	Description
CONTAINER	CONTAINER ID	Yes	No	ID
	FACILITY ID	No	Yes	ID
	CONTAINER TYPE ID	No	Yes	ID
CONTAINER TYPE	CONTAINER TYPE ID	Yes	No	ID
	DESCRIPTION	No	No	Description
CONTRACTOR	PARTY ID	Yes	Yes	ID
	ROLE TYPE ID	Yes	Yes	ID
CORPORATION	PARTY ID	Yes	Yes	ID
COST COMPONENT TYPE	COST COMPONENT TYPE ID	Yes	No	ID
	DESCRIPTION	No	No	Description
COUNTRY	GEO ID	Yes	Yes	ID
COUNTY	GEO ID	Yes	Yes	ID
COUNTY CITY	GEO ID	Yes	Yes	ID
CREDIT LINE	TRANSACTION ID	Yes	Yes	ID
CREDIT MEMO	TRANSACTION ID	Yes	Yes	ID
CURRENCY MEASURE	UOM ID	Yes	Yes	ID
CUSTOMER	CUSTOMER ID	Yes	No	ID
	PARTY ID	Yes	Yes	ID

ENTITY NAME	ATTRIBUTE NAME	PK?	FK?	DOMAIN
	ROLE TYPE ID	Yes	Yes	ID
CUSTOMER RELATIONSHIP	PARTY ID FROM	Yes	Yes	ID
	PARTY ID TO	Yes	Yes	ID
	FROM DATE	Yes	Yes	Datetime
	ROLE TYPE ID FROM	Yes	Yes	ID
	ROLE TYPE ID TO	Yes	Yes	ID
CUSTOMER REQUIREMENT	REQUIREMENT ID	Yes	Yes	ID
CUSTOMER RETURN	SHIPMENT ID	Yes	Yes	ID
CUSTOMER SERVICE CALL	COMMUNICATION EVENT PRP TYP ID	Yes	Yes	ID
	COMMUNICATION EVENT ID	Yes	Yes	ID
CUSTOMER SHIPMENT	SHIPMENT ID	Yes	Yes	ID
DEDUCTION	DEDUCTION ID	Yes	No	ID
	PAYMENT ID	No	Yes	ID
	DEDUCTION TYPE ID	No	Yes	ID
	AMOUNT	No	No	Currency amount
DEDUCTION TYPE	DEDUCTION TYPE ID	Yes	No	ID
	DESCRIPTION	No	No	Description
DEGREE	QUAL TYPE ID	Yes	Yes	ID
	PARTY ID	Yes	Yes	ID
DELIVERABLE	DELIVERABLE ID	Yes	No	ID
	DELIVERABLE TYPE ID	No	Yes	ID
	NAME	No	No	Name
	DESCRIPTION	No	No	Description
DELIVERABLE TYPE	DELIVERABLE TYPE ID	Yes	No	ID
	DESCRIPTION	No	No	Description
DEPARTMENT	PARTY ID	Yes	Yes	ID
	ROLE TYPE ID	Yes	Yes	ID
DEPOSIT	FINANCIAL ACCOUNT TRANS ID	Yes	Yes	ID
DEPRECIATION	TRANSACTION ID	Yes	Yes	ID
	ASSET ID	No	Yes	ID

ENTITY NAME	ATTRIBUTE NAME	PK?	FK?	DOMAIN
	FIXED ASSET ID	No	Yes	ID
DEPRECIATION METHOD	DEPRECIATION METHOD ID	Yes	No	ID
	DESCRIPTION	No	No	Description
	FORMULA	No	No	Long varchar
DESIRED FEATURE	DESIRED FEATURE ID	Yes	No	ID
	REQUIREMENT ID	Yes	Yes	ID
	PRODUCT FEATURE ID	No	Yes	ID
	OPTIONAL IND	No	No	Indicator
DIMENSION	PRODUCT FEATURE ID	Yes	Yes	ID
	UOM ID	No	Yes	ID
	NUMBER SPECIFIED	No	No	Numeric
DISBURSEMENT	PAYMENT ID	Yes	Yes	ID
DISBURSEMENT ACCTG TRANS	TRANSACTION ID	Yes	Yes	ID
DISCOUNT ADJUSTMENT	ORDER ADJUST SEQ ID	Yes	Yes	ID
DISCOUNT COMPONENT	PRICE COMPONENT ID	Yes	Yes	ID
DISTRIBUTION CHANNEL	PARTY ID	Yes	Yes	ID
	ROLE TYPE ID	Yes	Yes	ID
DISTRIBUTION CHANNEL RELATIONSHIP	PARTY ID TO	Yes	Yes	ID
	PARTY ID FROM	Yes	Yes	ID
	FROM DATE	Yes	Yes	Datetime
	ROLE TYPE ID FROM	Yes	Yes	ID
	ROLE TYPE ID TO	Yes	Yes	ID
DISTRUBUTOR	PARTY ID	Yes	Yes	ID
	ROLE TYPE ID	Yes	Yes	ID
DIVISION	PARTY ID	Yes	Yes	ID
	ROLE TYPE ID	Yes	Yes	ID
DOCUMENT	DOCUMENT ID	Yes	No	ID
	DOCUMENT TYPE ID	No	Yes	ID
	DATE CREATED	No	No	Datetime
	COMMENT	No	No	Comment

ENTITY NAME	ATTRIBUTE NAME	PK?	FK?	DOMAIN
	DOCUMENT LOCATION	No	No	Long varchar
	DOCUMENT TEXT	No	No	Long varchar
	IMAGE	No	No	Blob
DOCUMENT TYPE	DOCUMENT TYPE ID	Yes	No	ID
	DESCRIPTION	No	No	Description
DROP SHIPMENT	SHIPMENT ID	Yes	Yes	ID
EEOC CLASSIFICATION	FROM DATE	Yes	Yes	Datetime
	PARTY TYPE ID	Yes	Yes	ID
	PARTY ID	Yes	Yes	ID
ELECTRONIC ADDRESS	CONTACT MECHANISM ID	Yes	Yes	ID
	ELECTRONIC ADDRESS STRING	No	No	Long varchar
EMAIL COMMUNICATION	COMMUNICATION EVENT ID	Yes	Yes	ID
EMPLOYEE	PARTY ID	Yes	Yes	ID
	ROLE TYPE ID	Yes	Yes	ID
EMPLOYEE PERFORMANCE REVIEW	EMPLOYEE PARTY ID	Yes	Yes	ID
	PERF REVIEW ID	Yes	No	ID
	EMPLOYEE ROLE TYPE ID	Yes	Yes	ID
	MANAGER PARTY ID	No	Yes	ID
	MNAGER ROLED TYPE ID	No	Yes	ID
	PAYMENT ID	No	Yes	ID
	POSITION ID	No	Yes	ID
	PAY HISTORY PARTY ID FROM	No	Yes	ID
	PAY HISTORY FROM DATE	No	Yes	Datetime
	PAY HISTORY ROLE TYPE ID TO	No	Yes	ID
	PAY HISTORY ROLE TYPE ID FROM	No	Yes	ID
	FROM DATE	No	No	Datetime
	THRU DATE	No	No	Datetime
	COMMENTS	No	No	Comment
EMPLOYMENT	PARTY ID FROM	Yes	Yes	ID
	PARTY ID TO	Yes	Yes	ID
	FROM DATE	Yes	Yes	Datetime

ENTITY NAME	ATTRIBUTE NAME	PK?	FK?	DOMAIN
	ROLE TYPE ID TO	Yes	Yes	ID
	ROLE TYPE ID FROM	Yes	Yes	ID
	TERMINATION REASON ID	No	Yes	ID
	TERMINATION TYPE ID	No	Yes	ID
EMPLOYMENT AGREEMENT	AGREEMENT ID	Yes	Yes	ID
EMPLOYMENT APPLICATION	APPLICATION ID	Yes	No	ID
	POSITION ID	No	Yes	ID
	STATUS TYPE ID	No	Yes	ID
	EMPLOYMENT APPLICATION SOURCE TYPE ID	No	Yes	ID
	APPLYING PARTY ID	No	Yes	ID
	REFERRED BY PARTY ID	No	Yes	ID
	APPLICATION DATE	No	No	Datetime
EMPLOYMENT APPLICATION SOURCE TYPE	EMPLOYMENT APPLICATION SOURCE TYPE ID	Yes	No	ID
	DESCRIPTION	No	No	Description
EMPLOYMENT APPLICATION STATUS TYPE	STATUS TYPE ID	Yes	Yes	ID
END USER CUSTOMER	CUSTOMER ID	Yes	Yes	ID
	PARTY ID	Yes	Yes	ID
	ROLE TYPE ID	Yes	Yes	ID
EQUIPMENT	FIXED ASSET ID	Yes	Yes	ID
ESTIMATED LABOR COST	COST COMPONENT ID	Yes	Yes	ID
ESTIMATED MATERIALS COST	COST COMPONENT ID	Yes	Yes	ID
ESTIMATED OTHER COSTS	COST COMPONENT ID	Yes	Yes	ID
ESTIMATED PRODUCT COST	COST COMPONENT ID	Yes	No	ID
	PRODUCT ID	No	Yes	ID
	PARTY ID	No	Yes	ID

ENTITY NAME	ATTRIBUTE NAME	PK?	FK?	DOMAIN
	COST COMPONENT TYPE ID	No	Yes	ID
	PRODUCT FEATURE ID	No	Yes	ID
	FROM DATE	No	No	Datetime
	THRU DATE	No	No	Datetime
	COST	No	No	Currency amount
	GEO ID	No	Yes	ID
EXPORT DOCUMENTATION	DOCUMENT ID	Yes	Yes	ID
EXTERNAL ACCTG TRANS	TRANSACTION ID	Yes	Yes	ID
	PARTY ID	No	Yes	ID
FACE TO FACE COMMUNICATION	COMMUNICATION EVENT ID	Yes	Yes	ID
FACILITY	FACILITY ID	Yes	No	ID
	PART OF FACILITY	No	Yes	ID
	FACILITY TYPE ID	No	Yes	ID
	SQUARE FOOTAGE	No	No	Numeric
	DESCRIPTION	No	No	Description
	FACILITY NAME	No	No	Name
FACILITY CONTACT MECHANISM	FACILITY ID	Yes	Yes	ID
	CONTACT MECHANISM ID	Yes	Yes	ID
FACILITY ROLE	FACILITY ID	Yes	Yes	ID
	PARTY ID	Yes	Yes	ID
	ROLE TYPE ID	Yes	Yes	ID
FACILITY ROLE TYPE	FACILITY ROLE TYPE ID	Yes	No	ID
	DESCRIPTION	No	No	Description
FACILITY TYPE	FACILITY TYPE ID	Yes	No	ID
	DESCRIPTION	No	No	Description
FAMILY	PARTY ID	Yes	Yes	ID
FAMILY MEMBER	PARTY ID	Yes	Yes	ID
	ROLE TYPE ID	Yes	Yes	ID
FAX COMMUNICATION	COMMUNICATION EVENT ID	Yes	Yes	ID

ENTITY NAME	ATTRIBUTE NAME	PK?	FK?	DOMAIN
FEATURE INTERACTION DEPENDENCY	PRODUCT FEATURE ID OF	Yes	Yes	ID
	PRODUCT FEATURE ID FACTOR IN	Yes	Yes	ID
FEATURE INTERACTION INCOMPATIBILITY	PRODUCT FEATURE ID OF	Yes	Yes	ID
	PRODUCT FEATURE ID FACTOR IN	Yes	Yes	ID
FEE	ORDER ADJUST SEQ ID	Yes	Yes	ID
FINANCIAL ACCOUNT	FINANCIAL ACCOUNT TYPE ID	Yes	Yes	ID
	FINANCIAL ACCOUNT NAME	No	No	Name
FINANCIAL ACCOUNT ADJUSTMENT	FINANCIAL ACCOUNT TRANS ID	Yes	Yes	ID
FINANCIAL ACCOUNT ROLE	FINANCIAL ACCOUNT ID	No	Yes	ID
	PARTY ID	Yes	Yes	ID
	ROLE TYPE ID	Yes	Yes	ID
	FROM DATE	No	No	Datetime
	THRU DATE	No	No	Datetime
FINANCIAL ACCOUNT ROLE TYPE	ROLE TYPE ID	Yes	Yes	ID
FINANCIAL ACCOUNT TRANSACTION	FINANCIAL ACCOUNT ID	Yes	Yes	ID
	FINANCIAL ACCOUNT TRANS ID	Yes	No	ID
	PARTY ID	No	Yes	ID
	TRANSACTION DATE	No	No	Datetime
	ENTRY DATE	No	No	Datetime
FINANCIAL ACCOUNT TYPE	FINANCIAL ACCOUNT ID	Yes	No	ID
	DESCRIPTION	No	No	Description
FINANCIAL TERM	AGREEMENT TERM ID	Yes	Yes	ID
	TERM TYPE ID	Yes	Yes	ID
FINISHED GOOD	PART ID	Yes	Yes	ID
FIXED ASSET	FIXED ASSET ID	Yes	No	ID
	PARTY ID	No	Yes	ID
	ROLE TYPE ID	No	Yes	ID

ENTITY NAME	ATTRIBUTE NAME	PK?	FK?	DOMAIN
	UOM ID	No	Yes	ID
	FIXED ASSET TYPE ID	No	Yes	ID
	NAME	No	No	Name
	DATE ACQUIRED	No	No	Datetime
	DATE LAST SERVICED	No	No	Datetime
	DATE NEXT SERVICE	No	No	Datetime
	PRODUCTION CAPACITY	No	No	Floating point
FIXED ASSET DEPRECIATION METHOD	DEPRECIATION METHOD ID	Yes	Yes	ID
	FIXED ASSET ID	Yes	Yes	ID
	FROM DATE	No	No	Datetime
	THRU DATE	No	No	Datetime
FIXED ASSET TYPE	FIXED ASSET TYPE ID	Yes	No	ID
	DESCRIPTION	No	No	Description
FLOOR	FACILITY ID	Yes	Yes	ID
GENERAL LEDGER ACCOUNT	GENERAL LEDGER ACCOUNT ID	Yes	No	ID
	GENERAL LEDGER ACCOUNT TYPE ID	No	Yes	ID
	NAME	No	No	Name
	DESCRIPTION	No	No	Description
GENERAL LEDGER ACCOUNT TYPE	GENERAL LEDGER ACCOUNT TYPE ID	Yes	No	ID
	DESCRIPTION	No	No	Long varchar
GEOGRAPHIC BOUNDARY	GEO ID	Yes	Yes	ID
	GEO BOUNDARY TYPE ID	No	Yes	ID
	NAME	No	No	Name
	GEO CODE	No	No	Short varchar
	ABBREVIATION	No	No	Short varchar
GEOGRAPHIC BOUNDARY ASSOCIATION	GEO ID	Yes	Yes	ID
	GEO ID	Yes	Yes	ID

ENTITY NAME	ATTRIBUTE NAME	PK?	FK?	DOMAIN
GEOGRAPHIC BOUNDARY TYPE	GEO BOUNDARY TYPE ID	Yes	No	ID
	DESCRIPTION	No	No	Description
GL BUDGET XREF	FROM DATE	Yes	No	Datetime
	GENERAL LEDGER ACCOUNT ID	Yes	Yes	ID
	BUDGET ITEM TYPE ID	Yes	Yes	ID
	THRU DATE	No	No	Datetime
	ALLOCATION PERCENTAGE	No	No	Floating point
GOOD	PRODUCT ID	Yes	Yes	ID
	PART ID	No	Yes	ID
GOOD IDENTIFICATION	IDENTIFICATION TYPE ID	Yes	Yes	ID
	PRODUCT ID	Yes	Yes	ID
	ID VALUE	No	No	Long Varchar
GOVERNMENT AGENCY	PARTY ID	Yes	Yes	ID
HARDWARE FEATURE	PRODUCT FEATURE ID	Yes	Yes	ID
HAZARDOUS MATERIALS DOCUMENT	DOCUMENT ID	Yes	Yes	ID
HOUSEHOLD	PARTY ID	Yes	Yes	ID
	ROLE TYPE ID	Yes	Yes	ID
IDENTIFICATION TYPE	IDENTIFICATION TYPE ID	Yes	No	ID
	DESCRIPTION	No	No	Description
INCENTIVE	AGREEMENT TERM ID	Yes	Yes	ID
	TERM TYPE ID	Yes	Yes	ID
INCOME CLASSIFICATION	FROM DATE	Yes	Yes	Datetime
	PARTY TYPE ID	Yes	Yes	ID
	PARTY ID	Yes	Yes	ID
INCOMING SHIPMENT	SHIPMENT ID	Yes	Yes	ID
INDUSTRY CLASSIFICATION	FROM DATE	Yes	Yes	Datetime
INDUSTRY CLASSIFICATION	PARTY TYPE ID	Yes	Yes	ID
	PARTY ID	Yes	Yes	ID
INFORMAL	PARTY ID	Yes	Yes	ID

ENTITY NAME	ATTRIBUTE NAME	PK?	FK?	DOMAIN
ORGANIZATION				
INQUIRY	COMMUNICATION EVENT PRP TYP ID	Yes	Yes	ID
	COMMUNICATION EVENT ID	Yes	Yes	ID
INTERNAL ACCTG TRANS	TRANSACTION ID	Yes	Yes	ID
	PARTY ID	No	Yes	ID
	ROLE TYPE ID	No	Yes	ID
INTERNAL ORGANIZATION	PARTY ID	Yes	Yes	ID
	ROLE TYPE ID	Yes	Yes	ID
	INTERNAL ORGANIZATION ID	Yes	No	ID
INTERNAL REQUIREMENT	REQUIREMENT ID	Yes	Yes	ID
INVENTORY ITEM	INVENTORY ITEM ID	Yes	No	ID
	PART ID	No	Yes	ID
	PRODUCT ID	No	Yes	ID
	PARTY ID	No	Yes	ID
	STATUS TYPE ID	No	Yes	ID
	FACILITY ID	No	Yes	ID
	CONTAINER ID	No	Yes	ID
	LOT ID	No	Yes	ID
INVENTORY ITEM STATUS TYPE	STATUS TYPE ID	Yes	Yes	ID
INVENTORY ITEM VARIANCE	INVENTORY ITEM ID	Yes	Yes	ID
	PHYSICAL INVENTORY DATE	Yes	No	Datetime
	REASON ID	No	Yes	ID
	QUANTITY	No	No	Numeric
	COMMENT	No	No	Comment
INVESTMENT ACCOUNT	FINANCIAL ACCOUNT ID	Yes	Yes	ID
INVOICE	INVOICE ID	Yes	No	ID
	PARTY ID	No	Yes	ID
	ROLE TYPE ID	No	Yes	ID

ENTITY NAME	ATTRIBUTE NAME	PK?	FK?	DOMAIN
	BILLING ACCOUNT ID	No	Yes	ID
	CONTACT MECHANISM ID	No	Yes	ID
	INVOICE DATE	No	No	Datetime
	MESSAGE	No	No	Long varchar
	DESCRIPTION	No	No	Description
INVOICE ITEM	INVOICE ITEM SEQ ID	Yes	No	ID
	INVOICE ID	Yes	Yes	ID
	UOM ID	No	Yes	ID
	INVENTORY ITEM ID	No	Yes	ID
	PRODUCT FEATURE ID	No	Yes	ID
	INVOICE ITEM TYPE ID	No	Yes	ID
	PRODUCT ID	No	Yes	ID
	TAXABLE FLAG	No	No	Indicator
	QUANTITY	No	No	Numeric
	AMOUNT	No	No	Currency amount
	ITEM DESCRIPTION	No	No	Description
INVOICE ITEM TYPE	INVOICE ITEM TYPE ID	Yes	No	ID
	DESCRIPTION	No	No	Description
INVOICE ROLE	PARTY ID	Yes	Yes	ID
	INVOICE ID	Yes	Yes	ID
	ROLE TYPE ID	Yes	Yes	ID
	DATETIME	No	No	Datetime
	PERCENTAGE	No	No	Floating point
INVOICE ROLE TYPE	ROLE TYPE ID	Yes	Yes	ID
INVOICE STATUS	STATUS TYPE ID	Yes	Yes	ID
	INVOICE ID	Yes	Yes	ID
	STATUS DATE	Yes	No	Datetime
INVOICE STATUS TYPE	STATUS TYPE ID	Yes	No	ID
	DESCRIPTION	No	No	Description
INVOICE TERM	INVOICE TERM ID	Yes	No	ID
	TERM TYPE ID	Yes	Yes	ID
	INVOICE ITEM SEQ ID	No	Yes	ID

ENTITY NAME	ATTRIBUTE NAME	PK?	FK?	DOMAIN
	INVOICE ID	No	Yes	ID
	TERM VALUE	No	No	Numeric
ISBN	IDENTIFICATION TYPE ID	Yes	Yes	ID
	PRODUCT ID	Yes	Yes	ID
ITEM ISSUANCE	ITEM ISSUANCE ID	Yes	No	ID
	INVENTORY ITEM ID	No	Yes	ID
	PICKLIST ID	No	Yes	ID
	SHIPMENT ITEM SEQ ID	No	Yes	ID
	SHIPMENT ID	No	Yes	ID
	ISSUED DATE TIME	No	No	Datetime
	QUANTITY	No	No	Numeric
ITEM ISSUANCE ROLE	PARTY ID	Yes	Yes	ID
	ITEM ISSUANCE ID	Yes	Yes	ID
	ROLE TYPE ID	Yes	Yes	ID
ITEM ISSUANCE ROLE TYPE	ROLE TYPE ID	Yes	Yes	ID
ITEM VARIANCE ACCTG TRANS	TRANSACTION ID	Yes	Yes	ID
	INVENTORY ITEM ID	No	Yes	ID
	PHYSICAL INVENTORY DATE	No	Yes	Datetime
LEGAL ORGANIZATION	PARTY ID	Yes	Yes	ID
	FEDERAL TAX ID NUM	No	No	Numeric
LEGAL TERM	AGREEMENT TERM ID	Yes	Yes	ID
	TERM TYPE ID	Yes	Yes	ID
LETTER CORRESPONDENCE	COMMUNICATION EVENT ID	Yes	Yes	ID
LOT	LOT ID	Yes	No	ID
	CREATION DATE	No	No	Datetime
	QUANTITY	No	No	Numeric
	EXPIRATION DATE	No	No	Datetime
MAINTENANCE	WORK EFFORT ID	Yes	Yes	ID
MANAGER	PARTY ID	Yes	Yes	ID
	ROLE TYPE ID	Yes	Yes	ID

ENTITY NAME	ATTRIBUTE NAME	PK?	FK?	DOMAIN
MANIFEST	DOCUMENT ID	Yes	Yes	ID
MANUFACTURER ID NO	IDENTIFICATION TYPE ID	Yes	Yes	ID
	PRODUCT ID	Yes	Yes	ID
MANUFACTURER SUGGESTED PRICE	PRICE COMPONENT ID	Yes	Yes	ID
MARKET INTEREST	FROM DATE	Yes	No	Datetime
	PRODUCT CATEGORY ID	Yes	Yes	ID
	PARTY TYPE ID	Yes	Yes	ID
	THRU DATE	No	No	Datetime
MARKETING PACKAGE	PRODUCT ID FROM	Yes	Yes	ID
	PRODUCT ID TO	Yes	Yes	ID
	FROM DATE	Yes	Yes	Datetime
	QUANTITY USED	No	No	Numeric
	INSTRUCTION	No	No	Long varchar
MEETING	COMMUNICATION EVENT PRP TYP ID	Yes	Yes	ID
	COMMUNICATION EVENT ID	Yes	Yes	ID
MINORITY CLASSIFICATION	FROM DATE	Yes	Yes	Datetime
	PARTY TYPE ID	Yes	Yes	ID
	PARTY ID	Yes	Yes	ID
MISCELLANEOUS CHARGE	ORDER ADJUST SEQ ID	Yes	Yes	ID
NON SERIALIZED INVENTORY ITEM	INVENTORY ITEM ID	Yes	Yes	ID
	QUANTITY ON HAND	No	No	Numeric
NOTE	TRANSACTION ID	Yes	Yes	ID
OBLIGATION ACCTG TRANS	TRANSACTION ID	Yes	Yes	ID
OFFICE	FACILITY ID	Yes	Yes	ID
ONE TIME CHARGE	PRICE COMPONENT ID	Yes	Yes	ID
OPERATING BUDGET	BUDGET ID	Yes	Yes	ID
	BUDGET TYPE ID	Yes	Yes	ID
OPTIONAL FEATURE	PRODUCT ID	Yes	Yes	ID

ENTITY NAME	ATTRIBUTE NAME	PK?	FK?	DOMAIN
	FROM DATE	Yes	Yes	Datetime
	PRODUCT FEATURE ID	Yes	Yes	ID
ORDER	ORDER ID	Yes	No	ID
	ORDER DATE	No	No	Datetime
	ENTRY DATE	No	No	Datetime
ORDER ADJUSTMENT	ORDER ADJUST SEQ ID	Yes	No	ID
	ORDER ADJUST TYPE ID	No	Yes	ID
	ORDER ID	No	Yes	ID
	ORDER ITEM SEQ ID	No	Yes	ID
	AMOUNT	No	No	Currency amount
	PERCENTAGE	No	No	Floating point
ORDER ADJUSTMENT TYPE	ORDER ADJUST TYPE ID	Yes	No	ID
	DESCRIPTION	No	No	Description
ORDER CONTACT MECHANISM	CONTACT MECHANISM PURPOSE TYPE ID	Yes	Yes	ID
	ORDER ID	Yes	Yes	ID
	CONTACT MECHANISM ID	Yes	Yes	ID
ORDER ITEM	ORDER ID	Yes	Yes	ID
	ORDER ITEM SEQ ID	Yes	No	ID
	BUDGET ID	No	Yes	ID
	BUDGET ITEM SEQ ID	No	Yes	ID
	PRODUCT ID	No	Yes	ID
	QUOTED ITEM SEQ ID	No	Yes	ID
	QUOTE ID	No	Yes	ID
	PRODUCT FEATURE ID	No	Yes	ID
	QUANTITY	No	No	Numeric
	UNIT PRICE	No	No	Currency amount
	ESTIMATED DELIVERY DATE	No	No	Datetime
	SHIPPING INSTRUCTIONS	No	No	Long varchar
	ITEM DESCRIPTION	No	No	Description
	COMMENT	No	No	Comment

ENTITY NAME	ATTRIBUTE NAME	PK?	FK?	DOMAIN
ORDER ITEM ASSOCIATION	SALES ORDER ID	Yes	Yes	ID
	SO ITEM SEQ ID	Yes	Yes	ID
	PURCHASE ORDER ID	Yes	Yes	ID
	PO ITEM SEQ ID	Yes	Yes	ID
ORDER ITEM BILLING	INVOICE ITEM SEQ ID	Yes	Yes	ID
	INVOICE ID	Yes	Yes	ID
	ORDER ID	Yes	Yes	ID
	ORDER ITEM SEQ ID	Yes	Yes	ID
	QUANTITY	No	No	Numeric
	AMOUNT	No	No	Currency amount
ORDER ITEM CONTACT MECHANISM	CONTACT MECHANISM PURPOSE TYPE ID	Yes	Yes	ID
	CONTACT MECHANISM ID	Yes	Yes	ID
	ORDER ID	Yes	Yes	ID
	ORDER ITEM SEQ ID	Yes	Yes	ID
ORDER ITEM ROLE	ROLE TYPE ID	Yes	Yes	ID
	PARTY ID	Yes	Yes	ID
	ORDER ID	Yes	Yes	ID
ORDER ITEM ROLE TYPE	ROLE TYPE ID	Yes	Yes	ID
ORDER REQUIREMENT COMMITMENT	ORDER ID	Yes	Yes	ID
	ORDER ITEM SEQ ID	Yes	Yes	ID
	REQUIREMENT ID	Yes	Yes	ID
	QUANTITY	No	No	Numeric
ORDER ROLE	ORDER ID	Yes	Yes	ID
	PARTY ID	Yes	Yes	ID
	ROLE TYPE ID	Yes	Yes	ID
ORDER ROLE TYPE	ROLE TYPE ID	Yes	Yes	ID
ORDER SHIPMENT	SHIPMENT ITEM SEQ ID	Yes	Yes	ID
	SHIPMENT ID	Yes	Yes	ID
	ORDER ID	Yes	Yes	ID
	ORDER ITEM SEQ ID	Yes	Yes	ID

ENTITY NAME	ATTRIBUTE NAME	PK?	FK?	DOMAIN
	QUANTITY	No	No	Numeric
ORDER STATUS	ORDER STATUS ID	Yes	No	ID
	STATUS TYPE ID	No	Yes	ID
	ORDER ID	No	Yes	ID
	ORDER ITEM SEQ ID	No	Yes	ID
	STATUS DATETIME	No	No	Datetime
ORDER STATUS TYPE	STATUS TYPE ID	Yes	Yes	ID
ORDER TERM	ORDER TERM ID	Yes	No	ID
	TERM TYPE ID	No	Yes	ID
	ORDER ID	No	Yes	ID
	ORDER ITEM SEQ ID	No	Yes	ID
	TERM VALUE	No	No	Numeric
ORDER VALUE	ORDER VALUE ID	Yes	No	ID
	FROM AMOUNT	No	No	Currency amount
	THRU AMOUNT	No	No	Currency amount
ORGANIZATION	PARTY ID	Yes	Yes	ID
	NAME	No	No	Name
ORGANIZATION CLASSIFICATION	FROM DATE	Yes	Yes	Datetime
	PARTY TYPE ID	Yes	Yes	ID
	PARTY ID	Yes	Yes	ID
ORGANIZATION CONTACT RELATIONSHIP	PARTY ID FROM	Yes	Yes	ID
	PARTY ID TO	Yes	Yes	ID
	FROM DATE	Yes	Yes	Datetime
	ROLE TYPE ID TO	Yes	Yes	ID
	ROLE TYPE ID FROM	Yes	Yes	ID
ORGANIZATION GL ACCOUNT	INTERNAL ORGANIZATION ID	Yes	Yes	ID
	PARTY ID	Yes	Yes	ID
	GENERAL LEDGER ACCOUNT ID	Yes	Yes	ID
	ROLE TYPE ID	Yes	Yes	ID
	PRODUCT CATEGORY ID	No	Yes	ID

ENTITY NAME	ATTRIBUTE NAME	PK?	FK?	DOMAIN
	CUSTOMER ID	No	Yes	ID
	PRODUCT ID	No	Yes	ID
	FROM DATE	No	No	Datetime
	THRU DATE	No	No	Datetime
ORGANIZATION ROLE	PARTY ID	Yes	Yes	ID
	ROLE TYPE ID	Yes	Yes	ID
ORGANIZATION ROLLUP	PARTY ID TO	Yes	Yes	ID
	PARTY ID FROM	Yes	Yes	ID
	FROM DATE	Yes	Yes	Datetime
	ROLE TYPE ID FROM	Yes	Yes	ID
	ROLE TYPE ID TO	Yes	Yes	ID
ORGANIZATION UNIT	PARTY ID	Yes	Yes	ID
	ROLE TYPE ID	Yes	Yes	ID
OTHER AGREEMENT	AGREEMENT ID	Yes	Yes	ID
OTHER AGREEMENT TERM	AGREEMENT TERM ID	Yes	Yes	ID
	TERM TYPE ID	Yes	Yes	ID
OTHER FEATURE	PRODUCT FEATURE ID	Yes	Yes	ID
OTHER FIXED ASSET	FIXED ASSET ID	Yes	Yes	ID
	ASSET ID	Yes	Yes	ID
OTHER ID	IDENTIFICATION TYPE ID	Yes	Yes	ID
	PRODUCT ID	Yes	Yes	ID
OTHER INFORMAL ORGANIZATION	PARTY ID	Yes	Yes	ID
OTHER INTERNAL ACCTG TRANSACTION	TRANSACTION ID	Yes	Yes	ID
OTHER OBLIGATION	TRANSACTION ID	Yes	Yes	ID
OTHER ORGANIZATION UNIT	PARTY ID	Yes	Yes	ID
	ROLE TYPE ID	Yes	Yes	ID
OTHER QUOTE	QUOTE ID	Yes	Yes	ID
OTHER SHIPPING DOCUMENTS	DOCUMENT ID	Yes	Yes	ID

ENTITY NAME	ATTRIBUTE NAME	PK?	FK?	DOMAIN
OUTGOING SHIPMENT	SHIPMENT ID	Yes	Yes	ID
PACKAGING CONTENT	SHIPMENT PACKAGE ID	Yes	Yes	ID
	SHIPMENT ITEM SEQ ID	Yes	Yes	ID
	SHIPMENT ID	Yes	Yes	ID
	QUANTITY	No	No	Numeric
PACKAGING SLIP	DOCUMENT ID	Yes	Yes	ID
PARENT ORGANIZATION	PARTY ID	Yes	Yes	ID
	ROLE TYPE ID	Yes	Yes	ID
PART	PART ID	Yes	No	ID
	NAME	No	No	Name
PARTNER	PARTY ID	Yes	Yes	ID
	ROLE TYPE ID	Yes	Yes	ID
PARTNERSHIP	PARTY ID TO	Yes	Yes	ID
	PARTY ID FROM	Yes	Yes	ID
	FROM DATE	Yes	Yes	Datetime
	ROLE TYPE ID FROM	Yes	Yes	ID
	ROLE TYPE ID TO	Yes	Yes	ID
PARTY	PARTY ID	Yes	No	ID
PARTY ASSET ASSIGN-MENT STATUS TYPE	STATUS TYPE ID	Yes	Yes	ID
PARTY BENEFIT	PARTY ID TO	Yes	Yes	ID
	PARTY ID FROM	Yes	Yes	ID
	FROM DATE	Yes	Yes	Datetime
	ROLE TYPE ID TO	Yes	Yes	ID
	ROLE TYPE ID FROM	Yes	Yes	ID
	BENEFIT TYPE ID	Yes	Yes	ID
	PERIOD TYPE ID	No	Yes	ID
	THRU DATE	No	No	Datetime
	COST	No	No	Currency amount
	ACTUAL EMPLOYER PAID PERCENT	No	No	Floating point
	AVAILABLE TIME	No	No	Numeric

ENTITY NAME	ATTRIBUTE NAME	PK?	FK?	DOMAIN
PARTY CLASSIFICATION	FROM DATE	Yes	No	Datetime
	PARTY TYPE ID	Yes	Yes	ID
	PARTY ID	Yes	Yes	ID
	THRU DATE	No	No	Datetime
PARTY CONTACT MECHANISM	FROM DATE	Yes	No	Datetime
	CONTACT MECHANISM ID	Yes	Yes	ID
	PARTY ID	Yes	Yes	ID
	ROLE TYPE ID	No	Yes	ID
	THRU DATE	No	No	Datetime
	NON-SOLICITATION INDICATOR	No	No	Indicator
	EXTENSION	No	No	Very short
	COMMENT	No	No	Comment
PARTY CONTACT MECHANISM PURPOSE	FROM DATE	Yes	Yes	Datetime
	CONTACT MECHANISM PURPOSE ID	Yes	Yes	ID
	CONTACT MECHANISM ID	Yes	Yes	ID
	PARTY ID	Yes	Yes	ID
	THRU DATE	No	No	Datetime
PARTY FIXED ASSET ASSIGNMENT	PARTY ID	Yes	Yes	ID
	FIXED ASSET ID	Yes	Yes	ID
	STATUS TYPE ID	Yes	Yes	ID
	FROM DATE	No	No	Datetime
	THRU DATE	No	No	Datetime
	ALLOCATED DATE	No	No	Datetime
	COMMENT	No	No	Comment
PARTY POSTAL ADDRESS	FROM DATE	Yes	No	Datetime
	PARTY ID	Yes	Yes	ID
	CONTACT MECHANISM ID	Yes	Yes	ID
	THRU DATE	No	No	Datetime
	COMMENT	No	No	Comment

ENTITY NAME	ATTRIBUTE NAME	PK?	FK?	DOMAIN
PARTY QUALIFICATION	QUAL TYPE ID	Yes	Yes	ID
	PARTY ID	Yes	Yes	ID
	FROM DATE	No	No	Datetime
	THRU DATE	No	No	Datetime
PARTY RATE	FROM DATE	Yes	No	Datetime
	RATE TYPE ID	Yes	Yes	ID
	PARTY ID	Yes	Yes	ID
	THRU DATE	No	No	Datetime
	RATE	No	No	Currency amount
PARTY RELATIONSHIP	PARTY ID FROM	Yes	Yes	ID
	PARTY ID TO	Yes	Yes	ID
	FROM DATE	Yes	No	Datetime
	ROLE TYPE ID TO	Yes	Yes	ID
	ROLE TYPE ID FROM	Yes	Yes	ID
	STATUS TYPE ID	No	Yes	ID
	PRIORITY TYPE ID	No	Yes	ID
	PARTY RELATIONSHIP TYPE ID	No	Yes	ID
	THRU DATE	No	No	Datetime
	COMMENT	No	No	Comment
PARTY RELATIONSHIP STATUS TYPE	STATUS TYPE ID	Yes	Yes	ID
PARTY RELATIONSHIP TYPE	PARTY RELATIONSHIP TYPE ID	Yes	No	ID
	ROLE TYPE ID VALID TO	No	Yes	ID
	ROLE TYPE ID VALID FROM	No	Yes	ID
	DESCRIPTION	No	No	Description
	NAME	No	No	Name
PARTY ROLE	PARTY ID	Yes	Yes	ID
	ROLE TYPE ID	Yes	Yes	ID
	PARTY ROLE ID	Yes	No	ID
	FROM DATE	No	No	Datetime
	THRU DATE	No	No	Datetime
PARTY ROLE TYPE	ROLE TYPE ID	Yes	Yes	ID

ENTITY NAME	ATTRIBUTE NAME	PK?	FK?	DOMAIN
PARTY SKILL	PARTY ID	Yes	Yes	ID
	SKILL TYPE ID	Yes	Yes	ID
	YEARS EXPERIENCE	No	No	Numeric
	RATING	No	No	Numeric
	SKILL LEVEL	No	No	Numeric
	STARTED USING DATE	No	No	Datetime
PARTY TYPE	PARTY TYPE ID	Yes	No	ID
	DESCRIPTION	No	No	Description
PAY CHECK	PAYMENT ID	Yes	Yes	ID
	ROLE TYPE ID	No	Yes	ID
	PARTY ID	No	Yes	ID
	INTERNAL ORGANIZATION ID	No	Yes	ID
PAY GRADE	PAY GRADE ID	Yes	No	ID
	NAME	No	No	Name
	COMMENT	No	No	Comment
PAY HISTORY	PARTY ID FROM	Yes	Yes	ID
	PARTY ID TO	Yes	Yes	ID
	FROM DATE	Yes	Yes	Datetime
	ROLE TYPE ID TO	Yes	Yes	ID
	ROLE TYPE ID FROM	Yes	Yes	ID
	SALARY STEP SEQ ID	No	Yes	ID
	PAY GRADE ID	No	Yes	ID
	PERIOD TYPE ID	No	Yes	ID
	THRU DATE	No	No	Datetime
	AMOUNT	No	No	Currency amount
	COMMENT	No	No	Comment
PAYMENT	PAYMENT ID	Yes	No	ID
	PAYMENT TYPE ID	No	Yes	ID
	PAYMENT METHOD TYPE ID	No	Yes	ID
	PARTY ID TO	No	Yes	ID
	PARTY ID FROM	No	Yes	ID
	EFFECTIVE DATE	No	No	Datetime
	PAYMENT REF NUM	No	No	Numeric

ENTITY NAME	ATTRIBUTE NAME	PK?	FK?	DOMAIN
	AMOUNT	No	No	Currency amount
	COMMENT	No	No	Comment
PAYMENT ACCTG TRANS	TRANSACTION ID	Yes	Yes	ID
	PAYMENT ID	No	Yes	ID
PAYMENT APPLICATION	PAYMENT APPLICATION ID	Yes	No	ID
	PAYMENT ID	Yes	Yes	ID
	INVOICE ITEM SEQ ID	No	Yes	ID
	INVOICE ID	No	Yes	ID
	BILLING ACCOUNT ID	No	Yes	ID
	AMOUNT APPLIED	No	No	Currency amount
PAYMENT BUDGET ALLOCATION	BUDGET TYPE ID	Yes	Yes	ID
	BUDGET ID	Yes	Yes	ID
	BUDGET ITEM SEQ ID	Yes	Yes	ID
	PAYMENT ID	Yes	Yes	ID
	AMOUNT	No	No	Currency amount
PAYMENT METHOD TYPE	PAYMENT METHOD TYPE ID	Yes	No	ID
	DESCRIPTION	No	No	Description
PAYROLL PREFERENCE	PARTY ID	Yes	Yes	ID
	INTERNAL ORGANIZATION ID	Yes	Yes	ID
	PAYROLL PREFERENCE SEQ ID	Yes	No	ID
	ROLE TYPE ID	Yes	Yes	ID
	DEDUCTION TYPE ID	No	Yes	ID
	PAYMENT METHOD TYPE ID	No	Yes	ID
	PERIOD TYPE ID	No	Yes	ID
	FROM DATE	No	No	Datetime
	THRU DATE	No	No	Datetime
	PERCENTAGE	No	No	Floating point
	FLAT AMOUNT	No	No	Currency amount
	ROUTING NUMBER	No	No	Numeric
	ACCOUNT NUMBER	No	No	Numeric
	BANK NAME	No	No	Name

ENTITY NAME	ATTRIBUTE NAME	PK?	FK?	DOMAIN
PERF REVIEW ITEM TYPE	PERF REVIEW ITEM TYPE ID	Yes	No	ID
	DESCRIPTION	No	No	Description
PERFORMANCE NOTE	PARTY ID	Yes	Yes	ID
	ROLE TYPE ID	Yes	Yes	ID
	FROM DATE	No	No	Datetime
	THRU DATE	No	No	Datetime
	COMMUNICATION DATE	No	No	Datetime
	COMMENT	No	No	Comment
PERFORMANCE REVIEW ITEM	EMPLOYEE PARTY ID	Yes	Yes	ID
	PERF REVIEW SEQ ID	Yes	No	ID
	PERF REVIEW ID	Yes	Yes	ID
	EMPLOYEE ROLE TYPE ID	Yes	Yes	ID
	RATING TYPE ID	No	Yes	ID
	PERF REVIEW ITEM TYPE ID	No	Yes	ID
	COMMENT	No	No	Comment
PERIOD TYPE	PERIOD TYPE ID	Yes	No	ID
	DESCRIPTION	No	No	Description
PERSON	PARTY ID	Yes	Yes	ID
	CURRENT LAST NAME	No	No	Name
	CURRENT FIRST NAME	No	No	Name
	CURRENT MIDDLE NAME	No	No	Name
	CURRENT PERSONAL TITLE	No	No	Name
	CURRENT SUFFIX	No	No	Name
	CURRENT NICKNAME	No	No	Name
	GENDER	No	No	Indicator
	BIRTH DATE	No	No	Datetime
	HEIGHT	No	No	Numeric
	WEIGHT	No	No	Numeric
	MOTHER'S MAIDEN NAME	No	No	Name
	MARITAL STATUS	No	No	Indicator
	SOCIAL SECURITY NUMBER	No	No	Numeric

ENTITY NAME	ATTRIBUTE NAME	PK?	FK?	DOMAIN
	CURRENT PASSPORT NUMBER	No	No	Numeric
	CURRENT PASSPORT EXPIRE DATE	No	No	Datetime
	TOTAL YEARS WORK EXPERIENCE	No	No	Numeric
	COMMENT	No	No	Comment
PERSON CLASSIFICATION	FROM DATE	Yes	Yes	Datetime
	PARTY TYPE ID	Yes	Yes	ID
	PARTY ID	Yes	Yes	ID
PERSON ROLE	PARTY ID	Yes	Yes	ID
	ROLE TYPE ID	Yes	Yes	ID
PERSON TRAINING	TRAINING CLASS TYPE ID	Yes	Yes	ID
	PARTY ID	Yes	Yes	ID
	THRU DATE	No	No	Datetime
	FROM DATE	No	No	Datetime
PHASE	WORK EFFORT ID	Yes	Yes	ID
PHONE COMMUNICATION	COMMUNICATION EVENT ID	Yes	Yes	ID
PICKLIST	PICKLIST ID	Yes	No	ID
	DATE CREATED	No	No	Datetime
PICKLIST ITEM	INVENTORY ITEM ID	Yes	Yes	ID
	PICKLIST ID	Yes	Yes	ID
	QUANTITY	No	No	Numeric
PLANT	FACILITY ID	Yes	Yes	ID
PORT CHARGES DOCUMENT	DOCUMENT ID	Yes	Yes	ID
POSITION	POSITION ID	Yes	No	ID
	STATUS TYPE ID	No	Yes	ID
	PARTY ID	No	Yes	ID
	BUDGET ID	No	Yes	ID
	BUDGET ITEM SEQ ID	No	Yes	ID
	POSITION TYPE ID	No	Yes	ID
	ESTIMATED FROM DATE	No	No	Datetime
	ESTIMATED THRU DATE	No	No	Datetime

ENTITY NAME	ATTRIBUTE NAME	PK?	FK?	DOMAIN
	SALARY FLAG	No	No	Indicator
	EXEMPT FLAG	No	No	Indicator
	FULLTIME FLAG	No	No	Indicator
	TEMPORARY FLAG	No	No	Indicator
	ACTUAL FROM DATE	No	No	Datetime
	ACTUAL THRU DATE	No	No	Datetime
	BUDGET TYPE ID	No	Yes	ID
POSITION CLASSIFICATION TYPE	POSITION CLASS TYPE ID	Yes	No	ID
	DESCRIPTION	No	No	Description
POSITION FULFILLMENT	FROM DATE	Yes	No	Datetime
	PARTY ID	Yes	Yes	ID
	POSITION ID	Yes	Yes	ID
	THRU DATE	No	No	Datetime
	COMMENT	No	No	Comment
POSITION REPORTING STRUCTURE	POSITION ID REPORTING TO	Yes	Yes	ID
	POSITION ID MANAGED BY	Yes	Yes	ID
	FROM DATE	Yes	No	Datetime
	THRU DATE	No	No	Datetime
	COMMENT	No	No	Comment
	PRIMARY FLAG	No	No	Indicator
POSITION RESPONSIBILITY	FROM DATE	Yes	No	Datetime
	POSITION ID	Yes	Yes	ID
	RESPONSIBILITY TYPE ID	Yes	Yes	ID
	THRU DATE	No	No	Datetime
	COMMENT	No	No	Comment
POSITION STATUS TYPE	STATUS TYPE ID	Yes	Yes	ID
POSITION TYPE	POSITION TYPE ID	Yes	No	ID
	PARTY ID	No	Yes	ID
	ROLE TYPE ID	No	Yes	ID
	DESCRIPTION	No	No	Description

ENTITY NAME	ATTRIBUTE NAME	PK?	FK?	DOMAIN
POSITION TYPE CLASS	FROM DATE	Yes	No	Datetime
	POSITION CLASS TYPE ID	Yes	Yes	ID
	POSITION TYPE ID	Yes	Yes	ID
	THRU DATE	No	No	Datetime
	STANDARD HOURS PER WEEK	No	No	Numeric
	FROM DATE	Yes	No	Datetime
	RATE TYPE ID	Yes	Yes	ID
	POSITION TYPE ID	Yes	Yes	ID
	PERIOD TYPE ID	Yes	Yes	ID
	SALARY STEP SEQ ID	No	Yes	ID
	PAY GRADE ID	No	Yes	ID
	THRU DATE	No	No	Datetime
	RATE	No	No	Floating point
POSTAL ADDRESS	CONTACT MECHANISM ID	Yes	Yes	ID
	ADDRESS1	No	No	Long varchar
	ADDRESS2	No	No	Long varchar
	DIRECTIONS	No	No	Long varchar
POSTAL ADDRESS BOUNDARY	GEO ID	Yes	Yes	ID
	CONTACT MECHANISM ID	Yes	Yes	ID
POSTAL CODE	ID	Yes	Yes	ID
PREFERENCE TYPE	PREFERENCE TYPE ID	Yes	No	ID
	DESCRIPTION	No	No	Description
PRICE COMPONENT	PRICE COMPONENT ID	Yes	No	ID
	PARTY ID	No	Yes	ID
	PRODUCT FEATURE ID	No	Yes	ID
	PRODUCT ID	No	Yes	ID
	AGREEMENT ITEM SEQ ID	No	Yes	ID
	AGREEMENT ID	No	Yes	ID
	PRODUCT CATEGORY ID	No	Yes	ID
	PARTY TYPE ID	No	Yes	ID
	UOM ID	No	Yes	ID

ENTITY NAME	ATTRIBUTE NAME	PK?	FK?	DOMAIN
	SALE TYPE ID	No	Yes	ID
	ORDER VALUE ID	No	Yes	ID
	QUANTITY BREAK ID	No	Yes	ID
	FROM DATE	No	No	Datetime
	THRU DATE	No	No	Datetime
	PRICE	No	No	Currency amount
	PERCENT	No	No	Floating point
	COMMENT	No	No	Comment
	GEO ID	No	Yes	ID
PRIORITY TYPE	PRIORITY TYPE ID	Yes	No	ID
	DESCRIPTION	No	No	Description
PRODUCT	PRODUCT ID	Yes	No	ID
	PART ID	No	Yes	ID
	MANUFACTURER PARTY ID	No	Yes	ID
	UOM ID	No	Yes	ID
	NAME	No	No	Name
	INTRODUCTION DATE	No	No	Datetime
	SALES DISCONTINUATION DATE	No	No	Datetime
	SUPPORT DISCONTINUATION DATE	No	No	Datetime
	COMMENT	No	No	Comment
	DESCRIPTION	No	No	Description
PRODUCT AGREEMENT	AGREEMENT ID	Yes	Yes	ID
PRODUCT ASSOCIATION	PRODUCT ID FROM	Yes	Yes	ID
	PRODUCT ID TO	Yes	Yes	ID
	FROM DATE	Yes	No	Datetime
	THRU DATE	No	No	Datetime
	REASON	No	No	Long varchar
PRODUCT CATEGORY	PRODUCT CATEGORY ID	Yes	No	ID
	DESCRIPTION	No	No	Description
PRODUCT CATEGORY CLASSIFICATION	FROM DATE	Yes	No	Datetime
	PRODUCT CATEGORY ID	Yes	Yes	ID

ENTITY NAME	ATTRIBUTE NAME	PK?	FK?	DOMAIN
	PRODUCT ID	Yes	Yes	ID
	THRU DATE	No	No	Datetime
	PRIMARY FLAG	No	No	Indicator
	COMMENT	No	No	Comment
PRODUCT CATEGORY ROLLUP	PRODUCT TYPE ID MADE UP OF	Yes	Yes	ID
	PRODUCT TYPE ID PART OF	Yes	Yes	ID
PRODUCT COMPLEMENT	PRODUCT ID FROM	Yes	Yes	ID
	PRODUCT ID TO	Yes	Yes	ID
	FROM DATE	Yes	Yes	Datetime
	REASON	No	No	Long varchar
PRODUCT COMPONENT	PRODUCT ID FROM	Yes	Yes	ID
	PRODUCT ID TO	Yes	Yes	ID
	FROM DATE	Yes	Yes	Datetime
	QUANTITY USED	No	No	Numeric
	INSTRUCTION	No	No	Long varchar
	COMMENT	No	No	Comment
PRODUCT FEATURE	PRODUCT FEATURE ID	Yes	No	ID
	PRODUCT FEATURE CATEGORY ID	No	Yes	ID
	DESCRIPTION	No	No	Description
PRODUCT FEATURE APPLICABILITY	PRODUCT ID	Yes	Yes	ID
	FROM DATE	Yes	No	Datetime
	PRODUCT FEATURE ID	Yes	Yes	ID
	THRU DATE	No	No	Datetime
PRODUCT FEATURE CATEGORY	PRODUCT FEATURE CATEGORY ID	Yes	No	ID
	DESCRIPTION	No	No	Description
PRODUCT FEATURE INTERACTION	PRODUCT FEATURE ID FACTOR IN	Yes	Yes	ID
	PRODUCT FEATURE ID OF	Yes	Yes	ID
	PRODUCT ID	No	Yes	ID
PRODUCT	PRODUCT ID FROM	Yes	Yes	ID

ENTITY NAME	ATTRIBUTE NAME	PK?	FK?	DOMAIN
INCOMPATABILITY				
	PRODUCT ID TO	Yes	Yes	ID
	FROM DATE	Yes	Yes	Datetime
	REASON	No	No	Long varchar
PRODUCT INDUSTRY CATEGORIZATION	PRODUCT CATEGORY ID	Yes	Yes	ID
PRODUCT MATERIALS CATEGORIZATION	PRODUCT CATEGORY ID	Yes	Yes	ID
PRODUCT OBSOLESCENCE	FROM DATE	Yes	Yes	Datetime
	PRODUCT ID FROM	Yes	Yes	ID
	PRODUCT ID TO	Yes	Yes	ID
	SUPERCESSION DATE	No	No	Datetime
	REASON	No	No	Long varchar
PRODUCT ORDER ITEM	ORDER ID	Yes	Yes	ID
	ORDER ITEM SEQ ID	Yes	Yes	ID
	ENGAGEMENT ITEM SEQ ID	Yes	Yes	ID
	ENGAGEMENT ID	Yes	Yes	ID
	PRODUCT ID	No	Yes	ID
PRODUCT QUALITY	PRODUCT FEATURE ID	Yes	Yes	ID
PRODUCT QUOTE	QUOTE ID	Yes	Yes	ID
PRODUCT REQUIREMENT	REQUIREMENT ID	Yes	Yes	ID
	PRODUCT ID	No	Yes	ID
PRODUCT SUBSTITUTE	PRODUCT ID FROM	Yes	Yes	ID
	PRODUCT ID TO	Yes	Yes	ID
	FROM DATE	Yes	Yes	Datetime
	QUANTITY	No	No	Numeric
	COMMENT	No	No	Comment
PRODUCT USAGE CATEGORIZATION	PRODUCT CATEGORY ID	Yes	Yes	ID
PRODUCTION RUN	WORK EFFORT ID	Yes	Yes	ID
	QUANTITY TO PRODUCE	No	No	Numeric
	QUANTITY PRODUCED	No	No	Numeric

ENTITY NAME	ATTRIBUTE NAME	PK?	FK?	DOMAIN
	QUANTITY REJECTED	No	No	Numeric
PROGRAM	WORK EFFORT ID	Yes	Yes	ID
PROJECT	WORK EFFORT ID	Yes	Yes	ID
PROPERTY	FIXED ASSET ID	Yes	Yes	ID
PROPOSAL	QUOTE ID	Yes	Yes	ID
PROSPECT	PARTY ID	Yes	Yes	ID
	ROLE TYPE ID	Yes	Yes	ID
PROVINCE	GEO ID	Yes	Yes	ID
PURCHASE AGREEMENT	AGREEMENT ID	Yes	Yes	ID
PURCHASE INVOICE	INVOICE ID	Yes	Yes	ID
PURCHASE INVOICE ITEM	INVOICE ITEM SEQ ID	Yes	Yes	ID
	INVOICE ID	Yes	Yes	ID
PURCHASE ORDER	PURCHASE ORDER ID	Yes	No	ID
	ORDER ID	Yes	Yes	ID
PURCHASE ORDER ITEM	ORDER ID	Yes	Yes	ID
	ORDER ITEM SEQ ID	Yes	Yes	ID
	PART ID	No	Yes	ID
PURCHASE RETURN	SHIPMENT ID	Yes	Yes	ID
PURCHASE SHIPMENT	SHIPMENT ID	Yes	Yes	ID
QUALIFICATION TYPE	QUAL TYPE ID	Yes	No	ID
	DESCRIPTION	No	No	Description
QUANTITY BREAK	QUANTITY BREAK ID	Yes	No	ID
	FROM QUANTITY	No	No	Numeric
	THRU QUANTITY	No	No	Numeric
QUOTE	QUOTE ID	Yes	No	ID
	PARTY ID	No	Yes	ID
	ISSUE DATE	No	No	Datetime
	VALID FROM DATE	No	No	Datetime
	VALID THRU DATE	No	No	Datetime
	DESCRIPTION	No	No	Description
QUOTE ITEM	QUOTED ITEM SEQ ID	Yes	No	ID
	QUOTE ID	Yes	Yes	ID

ENTITY NAME	ATTRIBUTE NAME	PK?	FK?	DOMAIN
	PRODUCT FEATURE ID	No	Yes	ID
	DELIVERABLE TYPE ID	No	Yes	ID
	SKILL TYPE ID	No	Yes	ID
	UOM ID	No	Yes	ID
	PRODUCT ID	No	Yes	ID
	WORK EFFORT ID	No	Yes	ID
	REQUEST ITEM SEQ ID	No	Yes	ID
	REQUEST ID	No	Yes	ID
	QUANTITY	No	No	Numeric
	QUOTE UNIT PRICE	No	No	Currency amount
	ESTIMATED DELIVERY DATE	No	No	Datetime
	COMMENT	No	No	Comment
QUOTE ROLE	PARTY ID	Yes	Yes	ID
	QUOTE ID	Yes	Yes	ID
	ROLE TYPE ID	No	Yes	ID
QUOTE ROLE TYPE	ROLE TYPE ID	Yes	Yes	ID
QUOTE TERM	QUOTE TERM ID	Yes	No	ID
	TERM TYPE ID	No	Yes	ID
	QUOTED ITEM SEQ ID	No	Yes	ID
	QUOTE ID	No	Yes	ID
	TERM VALUE	No	No	Numeric
RATE TYPE	RATE TYPE ID	Yes	No	ID
	DESCRIPTION	No	No	Description
RATING TYPE	RATING TYPE ID	Yes	No	ID
	DESCRIPTION	No	No	Description
RAW MATERIAL	PART ID	Yes	Yes	ID
REASON	REASON ID	Yes	No	ID
	DESCRIPTION	No	No	Description
RECEIPT	PAYMENT ID	Yes	Yes	ID
	FINANCIAL ACCOUNT ID	No	Yes	ID
RECEIPT ACCTG TRANS	TRANSACTION ID	Yes	Yes	ID
RECURRING CHARGE	PRICE COMPONENT ID	Yes	Yes	ID

ENTITY NAME	ATTRIBUTE NAME	PK?	FK?	DOMAIN
	UOM ID	No	Yes	ID
REGION	GEO ID	Yes	Yes	ID
REGULATORY AGENCY	PARTY ID	Yes	Yes	ID
	ROLE TYPE ID	Yes	Yes	ID
REJECTION REASON	REJECTION ID	Yes	No	ID
	DESCRIPTION	No	No	Description
REORDER GUIDELINE	REORDER GUIDELINE ID	Yes	No	ID
	PRODUCT ID	Yes	Yes	ID
	ROLE TYPE ID	No	Yes	ID
	FACILITY ID	No	Yes	ID
	FROM DATE	No	No	Datetime
	THRU DATE	No	No	Datetime
	REORDER QUANTITY	No	No	Numeric
	REORDER LEVEL	No	No	Numeric
	PARTY ID	No	Yes	ID
	INTERNAL ORGANIZATION ID	No	Yes	ID
	GEOGRAPHIC LOCATION ID	No	Yes	ID
REQUEST	REQUEST ID	Yes	No	ID
	REQUEST DATE	No	No	Datetime
	RESPONSE REQUIRED DATE	No	No	Datetime
	DESCRIPTION	No	No	Description
REQUEST ITEM	REQUEST ITEM SEQ ID	Yes	No	ID
	REQUEST ID	Yes	Yes	ID
	REQUIRED BY DATE	No	No	Datetime
	QUANTITY	No	No	Numeric
	MAXIMUM AMOUNT	No	No	Currency amount
	DESCRIPTION	No	No	Description
REQUEST ROLE	REQUEST ID	Yes	Yes	ID
	PARTY ID	Yes	Yes	ID
	ROLE TYPE ID	Yes	Yes	ID
REQUEST ROLE TYPE	ROLE TYPE ID	Yes	Yes	ID
REQUIRED FEATURE	PRODUCT ID	Yes	Yes	ID

ENTITY NAME	ATTRIBUTE NAME	PK?	FK?	DOMAIN
	FROM DATE	Yes	Yes	Datetime
	PRODUCT FEATURE ID	Yes	Yes	ID
REQUIREMENT	REQUIREMENT ID	Yes	No	ID
	FACILITY ID	No	Yes	ID
	DESCRIPTION	No	No	Description
	REQUIREMENT CREATION DATE	No	No	Datetime
	REQUIRED BY DATE	No	No	Datetime
	ESTIMATED BUDGET	No	No	Currency amount
	QUANTITY	No	No	Numeric
	REASON	No	No	Long varchar
REQUIREMENT BUDGET ALLOCATION	BUDGET ID	Yes	Yes	ID
	BUDGET ITEM SEQ ID	Yes	Yes	ID
	REQUIREMENT ID	Yes	Yes	ID
	AMOUNT	No	No	Currency amount
REQUIREMENT REQUEST	REQUEST ITEM SEQ ID	Yes	Yes	ID
	REQUEST ID	Yes	Yes	ID
	REQUIREMENT ID	Yes	Yes	ID
REQUIREMENT ROLE	PARTY ID	Yes	Yes	ID
	FROM DATE	Yes	No	Datetime
	REQUIREMENT ID	Yes	Yes	ID
	ROLE TYPE ID	Yes	Yes	ID
	THRU DATE	No	No	Datetime
REQUIREMENT ROLE TYPE	ROLE TYPE ID	Yes	Yes	ID
REQUIREMENT STATUS	REQUIREMENT ID	Yes	Yes	ID
	STATUS TYPE ID	Yes	Yes	ID
	STATUS DATE	No	No	Datetime
REQUIREMENT STATUS TYPE	STATUS TYPE ID	Yes	Yes	ID
RESEARCH	WORK EFFORT ID	Yes	Yes	ID
RESPONDING PARTY	RESPONDING PARTY SEQ ID	Yes	No	ID

ENTITY NAME	ATTRIBUTE NAME	PK?	FK?	DOMAIN
	REQUEST ID	Yes	Yes	ID
	PARTY ID	Yes	Yes	ID
	CONTACT MECHANISM ID	No	Yes	ID
	DATE SENT	No	No	Datetime
RESPONSIBILITY TYPE	RESPONSIBILITY TYPE ID	Yes	No	ID
	DESCRIPTION	No	No	Description
RESUME	PARTY ID	Yes	Yes	ID
	RESUME ID	Yes	No	ID
	RESUME DATE	No	No	Datetime
	RESUME TEXT	No	No	Long varchar
RFI	REQUEST ID	Yes	Yes	ID
RFP	REQUEST ID	Yes	Yes	ID
RFQ	REQUEST ID	Yes	Yes	ID
ROLE TYPE	ROLE TYPE ID	Yes	No	ID
	DESCRIPTION	No	No	Description
ROOM	FACILITY ID	Yes	Yes	ID
SALARY STEP	SALARY STEP SEQ ID	Yes	No	ID
	PAY GRADE ID	Yes	Yes	ID
	AMOUNT	No	No	Currency amount
	DATE MODIFIED	No	No	Datetime
SALE TYPE	SALE TYPE ID	Yes	No	ID
	DESCRIPTION	No	No	Description
SALES ACCTG TRANS	TRANSACTION ID	Yes	Yes	ID
	INVOICE ID	No	Yes	ID
SALES AGREEMENT	AGREEMENT ID	Yes	Yes	ID
SALES FOLLOW UP	COMMUNICATION EVENT PRP TYP ID	Yes	Yes	ID
	COMMUNICATION EVENT ID	Yes	Yes	ID
SALES INVOICE	INVOICE ID	Yes	Yes	ID
SALES INVOICE ITEM	INVOICE ITEM SEQ ID	Yes	Yes	ID
	INVOICE ID	Yes	Yes	ID
SALES ORDER	ORDER ID	Yes	Yes	ID

ENTITY NAME	ATTRIBUTE NAME	PK?	FK?	DOMAIN
SALES ORDER ITEM	ORDER ID	Yes	Yes	ID
	ORDER ITEM SEQ ID	Yes	Yes	ID
	CORRESPONDING PO ID	No	No	Long varchar
SALES TAX	ORDER ADJUST SEQ ID	Yes	Yes	ID
SALES TAX LOOKUP	GEOGRAPHIC LOCATION ID	Yes	Yes	ID
	SALES TAX SEQ ID	Yes	No	ID
	PRODUCT CATEGORY ID	No	Yes	ID
	SALES TAX PERCENTAGE	No	No	Floating point
SALES TERRITORY	GEO ID	Yes	Yes	ID
SELECTABLE FEATURE	PRODUCT ID	Yes	Yes	ID
	FROM DATE	Yes	Yes	Datetime
	PRODUCT FEATURE ID	Yes	Yes	ID
SEMINAR	COMMUNICATION EVENT PRP TYP ID	Yes	Yes	ID
	COMMUNICATION EVENT ID	Yes	Yes	ID
SERIALIZED INVENTORY ITEM	INVENTORY ITEM ID	Yes	Yes	ID
	SERIAL NUM	No	No	Long varchar
SERVICE	PRODUCT ID	Yes	Yes	ID
SERVICE TERRITORY	GEO ID	Yes	Yes	ID
SHAREHOLDER	PARTY ID	Yes	Yes	ID
	ROLE TYPE ID	Yes	Yes	ID
SHIP TO CUSTOMER	CUSTOMER ID	Yes	Yes	ID
	PARTY ID	Yes	Yes	ID
	ROLE TYPE ID	Yes	Yes	ID
SHIPMENT	SHIPMENT ID	Yes	No	ID
	CONTACT MECHANISM ID	No	Yes	ID
	PARTY ID	No	Yes	ID
	ESTIMATED SHIP DATE	No	No	Datetime
	ESTIMATED READY DATE	No	No	Datetime
	ESTIMATED ARRIVAL DATE	No	No	Datetime
	ESTIMATED SHIP COST	No	No	Currency amount

ENTITY NAME	ATTRIBUTE NAME	PK?	FK?	DOMAIN
	ACTUAL SHIP COST	No	No	Currency amount
	LATEST CANCEL DATE	No	No	Datetime
	HANDLING INSTRUCTIONS	No	No	Long varchar
	LAST UPDATED	No	No	Datetime
SHIPMENT ITEM	SHIPMENT ITEM SEQ ID	Yes	No	ID
	SHIPMENT ID	Yes	Yes	ID
	PRODUCT ID	No	Yes	ID
	QUANTITY	No	No	Numeric
	SHIPMENTS CONTENT DESCRIPTION	No	No	Description
SHIPMENT ITEM BILLING	INVOICE ITEM SEQ ID	Yes	Yes	ID
	INVOICE ID	Yes	Yes	ID
	SHIPMENT ID	Yes	Yes	ID
SHIPMENT ITEM FEATURE	SHIPMENT ITEM SEQ ID	Yes	Yes	ID
	SHIPMENT ID	Yes	Yes	ID
	PRODUCT FEATURE ID	Yes	Yes	ID
SHIPMENT METHOD TYPE	SHIPMENT METHOD TYPE ID	Yes	No	ID
	DESCRIPTION	No	No	Description
SHIPMENT PACKAGE	SHIPMENT PACKAGE ID	Yes	No	ID
	DATE CREATED	No	No	Datetime
SHIPMENT RECEIPT	RECEIPT ID	Yes	No	ID
	INVENTORY ITEM ID	No	Yes	ID
	PRODUCT ID	No	Yes	ID
	SHIPMENT PACKAGE ID	No	Yes	ID
	ORDER ID	No	Yes	ID
	ORDER ITEM SEQ ID	No	Yes	ID
	REJECTION ID	No	Yes	ID
	DATETIME RECEIVED	No	No	Datetime
	ITEM DESCRIPTION	No	No	Description
	QUANTITY ACCEPTED	No	No	Numeric
	QUANTITY REJECTED	No	No	Numeric

ENTITY NAME	ATTRIBUTE NAME	PK?	FK?	DOMAIN
SHIPMENT RECEIPT ROLE	PARTY ID	Yes	Yes	ID
	RECEIPT ID	Yes	Yes	ID
	ROLE TYPE ID	Yes	Yes	ID
SHIPMENT RECEIPT ROLE TYPE	ROLE TYPE ID	Yes	Yes	ID
SHIPMENT ROUTE SEGMENT	SHIPMENT ROUTE SEGMENT ID	Yes	No	ID
	SHIPMENT ID	Yes	Yes	ID
	PARTY ID	No	Yes	ID
	ROLE TYPE ID	No	Yes	ID
	FIXED ASSET ID	No	Yes	ID
	FACILITY ID	No	Yes	ID
	SHIPMENT METHOD TYPE ID	No	Yes	ID
	ACTUAL START DATETIME	No	No	Datetime
	ACTUAL ARRIVAL DATETIME	No	No	Datetime
	ESTIMATED START DATETIME	No	No	Datetime
	ESTIMATED ARRIVAL DATE	No	No	Datetime
	START MILEAGE	No	No	Numeric
	END MILEAGE	No	No	Numeric
	FUEL USED	No	No	Numeric
SHIPMENT STATUS	SHIPMENT ID	Yes	Yes	ID
	STATUS TYPE ID	Yes	Yes	ID
	STATUS DATE	No	No	Datetime
SHIPMENT STATUS TYPE	STATUS TYPE ID	Yes	Yes	ID
SHIPPING AND HANDLING CHARGES	ORDER ADJUST SEQ ID	Yes	Yes	ID
SHIPPING DOCUMENT	DOCUMENT ID	Yes	Yes	ID
	SHIPMENT ITEM SEQ ID	No	Yes	ID
	SHIPMENT ID	No	Yes	ID
	SHIPMENT PACKAGE ID	No	Yes	ID
	DESCRIPTION	No	No	Description
SIZE	PRODUCT FEATURE ID	Yes	Yes	ID
SIZE CLASSIFICATION	FROM DATE	Yes	Yes	Datetime

ENTITY NAME	ATTRIBUTE NAME	PK?	FK?	DOMAIN
	PARTY TYPE ID	Yes	Yes	ID
	PARTY ID	Yes	Yes	ID
SKILL TYPE	SKILL TYPE ID	Yes	No	ID
	DESCRIPTION	No	No	Description
SKU	IDENTIFICATION TYPE ID	Yes	Yes	ID
	PRODUCT ID	Yes	Yes	ID
SOFTWARE FEATURE	PRODUCT FEATURE ID	Yes	Yes	ID
STANDARD FEATURE	PRODUCT ID	Yes	Yes	ID
	FROM DATE	Yes	Yes	Datetime
	PRODUCT FEATURE ID	Yes	Yes	ID
STANDARD TIME PERIOD	STANDARD TIME PERIOD ID	Yes	No	ID
	PERIOD TYPE ID	No	Yes	ID
	THRU DATE	No	No	Datetime
	FROM DATE	No	No	Datetime
STATE	GEO ID	Yes	Yes	ID
STATUS TYPE	STATUS TYPE ID	Yes	No	ID
	DESCRIPTION	No	No	Description
SUB AGREEMENT	AGREEMENT ITEM SEQ ID	Yes	Yes	ID
	AGREEMENT ID	Yes	Yes	ID
SUBASSEMBLY	PART ID	Yes	Yes	ID
SUBSIDIARY	PARTY ID	Yes	Yes	ID
	ROLE TYPE ID	Yes	Yes	ID
SUPPLIER	PARTY ID	Yes	Yes	ID
	ROLE TYPE ID	Yes	Yes	ID
SUPPLIER PRODUCT	AVAILABLE FROM DATE	Yes	No	Datetime
	PRODUCT ID	Yes	Yes	ID
	PARTY ID	Yes	Yes	ID
	PREFERENCE TYPE ID	No	Yes	ID
	RATING TYPE ID	No	Yes	ID
	AVAILABLE THRU DATE	No	No	Datetime
	STANDARD LEAD TIME	No	No	Datetime

ENTITY NAME	ATTRIBUTE NAME	PK?	FK?	DOMAIN
	COMMENT	No	No	Comment
SUPPLIER RELATIONSHIP	PARTY ID TO	Yes	Yes	ID
	PARTY ID FROM	Yes	Yes	ID
	FROM DATE	Yes	Yes	Datetime
	ROLE TYPE ID FROM	Yes	Yes	ID
	ROLE TYPE ID TO	Yes	Yes	ID
SUPPORT CALL	COMMUNICATION EVENT PRP TYP ID	Yes	Yes	ID
	COMMUNICATION EVENT ID	Yes	Yes	ID
SURCHARGE ADJUSTMENT	ORDER ADJUST SEQ ID	Yes	Yes	ID
SURCHARGE COMPONENT	PRICE COMPONENT ID	Yes	Yes	ID
TASK	WORK EFFORT ID	Yes	Yes	ID
TAX AND TARIFF DOCUMENT	DOCUMENT ID	Yes	Yes	ID
TAX DUE	TRANSACTION ID	Yes	Yes	ID
TEAM	PARTY ID	Yes	Yes	ID
TELECOMMUNICATIONS NUMBER	CONTACT MECHANISM ID	Yes	Yes	ID
	AREA CODE	No	No	Numeric
	CONTACT NUMBER	No	No	Short varchar
	COUNTRY CODE	No	No	Numeric
TERM TYPE	TERM TYPE ID	Yes	No	ID
	DESCRIPTION	No	No	Description
TERMINATION REASON	TERMINATION REASON ID	Yes	No	ID
	DESCRIPTION	No	No	Description
TERMINATION TYPE	TERMINATION TYPE ID	Yes	No	ID
	DESCRIPTION	No	No	Description
TERRITORY	GEO ID	Yes	Yes	ID
THRESHOLD	AGREEMENT TERM ID	Yes	Yes	ID
	TERM TYPE ID	Yes	Yes	ID
TIME ENTRY	TIME ENTRY ID	Yes	Yes	ID

ENTITY NAME	ATTRIBUTE NAME	PK?	FK?	DOMAIN
	PARTY ID	No	Yes	ID
	ROLE TYPE ID	No	Yes	ID
	FROM DATETIME	No	No	Datetime
	RATE TYPE ID	No	Yes	ID
	UOM ID	No	Yes	ID
	WORK EFFORT ID	No	Yes	ID
	THRU DATETIME	No	No	Datetime
	HOURS	No	No	Numeric
	COMMENT	No	No	Comment
	TIMESHEET ID	No	Yes	ID
TIME ENTRY BILLING	INVOICE ITEM SEQ ID	Yes	Yes	ID
	INVOICE ID	Yes	Yes	ID
	TIME ENTRY ID	Yes	Yes	ID
TIME FREQUENCY MEASURE	UOM ID	Yes	Yes	ID
TIMESHEET	TIMESHEET ID	Yes	No	ID
	PARTY ID	Yes	Yes	ID
	ROLE TYPE ID	Yes	Yes	ID
	FROM DATE	No	No	Datetime
	THRU DATE	No	No	Datetime
	COMMENT	No	No	Comment
TIMESHEET ROLE	TIMESHEET ID	Yes	Yes	ID
	ROLE TYPE ID	Yes	Yes	ID
	PARTY ID	Yes	Yes	ID
TIMESHEET ROLE TYPE	ROLE TYPE ID	Yes	Yes	ID
TRAINING CLASS TYPE	TRAINING CLASS TYPE ID	Yes	No	ID
	DESCRIPTION	No	No	Description
TRANSACTION DETAIL	TRANS SEQ DETAIL ID	Yes	No	ID
	TRANSACTION ID	Yes	Yes	ID
	ROLE TYPE ID	No	Yes	ID
	GENERAL LEDGER ACCOUNT ID	No	Yes	ID
	AMOUNT	No	No	Currency amount

ENTITY NAME	ATTRIBUTE NAME	PK?	FK?	DOMAIN
	DEBIT CREDIT FLAG	No	No	Indicator
	PARTY ID	No	Yes	ID
	INTERNAL ORGANIZATION ID	No	Yes	ID
TRANSFER	SHIPMENT ID	Yes	Yes	ID
UNEMPLOYMENT CLAIM	UNEMPLOYMENT CLAIM ID	Yes	No	ID
	UNEMPLOYMENT CLAIM DATE	No	No	Datetime
	DESCRIPTION	No	No	Description
	STATUS TYPE ID	No	Yes	ID
	ROLE TYPE ID TO	No	Yes	ID
	ROLE TYPE ID FROM	No	Yes	ID
	PARTY ID TO	No	Yes	ID
	PARTY ID FROM	No	Yes	ID
	FROM DATE	No	Yes	Datetime
UNEMPLOYMENT CLAIM STATUS TYPE	STATUS TYPE ID	Yes	Yes	ID
UNION	PARTY ID	Yes	Yes	ID
	ROLE TYPE ID	Yes	Yes	ID
UNIT OF MEASURE	UOM ID	Yes	No	ID
	ABBREVIATION	No	No	Short varchar
	DESCRIPTION	No	No	Description
UNIT OF MEASURE CONVERSION	UOM ID FROM	Yes	Yes	ID
	UOM TO	Yes	Yes	ID
	CONVERSION FACTOR	No	No	Floating point
UPCA	IDENTIFICATION TYPE ID	Yes	Yes	ID
	PRODUCT ID	Yes	Yes	ID
UPCE	IDENTIFICATION TYPE ID	Yes	Yes	ID
	PRODUCT ID	Yes	Yes	ID
UTILIZATION CHARGE	PRICE COMPONENT ID	Yes	Yes	ID
	UOM ID	No	Yes	ID
	QUANTITY	No	No	Numeric
VALID CONTACT MECHANISM ROLE	ROLE TYPE ID	Yes	Yes	ID

ENTITY NAME	ATTRIBUTE NAME	PK?	FK?	DOMAIN
	CONTACT MECHANISM TYPE ID	Yes	Yes	ID
VALID RESPONSIBILITY	FROM DATE	Yes	No	Datetime
	POSITION TYPE ID	Yes	Yes	ID
	RESPONSIBILITY TYPE ID	Yes	Yes	ID
	THRU DATE	No	No	Datetime
	COMMENT	No	No	Comment
VEHICLE	FIXED ASSET ID	Yes	Yes	ID
WAREHOUSE	FACILITY ID	Yes	Yes	ID
WEB SITE COMMUNICATION	COMMUNICATION EVENT ID	Yes	Yes	ID
WITHDRAWAL	FINANCIAL ACCOUNT TRANS ID	Yes	Yes	ID
	PAYMENT ID	No	Yes	ID
WORK EFF ASSET ASSIGN STATUS TYPE	STATUS TYPE ID	Yes	Yes	ID
WORK EFFORT	WORK EFFORT ID	Yes	No	ID
	WORK EFFORT PURPOSE TYPE ID	No	Yes	ID
	WORK EFFORT TYPE ID	No	Yes	ID
	ASSET ID	No	Yes	ID
	FIXED ASSET ID	No	Yes	ID
	FACILITY ID	No	Yes	ID
	NAME	No	No	Name
	DESCRIPTION	No	No	Description
	SCHEDULED START DATE	No	No	Datetime
	SCHEDULED COMPLETION DATE	No	No	Datetime
	TOTAL DOLLARS ALLOWED	No	No	Currency amount
	TOTAL HOURS ALLOWED	No	No	Numeric
	ESTIMATED HOURS	No	No	Numeric
	SPECIAL TERMS	No	No	Long varchar
	ACTUAL START DATETIME	No	No	Datetime
	ACTUAL COMPLETION DATETIME	No	No	Datetime
	ACTUAL HOURS	No	No	Numeric
WORK EFFORT ASSIGNMENT RATE	FROM DATE	Yes	Yes	Datetime

ENTITY NAME	ATTRIBUTE NAME	PK?	FK?	DOMAIN
	RATE TYPE ID	Yes	Yes	ID
	PARTY ID	Yes	Yes	ID
	WORK EFFORT ID	Yes	Yes	ID
	ROLE TYPE ID	Yes	Yes	ID
	THRU DATE	No	No	Datetime
	RATE	No	No	Currency amount
WORK EFFORT ASSOCIATION	WORK EFFORT ID	Yes	Yes	ID
WORK EFFORT BILLING	INVOICE ITEM SEQ ID	Yes	Yes	ID
	INVOICE ID	Yes	Yes	ID
	WORK EFFORT ID	Yes	Yes	ID
	PERCENTAGE	No	No	Floating point
WORK EFFORT BREAKDOWN	WORK EFFORT ID	Yes	Yes	ID
WORK EFFORT CONCURRENCY	WORK EFFORT ID	Yes	Yes	ID
WORK EFFORT DELIVERABLE PRODUCED	DELIVERABLE ID	Yes	Yes	ID
	WORK EFFORT ID	Yes	Yes	ID
WORK EFFORT DEPENDENCY	WORK EFFORT ID	Yes	Yes	ID
WORK EFFORT FIXED ASSET ASSIGNMENT	WORK EFFORT ID	Yes	Yes	ID
	FIXED ASSET ID	Yes	Yes	ID
	STATUS TYPE ID	No	Yes	ID
	FROM DATE	No	No	Datetime
	THRU DATE	No	No	Datetime
	ALLOCATED COST	No	No	Currency amount
	COMMENT	No	No	Comment
WORK EFFORT FIXED ASSET STANDARD	FIXED ASSET TYPE ID	Yes	Yes	ID
	WORK EFFORT TYPE ID	Yes	Yes	ID
	ESTIMATED QUANTITY	No	No	Numeric
	ESTIMATED DURATION	No	No	Datetime

ENTITY NAME	ATTRIBUTE NAME	PK?	FK?	DOMAIN
	ESTIMATED COST	No	No	Currency amount
WORK EFFORT GOOD STANDARD	PRODUCT ID	Yes	Yes	ID
	WORK EFFORT TYPE ID	Yes	Yes	ID
	ESTIMATED COST	No	No	Currency amount
	ESTIMATED QUANTITY	No	No	Numeric
WORK EFFORT INVENTORY ASSIGNMENT	INVENTORY ITEM ID	Yes	Yes	ID
	WORK EFFORT ID	Yes	Yes	ID
	QUANTITY	No	No	Numeric
WORK EFFORT INVENTORY PRODUCED	WORK EFFORT ID	Yes	Yes	ID
	INVENTORY ITEM ID	Yes	Yes	ID
WORK EFFORT PARTY ASSIGNMENT	ROLE TYPE ID	Yes	Yes	ID
	FROM DATE	Yes	No	Datetime
	PARTY ID	Yes	Yes	ID
	WORK EFFORT ID	Yes	Yes	ID
	FACILITY ID	No	Yes	ID
	THRU DATE	No	No	Datetime
	COMMENT	No	No	Comment
WORK EFFORT PRECEDENCY	WORK EFFORT ID	Yes	Yes	ID
WORK EFFORT PURPOSE TYPE	WORK EFFORT PURPOSE TYPE ID	Yes	No	ID
	DESCRIPTION	No	No	Description
WORK EFFORT ROLE TYPE	ROLE TYPE ID	Yes	Yes	ID
WORK EFFORT SKILL STANDARD	SKILL TYPE ID	Yes	Yes	ID
	WORK EFFORT TYPE ID	Yes	Yes	ID
	ESTIMATED NUM PEOPLE	No	No	Numeric
	ESTIMATED DURATION	No	No	Numeric
	ESTIMATED COST	No	No	Currency amount
WORK EFFORT STATUS	WORK EFFORT ID	Yes	Yes	ID

ENTITY NAME	ATTRIBUTE NAME	PK?	FK?	DOMAIN
	STATUS TYPE ID	Yes	Yes	ID
	DATETIME	No	No	Datetime
WORK EFFORT STATUS TYPE	STATUS TYPE ID	Yes	Yes	ID
WORK EFFORT TYPE	WORK EFFORT TYPE ID	Yes	No	ID
	PRODUCT ID	No	Yes	ID
	DELIVERABLE TYPE ID	No	Yes	ID
	FIXED ASSET TYPE ID	No	Yes	ID
	DESCRIPTION	No	No	Description
WORK EFFORT TYPE ASSOCIATION	WORK EFFORT TYPE ID FROM	Yes	Yes	ID
	WORK EFFORT TYPE ID TO	Yes	Yes	ID
WORK EFFORT TYPE BREAKDOWN	WORK EFFORT TYPE ID TO	Yes	Yes	ID
	WORK EFFORT TYPE ID FROM	Yes	Yes	ID
WORK EFFORT TYPE DEPENDENCY	WORK EFFORT TYPE ID TO	Yes	Yes	ID
	WORK EFFORT TYPE ID FROM	Yes	Yes	ID
WORK FLOW	WORK EFFORT ID	Yes	Yes	ID
WORK ORDER ITEM	ORDER ID	Yes	Yes	ID
	ORDER ITEM SEQ ID	Yes	Yes	ID
WORK ORDER ITEM FULFILLMENT	WORK EFFORT ID	Yes	Yes	ID
	ORDER ID	Yes	Yes	ID
	ORDER ITEM SEQ ID	Yes	Yes	ID
WORK REQUIREMENT	REQUIREMENT ID	Yes	Yes	ID
	DELIVERABLE ID	No	Yes	ID
	FIXED ASSET ID	No	Yes	ID
	PRODUCT ID	No	Yes	ID
WORK REQUIREMENT FULFILLMENT	REQUIREMENT ID	Yes	Yes	ID
	WORK EFFORT ID	Yes	Yes	ID
WORKER	PARTY ID	Yes	Yes	ID
	ROLE TYPE ID	Yes	Yes	ID

APPENDIX B

Data Warehouse Data Model Tables and Columns

This appendix lists information about the tables and columns from the data warehouse data model found in Chapters 12 through 14. This listing includes the table names, column names, primary key indicators, foreign key indicators, and the domain for each column.

Refer to Table A.1 for definitions of each domain in these appendices. The domain indicates a standard set of characteristics that can be applied to columns including its datatype and length. The domains and their application to the columns in these appendices provide guidelines for what datatype and length to use when physically implementing these models. The datatypes may vary depending on the target database management system. Of course, the datatype and length of each column should be adjusted as appropriate to meet the specific needs of the enterprise.

The domain definitions as they are applied to the columns in the appendices are used for the SQL code that is contained on the full-blown CD-ROM (sold separately).

Data Warehouse Data Model Tables and Column Listing

TABLE NAME	COLUMN NAME	PK?	FK?	DOMAIN
BUDGET DETAILS	BUDGET ID	Yes	No	ID
	BUDGET ITEM SEQ ID	Yes	No	ID
	PRODUCT ID	No	Yes	ID
	BUDGET REVISION SEQ ID	No	No	ID
	BUDGET ITEM TYPE ID	No	No	ID
	BUDGET ITEM TYPE DESCRIPTION	No	No	Description
	ORGANIZATION ID	No	Yes	ID
	ADDRESS ID	No	Yes	ID
	BUDGET PERIOD	No	No	Numeric
	BUDGET ITEM AMOUNT	No	No	Currency amount
	BUDGET ITEM EXPENDITURES	No	No	Currency amount
	BUDGET ITEM COMMITMENTS	No	No	Currency amount
	LOAD DATE	No	No	Datetime
CUSTOMER ADDRESSES	CUSTOMER ID	Yes	No	ID
	ADDRESS ID	Yes	No	ID
	INVOICE ID	No	Yes	ID
	INVOICE ITEM SEQ ID	No	Yes	ID
	ADDRESS LINE1	No	No	Long varchar
	ADDRESS LINE2	No	No	Long varchar
	POSTAL CODE	No	No	Short varchar
	SALES REP ID	No	Yes	ID
	GEO ID	No	Yes	ID
	LOAD DATE	No	No	Datetime
	SNAPSHOT DATE	No	Yes	Datetime
CUSTOMER INVOICES	INVOICE ID	Yes	No	ID
	INVOICE ITEM SEQ ID	Yes	No	ID
	BILLED TO CUSTOMER ID	No	Yes	ID
	SNAPSHOT DATE	No	Yes	Datetime
	CUSTOMER DEMOGRAPHICS ID	No	No	ID

TABLE NAME	COLUMN NAME	PK?	FK?	DOMAIN
	INVOICE DATE	No	No	Datetime
	BILLED TO CONTACT MECHANISM	No	No	Short varchar
	BILL TO ADDRESS ID	No	No	ID
	ORGANIZATION ID	No	No	ID
	ORG ADDRESS ID	No	No	ID
	ADDRESS ID	No	Yes	ID
	QUANTITY	No	No	Numeric
	AMOUNT	No	No	Currency amount
	EXTENDED AMOUNT	No	No	Currency amount
	PRODUCT COST	No	No	Currency amount
	LOAD DATE	No	No	Datetime
	PRODUCT ID	No	Yes	ID
CUSTOMER TYPES	CUSTOMER ID	Yes	Yes	ID
	CUSTOMER TYPE ID	Yes	No	ID
	SNAPSHOT DATE	Yes	Yes	Datetime
	CUSTOMER TYPE DESCRIPTION	No	No	Description
CUSTOMERS	CUSTOMER ID	Yes	No	ID
	SNAPSHOT DATE	Yes	No	Datetime
	CUSTOMER NAME	No	No	Name
	AGE	No	No	Numeric
	MARITAL STATUS	No	No	Indicator
	CREDIT RATING	No	No	Short varchar
EMPLOYEES	EMPLOYEE ID	Yes	No	ID
	SNAPSHOT DATE	Yes	No	Datetime
	LAST NAME	No	No	Name
	FIRST NAME	No	No	Name
	GENDER	No	No	Indicator
	EEOC TYPE ID	No	No	ID
	EEOC DESCRIPTION	No	No	Description
	AGE	No	No	Numeric
	YEARS EXPERIENCE	No	No	Numeric

TABLE NAME	COLUMN NAME	PK?	FK?	DOMAIN
	SOCIAL SECURITY NO	No	No	Numeric
GEOGRAPHIC BOUNDARIES	GEO ID	Yes	No	ID
	CITY NAME	No	No	Name
	STATE NAME	No	No	Name
	COUNTRY NAME	No	No	Name
	CITY ABBRV	No	No	Short varchar
	STATE ABBRV	No	No	Short varchar
	COUNTRY ABBRV	No	No	Short varchar
INTERNAL ORG ADDRESSES	ORGANIZATION ID	Yes	No	ID
	ADDRESS ID	Yes	No	ID
	ORG TYPE	No	No	Short varchar
	ORGANIZATION NAME	No	No	Long varchar
	ADDRESS LINE1	No	No	Long varchar
	ADDRESS LINE2	No	No	Long varchar
	POSTAL CODE	No	No	Short varchar
	GEO ID	No	Yes	ID
	PARENT ORG ID	No	No	ID
	LOAD DATE	No	No	Datetime
POSITIONS	ORGANIZATION ID	Yes	Yes	ID
	ADDRESS ID	Yes	Yes	ID
	EMPLOYEE ID	Yes	Yes	ID
	POSITION ID	Yes	No	ID
	FROM DATE	Yes	No	Datetime
	THRU DATE	No	No	Datetime
	SNAPSHOT DATE	No	Yes	Datetime
	POSITION TYPE ID	No	No	ID
	TITLE	No	No	Short varchar
	ANNUAL PAY	No	No	Currency amount
	SALARY FLAG	No	No	Indicator
	EXEMPT FLAG	No	No	Indicator

TABLE NAME	COLUMN NAME	PK?	FK?	DOMAIN
PRODUCT CATEGORIES	PRODUCT ID	Yes	Yes	ID
	CATEGORY ID	Yes	No	ID
	SNAPSHOT DATE	Yes	No	Datetime
	CATEGORY DESCRIPTION	No	No	Description
PRODUCT SNAPSHOTS	PRODUCT ID	Yes	Yes	ID
	SNAPSHOT DATE	Yes	No	Datetime
	MSRP	No	No	Currency amount
	UOM	No	No	Short varchar
	PRIMARY SUPPLIER NAME	No	No	Name
	SUPPLIER CITY NAME	No	No	Name
	SUPPLIER STATE ABBRV	No	No	Short varchar
	SUPPLIER COUNTRY NAME	No	No	Short varchar
PRODUCTS	PRODUCT ID	Yes	No	ID
	DESCRIPTION	No	No	Description
PURCHASE INVOICES	INVOICE ID	Yes	No	ID
	INVOICE ITEM SEQ ID	Yes	No	ID
	PRODUCT ID	No	Yes	ID
	INVOICE DATE	No	No	Datetime
	SUPPLIER ID	No	Yes	ID
	ADDRESS ID	No	Yes	ID
	BUDGET ID	No	Yes	ID
	BUDGET REVISION SEQ ID	No	No	ID
	BUDGET ITEM SEQ ID	No	Yes	ID
	QUANTITY	No	No	Numeric
	UNIT PRICE	No	No	Currency amount
	AMOUNT	No	No	Currency amount
	LOAD DATE	No	No	Datetime
SALES REPS	SALES REP ID	Yes	No	ID
	SNAPSHOT DATE	Yes	No	Datetime
	INVOICE ID	Yes	Yes	ID
	INVOICE ITEM SEQ ID	Yes	Yes	ID

TABLE NAME	COLUMN NAME	PK?	FK?	DOMAIN
	LAST NAME	No	No	Name
	FIRST NAME	No	No	Name
	MANAGER SALES REP ID	No	No	ID
SUPPLIER ADDRESSES	SUPPLIER ID	Yes	No	ID
	ADDRESS ID	Yes	No	ID
	SUPPLIER NAME	No	No	Name
	POSTAL CODE	No	No	Short varchar
	GEO ID	No	Yes	ID
	LOAD DATE	No	No	Datetime

Star Schema Design Tables and Columns

This appendix lists information about the tables and columns from the star schema designs found in Chapters 12 through 14. This listing includes the table names, column names, primary key indicators, foreign key indicators, and the domain for each column.

Refer to Table A.1 for definitions of each domain in these appendices. The domain indicates a standard set of characteristics that can be applied to columns, including its datatype and length. The domains and their application to the columns in these appendices provide guidelines for what datatype and length to use when physically implementing these models. The datatypes may vary depending on the target database management system. Of course, the datatype and length of each column should be adjusted as appropriate to meet the specific needs of the enterprise.

The domain definitions as they are applied to the columns in the appendices are used for the SQL code that is contained on the full-blown CD-ROM (sold separately).

Star Schema Designs Tables and Column Listing

TABLE NAME	COLUMN NAME	PK?	FK?	DOMAIN
ACCOUNT BALANCES	GL ACCOUNT ID	Yes	Yes	ID
	INTERNAL ORGANIZATION ID	Yes	Yes	ID
	MONTH ID	Yes	Yes	ID
	COUNTRY ID	Yes	Yes	ID
	BALANCE SHEET ACTUAL BALANCE	No	No	Currency amount
	BALANCE SHEET PLANNED BALANCE	No	No	Currency amount
	BALANCE SHEET VARIANCE	No	No	Currency amount
	BALANCE SHEET PERCENTAGE OF PLAN	No	No	Floating point
	INCOME STATEMENT ACTUAL BALANCE	No	No	Currency amount
	INCOME STATEMENT PLANNED BALANCE	No	No	Currency amount
	INCOME STATEMENT VARIANCE	No	No	Currency amount
	INCOME STATEMENT PERCENTAGE OF PLAN	No	No	Floating point
ADDRESSES	ADDRESS ID	Yes	No	ID
	ADDRESS LINE1	No	No	Long varchar
	ADDRESS LINE2	No	No	Long varchar
	CITY NAME	No	No	Long varchar
	STATE ABBRV	No	No	Very short
	POSTAL CODE	No	No	Short varchar
	COUNTRY NAME	No	No	Short varchar
CARRIERS	CARRIER ID	Yes	No	ID
	CARRIER NAME	No	No	Name
COST CENTERS	COST CENTER ID	Yes	No	ID
	COST CENTER NAME	No	No	Name
CUSTOMER DEMOGRAPHICS	CUSTOMER DEMOGRAPHICS ID	Yes	No	ID
	CREDIT RATING	No	No	Short varchar
	MARITAL STATUS	No	No	Short varchar

TABLE NAME	COLUMN NAME	PK?	FK?	DOMAIN
	AGE	No	No	Numeric
CUSTOMER INVOICES	INVOICE ID	Yes	No	ID
	INVOICE ITEM SEQ ID	Yes	No	ID
	CUSTOMER ID	No	Yes	ID
	INTERNAL ORGANIZATION ID	No	Yes	ID
	ADDRESS ID	No	Yes	ID
	DAY ID	No	Yes	ID
	SALES REP ID	No	Yes	ID
	MANAGER REP ID	No	Yes	ID
	CUSTOMER DEMOGRAPHICS ID	No	Yes	ID
	QUANTITY	No	No	Numeric
	GROSS SALES	No	No	Currency amount
	PRODUCT COST	No	No	Currency amount
	LOAD DATE	No	No	Datetime
CUSTOMER REP SALES	INTERNAL ORGANIZATION ID	Yes	Yes	ID
	ADDRESS ID	Yes	Yes	ID
	MONTH ID	Yes	Yes	ID
	SALES REP ID	Yes	Yes	ID
	MANAGER REP ID	Yes	Yes	ID
	CUSTOMER ID	Yes	Yes	ID
	GROSS SALES	No	No	Currency amount
CUSTOMER SALES	SALES REP ID	Yes	Yes	ID
	MANAGER REP ID	Yes	Yes	ID
	CUSTOMER DEMOGRAPHICS ID	Yes	Yes	ID
	INTERNAL ORGANIZATION ID	Yes	Yes	ID
	ADDRESS ID	Yes	Yes	ID
	CUSTOMER ID	Yes	Yes	ID
	DAY ID	Yes	Yes	ID
	PRODUCT ID	Yes	Yes	ID
	QUANTITY	No	No	Numeric
	GROSS SALES	No	No	Currency amount
	PRODUCT COST	No	No	Currency amount

TABLE NAME	COLUMN NAME	PK?	FK?	DOMAIN
CUSTOMERS	CUSTOMER ID	Yes	No	ID
	CUSTOMER NAME	No	No	Name
EEOC TYPES	EEOC TYPE ID	Yes	No	ID
	DESCRIPTION	No	No	Description
FACILITIES	FACILITY ID	Yes	No	ID
	FACILITY NAME	No	No	Name
	FACILITY ADDRESS	No	No	Short varchar
	GEO LEVEL 1	No	No	Short varchar
	GEO LEVEL 2	No	No	Short varchar
	GEO LEVEL 3	No	No	Short varchar
GENDERS	GENDER ID	Yes	No	ID
	DESCRIPTION	No	No	Description
GENERAL LEDGER ACCOUNTS	GL ACCOUNT ID	Yes	No	ID
	GL ACCOUNT NAME	No	No	Name
	GL ACCOUNT ID L2	No	No	ID
	GL ACCOUNT NAME L2	No	No	Name
	GL ACCOUNT ID L3	No	No	ID
	GL ACCOUNT NAME L3	No	No	Name
	GL ACCOUNT ID L4	No	No	ID
	GL ACCOUNT NAME L4	No	No	Name
GEOGRAPHIC BOUNDARIES	GEO ID	Yes	No	ID
	CITY NAME	No	No	Name
	STATE NAME	No	No	Name
	COUNTRY NAME	No	No	Name
	CITY ABBRV	No	No	Very short
	STATE ABBRV	No	No	Very short
	COUNTRY ABBRV	No	No	Very short
GOODS	PRODUCT ID	Yes	No	ID
	PRODUCT NAME	No	No	Name
	PRODUCT CATEGORY	No	No	Name

TABLE NAME	COLUMN NAME	PK?	FK?	DOMAIN
HUMAN RESOURCES FACT	MONTH ID	Yes	Yes	ID
	PAY GRADE ID	Yes	Yes	ID
	STATUS ID	Yes	Yes	ID
	ORGANIZATION ID	Yes	Yes	ID
	GENDER ID	Yes	Yes	ID
	LENGTH OF SERVICE ID	Yes	Yes	ID
	POSITION TYPE ID	Yes	Yes	ID
	EEOC TYPE ID	Yes	Yes	ID
	NUMBER OF EMPLOYEES	No	No	Numeric
	AVERAGE AGE	No	No	Numeric
	AVERAGE YEARS EXPERIENCE	No	No	Numeric
	AVERAGE YEARS EMPLOYED	No	No	Numeric
	AVERAGE ANNUAL PAY	No	No	Currency amount
INTERNAL ORGANIZATIONS	INTERNAL ORGANIZATION ID	Yes	No	ID
	INTERNAL ORGANIZATION NAME	No	No	Name
	LEVEL 1 NAME	No	No	Name
	LEVEL 1 ORG TYPE	No	No	Short varchar
	LEVEL 2 NAME	No	No	Name
	LEVEL 2 ORG TYPE	No	No	Short varchar
	LEVEL 3 NAME	No	No	Name
	LEVEL 3 ORG TYPE	No	No	Short varchar
	LEVEL 4 NAME	No	No	Name
	LEVEL 4 ORG TYPE	No	No	Short varchar
	LEVEL 5 NAME	No	No	Name
	LEVEL 5 ORG TYPE	No	No	Short varchar
INVENTORY ITEM FACT	FACILITY ID	Yes	Yes	ID
	INTERNAL ORGANIZATION ID	Yes	Yes	ID
	INVENTORY STATUS ID	Yes	Yes	ID
	PART ID	Yes	Yes	ID
	DAY ID	Yes	Yes	ID

TABLE NAME	COLUMN NAME	PK?	FK?	DOMAIN
	ORGANIZATION ID	Yes	Yes	ID
	QTY ON HAND	No	No	Numeric
	QTY COMMITTED	No	No	Numeric
	QTY SHIPPED	No	No	Numeric
	QTY RECEIVED	No	No	Numeric
	QTY ISSUED	No	No	Numeric
	QTY SCRAPPED	No	No	Numeric
	STANDARD COST	No	No	Currency amount
	ITEM VALUATION	No	No	Currency amount
INVENTORY STATUSES	INVENTORY STATUS ID	Yes	No	ID
	DESCRIPTION	No	No	Description
LENGTH OF SERVICES	LENGTH OF SERVICE ID	Yes	No	ID
	RANGE	No	No	Short varchar
LOCATIONS	COUNTRY ID	Yes	No	ID
	COUNTRY NAME	No	No	Name
	CONTINENT ID	No	No	ID
	CONTINENT NAME	No	No	Name
ORGANIZATIONS	ORGANIZATION ID	Yes	No	ID
	LEVEL1 NAME	No	No	Name
	LEVEL1 ORG TYPE	No	No	Short varchar
	LEVEL2 NAME	No	No	Name
	LEVEL2 ORG TYPE	No	No	Short varchar
	LEVEL3 NAME	No	No	Name
	LEVEL3 ORG TYPE	No	No	Short varchar
	LEVEL4 NAME	No	No	Name
	LEVEL4 ORG TYPE	No	No	Short varchar
	LEVEL5 NAME	No	No	Name
	LEVEL5 ORG TYPE	No	No	Short varchar
PARTS	PART ID	Yes	No	ID
	PART NAME	No	No	Name
PARTYS	PARTY ID	Yes	No	Short varchar
	WORKER	No	No	Short varchar

TABLE NAME	COLUMN NAME	PK?	FK?	DOMAIN
	PROJECT MANAGER	No	No	Long varchar
PAY GRADES	PAY GRADE ID	Yes	No	ID
	PAY GRADE	No	No	Description
POSITION TYPES	POSITION TYPE ID	Yes	No	ID
	POSITION TYPE	No	No	Description
	POSITION CLASS	No	No	Description
PRODUCTS	PRODUCT ID	Yes	No	ID
	PRODUCT DESCRIPTION	No	No	Description
	CATEGORY ID	No	No	ID
	CATEGORY DESCRIPTION	No	No	Description
PRODUCTS SALES	GEO ID	Yes	Yes	ID
	MONTH ID	Yes	Yes	ID
	PRODUCT ID	Yes	Yes	ID
	GROSS SALES	No	No	Currency amount
	QUANTITY	No	No	Numeric
	PRODUCT COST	No	No	Currency amount
	LOAD DATE	No	No	Datetime
PURCHASE ORDER FACT	SUPPLIER ID	Yes	Yes	ID
	PRODUCT ID	Yes	Yes	ID
	PERSON ID	Yes	Yes	ID
	INTERNAL ORGANIZATION ID	Yes	Yes	ID
	COST CENTER ID	Yes	Yes	ID
	WEEK ID	Yes	Yes	ID
	NUM OF PURCHASE ORDER ITEMS	No	No	Numeric
	PURCHASE ORDER ITEM PRICE	No	No	Currency amount
	QUANTITY	No	No	Numeric
	DISCOUNT	No	No	Currency amount
	AVERAGE DAYS DELIVERED	No	No	Numeric
	AVERAGE DAYS LATER THAN PROMISED	No	No	Numeric
	NUMBER OF PURCHASE ORDERS ON BACKORDER	No	No	Numeric

TABLE NAME	COLUMN NAME	PK?	FK?	DOMAIN
RESPONSIBLE PERSONS	PERSON ID	Yes	No	ID
	PERSON ROLE	No	No	Short varchar
	RESPONSIBLE PERSON NAME	No	No	Name
SALES REPS	SALES REP ID	Yes	No	ID
	MANAGER REP ID	Yes	No	ID
	SALES REP LAST NAME	No	No	Name
	SALES REP FIRST NAME	No	No	Name
	MANAGER LAST NAME	No	No	Name
	MANAGER FIRST NAME	No	No	Name
SHIP FROMS	SHIP FROM ADDRESS	Yes	No	Long varchar
	GEO LEVEL 1	No	No	Short varchar
	GEO LEVEL 2	No	No	Short varchar
	GEO LEVEL 3	No	No	Short varchar
SHIP TOS	SHIP TO ADDRESS	Yes	No	Long varchar
	GEO LEVEL 1	No	No	Short varchar
	GEO LEVEL 2	No	No	Short varchar
	GEO LEVEL 3	No	No	Short varchar
SHIPMENT FACT	PRODUCT ID	Yes	Yes	ID
	PERSON ID	Yes	Yes	ID
	SHIPMENT TYPE ID	Yes	Yes	ID
	CARRIER ID	Yes	Yes	ID
	SHIP FROM ADDRESS	Yes	Yes	Long varchar
	SHIP TO ADDRESS	Yes	Yes	Long varchar
	DAY ID	Yes	Yes	ID
	NUM OF SHIPMENTS	No	No	Numeric
	NUM LATE SHIPMENTS	No	No	Numeric
	AVERAGE DAYS LATE	No	No	Numeric
	QUANTITY SHIPPED	No	No	Numeric
	QUANTITY ACCEPTED	No	No	Numeric
	QUANTITY REJECTED	No	No	Numeric
	QUANTITY DAMAGED	No	No	Numeric
	FREIGHT AMOUNT	No	No	Currency amount

TABLE NAME	COLUMN NAME	PK?	FK?	DOMAIN
SHIPMENT TYPES	SHIPMENT TYPE ID	Yes	No	ID
	SHIPMENT METHOD	No	No	Short varchar
STATUSES	STATUS ID	Yes	No	ID
	DESCRIPTION	No	No	Description
SUPPLIERS	SUPPLIER ID	Yes	No	ID
	SUPPLIER NAME	No	No	Name
	SUPPLIER LOCATION	No	No	Long varchar
	GEO LEVEL 1 NAME	No	No	Name
	GEO LEVEL 2 NAME	No	No	Name
	GEO LEVEL 3 NAME	No	No	Name
TIME BY DAY	DAY ID	Yes	No	ID
	FISCAL YEAR	No	No	Very short
	QUARTER	No	No	Very short
	MONTH	No	No	Very short
	WEEK	No	No	Very short
	DAY	No	No	Very short
TIME BY MONTH	MONTH ID	Yes	No	ID
	MONTH	No	No	Very short
	QUARTER	No	No	Very short
	FISCAL YEAR	No	No	Very short
TIME BY WEEK	WEEK ID	Yes	No	ID
	WEEK	No	No	Very short
	MONTH	No	No	Very short
	QUARTER	No	No	Very short
	YEAR	No	No	Very short
WORK EFFORT FACILITIES	FACILITY ID	Yes	No	ID
	FACILITY NAME	No	No	Name
	GEO LEVEL 1	No	No	Short varchar
	GEO LEVEL 2	No	No	Short varchar
	GEO LEVEL 3	No	No	Short varchar
WORK EFFORT FACT	PARTY ID	Yes	Yes	Short varchar

TABLE NAME	COLUMN NAME	PK?	FK?	DOMAIN
	WORK EFFORT PURPOSE TYPE ID	Yes	Yes	ID
	EFFORT TYPE ID	Yes	Yes	ID
	FACILITY ID	Yes	Yes	ID
	DAY ID	Yes	Yes	ID
	NUM COMPLETED WORK EFFORTS	No	No	Numeric
	NUMBER OF WORK EFFORTS OVER TIME	No	No	Numeric
	AVG ESTIMATED TIME TO COMPLETE	No	No	Floating point
	AVG ACTUAL TIME TO COMPLETE	No	No	Floating point
	ESTIMATED TOT HOURS	No	No	Numeric
	ACT TOT HOURS	No	No	Numeric
	EST TOT COST	No	No	Currency amount
	ACT TOTAL COST	No	No	Currency amount
	EST TOT MATERIALS COST	No	No	Currency amount
	ACTUAL TOT MATERIALS COST	No	No	Currency amount
	EST LABOR COST	No	No	Currency amount
	ACT LABOR COST	No	No	Currency amount
WORK EFFORT PURPOSES	WORK EFFORT PURPOSE ID	Yes	No	ID
	DESCRIPTION	No	No	Description
WORK EFFORT TYPES	WORK EFFORT TYPE ID	Yes	No	ID
	DESCRIPTION	No	No	Description

Other Reusable Data Model and Data Warehouse Design Resources

Hopefully, it is evident that reusing data models and data warehouse designs is extremely valuable. There are many other sources for reusable data model and data warehouse design constructs. In order to design systems more quickly and with higher quality, it only makes sense to use whatever sources of models are available—for example, models from vendors, models available on Web sites, models available within application packages, models available within the enterprise itself, models available from people's past experiences, and models available from other publications. The following publications, while not exhaustive, provide some practical sources for reusable data models and data warehouse designs.

Reusable Data Model Resources

Barker, Richard. *CASE*Method*™ *Entity Relationship Modeling*. Addison-Wesley. 1989 (Note: this book focuses mostly on CASE*Method and data modeling conventions; however, it contains some useful data model constructs and ideas.)

Fowler, Martin. *Analysis Patterns: Reusable Object Models*. Addison-Wesley. 1997. (Note: Though this book is an object-oriented patterns book, many of these patterns apply to data modeling.)

Hay, David C. *Data Model Patterns: Conventions of Thought*. Dorset House. 1996.

Reingruber, Michael C., and William W. Gregory. *The Data Modeling Handbook: A Best-Practice Approach to Building Quality Data Models*.

Silverston, Len. *"Is Your Organization Too Unique to Use Universal Data Models?"* Data Management Review 8:8. September 1998.

Simsion, Graeme C. Revised and updated by Graham C. Witt & Graeme C. Simsion. *Data Modeling Essentials*. Coriolis. 2000.

Reusable Data Warehouse Design Resources

Adamson, Christopher, and Michael Venerable. *Data Warehouse Design Solutions*. John Wiley & Sons. 1998

Connely, McNeill, and Mosimann. *The Multi-Dimensional Manager, 24 Ways to Impact Your Bottom Line in 90 Days*. Cognos. 1997

Kimball, Ralph. *The Data Warehouse Toolkit: Practical Techniques for Building Dimensional Data Warehouses*. John Wiley & Sons. 2000.

Index

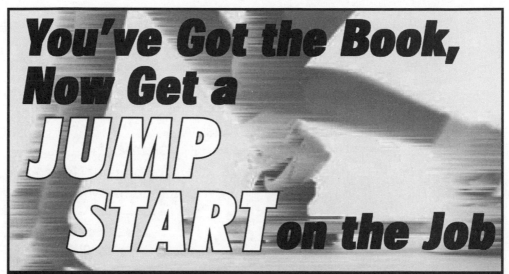

The CD-ROM

The accompanying CD-ROM product, which is included in the back of this book and needs to be licensed separately, provides all the SQL scripts needed to implement the data models described in this book, electronic versions of the diagrams contained in the book, and numerous reports with information about the models in the book. The CD-ROM in the back of the book also contains demos to illustrate what you can expect on the complete CD-ROM and includes directories **\v1 demo** and **\v2 demo,** which include a small sample of SQL code for a single data model from Volume 1 and a single data model from Volume 2. The full install of the CD-ROM contains the SQL code, diagrams, and reports for all the models in the book. The contents may be unlocked by contacting John Wiley & Sons via phone at (800) 825-8763 weekdays between 9 a.m. and 5 p.m. Eastern Standard Time, or online (http://silverston .wiley.com).

Both the demo and the complete CD-ROM include SQL scripts to implement the models, reports about the models, and electronic versions of the data models. SQL scripts are included that can be run in Oracle, SQL Server, and generic ODBC scripts that are included for use with other relational database management systems (RDBMSs). These SQL scripts may be used to either build a database or reverse-engineer the models into a CASE tool for further analysis and modifications.

The reports show a great deal of information and cross-referencing on the subject data areas, entities, attributes, tables, and columns. Electronic versions of the data model diagrams are included in Visio format and JPEG format. The JPEG files allow you to view all the models in an electronic manner. The Visio files allow you to modify the data model diagrams for your own purposes, if you have Visio 2000 software.

Within each of the root directories **\v1 cdrom**, **\v1 demo** and **\v2 demo,** are five more directories, three directories for each database platform, one for reports (**\reports**), and one for the diagrams (**\diagrams**)

Each of the three database-named directories contain SQL scripts for each supported database on the CD-ROM. SQL scripts for Oracle are found in the **\oracle** directory; Microsoft SQL Server in the **\sqlserver** directory; and generic OBDC scripts in the **\odbc** directory. Within each of these directories can be found three scripts. These subdirectories correspond to the logical data models, data warehouse data models, and star schema design models described in this book. The **\logicaldm** subdirectory contains the scripts to implement the logical data models that are part of the corporate data model described in Chapters 2 through 9. The **\dataware- house** subdirectory contains scripts to build the sample enterprise data warehouse described in Chapter 11. The **\starschema** subdirectory has the scripts to build the star schemas described in Chapters 12 through 14.

Within each of the subdirectories can be found files that contain the actual SQL code needed to build the described models. The files with a **.tab** extension can be used to build all the tables and referential integrity constraints for the model. The files with a **.ind** extension contain the SQL code to build all the indexes.

Using the Scripts

Using the scripts provided on the CD-ROM is quite simple. They can be used immediately if no changes are going to be made or they could be copied to a working directory on a hard drive or file server so they can be edited before execution. In either case, the scripts are ASCII files that can be loaded and executed from the standard SQL interface for the database selected (e.g., SQL*Plus for Oracle, ISQL/w for MS SQL Server). Be sure to execute the files (to build tables) before the **.ind** file (which builds indexes).

Most modeling tools have a reverse-engineering feature, which allows the extraction of object definitions from the database into the CASE tool. So once the models have been built in the target database, tools such as Oracle Designer/2000, ERwin, or StarDesignor can be used to reverse-engineer the definitions for further analysis or reengineering. Many popular CASE tools even have the ability to reverse-engineer directly from the SQL scripts.

Additional Information

This CD-ROM may be supplemented with the *Data Model Resource Industry Download*, which contains industry-specific model constructs for each of the eight industries. These are available for licensing at http://silverston.wiley.com. (See Volume 2 for details.)

Please read any additional notes and specific platform comments on the CD-ROM readme.htm file in the root directory of the CD-ROM.